# AUTHENTIC RESTORATION
## GUIDE

# CHEVELLE SS
# RESTORATION GUIDE

Paul A. Herd

MBI Publishing Company

*This book is dedicated to the memory of*
*my father, Thomas Adam Herd,*
*who inspired me to do what I wanted in life.*
*And who first introduced me to my never-ending*
*passion for the automobile.*

First published in 1992 by MBI Publishing Company, 729 Prospect Avenue, PO Box 1, Osceola, WI 54020-0001 USA

© Paul A. Herd, 1992

MBI Publishing Company books are also available at discounts in bulk quantity for industrial or sales-promotional use. For details write to Special Sales Manager at Motorbooks International Wholesalers & Distributors, 729 Prospect Avenue, PO Box 1, Osceola, WI 54020-0001 USA.

Library of Congress Cataloging-in-Publication Data
Herd, Paul A.
    Chevelle SS restoration guide, 1965–1972 / Paul A. Herd.
       p. cm.
    Includes index.
    ISBN 0-87938-569-3
    1. Chevelle automobile. 2. Automobiles—Conservation and restoration.
TL215.C48H46   1992
629.28'722—dc20         91-28695

**On the front cover:** A 1971 Chevelle SS convertible with Cowl Induction hood and 350 ci V–8 small-block, owner by Russ Werley of Hamburg, Pennsylvania. *Mike Mueller*

Printed in the United States of America

# Contents

# Acknowledgments

This book would not have been possible without the help of a number of people. I would like to thank all the individuals who allowed me to photograph their cars. A special thanks to Ed Witte at Classic Muscle Cars, Parts & Accessories for allowing me to photograph his inventory of original parts. Also a special thanks to Chevelle Classics, which supplied the replacement and reproduction parts featured in this book. And finally thanks to my photography assistant, K. O. Winston, and to all those at Chevrolet who provided me with information and original photographs.

# Introduction

During the mid sixties a new type of automobile was introduced—the muscle car. It was a simple idea: take a full-size car's engine, build it up and place it between the front frame rails of a midsize car.

The idea sounded unmarketable to the corporate brass, but when the demand for these factory hot rods exceeded all expectations the rush was on, as each manufacturer tried to outdo the other. First it was horsepower, then it was massive-cubic-inch blocks. In 1970 cubic inches and horsepower met as the pinnacle of the era when Chevrolet released a 454 ci Chevelle with a mind-bending 450 hp.

That period in time was decades ago, but the demand for these cars is still strong, and it is clear that no other car will ever have the same feel. Restoring muscle cars has become a favorite hobby—and for some a way of life.

The problem is that when dealing with cars that are more than twenty years old, information gets lost or misconstrued, resulting in incorrect cars being represented as correct. This is where this book comes in. It deals with America's favorite muscle car—the Chevelle Super Sport (SS).

After seeing so many incorrect cars at shows, I felt this book was needed. The information was drawn from factory manuals, original reports and photographs. Parts numbers, which are listed whenever possible, are the original numbers. This is because a part could still be available with that number, and as a guide to those who shop at a swap meet. Knowing the original part number enables you to correctly identify a piece as an SS part.

In some cases the part number or the part was changed during the course of the model year; whenever possible these changes and the date they occurred are noted.

Every effort was made to make sure all part numbers and facts are correct.

I wish you luck with your Chevelle SS. May you bring home all the trophies, and remember: you're not just restoring a car—you're restoring a piece of automotive history.

*Chapter 1*

# VIN Plates, Data Plates and Protect-O-Plates

## VIN Plates

### 1964

The VIN plates were stamped on a brightmetal tag riveted to the left front door hinge pillar in 1964. They consisted of twelve digits that indicated such facts as body style, engine type and assembly plant. All plates began with the number 4 to signify the 1964 model year. A typical 1964 VIN plate broke down as follows:

### 1964 VIN Plate Codes

| | | |
|---|---|---|
| First digit | Model year | 1964 |
| Second and third digits | Engine type | 57 Six-cylinder<br>58 V-8 |
| Fourth and fifth digits | Body style | 37 Two-door hardtop<br>67 Convertible |
| Sixth digit | Assembly plant | A Atlanta<br>B Baltimore<br>H Fremont<br>K Kansas City<br>L Los Angeles |
| Seventh-twelfth digits | Unit number | All plants began production at 100001 |

### 1965

The VIN plate location was the same in 1965 as in 1964, but the coding was changed. A thirteen-digit tag was now used and began with the number 1 to denote the manufacturer—Chevrolet. The new code deciphered as follows:

### 1965 VIN Plate Codes

| | | |
|---|---|---|
| First digit | Manufacturer | 1 Chevrolet |
| Second and third digits | Engine and model type | 37 Six-cylinder<br>38 V-8 |
| Fourth and fifth digits | Body style | 37 Sport coupe<br>67 Convertible |
| Sixth digit | Model year | 5 1965 |
| Seventh digit | Assembly Plant | A Atlanta<br>B Baltimore<br>G Farmingham |

| | | |
|---|---|---|
| | | K Kansas City<br>Z Fremont |
| Eighth-thirteenth digits | Unit number | All plants began at 100001 |

### 1966-1967

The 1966-67 VIN plates were the same as the 1965 plates except that the six-cylinder, code 37,

*In 1964 the VIN plate began with the number 4 indicating the model year.*

*The VIN plate was restyled in 1965.*

*The VIN was moved from the left front door hinge pillar to the instrument panel in 1968.*

5

## 1D80W2K500089

*The VIN was located in the same place but its style was changed in 1972.*

was eliminated and the coupe was now designated with the number 17 instead of 37. A Flint, Michigan, assembly plant was added in December 1965 for the 1966 model year only. Also, the sixth digit was changed accordingly: 6 for 1966 and 7 for 1967.

### 1968-1971

In 1968 the VIN plate was located on a bracket that was riveted to the underside of the instrument panel. The numbers were readable through the windshield on the driver's side.

Coding was the same in 1968 as in 1967 except that the coupe was again denoted by the number 37 and the El Camino two-door sedan pickup was added for the first time as an SS 396 model. The body style was signified by the code 80. The sixth digit was also changed to an 8 for 1968.

The SS model number was dropped in 1969 and made an option package on both the Malibu and 300 Deluxe coupes and the Malibu convertible. The SS 396 package for the sedan pickup was available only on the Custom El Camino. The following changes were made to the VIN plate:

### 1969 VIN Plate Codes

| | | |
|---|---|---|
| Second and third digits | Model type | 34 300 Deluxe based<br>36 Malibu based and Custom El Camino |
| Fourth and fifth digits | Body style | 37 Hardtop coupe |
| | | 27 Pillar coupe |
| | | 67 Convertible |
| | | 80 Pickup |
| Sixth digit | Model year | 9 1969 |
| Eighth-thirteenth digits | Unit number | All plants began at 300001 |

The 300 models and pillar coupe were dropped in 1970; all other body styles remained for 1970 and 1971. The sixth digit was changed with the model year. Assembly plants were again changed each year. Unit numbers began at 100001 both years at all plants.

In 1970 six plants assembled the cars.

### 1970 Assembly Plant Codes

A   Atlanta
B   Baltimore
F   Flint
K   Leeds, Missouri
L   Van Nuys, California
1   Oshawa, Canada
In 1971 five plants assembled the cars.

### 1971 Assembly Plant Codes

B   Baltimore
L   Van Nuys
K   Leeds
R   Arlington, Texas
1   Oshawa

### 1972

The VIN plate location was the same in 1972 as in 1971, but the hieroglyphics were changed. In fact this tag told more about the car than did those in previous years. And even though the SS was still not a model it could be used in determining a desirable SS 454, for the engine size and rating were coded into the plate and the 454 was available only with the SS package. The code broke down like this:

### 1972 VIN Plate Codes

| | | |
|---|---|---|
| First digit | Manufacturer | 1 Chevrolet |
| Second digit | Model | D Malibu |
| Third and fourth digits | Body style | 37 Coupe<br>67 Convertible<br>80 Pickup |
| Fifth digit | Engine | H 2 bbl 350 V-8<br>J 4 bbl 350 V-8<br>V 4 bbl 400 V-8<br>W 4 bbl 454 V-8 |
| Sixth digit | Model year | 2 1972 |
| Seventh digit | Assembly plant | Same as in 1971 |
| Eighth-thirteenth digits | Unit number | All plants began production at 500001 |

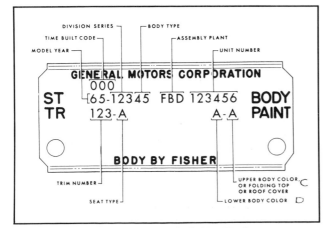

GENERAL MOTORS CORPORATION

DIVISION SERIES — BODY TYPE
TIME BUILT CODE — ASSEMBLY PLANT
MODEL YEAR — UNIT NUMBER

000
ST 65-12345 FBD 123456 BODY
TR 123-A A-A PAINT

BODY BY FISHER

TRIM NUMBER
SEAT TYPE
UPPER BODY COLOR, OR FOLDING TOP OR ROOF COVER — C
LOWER BODY COLOR — D

*This 1965 data plate was typical of 1964-67 plates.*

## Data Plates

### 1964-1967

Essential information can be obtained from the data plate, located on the left-hand side of the firewall. Such information about the original paint, the type and color of the interior, the color of the vinyl top if any and the build date can be found hidden in the symbols of this plate.

The data plate consisted of three important lines of information. The top line was the build code and listed the month (01 for January through 12 for December) and the week of the month (A for the first week through E for the fifth week) the car was assembled.

The second line was called the style body line. Information here must match that of the VIN plate. The model year began this line, followed by the model number and body style. In the center of this line was the assembly plant followed by the unit number.

The third line was the trim paint codes. Interior trim was designated with the letters *TR*. This code will tell you the original color and type of seats installed in the car; all 1964-1965 SSs were built with bucket seats. Following this was the paint code, which can also tell you the color of the top or if the car was two-toned.

### 1968-1972

The data tag for 1968 used the same layout as that for 1967, but the location was changed. The tag was now located on top of the cowl on the left-hand side below the rear edge of the hood. For 1969 the location was the same, but the layout was revised and the new layout was used throughout until 1972.

The first line was the style body line, the second was the trim paint line and the third was the build code. Deciphering was the same as in earlier years.

Cars built in Canada used a slightly different tag. Instead of Body by Fisher the words Made in Canada appeared at the top in bold letters. Also listed on this tag were the options that were installed on the car. The codes were the same as the RPO numbers of the options.

## Protect-O-Plate

### 1965-1972

A special metal card, the size of a credit card, was used from 1965 to 1972 to enable the service department to better repair the car. Listed in code on the card were all the options built on the car. This sounds like a blessing to the would-be restorer, but most of these cards were discarded after the warranty ran out.

This card was glued to the inside of the back cover of the owners manual at the factory. However, I have seen them in pouches on the radiator support wall and the glove compartment door. If you are lucky enough and your SS still has this card and you would like to decode it, you can find the information in an older parts catalog. Catalog 11 contains this information.

*Beginning in 1968 the data plate was riveted to the top of the cowl on the left-hand side. This plate is from a 1969 El Camino painted Glacier Blue with a blue bench seat interior. It was assembled at the Kansas City plant in the last week of January and was the 30,459th Chevelle built.*

*This 1965 SS was built in the last week of December at the Kansas City, Missouri, plant. It was the 8,323rd Chevelle to roll down the line. It was painted Ermine and came with a medium blue interior.*

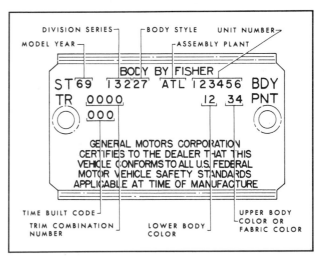

*The information was the same, but the style and location were changed in 1968.*

# Chapter 2

# Engines

## Cylinder Blocks

### 1964-1965

Two types of engines were used in both 1964 and 1965: an inline six-cylinder and the V-8 power-plant. The six-cylinder is not very popular with restorers. The standard V-8 engine both years was a two-barrel 283 ci small-block rated at 190 hp.

At the beginning of the 1964 model year only a single four-barrel 283 ci engine, RPO L77, was available as an optional powerplant. Then in April 1964 two 327 ci blocks were added: a 250 hp version, RPO L30, and a high-performance 300 hp version, RPO L74. All V-8 blocks had two-bolt mains. All blocks were identified by the casting date and suffix code. The suffix was stamped on a pad at the right front side of the cylinder block.

For a short time in 1965, the four-barrel version of the 283 ci engine was not available, but about two months after production began, it was reinstated.

All other engines returned. Also added were two new V-8s: a 327 ci engine and the 396 ci big-block, RPO L37, used in the Z16 option package.

The special high-performance 327 engine now available was rated at 350 hp. Most commonly known is the RPO L79 option, which used hydraulic lifters. For a short time another 327 with mechanical lifters, RPO L76, was listed, but it was never produced. The L79 block had four-bolt mains.

The 396 ci block was available only as part of the Z16 option package. Only one block was cast, and it should have four-bolt mains and should be coded with the suffix *IX*. The casting number was 3855962. This number was located at the rear of the block on the left-hand side of the bell housing. This block was used in conjunction with a four-speed manual transmission only.

All engines used an oil pan with a capacity of 4 quarts—5 quarts with an AC oil filter. The loop on the dipstick handle was painted entirely orange for 1964. The end of the loop was color-coded as follows for 1965:

*The horsepower numbers were increasing for the Chevelle Super Sport in 1965, its second year. Even the smallest cubic inches were still potent. The 327 ci mill was capable of 13 more horses than its cubic inches. But this engine didn't get its just rewards because of the awesome 396 ci engines. Phil Kunz/Bill Holder*

*Until the birth of the 396 ci engine, the 327 was the largest powerplant to be carried by the Super Sport. The engine carried a twin-snorkel air cleaner similar to the unit carried by the Z16 375 hp powerplant. Two versions of this engine were available; the L30 version produced 250 hp, and the L74 model provided a ground-pounding 300 horses. Phil Kunz/Bill Holder*

## 1965 Dipstick Handle Loop Colors

| | |
|---|---|
| All V-8s except 396 | Purple; brown after January 14, 1965 |
| 396 V-8 | Yellow |

All blocks should be painted Chevrolet Orange.

## 1964 Engine Suffix Codes

| Code | Engine Type | Transmission |
|---|---|---|
| J | 283/195 hp V-8 | 3-Speed Manual |
| JA | 283/195 hp V-8 | 4-Speed Manual |
| JD | 283/195 hp V-8 | Powerglide |
| JG | 283/220 hp V-8 | Powerglide |
| JII | 283/220 hp V-8 | Manual |
| JQ | 327/250 hp V-8 | Manual |
| SR | 327/250 hp V-8 | Powerglide |
| JR | 327/300 hp V-8 | Manual |
| SS | 327/300 hp V-8 | Powerglide |

## 1965 Engine Suffix Codes

| Code | Engine Type | Transmission |
|---|---|---|
| DA | 283/195 hp V-8 | 3-Speed Manual |
| DB | 283/195 hp V-8 | 4-Speed Manual |
| DE | 283/195 hp V-8 | Powerglide |
| EA | 327/250 hp V-8 | Manual |
| EE | 327/250 hp V-8 | Powerglide |
| EB | 327/300 hp V-8 | Manual |
| EF | 327/300 hp V-8 | Powerglide |
| EC | 327/350 hp V-8 | Manual only |
| ED | 327/350 hp V-8 | w/Transistor Ignition |
| IX | 396/375 hp Mark IV V-8 | Manual only |
| DG | 283/220 hp V-8 | 3-speed Manual |
| DH | 283/220 hp V-8 | Powerglide |

## 1966-1967

Only the 396 ci V-8 was available from the factory in both 1966 and 1967. Three different levels of horsepower were used: the RPO L35 325 hp version was standard; the RPO L34 360 hp (in 1966) or 350 hp (in 1967) version and the RPO L78 375 hp special performance version were optional. The L34 and L78 blocks had four-bolt mains and usually—but not always—had Hi Per Pass cast into the timing chain area. The casting number was the same for all in 1966, 3855961; however, some L34s and L78s did use casting number 3855962. The 1967 casting number was 3902406.

Some dealers installed a 427 ci engine for their customers, but if you cannot verify this it would be incorrect. A few SSs were converted by Motion Performance to use 427 ci engines in 1967. No records exist as to the number converted, but it is believed to be under 500.

The engine identification code was in same location as before; a total of twelve blocks were used in 1966, and fourteen in 1967. Three blocks in 1966 used a three-digit code; they were all on the

The big numbers were 396 and 375 for the Chevelle Super Sport in 1965. The 396 ci/375 hp powerplant was the go-power for the new Z16 Chevelle SS model. The new engine carried all the high performance goodies with cast iron heads, an 800 cfm Holley carb and a forged steel crank. Phil Kunz/Bill Holder

base L35 version. Two of these were with a Holley carburetor, and the letter H was added; the third was a version of the Powerglide with the Rochester. All other blocks used a two-digit code.

The oil pan capacity was 4 quarts—5 quarts if AC oil filter part number 5574279 was used. The dipstick, part number 3860316, was coded with yellow paint on the tip of the handle. The oil tube should have a natural metal appearance. Production engines were painted Chevrolet Orange.

## 1966-1967 Engine Suffix Codes

| Code | Engine Type | Transmission |
|---|---|---|
| ED | 396/325 hp V-8 | Manual |
| EH | 396/325 hp V-8 | Manual w/AIR |
| EK | 396/325 hp V-8 | Powerglide |
| EM | 396/325 hp V-8 | Powerglide w/AIR |
| EF | 396/360 hp V-8 | Manual |
| EJ | 396/360 hp V-8 | Manual w/AIR |
| EL | 396/360 hp V-8 | Powerglide |
| EN | 396/360 hp V-8 | Powerglide w/AIR |
| EG | 396/375 hp V-8 | Manual only |
| ET # | 396/325 hp V-8 | Turbo Hydra-Matic |
| EV # | 396/325 hp V-8 | Turbo Hydra-Matic w/AIR |
| EU # | 396/350 hp V-8 | Turbo Hydra-Matic |
| EW # | 396/350 hp V-8 | Turbo Hydra-Matic w/AIR |
| EX # | 396/375 hp V-8 | Manual w/AIR |

#-1967 only

PG-Powerglide two-speed automatic transmission

TH-Turbo Hydra-Matic three-speed automatic transmission

AIR-Air Injection Reactor (emission controls)

The standard 396 ci powerplant for 1966 was rated at 325 hp. It was basically the Z16 powerplant of the previous year, but it had been mellowed considerably and was a lot more streetable. There would also be 360 and 375 hp versions of the 396 engine available. The powerplants were one of the big reasons why the 1966 396-powered model sold over 72,000 units. Phil Kunz/Bill Holder

### 1968–1969

In 1968 the 396 ci V-8 remained the only engine available from the factory, with the same horsepower levels as in 1967. Again some dealers did install a 427 ci engine for their customers, but these were not factory approved and voided the warranty. The casting number for 1968 was 3916323, but some engines used casting number 3953440.

In 1969 the first factory-authorized engine conversion was available. Chevelles that were designated Central Office Production Order (COPO) came with a 425 hp 427 ci Corvette engine,

The popular 325 hp 396 ci powerplant was again available for the 1967 model year. Other 396 powerplants available with the SS that year included the L34 option, which was now producing an advertised 350 horses, but the L78 version kept all its 375 pounding ponies. That 396 figure on these cars certainly pushes the asking prices of these models far above their small-block brothers. Phil Kunz/Bill Holder

RPO L72. They were not converted at the factory but were shipped to dealers like Dana, Baldwin, Nickey and Yenko to be converted. Two blocks were used—one for the four-speed manual transmission, coded MQ, and the other for the Turbo Hydramatic 400, coded MP. The block casting number was 3963512, and its location was the same as on the 396 ci blocks.

Also near the end of the 1969 model year the 396 ci block was overbored to create 402 ci of displacement, although these were regarded as

The 360 hp version of the 396 motor was called the L34 version. The powerplant was basically the same engine as the 325 hp version, with the addition of a high-performance cam. Near the end of the model year, the L78 375 hp version of the 396 was offered. Needless to say, Super Sports powered with that latter engine will bring big dollars in the 1990s. Phil Kunz/Bill Holder

As in earlier years, the king of the powerplants for the Chevelle SS in 1968 was the 396 ci/375 hp powerhouse. An optional four-speed transmission could be ordered with this and the 350 hp version of this monster mill. Almost 4,800 Chevelle SSs were delivered with this powerplant under the hood and it took a while to get delivery from dealers. Phil Kunz/Bill Holder

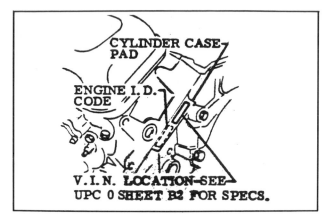

*1968 block identification and VIN location (396 ci engine only).*

## 1968 Engine Suffix Codes

| Code | Engine Type | Transmission |
|------|-------------|--------------|
| ED | 396/325 hp V-8 | Manual |
| EK | 396/325 hp V-8 | Powerglide |
| ET | 396/325 hp V-8 | Turbo Hydra-Matic |
| EF | 396/350 hp V-8 | Manual |
| EL | 396/350 hp V-8 | Powerglide |
| EU | 396/350 hp V-8 | Turbo Hydra-Matic |
| EG | 396/375 hp V-8 | Manual only |

## 1969 Engine Suffix Codes

| Code | Engine Type | Transmission |
|------|-------------|--------------|
| JA | 396/325 hp V-8 | Manual |
| JK | 396/325 hp V-8 | Turbo Hydra-Matic 400 |
| JC | 396/350 hp V-8 | Manual |
| JE | 396/350 hp V-8 | Turbo Hydra-Matic 400 |
| JD | 396/375 hp V-8 | Manual |
| KF | 396/375 hp V-8 | Turbo Hydra-Matic 400 |
| KG | 396/375 hp V-8 Alum. Head | Manual |
| KH | 396/375 hp V-8 Alum. Head | Turbo Hydra-Matic 400 |
| KD | 396/375 hp V-8 | Manual w/Heavy Duty Clutch |
| KI | 396/375 hp V-8 Alum. Head | Manual w/Heavy Duty Clutch |
| MQ | 427/425 hp V-8 COPO | Manual 4-Speed |
| MP | 427/425 hp V-8 COPO | Turbo Hydra-Matic 400 |
| CJA | 402/325 hp V-8 | Manual |
| CJK | 402/325 hp V-8 | Turbo Hydra-Matic 400 |
| CJC | 402/350 hp V-8 | Manual |
| CKF | 402/350 hp V-8 | Turbo Hydra-Matic 400 |
| CJD | 402/375 hp V-8 | Manual |
| CKF | 402/375 hp V-8 | Turbo Hydra-Matic 400 |
| CKG | 402/375 hp V-8 Alum. Head | Manual |
| CKH | 402/375 hp V-8 Alum. Head | Turbo Hydra-Matic 400 |

*Talk about your mighty powerplants! This 396 ci/375 hp mill could really get the job done for 1969 Chevelle SS buyers. The M13 three-speed transmission was a part of the SS 396 package. Almost 10,000 Chevelles carried the monster engine with a large number of them being Super Sports. Phil Kunz/Bill Holder*

396 ci engines. These blocks were distinguished by a three-letter suffix code; earlier blocks used only a two-letter suffix. The casting number for a true 396 ci block in 1969 was 3935440, and the casting number for the 402 ci 396 block was 3955272. The date when this change occurred varied from factory to factory.

With the 402 ci block came a new option, RPO L89, which was an L78 block with aluminum heads. Two different blocks were used: those with the manual transmission used suffix code CKG; those with the Turbo Hydra-matic used code CKH. However, some true 396 ci blocks were also equipped

*The L34 350 hp version of the 396 engine for 1969 was an awesome performer, but it was still just the second-place engine as far as performance was concerned. There were over 17,000 produced that model year. The M13 three-speed transmission came standard with the SS 396 powertrain equipment although the four-speed M20 could be ordered. Phil Kunz/Bill Holder*

11

*The standard powerplant for the 1970 Super Sport was the L34 350 hp version of the 396 ci engine. The powerplant, as was the case with all the 454 and 396 engines of that model year, carried the attractive chrome valve covers. This engine was tested by a number of the car magazines of the period who found it to be a 15-second performer in the quarter mile, somewhat behind its formidable Mopar and Ford competition. Phil Kunz/Bill Holder*

with the L89 option and used suffix codes KG with manual transmission and KH with the automatic.

Only seven blocks were used in 1968, and twenty-two blocks were available in 1969—more than in any other year. The oil level tube, part number 3928901, was the same both years and should have a natural metal appearance. The dipstick was listed as part number 3925599 and should be color-coded yellow on the tip of the handle. All blocks should be painted Chevrolet Orange.

Beginning in 1968 the car's VIN was stamped into the block next to the engine identification

*The 360 hp version of the 454 powerplant in 1970, the LS-5, certainly could not match its big brother LS-6, but there was performance aplenty with this mill. This powerplant used 10.25:1 compression ratio which made the engine more drivable. It will never have the desirability of the LS-6, but will certainly increase in value on the muscle car market in the coming years. Phil Kunz/Bill Holder*

stamp, on the right-hand side of the block where the head and block meet. This enables a restorer to verify if a block is original. The last eight digits of the VIN were used.

**1970-1972**

Still referred to as a 396 ci V-8, even though all blocks displaced 402 ci, the 325 hp version was dropped, and base power was the L34 350 hp engine for 1970. The 375 hp version with both conventional and aluminum heads continued. The 454 ci V-8 also made its first appearance in two forms:

*Here it is! The mighty LS-6 engine of 1970. The unbelievable 450 hp engine carried all the good stuff including a solid lift cam, forged steel crank, 11.25:1 compression heads, aluminum intake and a monstrous 780cfm Holley carb. Another 454 version was capable of 360 hp along with 350 and 375 horse versions of the 396 ci powerplant. A real powerpacked lineup to be sure. Phil Kunz/Bill Holder*

*The big-horse engine for the 1971 Chevelle Super Sport was the 365 hp 454 ci powerplant. Even though the engine had a considerably lower compression ratio than the 454 of only a year earlier, it still sported a five-horse higher rating. During this model year, General Motors started advertising its engine horsepower as net horsepower. For this engine, that amounted to 285 horses. Phil Kunz/Bill Holder*

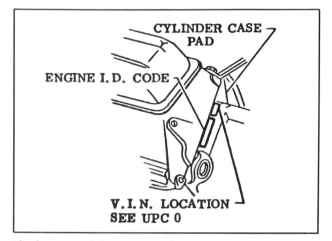

*The location of the VIN was determined by the assembly plant in 1970.*

*Note the incorrect placement of this valve cover decal. Both 283 ci engines used a single decal that should be positioned 6.969 in. from the centerline of the forward cover bolt, as measured from the rear edge of the decal.*

the RPO LS5 with 360 hp and the RPO LS6 with 450 hp. LS6 was not cast until the end of August 1969.

Nine different 396 (402 ci) blocks and four 454 ci blocks were used in 1970. The casting number for the 396 (402 ci) blocks was 3969854, and the casting number for the 454 blocks was 3963512.

Oil dipstick part number 3925599 and tube assembly part number 3928901 were used with all engines. The dipstick should be color-coded with yellow paint. The tube finish was the same as in previous years.

The 350 ci small-block was added in 1971 and continued into 1972 in two-barrel and four-barrel forms. The 396 name was replaced with the title Turbo-Jet 400, although the engine displaced 402 ci in both 1971 and 1972.

The 454 ci engine continued in 1971–72. LS6 was rated at 425 hp, and LS5 at 365 hp in 1971 and

## 1970 Engine Suffix Codes

| Code | Engine Type | Transmission |
|---|---|---|
| CTX | 396/350 hp V-8 | Manual 4-Speed |
| CTW | 396/350 hp V-8 | Turbo Hydra-Matic 400 |
| CTZ | 396/350 hp V-8 | Manual 4-Speed w/HDC |
| CKO | 396/375 hp V-8 | Manual |
| CTY | 396/375 hp V-8 | Turbo Hydra-Matic 400 |
| CKT | 396/375 hp V-8 Alum. Head | Manual |
| CKU | 396/375 hp V-8 Alum. Head | 4-Speed w/HDC |
| CKP | 396/375 hp V-8 Alum. Head | Turbo Hydra-Matic 400 |
| CKQ | 396/375 hp V-8 | 4-Speed w/HDC |
| CRT | 454/360 hp V-8 | Manual |
| CRQ | 454/360 hp V-8 | Turbo Hydra-Matic 400 |
| CRV | 454/450 hp V-8 | Manual |
| CRR | 454/450 hp V-8 | Turbo Hydra-Matic 400 HD |

## 1971 Engine Suffix Codes

| Code | Engine Type | Transmission |
|---|---|---|
| CGA | 350/245 hp V-8 | Manual |
| CGB | 350/245 hp V-8 | Powerglide |
| CGK | 350/270 hp V-8 | Manual |
| CJJ | 350/270 hp V-8 | Manual |
| CJD | 350/270 hp V-8 | Turbo Hydra-Matic 350 |
| CGL | 350/270 hp V-8 | Turbo Hydra-Matic 350 |
| CLB | 400/300 hp V-8 | Turbo Hydra-Matic 400 |
| CLP | 400/300 hp V-8 | Turbo Hydra-Matic 350 |
| CLS | 400/300 hp V-8 | 3-Speed Manual |
| CLL | 400/300 hp V-8 | 4-Speed Manual |
| CLR | 400/300 hp V-8 | Police Block |
| CPA | 454/365 hp V-8 | Manual 4-Speed |
| CPO | 454/365 hp V-8 | Turbo Hydra-Matic 400 |
| CPP | 454/425 hp V-8 | Manual |
| CPR | 454/425 hp V-8 | Turbo Hydra-Matic 400 |

## 1972 Engine Suffix Codes

| Code | Engine Type | Transmission |
|---|---|---|
| CTL | 350/165 hp V-8 | Turbo Hydra-Matic 350 |
| CKD | 350/175 hp V-8 | Turbo Hydra-Matic 350 |
| CKK | 350/165 hp V-8 | Manual |
| CKA | 350/175 hp V-8 | Manual |
| CLS | 400/240 hp V-8 | HD 3-Speed |
| CLA | 400/240 hp V-8 | Manual |
| CLB | 400/240 hp V-8 | Turbo Hydra-Matic 400 |
| CTB | 400/240 hp V-8 | Turbo Hydra-Matic w/AIR |
| CTH | 400/240 hp V-8 | 3-Speed |
| CPA | 454/270 hp V-8 | Manual 4-Speed |
| CRX | 454/270 hp V-8 | w/AIR |
| CPD | 454/270 hp V-8 | Turbo Hydra-Matic 400 |
| CRW | 454/270 hp V-8 | Turbo Hydra-Matic w/AIR |

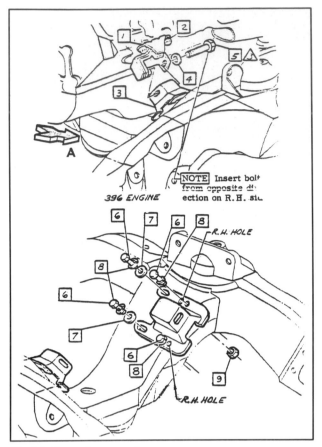

*Big-block engine mounts.*

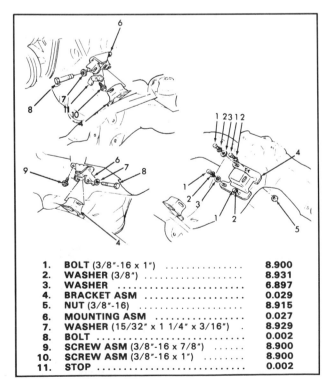

| | | | |
|---|---|---|---|
| 1. | BOLT (3/8"-16 x 1") | ............... | 8.900 |
| 2. | WASHER (3/8") | ................... | 8.931 |
| 3. | WASHER | ................... | 6.897 |
| 4. | BRACKET ASM | ................ | 0.029 |
| 5. | NUT (3/8"-16) | ................... | 8.915 |
| 6. | MOUNTING ASM | ................ | 0.027 |
| 7. | WASHER (15/32" x 1 1/4" x 3/16") | . | 8.929 |
| 8. | BOLT | ................... | 0.002 |
| 9. | SCREW ASM (3/8"-16 x 7/8") | ....... | 8.900 |
| 10. | SCREW ASM (3/8"-16 x 1") | ....... | 8.900 |
| 11. | STOP | ................... | 0.002 |

*Small-block engine mounts.*

270 hp in 1972. The LS6 option was canceled May 25, 1971. Casting numbers were the same in 1971 as in 1970, so no 1972 LS6s were made. In 1972 the Turbo-Jet 400 (402 ci) used casting number 3999290, and the 454 casting number 3999289.

Both 350s used dipstick part number 3951576 in both 1971 and 1972, and it was color-coded with green paint. The tube, part number 3876870, is recognizable by its curved shaped. The big-blocks used dipstick part number 3989391, and it was no longer color-coded.

The VIN can vary in location. In 1970 it was placed on the rear edge of the block on the left-hand side to the rear of the oil filter at all plants except Fremont, California, where it was located in the same place as before. In 1971 and 1972 either location was used. All blocks should be painted Chevrolet Orange.

The casting date is also useful in determining a block's model usage. It is located in one of two places. For 1965 blocks and true 396 blocks in 1969 it is located under the center freeze plug on the right-hand side. For all 402 ci and 454 ci blocks it is located on the right-hand side of the bell housing flange.

## Cylinder Heads

### 1964–1965

The 283 ci and 327 ci engines used cast-iron cylinder heads. All 283 engines used 1.725 in. diameter intake valves, part number 3989083, and 1.5 in. diameter exhaust valves, part number 6263778.

The larger 327 ci engine used two different sizes of valves in 1964. The L30 250 hp 327 used the same valves as the 283. The L74 300 hp high-performance 327 used a larger-diameter intake valve, part number 3989085. This valve was then installed in all the 1965 327s except the L79 350 hp version, which used 1.95 in. diameter valves, part number 3849814. Exhaust for all 327 engines except the 350 hp version in 1965 was listed as part number 6263778, and the 350 hp used part number 3849818. The special high-performance cylinder head was listed as part number 3987376 and used casting number 3849820.

Cast-iron cylinder heads were used on the 1965 L37 396 ci big-block engine. These were unique because they used the larger 2.19 in. diameter intake valves, part number 3864808; exhaust valves were the standard 1.72 in. diameter, part number 3860002. Closed-chamber-design cylinder heads, casting number 3856208, with large rectangular ports were used. The label Hi Perf was cast into this head on one runner.

Chromed valve covers part numbers 325173-LH and 325174-RH were standard. Chrome oil filler cap part number 3851735 was used on the right-hand valve cover.

## 1966-1967

Two different heads were used in 1966-67. The base and L34 360 hp engines used casting number 3872702, 3916323 in the last part of 1967, with oval ports and 2.06 in. diameter intake valves, part number 6263754 both years. The L78 375 hp engine used rectangular ports and larger 2.19 in. diameter valves which were slightly shorter in overall length; the casting numbers for this head were 3873858 in 1966 and 3904391 in 1967.

The exhaust valves for both heads used the same part number as in 1965. The cylinder heads should be painted Chevrolet Orange. Chrome valve covers were standard on all engines and used the same part number as in 1965.

## 1968-1969

The engine temperature switch, part number 1993426, was moved to the left cylinder head between the center exhaust ports in 1968, so earlier heads will not correctly interchange. The heads used the same valves and ports as before: the L35 and L34 engines used casting number 3917215, 3931063 in 1969, and the L78 engine used casting number 3919840 in both 1968 and 1969.

During late May 1968 the L89 option appeared. This used aluminum heads casting number 3919842 and the same type of ports and intake valves that the conventional L78 head used. However, it employed slightly different exhaust valves, part number 3879619, and AC-R43X1 spark plugs with a $^{13}/_{16}$ in. hex nut and full threads.

The COPO 427, L72, used the same head and casting number as the L78 396. All conventional heads should be painted Chevrolet Orange. The aluminum head should have a natural cast-aluminum appearance.

## 1970-1972

All heads were redesigned in 1970 to operate on low-octane fuels and now used an open chamber design. The walls around the spark plug were opened up and the combustion chamber was larger with this new design.

The temperature switch was also restyled. Part number 6489600 was standard, and it should be flat-black. When the gauge package, RPO U14, was ordered, the temperature switch was listed as part number 1513462 and was natural in appearance.

Spark plugs were also redesigned. Instead of the larger $^{13}/_{16}$ in. hex plugs, the new heads used $^5/_8$ in. hex plugs with a tapered seat and no washer.

The base L34 engine rated at 350 hp and the LS5 454 rated at 360 hp both used the same conventional heads, casting number 3964290, with oval ports and 2.06 in. diameter intake valves, part number 6263754. As before, these heads should have the label Pass stamped into them. Exhaust

*This decal identifies the Tonawanda engine plant. It was not used from 1965 to 1969 with chrome valve covers, as shown in this photo.*

valves were identical to those used in previous years.

The L78 option used the head with casting number 3964291, which had large rectangular ports and the same valves as before. The L89 aluminum head option continued and used casting number 3946074. Unlike conventional heads the aluminum heads still used the larger $^{13}/_{16}$ in. hex plugs with full threads and a washer gasket.

The LS6 used unique heads with 1.88 in. exhaust valves, part number 3946077, and 2.19 in. diameter intake valves, part number 3864808. The casting number was 3964292; replacement part number 3964286 is for the heads.

Chrome valve covers were standard on all engines until the end of the production run when the L34 and LS5 engines used steel valve covers painted Chevrolet Orange. These covers were used throughout till 1972 on all 400 and 454 Turbo-Jet engines except the LS6 in 1971, which used chrome-plated covers. The 350 engines used painted steel covers only.

### Steel Replacement Valve Cover Part Numbers

| | |
|---|---|
| 350 ci | 6272227 (replacement pair) |
| 400 (402 ci) & 454 ci | |
| LH | 338261 |
| RH | 338262 |

Combustion chambers were made even larger for 1971, which dropped horsepower on the LS6 engine, now rated at 425 hp—a loss of 25 ponies. The casting number was 3946074; replacement part number 6260482 is for the pair. The LS3 now rated at 300 hp and LS5 still shared the same head, casting number 3993820.

Only one set of heads was used with the 350 ci small-block engine, listed as replacement part number 14034808.

In 1972 the only big-block head was casting number 6272292, as the LS6 head was canceled. All cylinder heads except those for the 1970 L89 option should be painted Chevrolet Orange. The aluminum heads of the L89 option should have a natural cast appearance.

Big-block heads with rectangular ports had the label Hi Perf cast into them. The oval-port heads had Pass cast in. Heads for trucks had oval ports and the word Truck cast into them; they were not used on the Chevelle, not even the El Camino. The casting date was located on the end opposite the one with the casting number.

## Intake Manifold

### 1964-1972

A cast-iron intake manifold was used on all engines except those designated as special performance options—L37, L72, L78, L79, L89 and LS6—which used an aluminum intake.

Two different types of cast-iron intakes were used from 1964 to 1967. Each had the name of the original carburetor—Q-Jet, for Quadra Jet, or Holley—embossed into the valley just to the right of the right front runner of the intake. The casting number was located directly behind the carburetor. The casting date was in front of the distributor. It used a single letter of the alphabet (from A for January to L for December) to designate the month.

Aluminum intakes used only the Holley carburetor. The casting date was coded using a numerical system for the month instead of a lettering system. It was located either on the underside of the intake or near the front water neck.

The vehicle build date can be as much as four weeks from the intake casting date. Because of shipping delays from the Tonawanda plant in New York to the assembly plants, original SSs were built this way.

Be careful with casting dates: remember that the year of the casting may not match that of the model. For example, K 14 8 would have been cast November 14, 1968, and used on a 1969 model. Any date after August is for the following year.

| | | | | | | |
|---|---|---|---|---|---|---|
| 1. | CHOKE SHAFT AND LEVER KIT | 3.752 | 42. | RETAINER, Pump Discharge Ball | 3.826 |
| 2. | ROLL PIN, Pump & Lockout Levers | 8.940 | 43. | BALL, Pump Discharge | 3.825 |
| 3. | LOCKOUT LEVER, Air Valve | 3.757 | 44. | Part of Float Bowl Asm | N.S. |
| 4. | CLIP, Vacuum Brake Rod | 8.934 | 45. | SCREW, Diaphragm Retainer, Part of Float Bowl Asm | N.S. |
| 5. | CHOKE VALVE KIT | 3.752 | 46. | RETAINER, Float Needle Diaphragm Part of Float Bowl Asm | N.S. |
| 6. | SCREW, Choke Valve | 3.751 | 47. | Part of Float Bowl Asm. | N.S. |
| 7. | SCREW, Air Horn | 3.730 | 48. | NEEDLE & SEAT ASM | 3.814 |
| 8. | SECONDARY METERING ROD HOLDER KIT | 3.806 | 49. | FLOAT BOWL ASM | 3.734 |
| 9. | SCREW, Air Horn | 8.907 | 50. | SCREW, Vacuum Brake Control | 3.755 |
| 10. | SCREW, Air Horn | 3.730 | 51. | HOSE, Vacuum | 8.962 |
| 11. | ROLL PIN, Pump & Lockout Levers | 8.940 | 52. | VACUUM BRAKE CONTROL BRACKET | 3.750 |
| 12. | Part of Air Horn Asm | N.S. | 53. | ROD, Vacuum Brake | 3.755 |
| 13. | CLIP, Vacuum Brake Rod | 8.934 | 54. | CLIP, Pump Rod | 3.841 |
| 14. | Part of Air Horn Asm | N.S. | 55. | VACUUM BRAKE CONTROL ASM | 3.755 |
| 15. | Part of Idle Vent Valve Kit | N.S. | 56. | CAM, Fast Idle | 3.766 |
| 16. | LEVER, Pump Actuating | 3.842 | 57. | LOCKOUT LEVER, Secondary | 3.752 |
| 17. | ROLL PIN, Pump & Lockout Levers | 8.940 | 58. | FILTER NUT, Fuel Inlet | 3.740 |
| 18. | SCREW, Idle Vent Valve (Part of Idle Vent Valve Kit) | 3.852 | 59. | GASKET, Inlet Nut | 3.740 |
| 19. | VALVE, Idle Vent (Part of Idle Vent Valve Kit) | 3.852 | 60. | GASKET, Filter | 3.740 |
| | | | 61. | FILTER, Fuel Inlet | 3.740 |
| 20. | Part of Air Horn Asm | N.S. | 62. | SPRING, Inlet Filter | 3.740 |
| 21. | AIR HORN ASM | 3.730 | 63. | SPRING, Idle Stop Screw | 3.766 |
| 22. | METERING ROD, Secondary | 3.806 | 64. | SCREW, Idle Stop | 3.761 |
| 23. | Part of Float Bowl Asm | N.S. | 65. | GASKET, Throttle Body | 3.724 |
| 24. | PUMP ASM | 3.838 | 66. | THROTTLE BODY ASM | 3.729 |
| 25. | SPRING, Pump Return | 3.841 | 67. | LEVER, Fast Idle | 3.766 |
| 26. | GASKET, Air Horn | 3.724 | 68. | SCREW, Cam & Fast Idle Levers Attaching | 3.766 |
| 27. | FLOAT ASM | 3.745 | 69. | SPRING, Cam Follower Lever | 3.766 |
| 28. | HINGE PIN, Float | 3.814 | 70. | SPRING, Fast Idle Screw | 3.766 |
| 29. | SPRING, Metering Rod-Primary | 3.810 | 71. | SCREW, Fast Idle Adjusting | 3.766 |
| 30. | INSERT, Float Bowl | 3.734 | 72. | LEVER, Cam Follower | 3.766 |
| 31. | SCREW, Cover Attaching | 3.820 | 73. | SPRING, Idle Needle | 3.822 |
| 32. | COVER, Idle Compensator | 3.820 | 74. | NEEDLE, Idle Adjusting | 3.822 |
| 33. | IDLE COMPENSATOR ASM | 3.820 | 75. | SCREW, Throttle Body | 3.741 |
| 34. | GASKET, Idle Compensator | 3.724 | 76. | (Part of Throttle Body Asm) | N.S. |
| 35. | ROD, Choke | 3.752 | 77. | (Part of Throttle Body Asm) | N.S. |
| 36. | BAFFLE PLATE, Float Bowl | 3.740 | 78. | CLIP, Pump Rod | 3.841 |
| 37. | LEVER, Intermediate Choke | 3.752 | 79. | ROD, Pump | 3.843 |
| 38. | METERING ROD, Primary | 3.806 | | | |
| 39. | METERING JET, Primary | 3.792 | | | |
| 40. | POWER PISTON ASM | 3.858 | | | |
| 41. | SPRING, Power Piston | 3.859 | | | |

*Rochester four-barrel carburetor.*

## 1966-1972 Cast-Iron Manifold Casting Numbers

| | | |
|---|---|---|
| 1966-67 | Rochester carburetor | 3883948 |
| | Holley carburetor | 3966948 |
| 1968 | Rochester carburetor only | 3883948 |
| 1969 | Rochester carburetor only | 3931063 |
| 1970 | Rochester carburetor only | 3955287 |
| 1971-72 | Rochester carburetor only | |
| | L48 350 ci 4 bbl V-8 | 6262932* |
| | L65 350 ci 2 bbl V-8 | 3990948* |
| | LS3 400 (402 ci) Turbo-Jet V-8 | 3955287 |
| | LS5 454 Turbo-Jet V-8 | 3955287 |

*The correct replacement part number.

## 1965-1971 Aluminum Manifold Casting Numbers

| | | |
|---|---|---|
| 1965 | L37 375 hp 396 ci V-8 (Z16) | 3866963 |
| | L79 350 hp 327 ci V-8 | 3852570* |
| 1966-67 | L78 375 hp 396 ci V-8 | 3805069 |
| 1968 | L78 375 hp 396 ci V-8 | 3885069; 3933163† |
| 1969 | L72 COPO 425 hp 427 ci V-8 | 3933163 |
| | L78, L89 375 hp 396 ci V-8 | 3933163 |
| 1970-71 | L78, L89 375 hp 396 ci V-8 | 3963569 |
| | LS6 450 hp 454 ci V-8 | 3963569 |

*The part number.
†In the last half of the year.

Cast-iron manifolds should be painted Chevrolet Orange to match the engine. Aluminum manifolds should have a natural appearance. Polished aluminum intakes are incorrect for all years.

## Carburetors

### 1964-1965

The standard 283 ci V-8 used the two-barrel Rochester model 2GV carburetor in both 1964 and 1965. Part numbers varied according to the type of transmission installed. Vehicles with air conditioning also used different part numbers.

### 1964-1965 Carburetor Part Numbers

| Transmission | 1964 | 1965 |
|---|---|---|
| Manual | 7024101 | 7024101 |
| Powerglide automatic | 7024106; 7023108* | 7024110 |
| Manual w/AC | 7024102 | 7024103 |
| Powerglide automatic w/AC | 7024108 | 7024112 |

*After April 17, 1964.

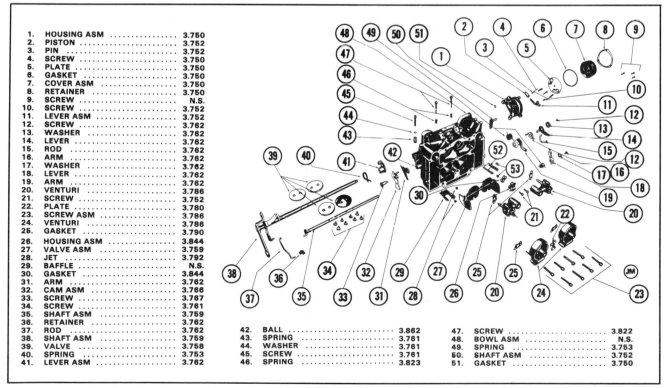

| | | |
|---|---|---|
| 1. | HOUSING ASM | 3.750 |
| 2. | PISTON | 3.752 |
| 3. | PIN | 3.752 |
| 4. | SCREW | 3.750 |
| 5. | PLATE | 3.750 |
| 6. | GASKET | 3.750 |
| 7. | COVER ASM | 3.750 |
| 8. | RETAINER | 3.750 |
| 9. | SCREW | N.S. |
| 10. | SCREW | 3.752 |
| 11. | LEVER ASM | 3.752 |
| 12. | SCREW | 3.762 |
| 13. | WASHER | 3.762 |
| 14. | LEVER | 3.762 |
| 15. | ROD | 3.762 |
| 16. | ARM | 3.762 |
| 17. | WASHER | 3.762 |
| 18. | LEVER | 3.762 |
| 19. | ARM | 3.762 |
| 20. | VENTURI | 3.786 |
| 21. | SCREW | 3.752 |
| 22. | PLATE | 3.780 |
| 23. | SCREW ASM | 3.786 |
| 24. | VENTURI | 3.786 |
| 25. | GASKET | 3.790 |
| 26. | HOUSING ASM | 3.844 |
| 27. | VALVE ASM | 3.759 |
| 28. | JET | 3.792 |
| 29. | BAFFLE | N.S. |
| 30. | GASKET | 3.844 |
| 31. | ARM | 3.762 |
| 32. | CAM ASM | 3.766 |
| 33. | SCREW | 3.767 |
| 34. | SCREW | 3.761 |
| 35. | SHAFT ASM | 3.759 |
| 36. | RETAINER | 3.762 |
| 37. | ROD | 3.762 |
| 38. | SHAFT ASM | 3.759 |
| 39. | VALVE | 3.758 |
| 40. | SPRING | 3.753 |
| 41. | LEVER ASM | 3.762 |

| | | |
|---|---|---|
| 42. | BALL | 3.862 |
| 43. | SPRING | 3.761 |
| 44. | WASHER | 3.761 |
| 45. | SCREW | 3.761 |
| 46. | SPRING | 3.823 |

| | | |
|---|---|---|
| 47. | SCREW | 3.822 |
| 48. | BOWL ASM | N.S. |
| 49. | SPRING | 3.753 |
| 50. | SHAFT ASM | 3.752 |
| 51. | GASKET | 3.750 |

*1964-66 Carter four-barrel carburetor bowl.*

The Rochester model 4GC four-barrel was used on the RPO L77 optional engine. Vehicles with manual transmission used part numbers 7024225 in 1964 and 7025127 in 1965, and those with automatic transmission used part numbers 7024226 in 1964 and 7025128 in 1965. With air conditioning, RPO C60, part number 7025128 was used both years.

Two types of carburetors were used on the L30 250 hp 327 ci V-8. Standard was the four-barrel Rochester 4GC model. The Carter model WCFB was optional, and the units for both years were identical. Cars with air conditioning used the Rochester carb only.

### 1964–1965 Rochester Carburetor Part Numbers

| Transmission | 1964 | 1965 |
| --- | --- | --- |
| Manual | 7024225 | 7025127 |
| Powerglide automatic | 7025124 | 7025128 |
| Manual w/AC | 7024220 | 7024220 |
| Powerglide automatic w/AC | 7025128 | 7025128 |

### 1964–1965 Carter Carburetor Part Numbers

| Transmission | 1964 | 1965 |
| --- | --- | --- |
| Manual | 36975 | 36975 |
| Powerglide automatic | 36985 | 36965 |

The Carter model AFB was used exclusively on the 300 hp 327 engine. Manual-transmission-equipped cars used part number 37215 SA, GM part number 3851761, and cars with automatic used part number 37205 SA, GM part number 3851771. Any other type of carburetor is incorrect. These part numbers were used both years.

The Holley model 4150 was used solely in 1965 on two engines: the L79 350 hp 327 and the L37 375 hp 396. The 327s used part number 3863150. The big-block 396 ci engine also used the 780 cfm Holley carburetor but used a different part number, 3878261; part number 3869933 was also used at the very beginning of production.

All three engines were available with four-speed manual transmission only.

### 1966–1967

Most 1966 SS 396s were equipped with the standard Rochester model 4MV four-barrel carburetor. The optional carburetor was the 585 cfm Holley. These carbs were used only on the L35 and L34 engines. The California L35 used a special Holley only, with provision for emission controls.

Special high-performance option L78 used a 780 cfm Holley model 4150, part numbers 3885067 in 1966 and 3916143 in 1967 only, except in California. A model 4160 was used in California; it was identical to the L34 carburetor.

### 1966 Rochester 4MV Carburetor Part Numbers

**Forty-nine States**

| | | |
| --- | --- | --- |
| L34 | Manual | 7026207 |
| | Powerglide automatic | 7026206 |
| L35 | Manual | 7026201 |
| | Powerglide automatic | 7026200 |

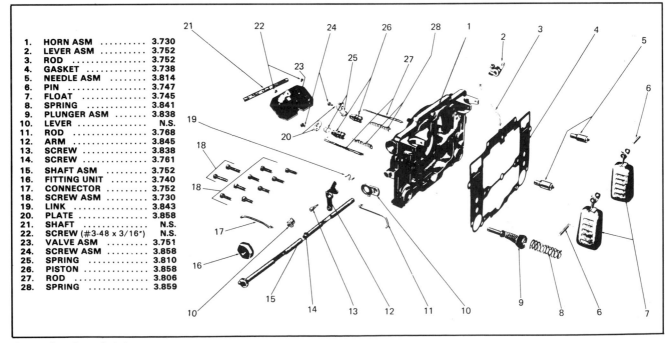

| | | | |
| --- | --- | --- | --- |
| 1. | HORN ASM | | 3.730 |
| 2. | LEVER ASM | | 3.752 |
| 3. | ROD | | 3.752 |
| 4. | GASKET | | 3.738 |
| 5. | NEEDLE ASM | | 3.814 |
| 6. | PIN | | 3.747 |
| 7. | FLOAT | | 3.745 |
| 8. | SPRING | | 3.841 |
| 9. | PLUNGER ASM | | 3.838 |
| 10. | LEVER | | N.S. |
| 11. | ROD | | 3.768 |
| 12. | ARM | | 3.845 |
| 13. | SCREW | | 3.838 |
| 14. | SCREW | | 3.761 |
| 15. | SHAFT ASM | | 3.752 |
| 16. | FITTING UNIT | | 3.740 |
| 17. | CONNECTOR | | 3.752 |
| 18. | SCREW ASM | | 3.730 |
| 19. | LINK | | 3.843 |
| 20. | PLATE | | 3.858 |
| 21. | SHAFT | | N.S. |
| 22. | SCREW (#3-48 x 3/16") | | N.S. |
| 23. | VALVE ASM | | 3.751 |
| 24. | SCREW ASM | | 3.858 |
| 25. | SPRING | | 3.810 |
| 26. | PISTON | | 3.858 |
| 27. | ROD | | 3.806 |
| 28. | SPRING | | 3.859 |

*Carter four-barrel air horn.*

## 1966 Holley 4160 Carburetor Part Numbers

**Forty-nine States**

| | | |
|---|---|---|
| L34 | Manual | 3886087 |
| | Powerglide automatic | 3886088 |
| L35 | Manual | 3874898 |
| | Powerglide automatic | 3874899 |

**California Only**

| | | |
|---|---|---|
| L34 | Manual & AIR | 3892339 |
| | Powerglide automatic & AIR | 3892338 |
| L35 | Manual & AIR | 7036201 |
| | Powerglide automatic & AIR | 7036200 |
| L78 | Manual & AIR | 3892339 |

The standard carburetor for the base L35 engine in 1967 was a Rochester model 4MV. A Holley model 4160 was optional. The L34 engine was standard with the Holley 4160. L78 used a Holley model 4150 rated at 780 cfm. California cars continued to use special carburetors.

## 1967 Rochester 4MV Carburetor Part Numbers

| | | |
|---|---|---|
| L35 | Manual | 7027201; 7027211* |
| | Automatic | 7027200; 7027210* |
| | Manual & AIR | 7037211 |
| | Automatic & AIR | 7037210 |

*After October 20, 1966.

## 1967 Holley 4160 Carburetor Part Numbers

| Transmission | | Holley Part Number | GM Part Number |
|---|---|---|---|
| L34 & L35 | Manual | R-3839 A | 3908957 |
| | Automatic | R-3838 A | 3908956 |
| | Manual & AIR* | R-3837 A | 3908959 |
| | Automatic & AIR* | R-3836 A | 3908958 |

*California only.

## 1968-1969

All engines except L78 used four-barrel Rochester model 4MV carburetors; L78 continued to use Holley part number 3923289. Other carburetors are listed below. AIR emissions were standard but could be deleted for credit, as RPO KD1, except in California. However, unlike versions in the previous years, this option did not affect the carburetor in any way.

## 1968 Carburetor Part Numbers

| | | |
|---|---|---|
| L34 | Manual | 7028217 |
| | Automatic | 7028216 |
| L35 | Manual | 7028211 |
| | Automatic | 7028210 |

Rochester continued to be the only carburetor available on the L35 and L34 engines in 1969. Two different carburetors were used with each engine.

## 1969 Rochester Carburetor Part Numbers

| | | |
|---|---|---|
| L34 | Manual | 7029201 |
| | Automatic | 7029200 |
| L35 | Manual | 7029215 |
| | Automatic | 7029204 |

The 1969 L78 engine and the COPO 427 engine used the same Holley carburetor, model 4150, part numbers 3959164 for manual and 3959165 for Turbo Hydra-matic.

## 1970-1972

The base L34 engine and the LS5 454 engine used the same Rochester carburetor, part numbers 7040205 with manual and 7040204 with the Turbo Hydra-matic. The L78, L89 and LS6 all used a four-barrel 800 cfm Holley carburetor, part number 3767477, except for SSs sold in California.

California cars were standard with Evaporative Emission Control (EEC) in 1970 and required special carburetors. The L34 and LS5 engines used

| | | |
|---|---|---|
| 1 | 3874886 | PIPE ASM - REAR |
| 2 | 3874886 | PIPE ASM - FRONT |
| 3 | 5651143 | FILTER ASM - FUEL |
| 4 | 142559 | ELBOW |
| 5 | 3874882 | PIPE ASM |
| 6 | 445673 | PLUG |
| 7 | 3874876 | SCREW ASM |
| 8 | 6440248 | FUEL PUMP ASM |
| 9 | 3874964 | TEE |
| 10 | 1345198 | GASKET |
| 11 | 3840712 | VALVE ASM |

*1965 396 ci fuel line, fuel filter and fuel pump.*

part numbers 7040505 with manual transmissions and 7040504 with the automatic. The LS6, L78 and L89 engines used part numbers 3967479 with the four-speed and 3967478 with the Turbo Hydra-matic.

Two-barrel Rochester model 2GV returned on the SS in 1971 and 1972. All other engines except the LS6 used the four-barrel Rochester model 4MV carburetor. The LS6 used a four-barrel Holley model 4150, part numbers 3986195 with manual transmission and 3986196 with the automatic. California cars used the same carburetors as those for the other forty-nine states in 1971.

## 1971-1972 Carburetor Part Numbers

| Engine | Transmission | 1971 | 1972 |
|---|---|---|---|
| 2 bbl 350 | Manual | 7041113 | 7042833 |
| | Automatic | 7041114 | 7042834 |

## 1971-1972 Carburetor Part Numbers

| Engine | Transmission | 1971 | 1972 |
|---|---|---|---|
| 4 bbl 350 | Manual | 7041213 | 7042903 |
| | Automatic | 7041212 | 7042902 |
| LS5 4 bbl 400 | Manual | 7041201 | 7042215 |
| | Automatic | 7041200 | 7042220 |

More emission controls were added to California cars in 1972, and again different carburetors were used. No big-block SSs were sold in California that year, as they could not pass the tough emission standards. The following carburetors were used:

## 1972 California Carburetor Part Numbers

| Engine | Transmission | Part Number |
|---|---|---|
| 2 bbl 350 | Manual | 7042113 |
| | Automatic | 7042114 |
| 4 bbl 350 | Manual | 7042203 |
| | Automatic | 7042202 |

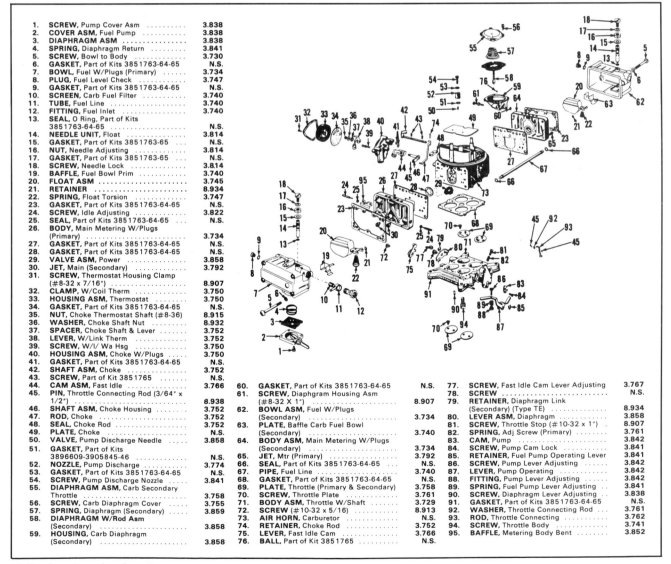

| No. | Description | Group |
|---|---|---|
| 1. | SCREW, Pump Cover Asm | 3.838 |
| 2. | COVER ASM, Fuel Pump | 3.838 |
| 3. | DIAPHRAGM ASM | 3.838 |
| 4. | SPRING, Diaphragm Return | 3.841 |
| 5. | SCREW, Bowl to Body | 3.730 |
| 6. | GASKET, Part of Kits 3851763-64-65 | N.S. |
| 7. | BOWL, Fuel W/Plugs (Primary) | 3.734 |
| 8. | PLUG, Fuel Level Check | 3.747 |
| 9. | GASKET, Part of Kits 3851763-64-65 | N.S. |
| 10. | SCREEN, Carb Fuel Filter | 3.740 |
| 11. | TUBE, Fuel Line | 3.740 |
| 12. | FITTING, Fuel Inlet | 3.740 |
| 13. | SEAL, O Ring, Part of Kits 3851763-64-65 | N.S. |
| 14. | NEEDLE UNIT, Float | 3.814 |
| 15. | GASKET, Part of Kits 3851763-65 | N.S. |
| 16. | NUT, Needle Adjusting | 3.814 |
| 17. | GASKET, Part of Kits 3851763-65 | N.S. |
| 18. | SCREW, Needle Lock | 3.814 |
| 19. | BAFFLE, Fuel Bowl Prim | 3.740 |
| 20. | FLOAT ASM | 3.745 |
| 21. | RETAINER | 8.934 |
| 22. | SPRING, Float Torsion | 3.747 |
| 23. | GASKET, Part of Kits 3851763-64-65 | N.S. |
| 24. | SCREW, Idle Adjusting | 3.822 |
| 25. | SEAL, Part of Kits 3851763-64-65 | N.S. |
| 26. | BODY, Main Metering W/Plugs (Primary) | 3.734 |
| 27. | GASKET, Part of Kits 3851763-64-65 | N.S. |
| 28. | GASKET, Part of Kits 3851763-64-65 | N.S. |
| 29. | VALVE ASM, Power | 3.858 |
| 30. | JET, Main (Secondary) | 3.792 |
| 31. | SCREW, Thermostat Housing Clamp (#8-32 x 7/16") | 8.907 |
| 32. | CLAMP, W/Coil Therm | 3.750 |
| 33. | HOUSING ASM, Thermostat | 3.750 |
| 34. | GASKET, Part of Kits 3851763-64-65 | N.S. |
| 35. | NUT, Choke Thermostat Shaft (#8-36) | 8.915 |
| 36. | WASHER, Choke Shaft Nut | 8.932 |
| 37. | SPACER, Choke Shaft & Lever | 3.752 |
| 38. | LEVER, W/Link Therm | 3.752 |
| 39. | SCREW, W/I/ Wa Hsg | 3.750 |
| 40. | HOUSING ASM, Choke W/Plugs | 3.750 |
| 41. | GASKET, Part of Kits 3851763-64-65 | N.S. |
| 42. | SHAFT ASM, Choke | 3.752 |
| 43. | SCREW, Part of Kit 3851765 | N.S. |
| 44. | CAM ASM, Fast Idle | 3.766 |
| 45. | PIN, Throttle Connecting Rod (3/64" x 1/2") | 8.938 |
| 46. | SHAFT ASM, Choke Housing | 3.752 |
| 47. | ROD, Choke | 3.752 |
| 48. | SEAL, Choke Rod | 3.752 |
| 49. | PLATE, Choke | N.S. |
| 50. | VALVE, Pump Discharge Needle | 3.858 |
| 51. | GASKET, Part of Kits 3896609-3905845-46 | N.S. |
| 52. | NOZZLE, Pump Discharge | 3.774 |
| 53. | GASKET, Part of Kits 3851763-64-65 | N.S. |
| 54. | SCREW, Pump Discharge Nozzle | 3.841 |
| 55. | DIAPHRAGM ASM, Carb Secondary Throttle | 3.758 |
| 56. | SCREW, Carb Diaphragm Cover | 3.755 |
| 57. | SPRING, Diaphragm (Secondary) | 3.859 |
| 58. | DIAPHRAGM W/Rod Asm (Secondary) | 3.858 |
| 59. | HOUSING, Carb Diaphragm (Secondary) | 3.858 |
| 60. | GASKET, Part of Kits 3851763-64-65 | N.S. |
| 61. | SCREW, Diaphgram Housing Asm (#8-32 X 1") | 8.907 |
| 62. | BOWL ASM, Fuel W/Plugs (Secondary) | 3.734 |
| 63. | PLATE, Baffle Carb Fuel Bowl (Secondary) | 3.740 |
| 64. | BODY ASM, Main Metering W/Plugs (Secondary) | 3.734 |
| 65. | JET, Mtr (Primary) | 3.792 |
| 66. | SEAL, Part of Kits 3851763-64-65 | N.S. |
| 67. | PIPE, Fuel Line | 3.740 |
| 68. | GASKET, Part of Kits 3851763-64-65 | N.S. |
| 69. | PLATE, Throttle (Primary & Secondary) | 3.758 |
| 70. | SCREW, Throttle Plate | 3.761 |
| 71. | BODY ASM, Throttle W/Shaft | 3.729 |
| 72. | SCREW (#10-32 x 5/16) | 8.913 |
| 73. | AIR HORN, Carburetor | N.S. |
| 74. | RETAINER, Choke Rod | 3.752 |
| 75. | LEVER, Fast Idle Cam | 3.766 |
| 76. | BALL, Part of Kit 3851765 | N.S. |
| 77. | SCREW, Fast Idle Cam Lever Adjusting | 3.767 |
| 78. | SCREW | N.S. |
| 79. | RETAINER, Diaphragm Link (Secondary) (Type TE) | 8.934 |
| 80. | LEVER ASM, Diaphragm | 3.858 |
| 81. | SCREW, Throttle Stop (#10-32 x 1") | 8.907 |
| 82. | SPRING, Adj Screw (Primary) | 3.761 |
| 83. | CAM, Pump | 3.842 |
| 84. | SCREW, Pump Cam Lock | 3.841 |
| 85. | RETAINER, Fuel Pump Operating Lever | 3.841 |
| 86. | SCREW, Pump Lever Adjusting | 3.842 |
| 87. | LEVER, Pump Operating | 3.842 |
| 88. | FITTING, Pump Lever Adjusting | 3.842 |
| 89. | SPRING, Fuel Pump Lever Adjusting | 3.841 |
| 90. | SCREW, Diaphragm Lever Adjusting | 3.838 |
| 91. | GASKET, Part of Kits 3851763-64-65 | N.S. |
| 92. | WASHER, Throttle Connecting Rod | 3.761 |
| 93. | ROD, Throttle Connecting | 3.762 |
| 94. | SCREW, Throttle Body | 3.741 |
| 95. | BAFFLE, Metering Body Bent | 3.852 |

*Holley four-barrel carburetor.*

## Accelerator Control

### 1964-1965

Accelerator rod part number 3837896 was used on all V-8 engines in 1964. It was threaded on one end, and that end attached to a swivel, part number 3758592, that mounted to the carburetor lever with a sleeve and bushing. The other end of the rod was attached to the pedal dash lever, part number 3853567, with a bushing sleeve and cotter pin. Be sure that the pin mounts on the outward left-hand side of the lever.

The kickback spring, part number 3785404, connected to the nose of the swivel and a tab on the oil fill spout. The long end of the spring should be assembled at the carburetor end.

The rod and the swivel should have a natural metal appearance. The spring should be white, and the dash lever flat-black.

For a short time in 1965 the same parts were again used on all V-8s except the L37 396 big-block. The rod was changed to part number 3860296 in November 1964. This rod differed in that it should turn freely in the bushing at the dash lever. The later rod provided for better throttle control and will interchange with the earlier design. Painting is the same as in 1964 except that the spring is blue.

The 396 ci engine used a unique rod assembly, part number 3874698. This rod was bent slightly at the carburetor end and threaded on the opposite end, where it mounted to a swivel that attached to the dash lever. A sleeve bushing and cotter pin secured the swivel to the lever. All of these were production parts.

The return spring was listed as part number 3871197. The long end of the spring was attached to the nose of the accelerator rod at the carburetor, and the other end to the lower hole in the generator bracket.

The rod, swivel and dash rod should be painted like those on production engines. The spring should be painted dark red.

### 1966-1967

In both 1966 and 1967 the throttle position was controlled by a rod, part number 3884868 in 1966, which was assembled like the one on the L37 engine in 1965. The return spring used the same part number and color as in 1965.

The rod was slightly redesigned in 1967 and used part number 3913411. The bushing and sleeve were no longer installed at the carburetor end. The rod was attached with a single cotter pin.

The location of the throttle return spring, part number 3913415, was also changed. The long end was attached in the bottom hole of the accelerator lever on the carburetor, and the short end to the coil bracket. The throttle rod should have a natural metal appearance. The return spring should be painted silver in 1967.

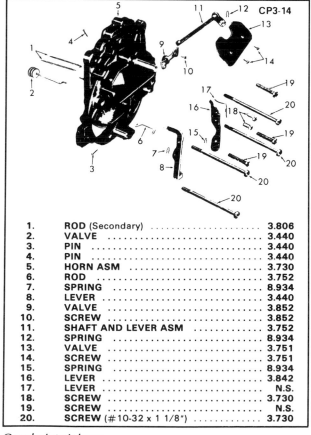

| 1. | ROD (Secondary) | 3.806 |
|---|---|---|
| 2. | VALVE | 3.440 |
| 3. | PIN | 3.440 |
| 4. | PIN | 3.440 |
| 5. | HORN ASM | 3.730 |
| 6. | ROD | 3.752 |
| 7. | SPRING | 8.934 |
| 8. | LEVER | 3.440 |
| 9. | VALVE | 3.852 |
| 10. | SCREW | 3.852 |
| 11. | SHAFT AND LEVER ASM | 3.752 |
| 12. | SPRING | 8.934 |
| 13. | VALVE | 3.751 |
| 14. | SCREW | 3.751 |
| 15. | SPRING | 8.934 |
| 16. | LEVER | 3.842 |
| 17. | LEVER | N.S. |
| 18. | SCREW | 3.730 |
| 19. | SCREW | N.S. |
| 20. | SCREW (#10-32 x 1 1/8″) | 3.730 |

*Quadrajet air horn.*

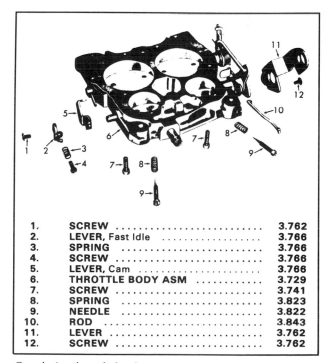

| 1. | SCREW | 3.762 |
|---|---|---|
| 2. | LEVER, Fast Idle | 3.766 |
| 3. | SPRING | 3.766 |
| 4. | SCREW | 3.766 |
| 5. | LEVER, Cam | 3.766 |
| 6. | THROTTLE BODY ASM | 3.729 |
| 7. | SCREW | 3.741 |
| 8. | SPRING | 3.823 |
| 9. | NEEDLE | 3.822 |
| 10. | ROD | 3.843 |
| 11. | LEVER | 3.762 |
| 12. | SCREW | 3.762 |

*Quadrajet throttle body.*

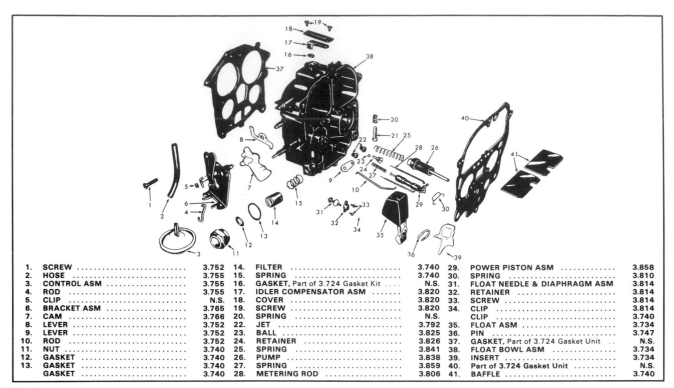

| | | | | | | | |
|---|---|---|---|---|---|---|---|
| 1. | SCREW | 3.752 | 14. | FILTER | 3.740 | 29. | POWER PISTON ASM | 3.858 |
| 2. | HOSE | 3.755 | 15. | SPRING | 3.740 | 30. | SPRING | 3.810 |
| 3. | CONTROL ASM | 3.755 | 16. | GASKET, Part of 3.724 Gasket Kit | N.S. | 31. | FLOAT NEEDLE & DIAPHRAGM ASM | 3.814 |
| 4. | ROD | 3.755 | 17. | IDLER COMPENSATOR ASM | 3.820 | 32. | RETAINER | 3.814 |
| 5. | CLIP | N.S. | 18. | COVER | 3.820 | 33. | SCREW | 3.814 |
| 6. | BRACKET ASM | 3.765 | 19. | SCREW | 3.820 | 34. | CLIP | 3.814 |
| 7. | CAM | 3.766 | 20. | SPRING | N.S. | | CLIP | 3.740 |
| 8. | LEVER | 3.752 | 22. | JET | 3.792 | 35. | FLOAT ASM | 3.734 |
| 9. | LEVER | 3.752 | 23. | BALL | 3.825 | 36. | PIN | 3.747 |
| 10. | ROD | 3.752 | 24. | RETAINER | 3.826 | 37. | GASKET, Part of 3.724 Gasket Unit | N.S. |
| 11. | NUT | 3.740 | 25. | SPRING | 3.841 | 38. | FLOAT BOWL ASM | 3.734 |
| 12. | GASKET | 3.740 | 26. | PUMP | 3.838 | 39. | INSERT | 3.734 |
| 13. | GASKET | 3.740 | 27. | SPRING | 3.859 | 40. | Part of 3.724 Gasket Unit | N.S. |
| | GASKET | 3.740 | 28. | METERING ROD | 3.806 | 41. | BAFFLE | 3.740 |

*Rochester float bowl.*

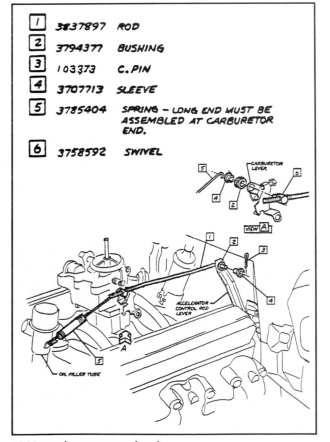

| 1 | 3837897 | ROD |
| 2 | 3794377 | BUSHING |
| 3 | 103373 | C. PIN |
| 4 | 3707713 | SLEEVE |
| 5 | 3785404 | SPRING - LONG END MUST BE ASSEMBLED AT CARBURETOR END. |
| 6 | 3758592 | SWIVEL |

*1964 accelerator control rod.*

### 1968-1972

A black-plastic-covered cable was used in 1968 to control the accelerator. The cable attached to the accelerator lever on the carburetor with a stud, washer and nut. This cable was supported by a bracket that mounted to the carburetor. The 1968 bracket used a design different from the one for other years. For 1968 the cable was routed through a hole in the bracket; from 1969 on, the cable was pressed into place by two fingers on the bracket that gripped the protective rubber grommets on the cable.

Brackets should be silver-cadmium-plated. This process creates the original natural metal look, and it can be used anywhere the natural metal look is needed—as long as the part is not subjected to heavy strain, since the plating process weakens the metal.

For 1968 and 1969 the return springs were in the same location as in 1967. For 1970-72 the springs were shorter and positioned between the accelerator lever on the carburetor and the cable support bracket. Cable, bracket and spring part numbers are listed below.

### 1968-1972 Accelerator Control Part Numbers

| Year | Cable | Bracket | Spring |
|---|---|---|---|
| 1968 | 3930793 | 3943667 | 3923501 |
| 1969 | 3949057 | 3949071 | 3923501 |

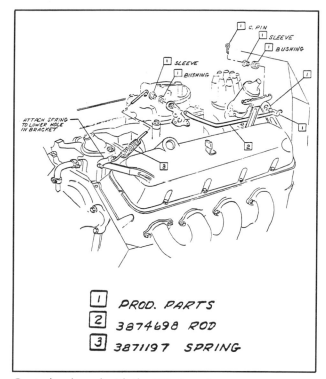

| 1 | PROD. PARTS |
| 2 | 3874698 ROD |
| 3 | 3871197 SPRING |

*Control rod used with the 396 ci engine.*

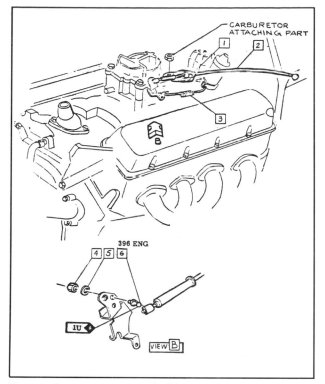

*The accelerator was controlled by a cable in 1968.*

## 1968-1972 Accelerator Control Part Numbers

| Year | Cable | Bracket | Spring |
|---|---|---|---|
| 1970 | 3972679 | 3972618; 3992361*; 3992376† | 3970274 |
| 1970-71 | | | |
| LS6 | 3972296 | 3980982 | 3970274 |
| 1971 | | | |
| L48 | 3972679 | 3992376 | 3970274 |
| L65 | 3973863 | 3972295‡ | 3952776 |
| LS3 & LS5 | 3972679 | 3992376 | 3970274 |
| 1972 | | | |
| L48 | 3973862 | 326564 | 3970274 |
| L65 | 3973863 | § | 6261815 |
| LS3 & LS5 | 3972679 | 326564 | 3970274 |

*From March 26, 1970, till May 19, 1970.

†From May 19, 1970, till the end of the model year.

‡Should be painted Chevrolet Orange.

§Used no part number, was part of the engine and should be painted Chevrolet Orange.

## Air Cleaners

### 1964-1965

All V-8 air cleaners in 1964 used the same design: they were cylindrical with a single air horn that was molded into the top portion of the assembly. For correctness the air horn should be positioned 35 degrees right of the centerline of the engine. Two different assemblies were available. The two-barrel 283 ci engine used part number 6419469, and all four-barrel engines used part number 6420857. All air cleaners were painted gloss-black.

Vehicles with closed engine ventilation, RPO K24, required different air cleaner assemblies. All four-barrel engines used part number 6419182, and the base V-8 used part number 6419470. These air cleaners were mandatory in California; the only difference was a provision in the base of the air

*The decal on this air cleaner is incorrect; no decal was used on the 1964-65 air cleaner assembly. The hose clamps are also incorrect; they should be tower clamps.*

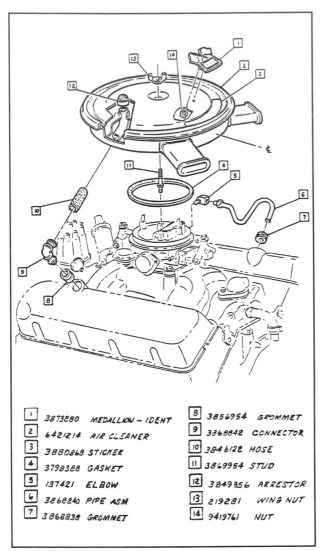

| | | | |
|---|---|---|---|
| 1 | 3873880 | MEDALLION – IDENT | |
| 2 | 6421214 | AIR CLEANER | |
| 3 | 3880868 | STICKER | |
| 4 | 3798388 | GASKET | |
| 5 | 137421 | ELBOW | |
| 6 | 3868840 | PIPE ASM | |
| 7 | 3868838 | GROMMET | |
| 8 | 3856954 | GROMMET | |
| 9 | 3868842 | CONNECTOR | |
| 10 | 3846122 | HOSE | |
| 11 | 3869954 | STUD | |
| 12 | 3849356 | ARRESTOR | |
| 13 | 219281 | WING NUT | |
| 14 | 9419761 | NUT | |

*Air cleaner assembly of the 1965 L37 engine.*

*Open element air cleaner used with the L34 and L78 engine options.*

cleaner for the ventilation hose. These air cleaners were also painted gloss-black.

Except on the L79 and L37 engines, the 1965 standard air cleaner was identical to the 1964 versions. The L79 assembly, part number 6420857, featured dual air horns, and the top and base were chrome-plated. Closed ventilation was standard.

A different design of air cleaner, part number 6421214, was used on the L37 396 ci engine. A dual air horn design was employed here, but the horns were molded into the base, which was painted gloss-black. The lid was chrome and held an engine identification medallion, part number 3873880; a decal is incorrect. A decal that read Turbo-Jet 375 Hp was placed below the medallion on the lid. Closed ventilation was standard with this air cleaner.

California cars used different air cleaners. Also, all states could order a new option Superlift

air shocks, RPO G67, which used a compressor that drew air from the air cleaner. Both RPO K24, closed ventilation, and G67 could be installed on the same car.

## 1964-1965 Air Cleaner Part Numbers

| | |
|---|---|
| Base 283 | 6420901 |
| L30, L74, L77 | 6420903 |
| L76, L79 | 6420857 |
| **With K24** | |
| Base 283 | 6420902 |
| L30, L74, L77 | 6420904 |
| **With G67** | |
| Base 283 | 6421577 |
| L30, L74, L77 | 6421579 |
| **With K24 and G67** | |
| Base 283 | 6421578 |
| L30, L74, L77 | 6421580 |
| L79 | 6421581 |

## 1966-1967

The standard air cleaner on the base L35 engine was listed as part number 6421312; part number 6421213 was also used at some plants. Both were cylindrical in design with a single air horn on the base portion. For correctness the air horn should be positioned 73 degrees left of the centerline of the engine. The base was painted gloss-black, and the lid was chrome-plated.

Both L34 and L78 used the same style of open element 14.16 in. diameter air cleaner with a chrome-plated top. The bases differed, however. L78 used part number 6423240 and was standard with closed ventilation, which provided a port for the crankcase ventilation hose from the valve cover. L34 used part number 6421773, and it was optional with K24 but then used part number 6421774, although it was identical to the L78 unit.

California SSs came with Air Injection Reactor (AIR) and closed ventilation emissions, which required air cleaners with extra provisions in the base for the hose. L35 used part number 6423268. The open element air cleaner, part number 6423269, was used on L34 with AIR; it can be identified by the hose port on the right-hand side and a clip on the left-hand side that supported a carburetor hose. For more details see the Emissions section later in this chapter.

For 1967 the air cleaners for the forty-nine states were unchanged except that closed ventilation was standard on L34 and used the L78 air cleaner. California SSs once again were mandatory with AIR emissions, RPO K19. The L35 assembly was unchanged and used the same part number. The L34 air cleaner was still of the open element design, but the clip on the base was eliminated, as was the hose it supported.

## 1967 Air Cleaner Part Numbers
| | |
|---|---|
| L34 & L78 | 6423907 |
| L34 w/AIR | 6423908 |
| L35 | 6423266 |
| L35 w/K24 | 6423267 |
| L35 w/AIR | 6423268 |

### 1968-1969
Air cleaners in 1968 were similar in design to those in previous years, but the air horn on the L35 engine was positioned by a slot in the carburetor. All fifty states were now standard with AIR emissions, but no special air cleaner was used. Closed ventilation was optional on the L35 engine, but again the standard air cleaner was used. When the closed ventilation option—now known as RPO KD5—was selected, the air cleaner was modified. See the Emissions section later in this chapter for further details.

## 1968 Air Cleaner Part Numbers
| | |
|---|---|
| L34 & L78 | 6423907 |
| L35 | 6483662 |
| L35 w/automatic | 6424428 |

Nothing, including part numbers, was changed in 1969, except when automatic transmission was ordered; then all engines used a closed-style assembly, part number 6484590. This assembly was similar to the one used on the L35 engine. It is recognizable by the thermo-mag unit on the snorkel.

The air cleaner used on the COPO 427 Chevelle was the L78 air cleaner. In addition to the production engine decals, each building dealer also used its own logo.

### 1970-1972
The open element air cleaner, part number 6485239, was used throughout 1970 on the new base L34 engine. The L78 and L89 engines began

production with the same open element filter. However, after February 1970 it was replaced with a closed style with dual air horns, listed as part number 6485257. The lids were chrome-plated, while the base was painted 30 degree gloss black.

The LS5 454 engine used a single air horn air cleaner, part number 6485252, and should be painted gloss-black, including the lid. The LS6 engine used the same dual air horn assembly as on the L78 option. This was the standard air cleaner and is rare, as most LS6s came with cowl induction RPO ZL2, which is covered later in this chapter. Of the LS6s built, probably fewer than 200 used the standard air cleaner.

For 1971 the standard air cleaner was re-shifted. The RPO LS3 used the LS5 air cleaner, which was unchanged and had the same part number as it did in 1970. The LS6 continued to used the same standard dual air horn cleaner as it did in 1970.

The 350 small-block used two different air cleaners. The two-barrel, RPO L65, used part number 6485900, and the four-barrel, RPO L48, used part number 6485240. Both were of the closed single air horn design and were painted gloss-black.

In 1972 the LS3 and 350 ci engines used the same air cleaner as before. The LS6 option was

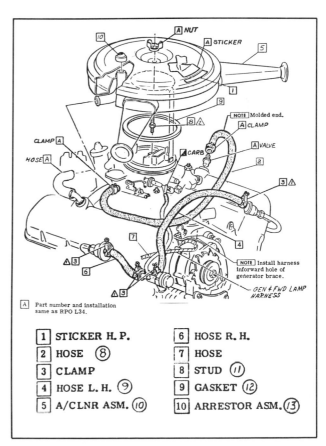

| | | | |
|---|---|---|---|
| 1 | STICKER H. P. | 6 | HOSE R. H. |
| 2 | HOSE ⑧ | 7 | HOSE |
| 3 | CLAMP | 8 | STUD ⑪ |
| 4 | HOSE L. H. ⑨ | 9 | GASKET ⑫ |
| 5 | A/CLNR ASM. ⑩ | 10 | ARRESTOR ASM. ⑬ |

*Standard air cleaner for the LS-6 engine.*

25

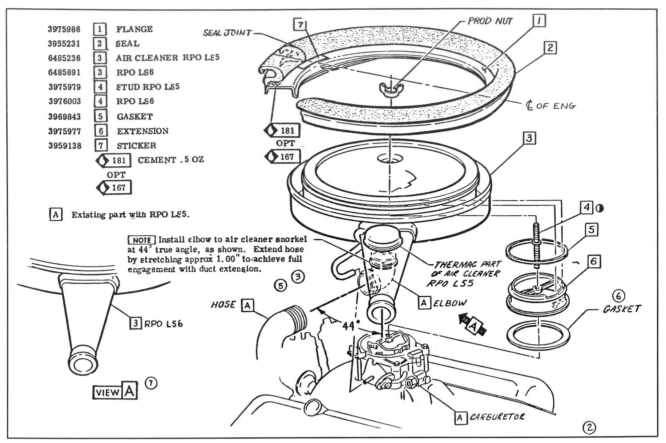

| 3975986 | [1] | FLANGE |
| 3955231 | [2] | SEAL |
| 6485236 | [3] | AIR CLEANER RPO LS5 |
| 6485891 | [3] | RPO LS6 |
| 3975979 | [4] | STUD RPO LS5 |
| 3976003 | [4] | RPO LS6 |
| 3969843 | [5] | GASKET |
| 3975977 | [6] | EXTENSION |
| 3959138 | [7] | STICKER |
| | 181 | CEMENT .5 OZ |
| | OPT | |
| | 167 | |

[A]  Existing part with RPO LS5.

[NOTE] Install elbow to air cleaner snorkel at 44° true angle, as shown. Extend hose by stretching approx 1.00" to achieve full engagement with duct extension.

*1970-72 cowl induction air cleaner assembly.*

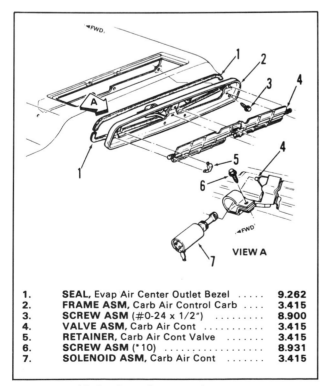

| | | | |
|---|---|---|---|
| 1. | SEAL, Evap Air Center Outlet Bezel | . . . . | 9.262 |
| 2. | FRAME ASM, Carb Air Control Carb | . . . . | 3.415 |
| 3. | SCREW ASM (#0-24 x 1/2") | . . . . . . . . | 8.900 |
| 4. | VALVE ASM, Carb Air Cont | . . . . . . . . . . | 3.415 |
| 5. | RETAINER, Carb Air Cont Valve | . . . . . . . | 3.415 |
| 6. | SCREW ASM (*10) | . . . . . . . . . . . . . . . . | 8.931 |
| 7. | SOLENOID ASM, Carb Air Cont | . . . . . . . | 3.415 |

*1970-72 cowl induction valve control.*

canceled, and the LS5 used a dual-air-style air cleaner, part number 6485248. This air cleaner was replaced with part number 6485254 midway through the year. With air conditioning, part number 6487394 was used. Both air cleaners should be painted gloss-black.

## Cowl Induction

### 1970-1972

A dealer-installed "special order" cowl induction system was available on the Chevelle in 1967-68. It was similar in design to the one used on the 1967-68 Camaro Z28, as it used ducting to draw air in from the passenger's side of the cowl.

Better known and more common was the ZL2 system used on the 1970-72 Chevelle SSs. It was available only on the big-block engines from the factory—on the 454 only in 1971 and 1972—but some dealers installed it for their customers, even on the 350 small-block. This last was not a General Motors authorized option, and unless original paperwork indicates it was done by the dealer, cowl induction would be incorrect on the small-block.

Only one special air cleaner was used in 1970. Listed as part number 6485235 it was painted

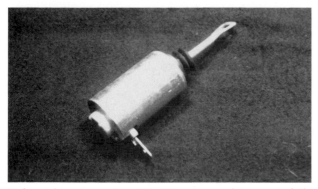

*Solenoid part number 1114427 was used to control the valve assembly.*

*Solenoid installed into the frame.*

gloss-black, including the lid. No evidence indicates that a chrome lid was optional from the factory. In 1971 two air cleaners were available. The LS5 used part number 6485236, and the LS6 used part number 6485891, which featured no thermo-mag housing on the snorkel. The LS5 continued into 1972 unchanged; the LS6 was dropped May 25, 1971.

A metal flange, part number 3975986, was the same all three years and was used to fill in the open area. A rubber seal, part number 3955231, was glued to the flange. A joint should be in the seal, and a small Rear sticker was centered on the flange at this seal. The flange should be gloss-black, and the rubber seal a natural look.

An extension, part number 3975977, was used on top of the carburetor to set the air cleaner up into the hood dome. The extension was secured with the carburetor stud, and gaskets were used on each side of the extension. L78 and LS6 used a slightly longer stud in 1970.

Often called a "flapper" because of the way it moves a valve, part number 3955226 controlled the airflow into the carburetor. It was mounted in a frame housing, part number 3975984, with three small retainers, part number 3955227. The frame assembly was attached to the underside of the domed hood with six 10-24×½ in. screws. For correctness a seal should be used between the frame and the hood and should be wrapped around the perimeter of the frame. Both the frame and the valve should be painted 0 degree gloss-black.

The position of the flapper was controlled by an electronic airflow solenoid, part number 1114427, which was held by a bracket on the back of the frame assembly with number 10 screws. The eye of the solenoid connected over the valve control arm.

The correct procedure for installing the solenoid is this: With the solenoid in the bracket and attached to the valve in the closed position, hold the plunger down, then pull back to remove all end play and torque down using 20–30 lb-ft of torque.

When air was needed, engine vacuum was used to lift the hood door with the assistance of an actuator, part number 1998970, which should have a natural finish. The inlet tube of the actuator should point to the right-hand side of the car when it is installed correctly in the support, part number 3968554. An arrow indicated the front of the support. The actuator was secured to the support with two 24 thread number 10 nuts; in 1972 a washer was also used. The support should be painted gloss-black.

A small length of black rubber hose was routed from the inlet stem of the actuator to the black side of a smaller valve, part number 6440776; the gold side of this valve was connected to a fitting in the intake manifold. Several different brass fittings were used, with the part number depending on the other accessories installed on the car.

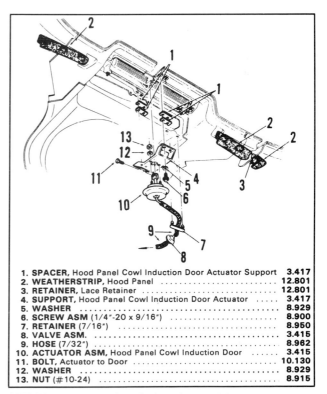

| | |
|---|---|
| 1. SPACER, Hood Panel Cowl Induction Door Actuator Support | 3.417 |
| 2. WEATHERSTRIP, Hood Panel | 12.801 |
| 3. RETAINER, Lace Retainer | 12.801 |
| 4. SUPPORT, Hood Panel Cowl Induction Door Actuator | 3.417 |
| 5. WASHER | 8.929 |
| 6. SCREW ASM (1/4"-20 x 9/16") | 8.900 |
| 7. RETAINER (7/16") | 8.950 |
| 8. VALVE ASM. | 3.415 |
| 9. HOSE (7/32") | 8.962 |
| 10. ACTUATOR ASM, Hood Panel Cowl Induction Door | 3.415 |
| 11. BOLT, Actuator to Door | 10.130 |
| 12. WASHER | 8.929 |
| 13. NUT (#10-24) | 8.915 |

*1970-72 actuator and underhood assemblies.*

## 1970-1972 Cowl Induction Brass Fitting Part Numbers

| Year | Fitting | Part Number |
|------|---------|-------------|
| 1970 | Power brakes | 3905372 |
| | Power brakes & AC or automatic | 3905374 |
| | Power brakes & AC & automatic | 3905376 |
| 1970-72 | No other accessories | 3891523 |
| | Automatic or AC | 3891524 |
| | Automatic & AC | 3891048 |

Two different hoods were available. Most 1970 models used part number 3365951, but those built after May 3, 1970, used part number 3987028, which was employed throughout unchanged till 1972. Both hoods featured a cutout at the rear edge. The cowl hood door, part number 3968539, was used all three years on both hoods. It should be painted to match the hood and should fit flush when in the closed position.

Spacers part number 396556 were used as needed on the door and actuator to position the hood door. The door was held to the hood with two hinge-supports part number 3968555 and four 1/4-20X9/16 in. screws. The underside of the hood door should be painted gloss-black.

Sport stripes and hood hold-down pins were part of the package all three years. Hood pins were used only on cars with cowl induction in 1970. They were made part of the SS package in 1971 and 1972.

The wiring harness for the cowl induction was listed as part number 8901587 all three years. Two leads were routed to the fuse panel: the ignition (pink) lead was plugged into the bottom right-hand receptacle; the accessory (tan) lead was plugged into the receptacle above the ignition lead.

Two other wires connected to a switch, part number 1233031, mounted on the accelerator rod with a special bracket, part number 3972676. This bracket should be painted 30 degree gloss-black.

A total of four other leads were routed through a special drilled hole in the firewall. Three leads went to a relay, part number 4540898, mounted on the firewall. The other lead was routed along with the engine harness to the valve solenoid. A special rubber grommet, part number 3955229, was used on the underside of the hood to protect the lead.

## Exhaust Systems

### 1964-1965

The base V-8 engine was standard with a single exhaust system in 1964. The head pipe was listed as part number 3840868, and a muffler as part number 3981942. The muffler was 17 in. in overall length and was the same one used on later six-cylinder systems. The tailpipe was listed as part number 3853651. In 1965 the muffler was increased to 21.25 in. in overall length and used part number 39819747. The head pipe was now listed as 3840868, and the tailpipe was the same.

Dual exhaust was not available as an option for the base V-8 in 1964. An optional dual exhaust system was available in 1965 as RPO N10. The head pipes for this option were listed as part numbers 3864735-LH and 3864736-RH, and the hanger as part number 1359887. Resonators were placed at the ends of each tailpipe; the original part numbers, 38663961-LH and 3863962-RH, included

*Actuator. Note the correct mounting position.*

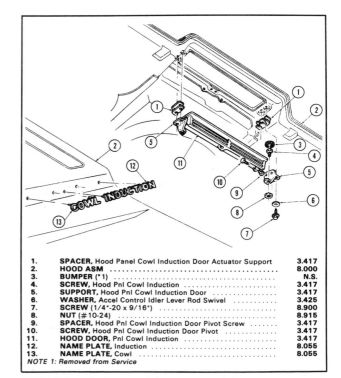

| | | |
|---|---|---|
| 1. | SPACER, Hood Panel Cowl Induction Door Actuator Support | 3.417 |
| 2. | HOOD ASM .......................................... | 8.000 |
| 3. | BUMPER (*1) ........................................ | N.S. |
| 4. | SCREW, Hood Pnl Cowl Induction ..................... | 3.417 |
| 5. | SUPPORT, Hood Pnl Cowl Induction Door .............. | 3.417 |
| 6. | WASHER, Accel Control Idler Lever Rod Swivel ......... | 3.425 |
| 7. | SCREW (1/4"-20 x 9/16") ............................ | 8.900 |
| 8. | NUT (#10-24) ....................................... | 8.915 |
| 9. | SPACER, Hood Pnl Cowl Induction Door Pivot Screw ....... | 3.417 |
| 10. | SCREW, Hood Pnl Cowl Induction Door Pivot .............. | 3.417 |
| 11. | HOOD DOOR, Pnl Cowl Induction ....................... | 3.417 |
| 12. | NAME PLATE, Induction ............................... | 8.055 |
| 13. | NAME PLATE, Cowl .................................... | 8.055 |
| NOTE 1: Removed from Service | | |

*1970-72 hood, door and dome nameplates.*

the tailpipes, which exited below the quarter panels. No chrome extensions were used.

All other V-8 engine options were standard with dual exhaust in 1964. The L77 and L30 engines used the same part numbers. The head pipes were listed as 3840878-LH and 33840879-RH; the muffler was 21.25 in. in overall length and was again listed as the part number 39819747. Tailpipes part numbers 3840877-LH and 3840878-RH exited under the rear quarter panels. The tailpipes were changed to part numbers 3857387-LH and 3857388-RH in 1965 but exited in the same place. No chrome extensions were used either year.

The L74 engine used larger 2 in. outside diameter (OD) exhaust pipes in 1964. The head pipes were listed as part numbers 3857377-LH and 3857378-RH. The tailpipes were also larger in diameter, and they were listed as part numbers 3857385-LH and 3857386-RH and exited farther back under the rear quarter panels. In 1965 the part numbers were the same as for the L30 engine. No chrome extensions were used.

The L37 engine used a set of specially designed exhaust manifolds that had rounder edges and no provisions for AIR emissions, as in 1966-72. The casting numbers were 3869925-LH and 3868874-RH. These were found on the outer side. The casting date was found on the inner face of the manifold, next to the cylinder head. It used the same letter code used with cast-iron intake manifolds. The head pipes were large 2.5 in. OD units, and the tailpipes were 2.25 in. OD units and exited under the rear fenders. No chrome extension was used.

### 1964-1965 L37 Engine Exhaust System Part Numbers

Muffler | 335219
Head pipes |
LH | 3872835
RH | 3872836
Tailpipes |
LH | 3876971
RH | 3876972
Hangers |
LH | 3876973
RH | 3876974

### 1966-1967

All SS 396s were standard with dual exhaust in 1966-67. Head pipes were the same diameter as in 1965 on the L37 engine. The tailpipes were smaller—2 in. OD. Exhaust manifolds were redesigned, and all manifolds, except those in early 1966, had provisions for AIR emissions, even those on cars not sold in California.

Casting numbers for 1966 manifolds with AIR were 3904399-LH and 3872770-RH; manifolds without the AIR provision drilled in them used a different set of casting numbers, 3904399-LH and 3872770-RH. For 1967, only one set of casting numbers was used for both AIR and non-AIR cars; they were 3909879-LH and 3909880-RH. The casting date should be no more than four weeks from the vehicle's build date. Manifolds should be painted dark cast-iron-gray. This simulates the look of a natural cast-iron finish.

Mufflers were 21.25 in. in length and should have a natural aluminum appearance. Tailpipes exited under the rear quarter panels behind the rear wheels. No chrome tailpipe extensions were used either year.

### 1966-1967 Exhaust System Part Numbers

| Part | 1966 | 1967 |
| --- | --- | --- |
| Muffler | 335219 | 335219 |
| Head pipes | | |
| LH | 3872835 | 3904047 |
| RH | 3872836 | 3900592 |
| Tailpipes | | |
| LH | 3901731 | 3901731 |
| RH | 3901732 | 3901732 |
| Rear hangers | | |
| LH | 3901731; 3901727* | 3901727 |
| RH | 3901732; 3901728* | 3901728 |

*After February 1, 1966.

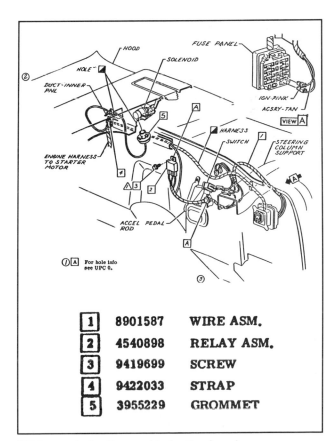

| 1 | 8901587 | WIRE ASM. |
| 2 | 4540898 | RELAY ASM. |
| 3 | 9419699 | SCREW |
| 4 | 9422033 | STRAP |
| 5 | 3955229 | GROMMET |

*Wiring route for the cowl induction hood.*

Pipes should be a natural metal finish except the section of tailpipe from the hanger to the end of the pipe, which should be painted gloss-black.

## 1968-1969

The exhaust system was redesigned for the new body in 1968, and large, oval-shaped chrome exhaust extensions, part number 3956756, were used on all engines. However, early cars with the L35 engine were not available with chrome extensions as standard equipment; this change occurred in late December 1967.

These chrome extensions were used unchanged with all dual exhaust systems till 1972. They were not used on the pickup, however, so it is incorrect for an El Camino to have chrome exhaust extensions.

The left-hand exhaust manifold used the same casting number in both 1968 and 1969 as in 1967. The right-hand unit was changed to casting number 3916178 in 1968. Even though the casting numbers are the same, be sure the casting date agrees with the model year of your Chevelle. Remember to match the actual casting date, and not the model year. These manifolds were also used on the COPO 427 Chevelle in 1969.

### 1968-1969 Exhaust System Part Numbers

| Muffler | 335219 |
| --- | --- |
| Head pipes | |
| LH | 3930765; 3930767* |
| RH | 3930766; 3930368* |

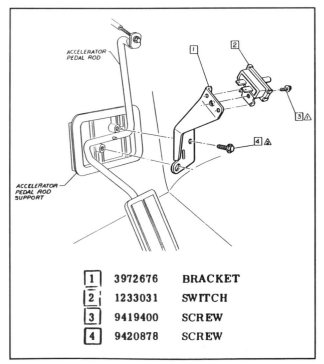

| | | |
| --- | --- | --- |
| 1 | 3972676 | BRACKET |
| 2 | 1233031 | SWITCH |
| 3 | 9419400 | SCREW |
| 4 | 9420878 | SCREW |

*Kick-down hood duct switch and pedal bracket.*

| Tailpipes | |
| --- | --- |
| LH | 3956757 |
| RH | 3956758 |
| Hangers | |
| LH (rear) | 3853659 |
| RH (rear) | 3853660 |

*Pickup only.

Part numbers remained the same in 1969 except that the pickup used special tailpipes, part numbers 3925103-LH and 3925104-RH, that exited at the side with no chrome extensions.

Chamber exhaust was standard on the 1969 L34 models till mid December 1968 when it was made optional. Listed as RPO NC8 it was available on all engines but was not on the pickup. Manifolds were the same as with the production exhaust.

The system consisted of two round front mufflers that were specially baffled—with eight rows of eleven baffles. These were listed as part numbers 3956749-LH and 3956750-RH and were 45 in. in overall length. Two shorter baffled mufflers, part numbers 3956751-LH and 3956752-RH, were molded to the ends of the tailpipes. Chrome extensions were also used with this setup; their part number was the same as with nonchambered exhaust systems.

The NC8 system used uniquely styled head pipes. At the front where they bolted to the manifold they measured 2.25 in. OD; at the rear where they connected to the mufflers they measured 2 in. OD. Replacement part numbers were 3956747-LH and 3956748-RH. The tailpipes measured 2 in. OD. They were combined with the rear mufflers and included with them. This was a fairly rare option, as it was canceled on May 19, 1969.

Head pipes and tailpipes should be painted flat-black with a quality high-temperature enamel paint. Production mufflers should have a dull metal appearance. The chamber exhaust mufflers should have a natural finish, as should the pipes.

## 1970-1972

Tailpipes were redesigned and used resonators at their ends in 1970. Dual exhaust was still standard on all big-block engines throughout till 1972. The mufflers emptied out into tailpipes part numbers 3973857-LH 3973858-RH with a resonator and chrome extension. The resonator should be shaped like a small straight-through muffler and not canister-shaped; the canister-shaped resonator was used only on the Monte Carlo and would be incorrect on the Chevelle.

The El Camino used a special resonator, part number 3982177, that looked like the production muffler but was mounted horizontally behind the rear axle. The tailpipes exited under the sides of the bed. No chrome extensions were used on the El Camino.

A single exhaust was standard on the 350 equipped SSs in 1971 and 1972. A Y-shaped head

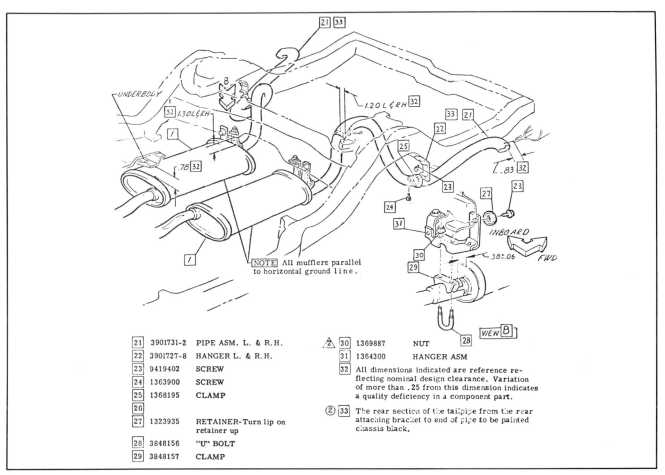

| | | | | | | |
|---|---|---|---|---|---|---|
| 21 | 3901731-2 | PIPE ASM. L. & R.H. | | 30 | 1369887 | NUT |
| 22 | 3901727-8 | HANGER L. & R.H. | | 31 | 1364300 | HANGER ASM |
| 23 | 9419402 | SCREW | | 32 | All dimensions indicated are reference reflecting nominal design clearance. Variation of more than .25 from this dimension indicates a quality deficiency in a component part. | |
| 24 | 1363900 | SCREW | | | | |
| 25 | 1368195 | CLAMP | | | | |
| 26 | | | | 33 | The rear section of the tailpipe from the rear attaching bracket to end of pipe to be painted chassis black. | |
| 27 | 1323935 | RETAINER-Turn lip on retainer up | | | | |
| 28 | 3848156 | "U" BOLT | | | | |
| 29 | 3848157 | CLAMP | | | | |

*Rear portion of the standard 1966 dual exhaust setup, also typical of 1967.*

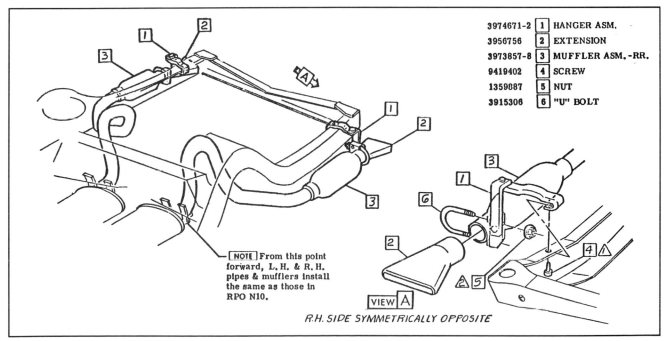

| | | |
|---|---|---|
| 3974671-2 | 1 | HANGER ASM. |
| 3956756 | 2 | EXTENSION |
| 3973857-8 | 3 | MUFFLER ASM.-RR. |
| 9419402 | 4 | SCREW |
| 1359887 | 5 | NUT |
| 3915306 | 6 | "U" BOLT |

*Resonators were part of the tailpipes for 1970.*

*A chrome exhaust extension was standard with dual exhaust from 1970 to 1972.*

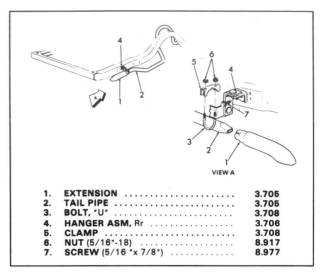

| | | |
|---|---|---|
| 1. | EXTENSION | 3.705 |
| 2. | TAIL PIPE | 3.705 |
| 3. | BOLT, "U" | 3.708 |
| 4. | HANGER ASM, Rr | 3.706 |
| 5. | CLAMP | 3.708 |
| 6. | NUT (5/16"-18) | 8.917 |
| 7. | SCREW (5/16 "x 7/8") | 8.977 |

*1971 and 1972 dual exhaust system.*

pipe with a 2 in. OD crossover pipe routed the exhaust into the muffler. A single tailpipe exited at the right rear of the car. No chrome extension was used.

Manifolds for 1970 used the same casting numbers as for 1969 on all engines. In 1971 the big-blocks used casting numbers 3989343-LH and 3989310-RH—part numbers 340293 and 353028, respectively; these same manifolds were also used in 1972.

The 350 ci engine used the same manifolds as the 307 engine, and these were listed as part numbers 336710-LH and 346222-RH for both 1971 and 1972. As before, be sure the casting date agrees with the model year of your SS.

### 1971–1972 Exhaust System Part Numbers

| Part | Dual Exhaust | Single Exhaust |
|---|---|---|
| Muffler | 3983320 | 1240538 |
| Head pipe | | 3983321; |
| LH | 3930765; | 3983322* |
| | 3930767* | |
| RH | 3930766; | |
| | 3930368* | |
| Crossover | | |
| pipe | NA | 3993787 |
| Tailpipes | | 3973804; |
| LH | 3974755; | 3973835* |
| | 3982173* | |
| RH | 3974756; | |
| | 3982174* | |
| Hangers | | 3949752; |
| LH | 3974671; | 3853659 (front); |
| | 3982179* | 1382595 (rear) |
| RH | 3974672; | |
| | 3982180* | |

*Pickup only.

### Emissions

#### 1964–1972

Emissions are not usually covered in restoration guides, but they are a vital part if you want

correctness. Every SS built used some kind of emission controls.

The most common emission control system was Positive Crankcase Ventilation, or PCV valve, which was available in two different styles. Standard was the open style, which used a vented-meshed oil cap. On 1964 and 1965 small-blocks the oil cap was at the front of the engine and should be painted gloss-black.

The other style was optional in the forty-nine states and mandatory in California in 1964 and 1965. This was the closed crankcase ventilation system, K24, which used a special air cleaner with provisions for the ventilation hoses. The system was unique in 1964 and 1965: a hose, part number 3846107, was routed from the oil fill tube, part number 3846123, and the carburetor, and was supported by a clip, part number 3846117. A short piece of rubber hose was routed to a curved tube, part number 3846180, which replaced the production adapter in the rear portion of the intake manifold. This pipe was also supported by a clip that was part of the assembly.

A different oil fill cap was also used. Listed as part number 3714893, it was flatter and thinner than the production part. The cap should have a natural metal appearance; the tube, support clips and oil filler tube should be painted gloss-black.

Some engines, such as the L79 and L37 units in 1965, were standard with this system, but the design was different. On the L79 engine the oil filler tube was listed as part number 3846102 with cap part number 3714893. A preformed hose, part number 3849984, was routed behind the fuel line and to a provision on the left-hand side of the carburetor. A small ring clamp was used to retain it at both ends. Another hose was mounted to the bottom of the air cleaner, then routed to a tube assembly, part number 3849733, which was supported by a clip at the distributor.

The L37 engine used a curved pipe assembly, part number 3868840, that was placed in a rubber grommet in the left-hand valve cover. This pipe was then connected to an elbow, part number 137421, that was screwed into the carburetor. On the opposite side a black plastic elbow was placed in a rubber grommet in the valve cover. A rubber hose was slipped over the end and routed to the port on the underside of the air cleaner. The pipe assembly and elbow should have a natural look.

In 1966 the PCV system was basically the same as it was on the L37 in 1965, but the pipe was replaced with a valve and the hose route was dependent on the type of carburetor used. The Holley was connected to the right side and incorporated an extra clip, part number 3846117, for support at the front of the carburetor. In 1966 it was standard on the L78, and in 1967 it was standard on all SS engines except the base L35.

Beginning in 1968 the production air cleaner was modified on the L35 engine to accommodate the closed ventilation option, now called RPO KD5. A 0.9375 in. diameter hole was drilled into the base and a pipe, part number 3927731, was bolted in place along with a cotter pin. The existing tube was removed and a plug was inserted into the opening.

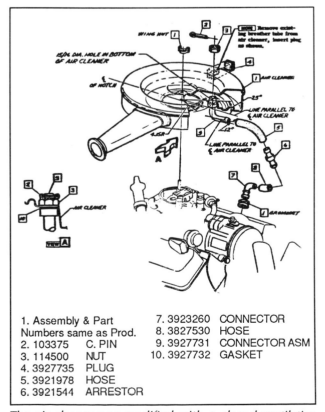

| | | |
|---|---|---|
| 1. Assembly & Part Numbers same as Prod. | 7. 3923260 | CONNECTOR |
| 2. 103375 C. PIN | 8. 3827530 | HOSE |
| 3. 114500 NUT | 9. 3927731 | CONNECTOR ASM |
| 4. 3927735 PLUG | 10. 3927732 | GASKET |
| 5. 3921978 HOSE | | |
| 6. 3921544 ARRESTOR | | |

*The air cleaner was modified with a closed ventilation option on the L35 engine.*

The closed ventilation system was standard on all SS engines from 1970 on. On the L78 and L89 engines when the open element filter was used, a short piece of hose was connected to the elbow with the right-hand valve cover and to the air cleaner and was secured with tower clips at each end. When the dual air horn assembly was used, a preformed hose was installed and the clamps were eliminated.

## AIR

### 1966-1972

The AIR system was a mandatory option, RPO K19, on all California SS 396s in 1966 and 1967, then as standard equipment from 1968 on. However, it could be deleted for the forty-nine states.

This system used a special air compressor pump to inject compressed air into the exhaust through a maze of valves and hoses. Special carburetors and distributors were also available with this option and cannot be interchanged with non-AIR applications. The pump was in an aluminum housing and should have a dull natural appearance. However, the back portion of the pump should be painted gloss-black.

### 1966-1972 AIR Pump Part Numbers
| | |
|---|---|
| 1966-67 | 5696104* |
| 1968-69 | 7801512 |
| 1970-71 | 7806686 |
| 1972 | 7817809 |

*For California only, and fits all V-8 engines.

For correctness, in 1966 and 1967 the outlet and inlet hoses should be installed with the part numbers next to the pump and readable from the left-hand side of the car. In 1968 and 1969 the pump pulley, part number 3927116, should be installed with the part number facing forward. The pulley should have a natural finish. All hoses were secured with tower clamps at both ends.

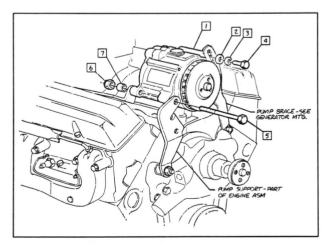

*Positioning and mounting of a reactor pump.*

## 1966-1967 AIR Hose Part Numbers

| Engine Hose | 1966 | 1967 |
|---|---|---|
| L35 Inlet | 3883233 | 3902346 |
| Outlet | | |
| LH | 3889379 | 3889379 |
| RH | 3889352 | 3902340 |

To prevent backfiring, a diverter valve was used. This valve would monitor manifold vacuum pressure and would cease the flow of air into the exhaust during fuel-rich periods. When the engine was not under load the valve would divert the airflow to the pump's muffler. When the engine was operating under load the airflow would be expelled through a relief valve. The diverter valve should have a natural finish.

## Evaporative Emission Control

### 1970-1972

The EEC system was designed to trap fuel vapors from escaping into the air. It was first used on all California SSs in 1970 and required a smaller 18 gallon gas tank; part number 3967796; the pickup used a 24 gallon tank, part number 3970269. The system was modified in April 1970 and began production nationwide, and it remained basically the same from 1970 to 1972.

Fuel vapors were directed through pipes along the side of the frame rail from the gas tank to a canister, part number 7028129, mounted in a support, part number 3974652, on the left front frame rail. This canister contained activated charcoal; the fuel vapors were trapped here when the engine was not running, then burned again when the car was started.

## 1971-1972 Fuel Vapor Line Part Numbers

| Body Style | 1971 | 1972 |
|---|---|---|
| Coupe | 3992449 | 6263659 |
| Convertible | 3992450 | 6263658 |
| Pickup | 3992454 | 6263661 |

Hoses from the canister were routed to the carburetor and the PCV valve on the valve cover. Carburetors were redesigned to support the EEC system. Part numbers were listed as follows. These carburetors must be used with the EEC option.

## 1970-1972 EEC System Carburetor Part Numbers

| L34 | |
|---|---|
| Manual | 7040505 |
| Automatic | 7040504 |
| L78, L89 & LS6 | |
| Manual | 3967479 |
| Automatic | 3969894 |
| LS5 | |
| Manual | 7040501; 7040521* |
| Automatic | 7040500 |

*After the second week in March 1970.

Notice that the L34 and LS5 engines used Rochester carburetors, and the L78, L89 and LS6 engines used Holley four-barrels. Also notice that with the EEC option the LS5 did not use the same carburetors as the L34.

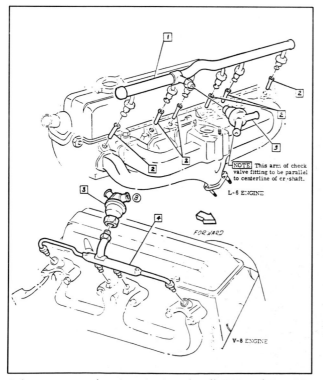

*Exhaust gas combustion air pipes for all 1966 and 1967 SSs.*

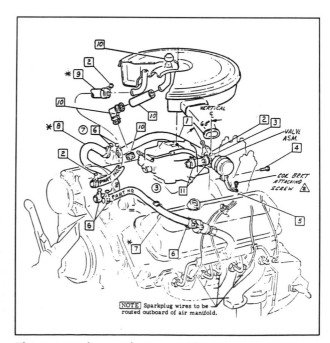

*The part numbers on hoses must be next to the air pump, as shown here.*

Also installed with this setup was a heat shield, part numbers 3969837 with the Rochesters and 3969835 with the Holleys, under the carburetor. A special choke assembly was also used with this form of emissions. Two different units were employed, part number 3967468 with the Rochesters and part number 3967494 with the Holleys.

Early 1971 models used canister part number 7028129 and support part number 3974652, which mounted like the 1970 unit. After the third week in February 1971 the part number was changed to 7030541, and the support was also redesigned. Listed as part number 3992371, the new support was mounted to the left-hand corner of the radiator support wall.

The canister was changed to part number 7030605 in 1972, but the support was identical to that used in the last part of the 1971 model year. The canister should be flat-black and the support gloss-black for all three years.

In 1972 a tee was used at the carburetor to route to the vacuum and at the carburetor body. This tee should be black plastic. Hoses were also bundled together differently: in 1971 the clip, part number 3977988, was positioned on the top of the left front fender wheelwell; in 1972 this clip was moved down and positioned on the side of the wheelwell.

## Cooling Systems

### 1964-1965

Four radiators were installed in the 1964 Malibu SS with a V-8 engine. Both 283 ci engines

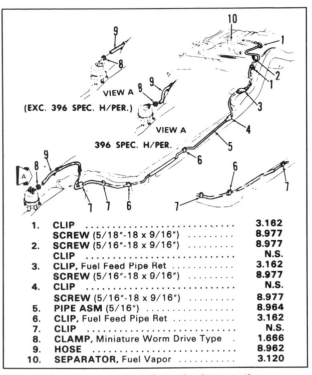

| | | |
|---|---|---|
| 1. | CLIP . . . . . . . . . . . . . . . . . . . . . . . . . . | 3.162 |
| | SCREW (5/18"-18 x 9/16") . . . . . . . . | 8.977 |
| 2. | SCREW (5/16"-18 x 9/16") . . . . . . . . | 8.977 |
| | CLIP . . . . . . . . . . . . . . . . . . . . . . . . . . | N.S. |
| 3. | CLIP, Fuel Feed Pipe Ret . . . . . . . . . . | 3.162 |
| | SCREW (5/16"-18 x 9/16") . . . . . . . . | 8.977 |
| 4. | CLIP . . . . . . . . . . . . . . . . . . . . . . . . . . | N.S. |
| | SCREW (5/16"-18 x 9/16") . . . . . . . . | 8.977 |
| 5. | PIPE ASM (5/16") . . . . . . . . . . . . . . | 8.964 |
| 6. | CLIP, Fuel Feed Pipe Ret . . . . . . . . . . | 3.162 |
| 7. | CLIP . . . . . . . . . . . . . . . . . . . . . . . . . . | N.S. |
| 8. | CLAMP, Miniature Worm Drive Type . | 1.666 |
| 9. | HOSE . . . . . . . . . . . . . . . . . . . . . . . . | 8.962 |
| 10. | SEPARATOR, Fuel Vapor . . . . . . . . . . | 3.120 |

*The EEC lines were routed along the frame rails.*

used the same radiator body with a 1.26 in. core and 357 sq in. of frontal area. The base 283 ci V-8 used a four-blade steel fan, part number 3839282, and the optional V-8s used a five-blade clutch-driven unit, part number 3789562. The clutch assembly was listed as part number 3814137; this system was also optional, as RPO K02, on the base V-8. Both fan assemblies should be painted gloss-black, and the clutch assembly should be cadmium gold.

When an automatic transmission was selected, a radiator body with provisions for the cooling lines

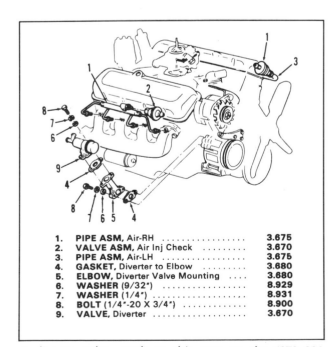

| | | |
|---|---|---|
| 1. | PIPE ASM, Air-RH . . . . . . . . . . . . . . | 3.675 |
| 2. | VALVE ASM, Air Inj Check . . . . . . . . | 3.670 |
| 3. | PIPE ASM, Air-LH . . . . . . . . . . . . . . | 3.675 |
| 4. | GASKET, Diverter to Elbow . . . . . . . . | 3.680 |
| 5. | ELBOW, Diverter Valve Mounting . . . . | 3.680 |
| 6. | WASHER (9/32") . . . . . . . . . . . . . . . . | 8.929 |
| 7. | WASHER (1/4") . . . . . . . . . . . . . . . . | 8.931 |
| 8. | BOLT (1/4"-20 X 3/4") . . . . . . . . . . . | 8.900 |
| 9. | VALVE, Diverter . . . . . . . . . . . . . . . . | 3.670 |

*A diverter valve, such as this one on the 1970 396, prevented backfiring.*

*The canister was imprinted with the Rochester name.*

in the bottom was used; it was listed as part number 3159118, and it was used with all engines. When air conditioning was ordered, part of the package was a heavy-duty radiator. Two shells were used. These heavy-duty radiators were also available without air conditioning as RPO V01. Both were larger, with a 1.98 in. core and 391 sq in. of frontal area.

### 1964 Radiator Part Numbers

| | |
|---|---|
| Manual | 3002011 |
| Automatic | 3002019 |

Radiators were the same in 1965 except on the L79 engine, which was standard with the heavy-duty assembly, and on the L37 engine, which used

### 1964 V-8 Radiator Hoses

| Part Number | Part Name | Ref. Note |
|---|---|---|
| 3850687 | Upper Hose | 1 |
| 3839301 | Lower Hose | 1 |
| 3839302 | Upper Hose | 2 |
| 3839303 | Lower Hose | 2,3 |
| 3850688 | Upper Hose | 3 |
| 9411656 | Upper Hose Clamp | 1,2,3 |
| 274765 | Lower Hose Clamp | 1,2,3 |

1-Standard hoses
2-Used only with RPO C60
3-Used with V01

All clamps are tower type and should be positioned so they don't interfere with fans.

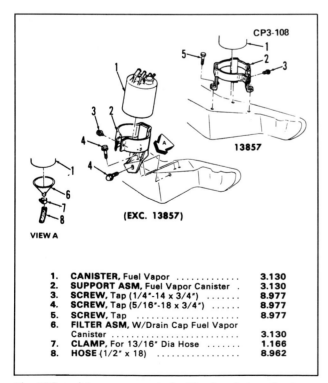

| | | |
|---|---|---|
| 1. | CANISTER, Fuel Vapor .............. | 3.130 |
| 2. | SUPPORT ASM, Fuel Vapor Canister . | 3.130 |
| 3. | SCREW, Tap (1/4"-14 x 3/4") ....... | 8.977 |
| 4. | SCREW, Tap (5/16"-18 x 3/4") ...... | 8.977 |
| 5. | SCREW, Tap ................... | 8.977 |
| 6. | FILTER ASM, W/Drain Cap Fuel Vapor Canister ........................ | 3.130 |
| 7. | CLAMP, For 13/16" Dia Hose ....... | 1.166 |
| 8. | HOSE (1/2" x 18) ................ | 8.962 |

*The EEC canister was mounted with a bracket on the frame rail.*

radiator body part number 3005620 only. A round metal shroud, part number 3861760, was used on the L37, and it should be spot welded to the shroud frame nine times on each side. The cap was rated at 15 psi and was located in the center of the top of the core. The fan was the clutch-driven unit with five blades; part numbers and colors were the same as in 1964.

### 1966-1967

No shroud was used in either 1966 or 1967 on the L35 and L34 engines with the standard radiator. Nor was it used on the L78 engine in 1966. However, in 1967 a one-piece gloss-black shroud, part number 3891464, was standard on the L78 engine. When air conditioning, RPO C60, or the heavy-duty radiator, RPO V01, was ordered, the one-piece shroud was included.

### 1965 V-8 Radiator Hoses

| Part Number | Part Name | Ref. Note |
|---|---|---|
| 3850687 | Inlet Hose | 1,4 |
| 3839301 | Outlet Hose | 1,4 |
| 3863106 | Inlet Hose | 5 |
| 3870312 | Inlet Hose | 6 |
| 3870311 | Outlet Hose | 5 |
| 3850688 | Inlet Hose | 2,3 |
| 3839303 | Outlet Hose | 2,3 |
| 9411656 | Inlet Hose Clamp | 1,2,3,5 |
| 274765 | Outlet Hose Clamp | 1,2,3 |
| 3870311 | Outlet Hose Clamp | 5 |

1-Standard hoses
2-With C60
3-With V01
4-Hose must be installed with "RAD" pointing to radiator
5-L37 396 ci V-8 only
6-Early L37 only

All clamps are tower type

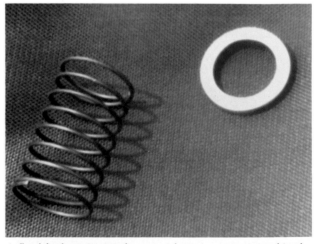

*A flat-black spring and a natural retainer were used in the canister under the cap.*

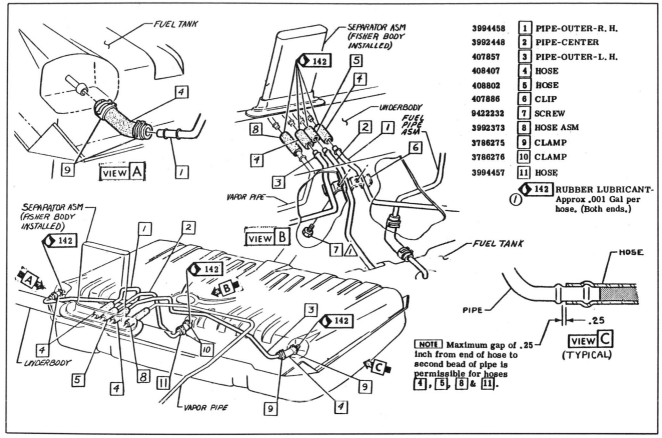

| | | | |
|---|---|---|---|
| 3994458 | 1 | PIPE-OUTER-R. H. |
| 3992448 | 2 | PIPE-CENTER |
| 407857 | 3 | PIPE-OUTER-L. H. |
| 408407 | 4 | HOSE |
| 408802 | 5 | HOSE |
| 407886 | 6 | CLIP |
| 9422232 | 7 | SCREW |
| 3992373 | 8 | HOSE ASM |
| 3786275 | 9 | CLAMP |
| 3786276 | 10 | CLAMP |
| 3994457 | 11 | HOSE |

◆142 RUBBER LUBRICANT-
Approx .001 Gal per
hose. (Both ends.)

NOTE Maximum gap of .25
inch from end of hose to
second bead of pipe is
permissible for hoses
4, 5, 8 & 11.

VIEW C
(TYPICAL)

Special gas tanks with provisions for the emission control
hoses must be used.

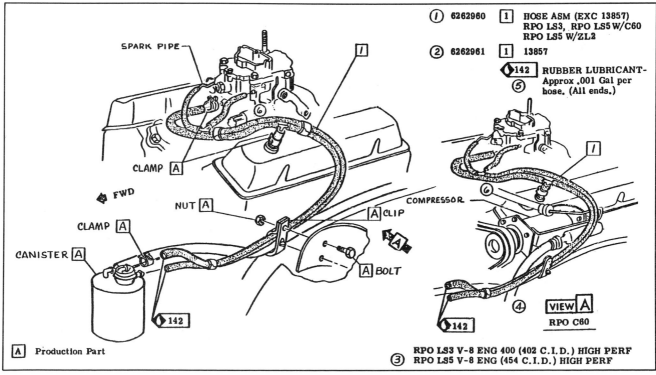

① 6262960 | 1 | HOSE ASM (EXC 13857)
RPO LS3, RPO LS5 W/C60
RPO LS5 W/ZL2

② 6262961 | 1 | 13857

◆142 RUBBER LUBRICANT-
Approx .001 Gal per
hose. (All ends.)

A  Production Part

RPO LS3 V-8 ENG 400 (402 C.I.D.) HIGH PERF
③ RPO LS5 V-8 ENG (454 C.I.D.) HIGH PERF

*1971-72 original EEC hose routes.*

37

The standard cap was now rated at 15 psi and listed as part number 3887586, and it should have a natural appearance. The cap location for both years was left of the center of the top of the core. An overflow hose was routed down the left-hand side of the core and supported by two clips.

A 17.62 in. diameter four-blade fan was standard with all engines except the L78, which used a five-blade clutch-driven unit. The larger 18 in. diameter five-blade fan, part number 3863137, used a gold cadmium clutch, and the outer geared ring—listed as part number 3857530, 3916142 in 1967—should have a natural metal appearance. Both fans should be painted gloss-black. The spacer, part number 3876828, behind the fan should have a natural appearance. A different spacer, listed as part number 3857042, was used with the 1967 L78 engine. This spacer was also used in all cars equipped with air conditioning and in those with the V01 heavy-duty radiator option.

## 1968-1969

A gloss-black fiberglass shroud, part number 3920110, was standard equipment on all engines in 1968. Two small clips along the bottom of the radiator helped support the shroud. A metal tray, part number 3917438, topped the radiator core, and rubber pads, part number 3917441, were used

## 1966-1967 V-8 Radiator Hoses

| Part Number | Part Name | Years Used | Ref. Note |
|---|---|---|---|
| 3880813 | Inlet (upper) Hose | 1966 | 1,2 |
| 3880814 | Inlet (upper) Hose | 1967 | 1,2 |
| 3881814 | Outlet (lower) Hose | Both | 1,2 |
| 3882884 | Inlet (upper) Hose | 1966 | 4,5 |
| 3880813 | Inlet (upper) Hose | 1967 | 3,4,5 |
| 3881857 | Outlet (lower) Hose | Both | 3,4,5 |
| 9411656 | Inlet Hose Clamp | Both | All |
| 274765 | Outlet Hose Clamp | Both | All |

    1-Production parts
    2-L34 engine
    3-L78 engine
    4-C60
    5-V01

Clamps are tower type and should be positioned so there is no interference with fan, except upper hose clamp next to thermostat housing, which should be positioned 330 degrees inward toward radiator.

All hoses should be installed so that "RAD" and the arrow point to radiator.

## 1968-1969 Radiator Hoses

| Part Number | Part Name | With Options |
|---|---|---|
| 3917227 | Inlet Hose | Standard except L78, L78, A/C and V01 |
| 3937733 | Outlet Hose | Standard * except L78 A/C, L78 and V01 |
| 9411656 | Inlet Hose Clamp | Tower clips all |
| 274765 | Outlet Hose Clamp | Tower clamp next to engine only |
| 9411656 | | Next to Radiator, all options |

    *-Part Number 3937733 was used till November 22, 1967; Clamp 274765 was used at both ends of this hose.

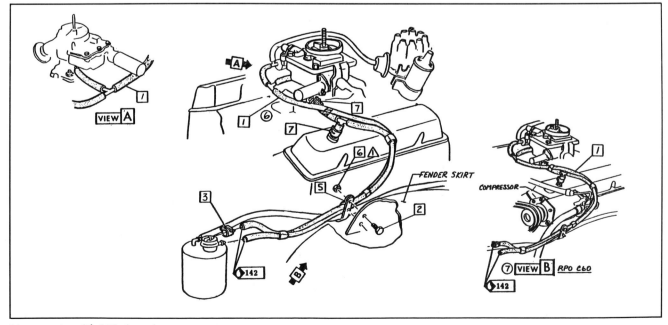

*Hose route with 350 ci engines.*

between the tray and the core. Rubber pads were also used under all radiators.

The overflow hose was now routed down the back side of the core on the right-hand side. The pressure cap was the RC-15 unit and used the same part number as in 1967. The cap was located on the far right-hand side of the top of the core.

The four-blade fan was still standard on all engines except the L78, which used a clutch-driven unit. The L78 fan still measured 18 in. in diameter but now had seven blades. It was listed as part number 3931002, and colors for the clutch, part number 3931003, were the same as in 1967.

Few changes marked the 1969 models. The radiator tray was now listed as part number 3930166 except on the L78, which used part number 3975385. The L78 tray was also used with air conditioning and the V01 option.

### 1970-1972

In 1970 all radiators were the same size in frontal area—480 sq in.—but the L34 and LS5 engines used a radiator with a 1.26 in. thick core, whereas the L78, L89 and LS6 engines used the heavy-duty radiator with a thicker 2.70 in. core. This radiator was also optional on the L34 and LS5 engines and included with air conditioning.

The top tray was the same as in 1969. On this gloss-black tray the tune-up and cooling system decals were placed. An SS headed for California also included an emission decal in between the other two.

In 1971 and 1972 a total of eight radiators were available. The 350 engines with the standard radiator had a core width of 1.26 in., but when the heavy-duty radiator was installed, the 350s used two different cores. Those with manual transmission used the same core width as the standard unit. Those with automatic transmissions used a core width of 1.198 in.

The LS3 and LS5 engines used the same radiators, but the LS6 used the heavy-duty 2.7 in. wide core. This radiator was also optional on the LS3 and LS5 engines and as part of the air conditioning package.

### 1970-1972 V-8 Radiator Hoses

| Part Number | Part Name | Ref. Note |
|---|---|---|
| 3986380 | Inlet Hose | 350 ci V-8 |
| 3917227 | Inlet Hose | LS3 and LS5 |
| 3989342 | Inlet Hose | HD/C60 and LS6 |
| 3959488 | Outlet Hose | 350 ci V-8 |
| 3992083 | Outlet Hose | LS3 and LS5 |
| 3989342 | Outlet Hose | LS6 and LS3/LS5 w/C60 or V01 |
| 9411656 | Tower Clamp | |
| 274765 | Tower Clamp | Used only on outlet hose next to block |

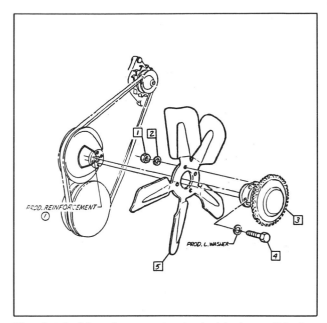

*The clutch-driven fan was standard with air conditioning.*

Shrouds were redesigned in 1971 and were now in two parts that were stapled together using three staples for each side. Many replacement shrouds are one-piece and are incorrect for 1971 and 1972 Chevelles.

### 1971-1972 Shroud Part Numbers

| Engine | Upper | Lower |
|---|---|---|
| L48, L65 | 3986905 | 6261917 |
| LS3, LS5 | 3986907 | 6261918 |
| LS6* & V01 | 3986924 | 6261918 |

*For 1971 only.

Pads were used under the tray and the radiator. Part numbers were listed according to engine size and accessories.

### 1971-1972 Pad Part Numbers

| Engine | Upper | Lower |
|---|---|---|
| L48, L65 | 3966804 | 3966804 |
| LS3, LS5 | | |
| LH | 3966800 | 3966800 |
| RH | 3966812 | 3966812 |
| W/C60 | 3966812 | 3966812 |
| LS6* & V01 | | |
| LH | 3966800 | 3966800 |
| RH | 3966812 | 3966812 |

*For 1971 only.

## Camshafts

### 1964-1972

Except for the L72, L78, L89 and LS6 special performance engines, all SS engines used hydraulic camshafts. The others, including the L76 engine in 1965, used a mechanical cam.

# Chapter 3

# Transmissions and Drivetrain

## Three-speed Manual Transmissions

### 1964-1965

A synchromesh three-speed manual transmission was standard on all Chevelles and all 1964 and 1965 engines except the 1965 L37. The transmission should have the code W stamped on the rear face of the upper right-hand corner. Following this was the date of manufacture: the month was coded with a single letter (from A for January to L for December); after that was the day of the month; then came the last digit of the year. The final number was the shift. So, for example, a transmission with the production code WC1261 would have been built at the Warner plant (W) in March (C) on the twelfth day (12) in 1966 (6) by the first shift (1).

Optional only on six-cylinders and the base two-barrel 283 ci V-8 was the RPO M10 overdrive three-speed manual transmission, which was coded the same as the standard unit. It was distinguished from other three-speeds by the addition of a solenoid on the left-hand side of the unit. When this transmission was used, an indicator light was placed on the underside of the instrument panel.

All transmissions should be painted cast-iron-gray, and the code should be stenciled in yellow paint on the right-hand side of the case.

### 1966-1967

The Warner T-16 fully synchronized three-speed manual transmission was standard on all Chevelles, including the SS 396, in 1966. A three-speed heavy-duty transmission manufactured at the Saginaw plant was optional, as RPO M13, for the SS only. In the fourth week of August 1965 the heavy-duty Saginaw unit became the standard transmission for the SS model.

The location and explanation of the Warner transmission assembly code were the same as in 1965. The Saginaw unit was coded with the letter S on a square boss on the left side of the transmission below and to the rear of the cover. Following this code was the date of manufacture—year, month, day—and the shift. The date was straightforward with no special codes; the shift was represented by either a D for day or an N for night. So, for example, the code S60521N would indicate a Saginaw transmission (S) built in 1966 (6) on May (05) 21 (21) by the night shift (N).

The Saginaw transmission was used unchanged in 1967. The L35 engine used part number 3890533 and the L34 and L78 engines used part number 3890536 in both 1966 and 1967.

### 1968-1969

The Saginaw transmission was still being used as standard equipment in 1968, but the identification stamp was changed. Its location was the same as in 1966. The code should begin with the letters QB to indicate the three-speed transmission followed by an S for the Saginaw assembly plant. Next was the last digit of the year followed by the date of manufacture, which included the month, designated by a single letter (see the following chart), and the day, designated by a two-digit number. Finally came the shift, coded as a D for day or an N for night. For example, the code QBS8D04D would indicate a three-speed transmission (QB) built in the Saginaw plant (S) in 1968 (8) on April (D) 4 (04) by the day shift (D).

### 1968-1969 Three-speed Manual Month Codes

| | |
|---|---|
| A | January |
| B | February |
| C | March |
| D | April |
| E | May |
| H | June |
| K | July |
| M | August |
| P | September |
| R | October |
| S | November |
| T | December |

The last eight digits of the VIN preceded by the number 1 were stamped into a pad on the upper left-hand corner of the right-hand side of the case. The number 1 indicated a Chevrolet transmission.

The identification code was changed to QP in 1969. Its location was the same as in previous years. However, late 1969 models used a heavy-duty three-speed transmission manufactured at the Muncie plant. This transmission should be coded with the letter *H* on a machined surface on the left-hand side of the case just below the side

cover and should have the name General Motors Corp cast into the side.

Both transmissions should be painted medium cast-iron-gray and should have the letter codes stenciled in yellow paint on the left-hand side.

### 1970–1972

No three-speed manual transmission was available in 1970; it was not part of either SS pack-

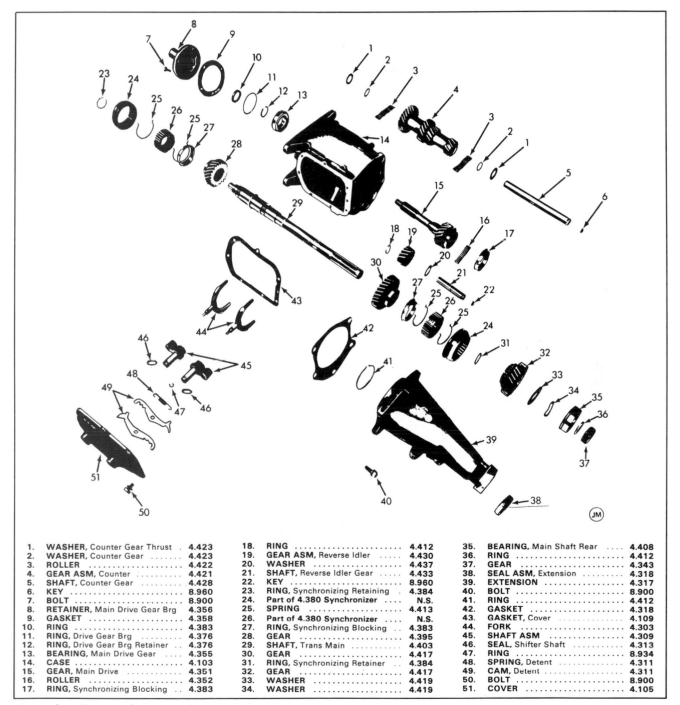

| | | | |
|---|---|---|---|
| 1. | WASHER, Counter Gear Thrust | 4.423 |
| 2. | WASHER, Counter Gear | 4.423 |
| 3. | ROLLER | 4.422 |
| 4. | GEAR ASM, Counter | 4.421 |
| 5. | SHAFT, Counter Gear | 4.428 |
| 6. | KEY | 8.960 |
| 7. | BOLT | 8.900 |
| 8. | RETAINER, Main Drive Gear Brg | 4.356 |
| 9. | GASKET | 4.358 |
| 10. | RING | 4.383 |
| 11. | RING, Drive Gear Brg | 4.376 |
| 12. | RING, Drive Gear Brg Retainer | 4.376 |
| 13. | BEARING, Main Drive Gear | 4.355 |
| 14. | CASE | 4.103 |
| 15. | GEAR, Main Drive | 4.351 |
| 16. | ROLLER | 4.352 |
| 17. | RING, Synchronizing Blocking | 4.383 |

| | | | |
|---|---|---|---|
| 18. | RING | 4.412 |
| 19. | GEAR ASM, Reverse Idler | 4.430 |
| 20. | WASHER | 4.437 |
| 21. | SHAFT, Reverse Idler Gear | 4.433 |
| 22. | KEY | 8.960 |
| 23. | RING, Synchronizing Retaining | 4.384 |
| 24. | Part of 4.380 Synchronizer | N.S. |
| 25. | SPRING | 4.413 |
| 26. | Part of 4.380 Synchronizer | N.S. |
| 27. | RING, Synchronizing Blocking | 4.383 |
| 28. | GEAR | 4.395 |
| 29. | SHAFT, Trans Main | 4.403 |
| 30. | GEAR | 4.417 |
| 31. | RING, Synchronizing Retainer | 4.384 |
| 32. | GEAR | 4.417 |
| 33. | WASHER | 4.419 |
| 34. | WASHER | 4.419 |

| | | | |
|---|---|---|---|
| 35. | BEARING, Main Shaft Rear | 4.408 |
| 36. | RING | 4.412 |
| 37. | GEAR | 4.343 |
| 38. | SEAL ASM, Extension | 4.318 |
| 39. | EXTENSION | 4.317 |
| 40. | BOLT | 8.900 |
| 41. | RING | 4.412 |
| 42. | GASKET | 4.318 |
| 43. | GASKET, Cover | 4.109 |
| 44. | FORK | 4.303 |
| 45. | SHAFT ASM | 4.309 |
| 46. | SEAL, Shifter Shaft | 4.313 |
| 47. | RING | 8.934 |
| 48. | SPRING, Detent | 4.311 |
| 49. | CAM, Detent | 4.311 |
| 50. | BOLT | 8.900 |
| 51. | COVER | 4.105 |

*Heavy-duty Saginaw three-speed transmission.*

age. For the standard transmission see the Four-speed and Turbo Hydra-matic sections later in this chapter.

The three-speed manual transmission returned in 1971 for all SS packages except the SS 454, which used the same transmissions as in 1970.

Not all SSs came with the heavy-duty unit; it was only standard on the SS 400 package. Both the SS 350 packages used the production three-speed transmission as standard equipment.

The heavy-duty three-speed was optional, as RPO MC1, for the L48 engine in early 1971, can-

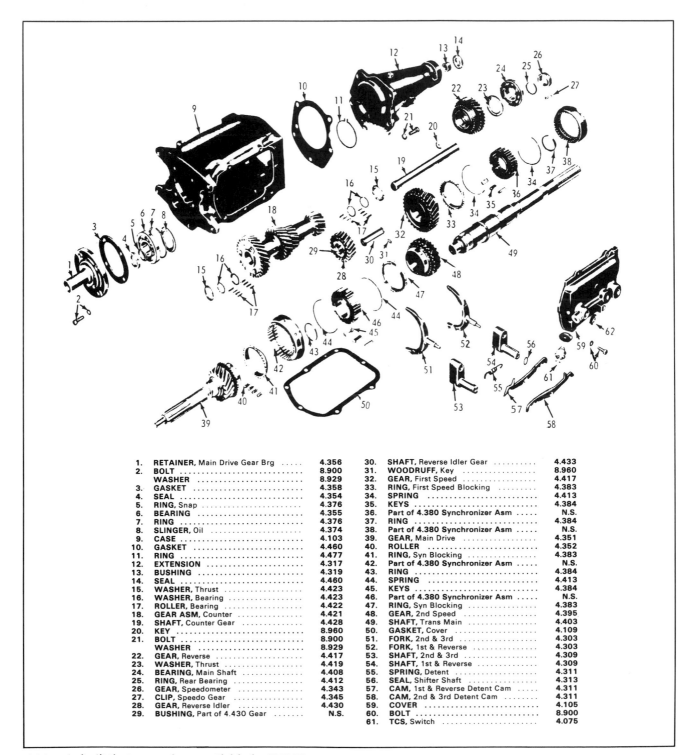

| 1. | RETAINER, Main Drive Gear Brg | 4.356 |
| 2. | BOLT | 8.900 |
| | WASHER | 8.929 |
| 3. | GASKET | 4.358 |
| 4. | SEAL | 4.354 |
| 5. | RING, Snap | 4.376 |
| 6. | BEARING | 4.355 |
| 7. | RING | 4.376 |
| 8. | SLINGER, Oil | 4.374 |
| 9. | CASE | 4.103 |
| 10. | GASKET | 4.460 |
| 11. | RING | 4.477 |
| 12. | EXTENSION | 4.317 |
| 13. | BUSHING | 4.319 |
| 14. | SEAL | 4.460 |
| 15. | WASHER, Thrust | 4.423 |
| 16. | WASHER, Bearing | 4.423 |
| 17. | ROLLER, Bearing | 4.422 |
| 18. | GEAR ASM, Counter | 4.421 |
| 19. | SHAFT, Counter Gear | 4.428 |
| 20. | KEY | 8.960 |
| 21. | BOLT | 8.900 |
| | WASHER | 8.929 |
| 22. | GEAR, Reverse | 4.417 |
| 23. | WASHER, Thrust | 4.419 |
| 24. | BEARING, Main Shaft | 4.408 |
| 25. | RING, Rear Bearing | 4.412 |
| 26. | GEAR, Speedometer | 4.343 |
| 27. | CLIP, Speedo Gear | 4.345 |
| 28. | GEAR, Reverse Idler | 4.430 |
| 29. | BUSHING, Part of 4.430 Gear | N.S. |
| 30. | SHAFT, Reverse Idler Gear | 4.433 |
| 31. | WOODRUFF, Key | 8.960 |
| 32. | GEAR, First Speed | 4.417 |
| 33. | RING, First Speed Blocking | 4.383 |
| 34. | SPRING | 4.413 |
| 35. | KEYS | 4.384 |
| 36. | Part of 4.380 Synchronizer Asm | N.S. |
| 37. | RING | 4.384 |
| 38. | Part of 4.380 Synchronizer Asm | N.S. |
| 39. | GEAR, Main Drive | 4.351 |
| 40. | ROLLER | 4.352 |
| 41. | RING, Syn Blocking | 4.383 |
| 42. | Part of 4.380 Synchronizer Asm | N.S. |
| 43. | RING | 4.384 |
| 44. | SPRING | 4.413 |
| 45. | KEYS | 4.384 |
| 46. | Part of 4.380 Synchronizer Asm | N.S. |
| 47. | RING, Syn Blocking | 4.383 |
| 48. | GEAR, 2nd Speed | 4.395 |
| 49. | SHAFT, Trans Main | 4.403 |
| 50. | GASKET, Cover | 4.109 |
| 51. | FORK, 2nd & 3rd | 4.303 |
| 52. | FORK, 1st & Reverse | 4.303 |
| 53. | SHAFT, 2nd & 3rd | 4.309 |
| 54. | SHAFT, 1st & Reverse | 4.309 |
| 55. | SPRING, Detent | 4.311 |
| 56. | SEAL, Shifter Shaft | 4.313 |
| 57. | CAM, 1st & Reverse Detent Cam | 4.311 |
| 58. | CAM, 2nd & 3rd Detent Cam | 4.311 |
| 59. | COVER | 4.105 |
| 60. | BOLT | 8.900 |
| 61. | TCS, Switch | 4.075 |

*A Muncie-built three-speed was available for 1969-72.*

celed during production of 1971 models in the third week of September 1970 and then then reinstated in 1972. The L65 engine was never available with this transmission.

Identification for the heavy-duty transmission was the code H, and identification for the regular transmission was the code S. Both transmissions were manufactured at the Muncie plant. Both codes are found stamped on a machined surface on the left-hand side of the case just below the side cover. Codes for the date of manufacture were the same as in 1968-69. Transmission codes were identical in 1972 except that the fourth digit was changed to a 2 for 1972 models.

The last eight digits of the VIN were stamped on a pad in the upper left-hand corner of the right side of the case on the production unit. On the heavy-duty three-speed assembly they were stamped vertically on a boss on the right-hand side of the transmission where the case and extension met when used with the LS3 engine and on a boss on the case in the upper right-hand corner for cars with the L48 engine.

## Four-speed Manual Transmissions

### 1964-1965

Two four speed transmissions were available on the 1964 Malibu SS. The wide ratio, RPO M20, and the close ratio, RPO M21, were both built at Muncie.

### 1964 Four-speed Gear Ratios

| Gear | M20 | M21 |
|------|------|------|
| 1st | 2.56 | 2.20 |
| 2nd | 1.91 | 1.64 |
| 3rd | 1.48 | 1.28 |
| 4th | 1.00 | 1.00 |

Both transmissions were housed in an aluminum case and coded with the letter P on the top right side of the case. The production date followed, with the last digit of the year followed by a single letter designating the month (see the 1968-1969 Three-speed Manual Month Codes chart) and a two-digit number designating the day. The shift came last, indicated by either a D for day or an N for night.

No changes appeared in 1965. The M20 transmission was standard with the Z16 package, and the close-ratio M21 was optional but only with 3.73, 4.11 and 4.56 rear end gear ratios.

### 1966-1967

The Muncie transmissions returned and used the same code in 1966. The M20 wide ratio—part number 3870357, 3890534 with L78—was available with all engines including the base. The M21 close ratio, part number 3877459, was available with the L34 and L78 engines with 3.31, 3.55, 4.10,

4.56 and 4.88 rear end gear ratios only. Air conditioning, C60, was also not available with this transmission owing to rear end gearing.

In both 1966 and 1967 Muncie transmissions were still coded with the letter P in the same location as before. The M20 transmission was available with all three engines again in 1967. The M21 close-ratio transmission was still available only with the optional powerplants. Air conditioning became available with the M21 transmission; the only rear end gear ratio used was 3.07, which was standard with air conditioning with all four-speed transmissions.

Part numbers were the same in early 1967 as in 1966, but after January 1967 the M21 used part number 3879668. Finishing should be natural.

Beginning in 1966 a special heavy-duty 4-speed transmission became optional. It was coded RPO M22. This option was available only with the L78 engine with no air conditioning. A total of twelve cars had this option in 1966. The production number for 1967 is not known.

### 1968-1969

All four-speed transmissions in 1968 were coded HI, and those used on the SS 396 should also be coded with the letter P in the third digit. This code indicated the manufacturer, in this case Muncie. The build date codes were the same as for the three-speed unit.

The M20 wide-ratio transmission—part number 3919390, 3915079 with L34 and L78—was available with all three engine choices. The M21 close-ratio transmission, part number 3915085, was available only with the L34 and L78 engines.

Like the three-speed transmission, the four-speeds were also stamped with the car's VIN beginning in 1968. This stamp must be vertical on the right-hand side, on a boss where the case meets the extension. It should begin with the number 1 followed by the last eight digits of the car's VIN plate.

Gear ratios were revised for the M21 transmission. The ratio 3.55 was standard except when air conditioning was ordered; then 3.07 was standard. Optional ratios were 3.31, 3.73 and 4.10. A 2.73 ratio was available as a special order, but few cars were built with it, as gears that high defeated the purpose of a close-ratio transmission.

The code was changed to HU for 1969. The M20 wide-ratio transmission was listed as part numbers 3950301 with the L35 engine and 3946767 with the other engines including the COPO 427 Chevelle. The M21 close-ratio transmission was part number 3946798 for all engines except the base. The VIN was again stamped into the case of both transmissions at the same location.

The 2.73 ratio was no longer available for either four-speed and the 3.07 ratio became a special order. Air-conditioned cars used the same ratios as cars without air conditioning.

The M22 transmission remained optional in both years for the L78 engine (only when without air conditioning). As before, it had the same gear ratios as the M21 but with beefier components. A total of 1,049 L78s had this in 1968, and 1,276 had it in 1969.

## 1970–1972

In 1970 the M20 wide-ratio unit was the standard manual transmission on the SS 396 models. The M21 close-ratio transmission was standard on the SS 454s and optional on the SS 396 package.

Both transmissions were coded with the letters *WC*. The standard 3.31 gears were used with and without air conditioning with both transmissions.

All transmissions were stamped with the car's VIN. In cars with the L34 engine this stamping was in the same location as in 1969, but in cars with a 454 engine it was located on a pad on the upper left-hand corner of the right-hand side of the case.

The M21 transmission was replaced with a heavy-duty M22 transmission, which was optional in 1970 and was the standard manual transmission with the SS 454 package in 1971. This unit was coded with the letter *P* in both 1971 and 1972. The M22 transmission had the same ratio as the M21 close-ratio unit that preceded it. This transmission was not available as an option for the 400 Turbo-Jet or 350 Turbo-Fire engines. The M21 close-ratio transmission was canceled.

Only the M20 wide-ratio four-speed transmission was available with the LS3 400 Turbo-Jet and L48 350 ci engines. The L65 was also optional with the M20 but used different gear ratios and a cast-iron case; it was coded with the letter *R* in both 1971 and 1972. However, in 1972 the M20 transmission was used with all 350 ci engines.

All four-speeds in 1971 began with the same two letters: *WO*. The third digit, either *R* or *P*, was used to identify the type.

In 1971 the VIN was stamped as before, with the L48 and L65 engines using the same location as the 454. In early 1972 the VIN stamp was located on a pad for the big-blocks and on the boss for the two small-blocks. After mid January this procedure was reversed, and cars equipped with the 400 and 454 Turbo-Jets had the VIN stamped on the boss of the case next to the extension. The numerals must be vertical to be correct.

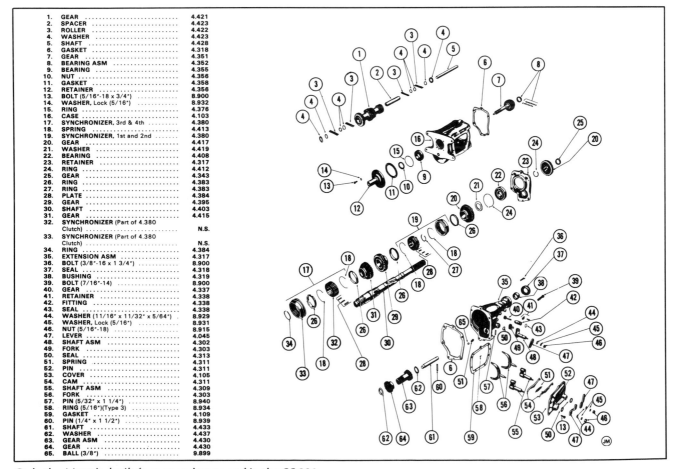

| | | |
|---|---|---|
| 1. | GEAR | 4.421 |
| 2. | SPACER | 4.423 |
| 3. | ROLLER | 4.422 |
| 4. | WASHER | 4.423 |
| 5. | SHAFT | 4.428 |
| 6. | GASKET | 4.318 |
| 7. | GEAR | 4.351 |
| 8. | BEARING ASM | 4.352 |
| 9. | BEARING | 4.355 |
| 10. | NUT | 4.356 |
| 11. | GASKET | 4.358 |
| 12. | RETAINER | 4.356 |
| 13. | BOLT (5/16"-18 x 3/4") | 8.900 |
| 14. | WASHER, Lock (5/16") | 8.932 |
| 15. | RING | 4.376 |
| 16. | CASE | 4.103 |
| 17. | SYNCHRONIZER, 3rd & 4th | 4.380 |
| 18. | SPRING | 4.413 |
| 19. | SYNCHRONIZER, 1st and 2nd | 4.380 |
| 20. | GEAR | 4.417 |
| 21. | WASHER | 4.419 |
| 22. | BEARING | 4.408 |
| 23. | RETAINER | 4.317 |
| 24. | RING | 4.412 |
| 25. | GEAR | 4.343 |
| 26. | RING | 4.383 |
| 27. | RING | 4.383 |
| 28. | PLATE | 4.384 |
| 29. | GEAR | 4.395 |
| 30. | SHAFT | 4.403 |
| 31. | GEAR | 4.415 |
| 32. | SYNCHRONIZER (Part of 4.380 Clutch) | N.S. |
| 33. | SYNCHRONIZER (Part of 4.380 Clutch) | N.S. |
| 34. | RING | 4.384 |
| 35. | EXTENSION ASM | 4.317 |
| 36. | BOLT (3/8"-16 x 1 3/4") | 8.900 |
| 37. | SEAL | 4.318 |
| 38. | BUSHING | 4.319 |
| 39. | BOLT (7/16"-14) | 8.900 |
| 40. | GEAR | 4.337 |
| 41. | RETAINER | 4.338 |
| 42. | FITTING | 4.338 |
| 43. | SEAL | 4.338 |
| 44. | WASHER (11/16" x 11/32" x 5/64") | 8.929 |
| 45. | WASHER, Lock (5/16") | 8.931 |
| 46. | NUT (5/16"-18) | 8.915 |
| 47. | LEVER | 4.045 |
| 48. | SHAFT ASM | 4.302 |
| 49. | FORK | 4.303 |
| 50. | SEAL | 4.313 |
| 51. | SPRING | 4.311 |
| 52. | PIN | 4.311 |
| 53. | COVER | 4.105 |
| 54. | CAM | 4.311 |
| 55. | SHAFT ASM | 4.309 |
| 56. | FORK | 4.303 |
| 57. | PIN (5/32" x 1 1/4") | 8.940 |
| 58. | RING (5/16")(Type 3) | 8.934 |
| 59. | GASKET | 4.109 |
| 60. | PIN (1/4" x 1 1/2") | 8.939 |
| 61. | SHAFT | 4.433 |
| 62. | WASHER | 4.437 |
| 63. | GEAR ASM | 4.430 |
| 64. | GEAR | 4.430 |
| 65. | BALL (3/8") | 9.899 |

*Only the Muncie-built four-speed was used in the SS 396.*

All four-speeds from 1964 on had the code stenciled in yellow paint on the right-hand side of the case. This was done to help distinguish them at the assembly plant. The letters should be 2 in. in height and in block form for correctness.

## Manual Transmission Clutch Plate, Pedal

### 1964-1965

All V-8s in 1964 used a 10.4 in. disc with a pressure plate rating of 2,300 pounds, except for the 283 ci engines with a three-speed transmission. These engines used a 10.1 in. disc with a pressure plate rating of 1,950 pounds.

The discs and pressure plates remained the same in 1965 with the addition of the 11 in. disc and 2,600 pound rated pressure plate used on the 396 engine. Instead of the regular 12.75 in. diameter flywheel with 153 teeth, a larger 14 in. diameter flywheel with 168 teeth was used with the 396 ci engine.

The pedal was listed as part number 3841214 and was finished in 60 degree gloss-black non-acrylic lacquer paint both years. The correct paint part numbers were Ditzler DL-9248 and Rinshed Mason 400. The cover, part number 3858198, was also used both years with no trim plate.

### 1966-1967

All engines used an 11 in. centrifugal dry disc and a pressure plate with a rating of 2,750 pounds

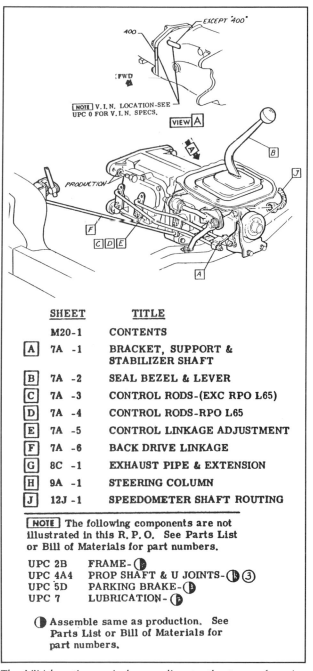

| SHEET | TITLE | |
|-------|-------|--|
| M20-1 | CONTENTS | |
| [A] 7A -1 | BRACKET, SUPPORT & STABILIZER SHAFT | |
| [B] 7A -2 | SEAL BEZEL & LEVER | |
| [C] 7A -3 | CONTROL RODS-(EXC RPO L65) | |
| [D] 7A -4 | CONTROL RODS-RPO L65 | |
| [E] 7A -5 | CONTROL LINKAGE ADJUSTMENT | |
| [F] 7A -6 | BACK DRIVE LINKAGE | |
| [G] 8C -1 | EXHAUST PIPE & EXTENSION | |
| [H] 9A -1 | STEERING COLUMN | |
| [J] 12J -1 | SPEEDOMETER SHAFT ROUTING | |

[NOTE] The following components are not illustrated in this R. P. O. See Parts List or Bill of Materials for part numbers.

UPC 2B    FRAME-◑

UPC 4A4   PROP SHAFT & U JOINTS-◑③

UPC 5D    PARKING BRAKE-◑

UPC 7     LUBRICATION-◑

◑ Assemble same as production. See Parts List or Bill of Materials for part numbers.

*The VIN location varied according to the type of engine used. Note that the 400 is the 402 ci big-block.*

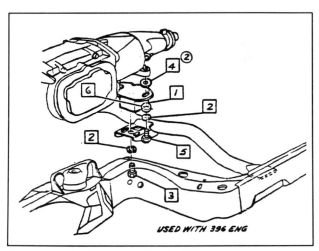

*Rear transmission mount for the SS 396.*

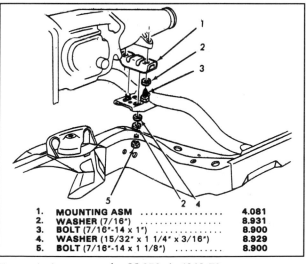

| | | |
|---|---|---|
| 1. | MOUNTING ASM | 4.081 |
| 2. | WASHER (7/16") | 8.931 |
| 3. | BOLT (7/16"-14 x 1") | 8.900 |
| 4. | WASHER (15/32" x 1 1/4" x 3/16") | 8.929 |
| 5. | BOLT (7/16"-14 x 1 1/8") | 8.900 |

*Transmission mount for SS 350s in 1969-70.*

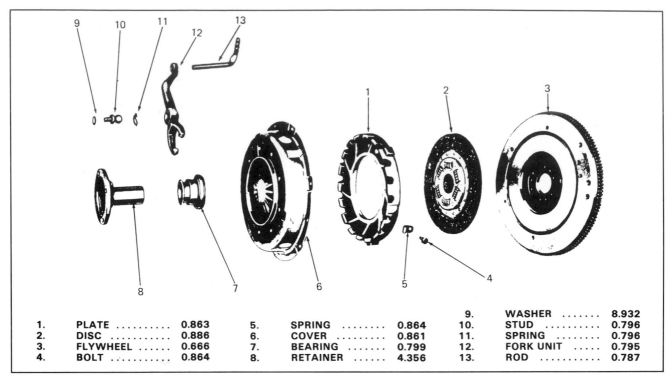

| | | | | | | | | | |
|---|---|---|---|---|---|---|---|---|---|
| 1. | PLATE | 0.863 | 5. | SPRING | 0.864 | 9. | WASHER | 8.932 |
| 2. | DISC | 0.886 | 6. | COVER | 0.861 | 10. | STUD | 0.796 |
| 3. | FLYWHEEL | 0.666 | 7. | BEARING | 0.799 | 11. | SPRING | 0.796 |
| 4. | BOLT | 0.864 | 8. | RETAINER | 4.356 | 12. | FORK UNIT | 0.795 |
| | | | | | | 13. | ROD | 0.787 |

*Chevelle clutch and flywheel.*

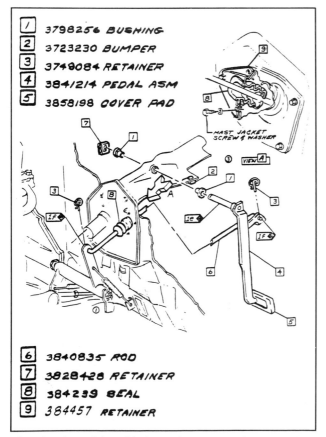

1. 3798256 BUSHING
2. 3723230 BUMPER
3. 3749084 RETAINER
4. 384/214 PEDAL ASM
5. 3858198 COVER PAD
6. 3840835 ROD
7. 3828428 RETAINER
8. 384239 SEAL
9. 384457 RETAINER

*The clutch pedal and linkage design was the same from 1964 to 1967.*

in 1966-67. The flywheel was identical to the one used on the Z16 Chevelle in 1965.

The 1966 pedal assembly was identical to that used in 1964-65, but the part number was changed to 3900527 in 1967. The cover used the same part number as before and came with no trim in either 1966 or 1967.

**1968-1969**

The discs were basically the same in 1968-69 as in 1967. The pressure plate was changed to a 2,800 pound rate in 1969. Pedals were redesigned in 1968 and listed as part number 3904302, and they will not interchange with earlier models. Also changed were the rod and the boot. The pedal was listed as part number 3965777 in 1969. The same cover, part number 3858198, with no trim plate was used both years.

The finish on the 1968-69 pedal should be 30 degree gloss-black acrylic lacquer instead of 60 degree gloss-black nonacrylic lacquer. The correct paint part numbers were Ditzler 9317, Rinshed Mason 168C41 and DuPont 4428L.

**1970-1972**

Discs were 11 in. for all engines in 1970. Pressure plates for all but the high-performance engines—L78, L89, LS6—were rated at 2,750 pounds; the high-performance engines used a 2,800 pound-rated pressure plate.

In 1971 the L48 engine used the same disc as the LS3 and LS5 engines, and the L65 engine used a

10.3 in. clutch. The pressure plate rate was also different at 2,300 pounds. In 1972 both the L65 and L48 engines used the smaller 10.3 in. disc and the 2,300 pound pressure plate.

The pedal assembly part number and finish for 1970 and 1971 were identical to those used in 1969. The pedal was changed to part number 3967183 in 1972, but the finish was the same as in 1971. The same cover, part number 3858198, was used all three years with no trim.

## Powerglide Automatic Transmissions

### 1964-1965

A two-speed automatic transmission was listed as RPO M35 in both 1964 and 1965. In 1964 two different transmissions were available with the V-8 engine. All 283 ci equipped cars used the same transmission—part number 3837494, 3864436 in 1965. The 327 ci engined cars used part number 3858745, 3848984 in 1965. All transmissions used the same 11.75 in. diameter torque converter, part number 3789959.

Both transmissions were coded with the letter T found stamped on the bottom of the oil pan both years. Following this code was a series of numbers that indicated the date and the shift on which the transmission was built. For example, T40430D would be a Powerglide built in 1964 on April 30 by the day shift.

The cooling lines should have a natural metal appearance. The same part numbers were used both years: 3846871 for the inlet and 3846874 for the outlet. The lines were routed along the right-hand side frame rail and supported with two clips. The inlet pipe must also bend around behind the fan for correctness. A radiator with provisions for the cooling lines was also used.

Modulator line part number 3854287 was routed along the left-hand side of the transmission, supported with two clips, to a connector in the intake manifold. At each end of this line a short piece of hose with no clamps was used. This line should also have a natural appearance.

The only available ratio for the rear axle was 3.08 with all V-8 engines. In February 1965 this was revised and the L77 engine used 3.36 gears; the L30 and L74 engines used 3.70 gears all year. The L79 and L37 engines were not available with the Powerglide option.

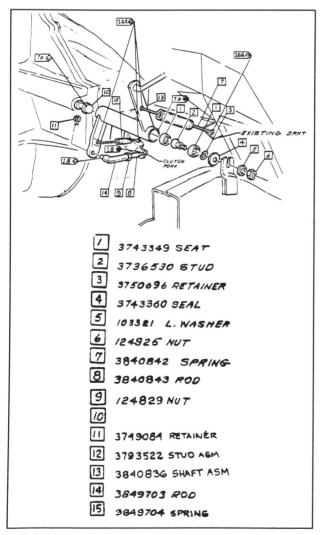

| | |
|---|---|
| 1 | 3743349 SEAT |
| 2 | 3736530 STUD |
| 3 | 3750696 RETAINER |
| 4 | 3743360 SEAL |
| 5 | 103321 L. WASHER |
| 6 | 124926 NUT |
| 7 | 3840842 SPRING |
| 8 | 3840843 ROD |
| 9 | 124829 NUT |
| 10 | |
| 11 | 3749084 RETAINER |
| 12 | 3793522 STUD ASM |
| 13 | 3840836 SHAFT ASM |
| 14 | 3849703 ROD |
| 15 | 3849704 SPRING |

*1964-67 clutch shaft and pushrod.*

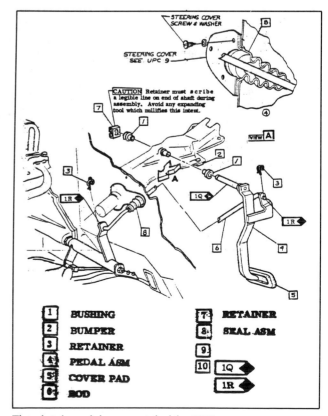

| | | | |
|---|---|---|---|
| 1 | BUSHING | 7 | RETAINER |
| 2 | BUMPER | 8 | SEAL ASM |
| 3 | RETAINER | 9 | |
| 4 | PEDAL ASM | 10 | 1Q |
| 5 | COVER PAD | | 1R |
| 6 | ROD | | |

*The clutch pedal was restyled for 1968.*

The one-piece aluminum case should have a dirty gray (natural aluminum) appearance. The oil pan and underpan should both be painted gloss-black.

A splash shield, part number 3884843, and extension, part number 3884844, were added to the front left-hand side of the transmission in the fourth week of April 1965. For correctness the extension must be stapled to the shield in four places.

### 1966-1968

The two-speed automatic transmission, M35, continued to be offered in the 1966 SS. Two trans-

missions were available: L35 used part number 3883906 with a stall speed of 1880 rpm; the other transmission, part number 3890560, had a converter with a lower stall speed of 1860 rpm.

The code was the same as before in 1965, but the build date was changed accordingly. The code was now stamped on the right side of the oil pan. A larger converter underpan, part number 3831527, was used on both transmissions, as was a splash shield.

The cooling lines—inlet part number 3880560 and outlet part number 3880562—were now rerouted along the bottom right-hand side of the engine block. They were again supported by two clips. The first clip should be located 8 in. from the rear edge of the radiator, and the next clip 29 in. from the first clip. The lines should have a natural appearance, and the clips should be gloss-black.

The radiator was also redesigned: the cooling provisions were closer together on the bottom rear of the core. Thus, this radiator will not interchange with 1964-65 models.

Modulator line part number 3905424 was used on the SS. It too was rerouted up and over the transmission to the right-hand side. A natural metal clip held the line and the oil fill tube together. Vacuum was drawn by a T-connector—part number 3891523, 3891525 with power brakes—in the intake manifold.

The standard rear end ratio was 3.31 on the base L35 engine and 3.73 with the L34 engine. With air conditioning, 3.07 gears were used. Optional gear ratios of 3.55, 3.73 and 4.10 were available.

The same code and code location were used again in 1967. The L35 transmission was now listed as part number 3904512, and the L34 transmission as part number 3895724, although part number 3895723 was used for two months. The L78 engine was not available with an automatic transmission in either 1966 or 1967. The cooling and modulator lines were identical to those used in 1965.

The year 1968 was the last one the Powerglide automatic transmission, M35, was available on the Chevelle SS 396. The code should be the letters *TG* followed by the plant of manufacture, then the model year and date of assembly, and finally the shift. The month was indicated by a single letter (see the 1968-1969 Three-speed Manual Month Codes chart).

The base L35 engine used part number 3919339, and the optional L34 powerplant used part number 3919342. Modulator line part number 3920777 was routed as in 1966-67. The vacuum T-connector in the intake manifold must be aligned at 90 degrees from the centerline of the engine.

The cooling lines—inlet part number 3931428 and outlet part number 3931430—were rerouted because the provisions were now on the back of the core on the right-hand side. Both lines were routed behind the starter motor, then along the oil pan

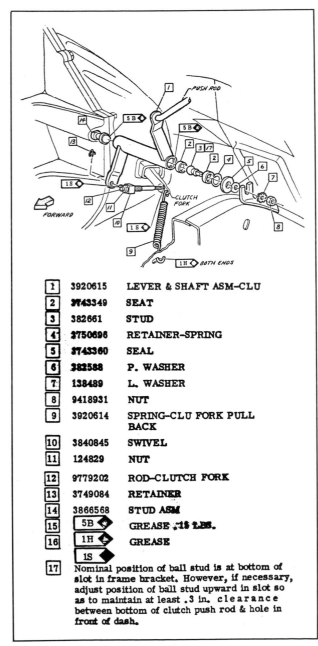

| | | |
|---|---|---|
| 1 | 3920615 | LEVER & SHAFT ASM–CLU |
| 2 | 3743349 | SEAT |
| 3 | 382661 | STUD |
| 4 | 3750698 | RETAINER–SPRING |
| 5 | 3743360 | SEAL |
| 6 | 382588 | P. WASHER |
| 7 | 138489 | L. WASHER |
| 8 | 9418931 | NUT |
| 9 | 3920614 | SPRING–CLU FORK PULL BACK |
| 10 | 3840845 | SWIVEL |
| 11 | 124829 | NUT |
| 12 | 9779202 | ROD–CLUTCH FORK |
| 13 | 3749084 | RETAINER |
| 14 | 3866568 | STUD ASM |
| 15 | 5B | GREASE .15 LBS. |
| 16 | 1H | GREASE |
| | 1S | |
| 17 | | Nominal position of ball stud is at bottom of slot in frame bracket. However, if necessary, adjust position of ball stud upward in slot so as to maintain at least .3 in. clearance between bottom of clutch push rod & hole in front of dash. |

*The shaft and pushrod were also restyled for 1968.*

rail, behind the fuel pump and to the radiator. They were supported by two clips, one at the front of the engine and the other behind the starter. The lines were also supported by a clip on the oil pan. A special spacer, part number 1362766, was also used here. Minimum clearance between the lines and the lower radiator hose was 1.02 in.

Gear ratios were the same for both 1967 and 1968. The standard ratio with air conditioning was 3.07; this was also the standard ratio with the base L35 engine. The optional L34 engine used 3.31 as the standard ratio. Optional gear ratios were 3.55, 3.73 and 4.10.

Finishing for all three years should be done according to 1965 directions. At some factories units built for use on the SS 396 had the engine option number painted on the bell housing in yellow paint.

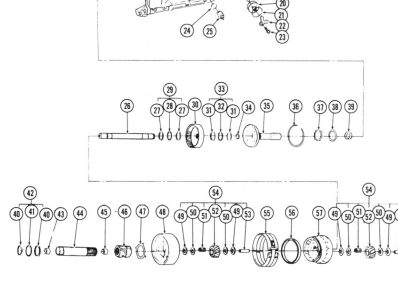

| 41. | BEARING, Center Support to Sun Gear Thrust | N.S. |
| 42. | BEARING & RACES KIT, Center Support to Sun Gear Thrust | 4.159 |
| 43. | BUSHING, Sun Gear Shaft | 4.161 |
| 44. | SHAFT ASM, Sun Gear-Includes Bushings | 4.161 |
| 45. | BUSHING, Sun Gear Shaft | 4.161 |
| 46. | GEAR, Sun | 4.159 |
| 47. | WASHER, Reaction Carrier to Output Carrier | 4.176 |
| 48. | CARRIER ASM, Reaction-Complete | 4.175 |
| 49. | WASHER, Pinion Thrust-Bronze | N.S. |
| 50. | WASHER, Pinion Thrust-Steel | N.S. |
| 51. | BEARING, Output & Reaction Carrier Roller | N.S. |
| 52. | PINION, Planet | N.S. |
| 53. | PIN, Planet Pinion | N.S. |
| 54. | PINION KIT, Output & Reaction Carrier | 4.175 |
| 55. | BAND ASM, Rear Brake-Complete | 4.251 |
| 56. | RING, Front Internal Gear | 4.176 |
| 57. | CARRIER ASM, Output-Complete | 4.175 |

| 1. | RETAINER, Vacuum Modulator | 4.205 |
| 2. | BOLT, Retainer to Case (5/16"-18 x 9/16") | 8.900 |
| 3. | MODULATOR ASM, Vacuum | 4.205 |
| 4. | SEAL, Vacuum Modulator | 4.205 |
| 5. | VALVE, Vacuum Modulator | 4.205 |
| 6. | BOLT, Governor Cover to Case (5/16"-18 x 9/16") | 8.900 |
| 7. | COVER, Governor | 4.256 |
| 8. | GASKET, Governor Cover | 4.256 |
| 9. | GOVERNOR ASM, Trans | 4.256 |
| 10. | CASE, Trans | N.S. |
| 11. | BUSHING, Trans Case | 4.104 |
| 12. | CASE ASM, Trans | 4.103 |
| 13. | SEAL, Case Extension to Case | 4.318 |
| 14. | BOLT, Extension to Case (3/8"-16 x 1") | 8.900 |
| 15. | EXTENSION, Case | N.S. |
| 16. | BUSHING, Case Extension | 4.319 |
| 17. | EXTENSION ASM, Case | 4.317 |
| 18. | SEAL, Case Extension Oil | 4.318 |
| 19. | GEAR, Speedometer Driven | 4.337 |
| 20. | SLEEVE & SEAL ASM, Speedometer Driven Gear | 4.338 |
| 21. | SEAL, Speedo Gear Sleeve to Case | 4.338 |
| 22. | RETAINER, Speedo Driven Gear Sleeve | 4.338 |
| 23. | BOLT, Retainer to Case (5/16"-18 x 5/8") | 8.900 |
| 24. | SEAL, Connector to Case | 4.205 |
| 25. | CONNECTOR, Downshift Solenoid Valve-Single Male | 4.265 |
| 26. | SHAFT & PLUG ASM, Trans Main | 4.172 |
| 27. | RACE, Sun Gear to Rear Internal Gear Thrust Brg | N.S. |
| 28. | BEARING, Sun Gear to Rear Internal Gear Thrust | N.S. |
| 29. | BEARING & RACES KIT, Sun Gear to Rear Internal Gear Thrust | 4.159 |
| 30. | GEAR, Rear Internal Main Shaft | 4.187 |
| 31. | RACE, Rear Internal Gear to Output Shaft Bearing | N.S. |
| 32. | BEARING, Rear Internal Gear to Output Shaft | N.S. |
| 33. | BEARING & RACES KIT, Rr Internal Gear to Output Shaft | 4.187 |
| 34. | RING, Mainshaft Snap | 4.172 |
| 35. | SHAFT & PLUG ASM, Output | 4.175 |
| 36. | RING, Output Shaft to Front Internal Gear-Snap | 4.176 |
| 37. | WASHER, Output Shaft to Case Thrust | 4.176 |
| 38. | WASHER, Output Shaft to Case-Selective (.078 to .122) | 4.176 |
| 39. | GEAR, Speedometer Drive | 4.343 |
| 40. | RACE, Center Support to Sun Gear Thrust Bearing | N.S. |

*Turbo Hydra-matic 375 400 automatic transmission.*

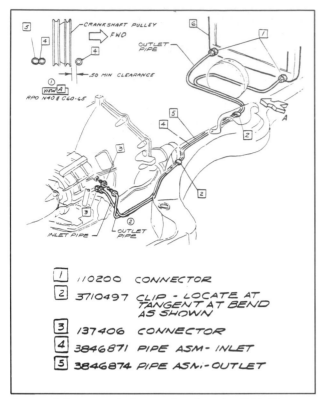

*Route of the transmission cooling lines for 1964-65.*

| | | |
|---|---|---|
| 1 | 110200 | CONNECTOR |
| 2 | 3710497 | CLIP - LOCATE AT TANGENT AT BEND AS SHOWN |
| 3 | 137406 | CONNECTOR |
| 4 | 3846871 | PIPE ASM - INLET |
| 5 | 3846874 | PIPE ASM - OUTLET |

*The cooling lines were revised in 1966.*

| | | |
|---|---|---|
| 1 | 3007618 | BODY ASM RADIATOR |
| | 3007615 | -RPO L30 & RPO L77 ④ |
| | 3007621 | -RPO L34 & RPO L35 |
| 2 | 3710497 | CLIP |
| 3 | 3863971 | PIPE ASM-INLET EXC RPO L34 & L35 |
| | 3880560 | -RPO L34 & RPO L35 |
| 4 | 3863972 | PIPE ASM-OUTLET EXC RPO L34 & L35 |
| | 3880562 | -RPO L34 & RPO L35 |

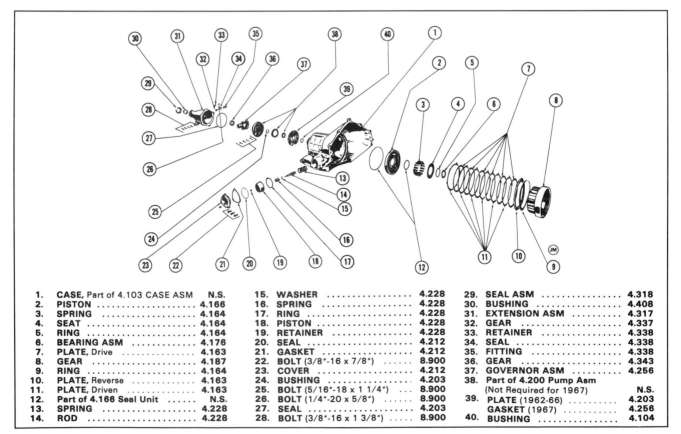

| | | | | | |
|---|---|---|---|---|---|
| 1. | CASE, Part of 4.103 CASE ASM N.S. | 15. | WASHER ..... 4.228 | 29. | SEAL ASM ..... 4.318 |
| 2. | PISTON ..... 4.166 | 16. | SPRING ..... 4.228 | 30. | BUSHING ..... 4.408 |
| 3. | SPRING ..... 4.164 | 17. | RING ..... 4.228 | 31. | EXTENSION ASM ..... 4.317 |
| 4. | SEAT ..... 4.164 | 18. | PISTON ..... 4.228 | 32. | GEAR ..... 4.337 |
| 5. | RING ..... 4.164 | 19. | RETAINER ..... 4.228 | 33. | RETAINER ..... 4.338 |
| 6. | BEARING ASM ..... 4.176 | 20. | SEAL ..... 4.212 | 34. | SEAL ..... 4.338 |
| 7. | PLATE, Drive ..... 4.163 | 21. | GASKET ..... 4.212 | 35. | FITTING ..... 4.338 |
| 8. | GEAR ..... 4.187 | 22. | BOLT (3/8"-16 x 7/8") ..... 8.900 | 36. | GEAR ..... 4.343 |
| 9. | RING ..... 4.164 | 23. | COVER ..... 4.212 | 37. | GOVERNOR ASM ..... 4.256 |
| 10. | PLATE, Reverse ..... 4.163 | 24. | BUSHING ..... 4.203 | 38. | Part of 4.200 Pump Asm (Not Required for 1967) N.S. |
| 11. | PLATE, Driven ..... 4.163 | 25. | BOLT (5/16"-18 x 1 1/4") ..... 8.900 | 39. | PLATE (1962-66) ..... 4.203 |
| 12. | Part of 4.166 Seal Unit ..... N.S. | 26. | BOLT (1/4"-20 x 5/8") ..... 8.900 | | GASKET (1967) ..... 4.256 |
| 13. | SPRING ..... 4.228 | 27. | SEAL ..... 4.203 | 40. | BUSHING ..... 4.104 |
| 14. | ROD ..... 4.228 | 28. | BOLT (3/8"-16 x 1 3/8") ..... 8.900 | | |

*Transmission case.*

## Turbo Hydra-matic Automatic Transmissions

### 1967-1968

A three-speed automatic became available for the SS 396 only in 1967. It was known as the Turbo 400 transmission and it was listed as RPO M40. This transmission was coded with the letters *CC* on a tag on the right-hand side of the case and was made at the Ypsilanti, Michigan, plant.

The stall speed was rated at 2100 rpm and the converter was 12.83 in. in diameter. Owing to the extra overall length of the Turbo 400 transmission, the support member, part number 3838040, was moved back. In the convertible or pickup a special bracket, part number 383043, had to be welded into place for the support. A shorter drive shaft, part number 7801646, was also needed. The El Camino used a different drive shaft, part number 7802607. This shaft was 6 in. shorter than the production part but was 4 in. longer than the drive shaft used in the coupe and convertible.

The standard gear ratio for the Turbo 400 transmission was 2.73 on the base L35 engine and 3.07 on the L34 engine. The L78 engine was not available with automatic transmission in either 1967 or 1968. When air conditioning was ordered, the gear ratio was 3.07, which was also a performance option for the L35 engine without air conditioning. A performance option on the L34 without air conditoning was listed as a 3.31 ratio; this ratio was available as a special order option with the L35 engine.

Modular line part number 3915021 was routed up the right-hand side of the case to a connector in the intake manifold. The cooling lines—inlet part number 3909604 and outlet part number 3909605—were routed much as they were on the Powerglide but higher up. The lines were supported by two gloss-black clips. The first clip should be located 6.75 in. from the rear edge of the radiator. The next clip was 28 in. from the first clip.

Both the modulator line and the cooling lines should have a natural appearance. Two small rubber hoses were used at each end of the modulator line. No clamps were used. These small hoses were known for slipping off the modulator line. If your car will not shift automatically in drive but can be force shifted, this may be its problem, but more often the culprit is the hose that connects to the transmission. Replace the hose back on the pipe, and the transmission should shift normally again.

The case should have a natural dull aluminum appearance. The oil pan and the converter pan, part number 3868810, should be painted gloss-black.

A few late-model 1967 SS 396s used the second-design oil pan. It can be identified by two stamped bosses in the bottom of the pan, and its shape was also slightly different. The first design

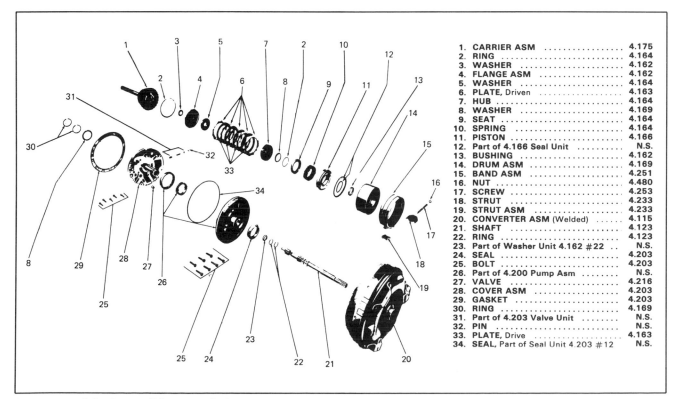

| 1. CARRIER ASM | 4.175 |
|---|---|
| 2. RING | 4.164 |
| 3. WASHER | 4.162 |
| 4. FLANGE ASM | 4.162 |
| 5. WASHER | 4.164 |
| 6. PLATE, Driven | 4.163 |
| 7. HUB | 4.164 |
| 8. WASHER | 4.169 |
| 9. SEAT | 4.164 |
| 10. SPRING | 4.164 |
| 11. PISTON | 4.166 |
| 12. Part of 4.166 Seal Unit | N.S. |
| 13. BUSHING | 4.162 |
| 14. DRUM ASM | 4.169 |
| 15. BAND ASM | 4.251 |
| 16. NUT | 4.480 |
| 17. SCREW | 4.253 |
| 18. STRUT | 4.233 |
| 19. STRUT ASM | 4.233 |
| 20. CONVERTER ASM (Welded) | 4.115 |
| 21. SHAFT | 4.123 |
| 22. RING | 4.123 |
| 23. Part of Washer Unit 4.162 #22 | N.S. |
| 24. SEAL | 4.203 |
| 25. BOLT | 4.203 |
| 26. Part of 4.200 Pump Asm | N.S. |
| 27. VALVE | 4.216 |
| 28. COVER ASM | 4.203 |
| 29. GASKET | 4.203 |
| 30. RING | 4.169 |
| 31. Part of 4.203 Valve Unit | N.S. |
| 32. PIN | N.S. |
| 33. PLATE, Drive | 4.163 |
| 34. SEAL, Part of Seal Unit 4.203 #12 | N.S. |

*Inner parts of the Powerglide transmission.*

used three stamped bosses in the pan. The first design was listed as part number 8623778, and the second design as part number 8625766.

Various other parts were also changed with the second design.

## 1967–1969 Turbo Hydra-matic Part Numbers

| Part | First Design | Second Design |
|---|---|---|
| Filter | 6259422 | 6437741 |
| Filter retaining bolt | None | 8625769 |
| Grommet to oil pump pipe | None | 6437746 |

## 1967–1969 Turbo Hydra-matic Part Numbers

| Part | First Design | Second Design |
|---|---|---|
| Oil pump intake pipe | None | 8625428 |

The M40 Turbo 400 automatic transmission, part number 8626225, continued to be offered on the SS 396 only in 1968. Its code and the location of its tag were the same as before.

The cooling lines—inlet part number 3931424 and outlet part number 3931426—were routed much like the Powerglide lines except that no spacer was used and the clip behind the starter was mounted farther back.

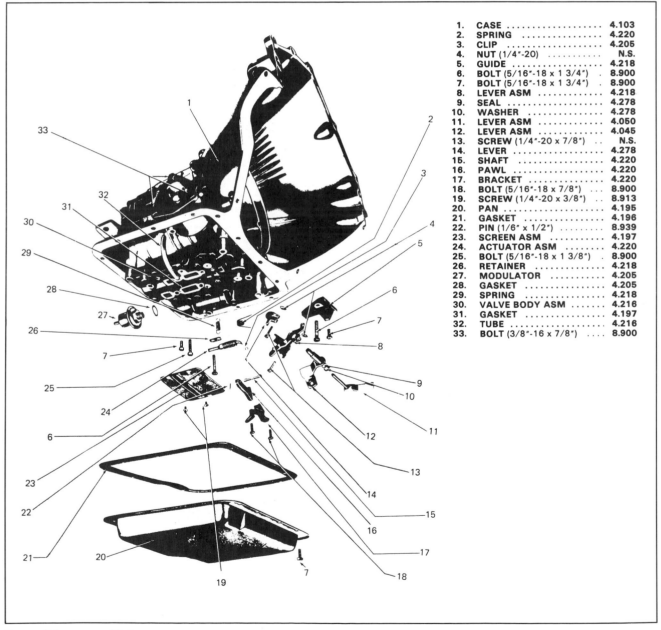

| 1. | CASE | 4.103 |
|---|---|---|
| 2. | SPRING | 4.220 |
| 3. | CLIP | 4.205 |
| 4. | NUT (1/4"-20) | N.S. |
| 5. | GUIDE | 4.218 |
| 6. | BOLT (5/16"-18 x 1 3/4") | 8.900 |
| 7. | BOLT (5/16"-18 x 1 3/4") | 8.900 |
| 8. | LEVER ASM | 4.218 |
| 9. | SEAL | 4.278 |
| 10. | WASHER | 4.278 |
| 11. | LEVER ASM | 4.050 |
| 12. | LEVER ASM | 4.045 |
| 13. | SCREW (1/4"-20 x 7/8") | N.S. |
| 14. | LEVER | 4.278 |
| 15. | SHAFT | 4.220 |
| 16. | PAWL | 4.220 |
| 17. | BRACKET | 4.220 |
| 18. | BOLT (5/16"-18 x 7/8") | 8.900 |
| 19. | SCREW (1/4"-20 x 3/8") | 8.913 |
| 20. | PAN | 4.195 |
| 21. | GASKET | 4.196 |
| 22. | PIN (1/6" x 1/2") | 8.939 |
| 23. | SCREEN ASM | 4.197 |
| 24. | ACTUATOR ASM | 4.220 |
| 25. | BOLT (5/16"-18 x 1 3/8") | 8.900 |
| 26. | RETAINER | 4.218 |
| 27. | MODULATOR | 4.205 |
| 28. | GASKET | 4.205 |
| 29. | SPRING | 4.218 |
| 30. | VALVE BODY ASM | 4.216 |
| 31. | GASKET | 4.197 |
| 32. | TUBE | 4.216 |
| 33. | BOLT (3/8"-16 x 7/8") | 8.900 |

*Powerglide case and linkage.*

Rear end ratios remained the same as in 1967, but a 2.56 ratio was available on the base engine without air conditioning as an economy option.

Like all other transmissions the Turbo Hydra-matic 400 was stamped with the car's VIN beginning in 1968. The stamping was located on a pad on the right side of the case just above the pan. It should begin with the number 1, as does the stamping for manual transmissions.

### 1969-1972

The only optional automatic transmission available for the 1969 SS 396 was the M40 Turbo 400 unit. Four separate transmissions were used according to the engine. The base L35 engine used part number 8626464, and the L34 engine part number 8626466. For the first time the L78 engine came with M40. It started with part number 8626536 and then, beginning in the fourth week in April 1969, used part number 8626605.

All transmissions were coded with the letters *CA* on a tag on the right-hand side of the case. The torque converter was smaller at 12.2 in. in diameter. The car's VIN was stamped on the transmission in the same location and manner as in 1968.

The cooling lines—inlet part number 3945485, code CM, and outlet part number 3945486, code CN—were routed as in 1968, but the clip behind the starter was moved back toward the transmission. The codes were listed on white tape with red letters 3 in. from the radiator.

All 396 ci engines with automatic transmissions in 1969 used a closed air cleaner assembly, part number 6484590, with a single air horn. This horn was connected to a ducting system that drew hot air from the right-hand exhaust manifold into the carburetor.

### 1969-1972 Turbo Hydra-matic Ducting System Part Numbers

| | |
|---|---|
| Hose | 3952317 |
| Duct assembly | 3916177 |
| Extension between hose & duct | 3964265 |

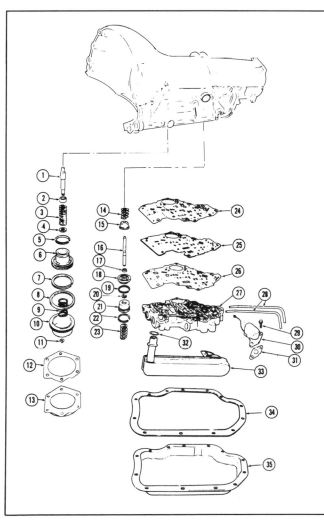

| | | | |
|---|---|---|---|
| 1. | **PIN,** Rr Servo Rear Band Apply | ...... | 4.241 |
| 2. | **RETAINER,** Rr Servo Piston Spring | ... | 4.247 |
| 3. | **SPRING,** Rr Servo | ............... | 4.246 |
| 4. | **WASHER,** Rr Servo Piston | ......... | 4.241 |
| 5. | **RING,** Accum Piston Oil Seal-Inr | ..... | 4.242 |
| 6. | **PISTON,** Accum | ................... | 4.241 |
| 7. | **RING,** Accum Piston Oil Seal-Otr | ..... | 4.242 |
| 8. | **SEAL,** Rr Servo Piston | ............. | 4.242 |
| 9. | **SPRING,** Rr Accum | ............... | 4.246 |
| 10. | **PISTON,** Servo-Rr | ............... | 4.241 |
| 11. | **RING,** Servo Piston Retainer-Snap | .... | N.S. |
| 12. | **GASKET,** Rr Servo Cover | .......... | 4.241 |
| 13. | **COVER,** Rr Servo | ................ | 4.241 |
| 14. | **SPRING,** Frt Servo | ............... | 4.228 |
| 15. | **RETAINER,** Frt Servo Spring | ........ | 4.226 |
| 16. | **PIN,** Frt Servo Piston | ............. | 4.228 |
| 17. | **WASHER,** Servo Piston | ........... | 4.228 |
| 18. | **PISTON,** Frt Servo | ............... | 4.228 |
| 19. | **RING,** Frt Servo Piston Oil Seal | ...... | 4.229 |
| 20. | **RING,** Frt Servo Ret-Snap | ......... | 4.246 |
| 21. | **PISTON,** Accum Frt | .............. | 4.228 |
| 22. | **RING,** Accum Piston Oil Seal | ....... | 4.229 |
| 23. | **SPRING,** Accum Piston-Frt | ......... | 4.246 |
| 24. | **GASKET,** Case to Spacer | .......... | 4.265 |
| 25. | **SPACER,** Valve Body | ............. | 4.265 |
| 26. | **GASKET,** Valve Body to Spacer | ..... | 4.265 |
| 27. | **VALVE ASM,** Trans Control | ........ | 4.265 |
| 28. | **PIPE,** Governor Oil | .............. | 4.248 |
| 29. | **BOLT** (1/4"-20 x 3/4") | ........... | 8.900 |
| 30. | **SOLENOID,** Trans | ............... | 4.265 |
| 31. | **GASKET,** Solenoid Valve | .......... | 4.265 |
| 32. | **SEAL,** Oil Suction Pipe to Case | ...... | 4.197 |
| 33. | **FILTER,** Trans Oil | ................ | 4.197 |
| 34. | **GASKET,** Trans Oil Pan | ........... | 4.196 |
| 35. | **PAN,** Trans Oil | .................. | 4.195 |

*Turbo Hydra-matic transmission servos and control valve.*

## 1969–1972 Turbo Hydra-matic Ducting System Part Numbers

| | |
|---|---|
| Threaded elbow | 3946083 |
| Clamp to attach hose to elbow | 451216 |
| Extension bolt | 9419049 |

When installed, the duct must be pushed back over the exhaust manifold till the dimple on the end of the duct snaps into place over the rib on the manifold. Duct, extension, elbow and air cleaner base should be painted gloss-black.

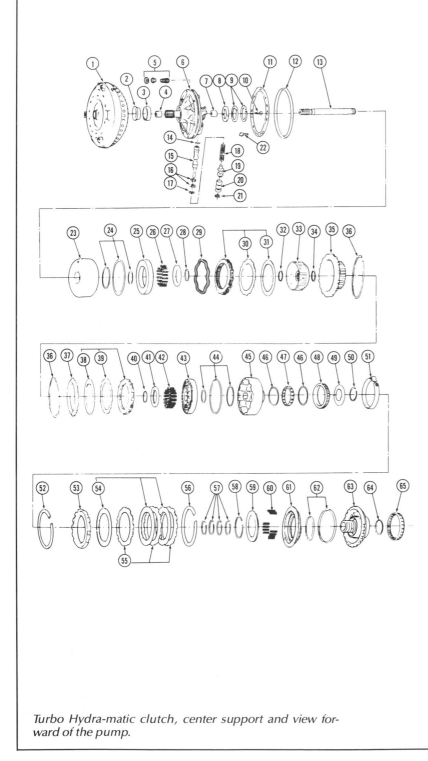

| | | |
|---|---|---|
| 1. | **CONVERTER ASM** | 4.115 |
| 2. | **SEAL,** Pump Body | 4.226 |
| 3. | **BUSHING,** Pump Body | 4.226 |
| 4. | **BUSHING,** Oil Pump Stator Shaft | 4.226 |
| 5. | Part of Pump Asm | N.S. |
| 6. | **PUMP ASM,** Trans Complete | 4.224 |
| 7. | **BUSHING,** Oil Pump Stator Shaft | 4.226 |
| 8. | **WASHER,** Pump Cvr to Forward Clutch Drum (.060 to .130) | 4.169 |
| 9. | **RING,** Front Pump to Forward Clutch | 4.162 |
| 10. | **BOLT,** Pump to Stator (5/16"-18 x 1 1/2") | 8.900 |
| 11. | **GASKET,** Pump Cover to Case | 4.226 |
| 12. | **SEAL,** Oil Pump to Case | 4.226 |
| 13. | **SHAFT,** Trans Turbine | 4.123 |
| 14. | **PIN,** Trans Oil Pump (.13 Dia x 1.33 Straight) | 4.226 |
| 15. | **VALVE & PLUG ASM,** Pressure Regulator | 4.216 |
| 16. | **SPACER,** Pressure Regulator Valve | 4.216 |
| 17. | **WASHER,** Pressure Regulator Valve Spring Retainer | 4.216 |
| 18. | **SPRING,** Pressure Regulator Valve | 4.216 |
| 19. | **VALVE KIT,** Pressure Regulator Boost | 4.216 |
| 20. | **BUSHING,** Pressure Regulator Boost Valve Part of #19 | N.S. |
| 21. | **RING,** Regulator Bushing Retaining | 4.162 |
| 22. | **BOLT ASM KIT,** Pump to Case | 4.226 |
| 23. | **HOUSING,** Forward Clutch | 4.169 |
| 24. | **SEALS KIT,** Forward & Direct Piston | 4.166 |
| 25. | **PISTON,** Forward Clutch | 4.166 |
| 26. | **SPRING,** Forward Clutch Piston Release-Blue | 4.164 |
| 27. | **RETAINER,** Clutch Piston Spring | 4.164 |
| 28. | **RING,** Retainer to Clutch Housing-Snap | 4.164 |
| 29. | **PLATE,** Forward Clutch Driven-Wave | 4.163 |
| 30. | **PLATE,** Forward Clutch Driven | 4.163 |
| 31. | **PLATE,** Forward & Direct Clutch Drive | 4.163 |
| 32. | **WASHER,** Clutch Hub to Clutch Housing Thrust | N.S. |
| 33. | **HUB,** Forward Clutch | 4.164 |
| 34. | **WASHER,** Clutch Hub to Direct Clutch Thrust | 4.164 |
| 35. | **HUB,** Direct Clutch | 4.164 |
| 36. | **RING,** Forward & Direct Clutch-Snap | 4.164 |
| 37. | **PLATE,** Direct Clutch Backing | 4.163 |
| 38. | **PLATE,** Forward & Direct Clutch Drive | 4.163 |
| 39. | **PLATE,** Direct Clutch Driven | 4.163 |
| 40. | **RING,** Retainer to Clutch Housing-Snap | 4.164 |
| 41. | **RETAINER,** Clutch Piston Spring | 4.164 |
| 42. | **SPRING,** Direct Clutch Piston Release-Black | 4.164 |
| 43. | **PISTON ASM,** Direct Clutch | 4.166 |
| 44. | **SEALS KIT,** Forward & Direct Clutch Piston | 4.166 |
| 45. | **HOUSING & RACE,** Direct Clutch | 4.169 |
| 46. | **BUSHINGS,** Intermediate Clutch Sprag (Part of #47) | N.S. |
| 47. | **SPRAG & BUSHING,** Intermediate Clutch | 4.167 |
| 48. | **RACE,** Intermediate Clutch Outer | 4.168 |
| 49. | **RETAINER,** Intermediate Clutch | 4.167 |
| 50. | **RING,** Inter Clutch Sprag Ret to Dir Clutch Hsg-Snap | 4.167 |
| 51. | **BAND ASM,** Trans Brake-Front | 4.251 |
| 52. | **RING,** Intermediate Clutch Retaining-Snap | 4.164 |
| 53. | **PLATE,** Intermediate Clutch Backing | 4.163 |
| 54. | **PLATE,** Intermediate Clutch Driving | 4.163 |
| 55. | **PLATE,** Intermediate Clutch Reaction | 4.163 |
| 56. | **RING,** Center Support to Case-Snap | 4.162 |
| 57. | **RING,** Center Support & Direct Clutch Oil Seal | 4.162 |
| 58. | **RING,** Inter Clutch Spring Retainer to Support-Snap | 4.164 |
| 59. | **RETAINER,** Intermediate Clutch Spring | 4.164 |
| 60. | **SPRING,** Intermediate Clutch Release | 4.164 |
| 61. | **PISTON,** Intermediate Clutch | 4.166 |
| 62. | **SEALS KIT,** Intermediate Clutch Piston | 4.166 |
| 63. | **SUPPORT & RACE ASM,** Trans Center | 4.162 |
| 64. | **WASHER,** Support to Reaction Drum-Thrust | 4.162 |
| 65. | **SPRAG ASM,** Trans Low Clutch | 4.180 |

*Turbo Hydra-matic clutch, center support and view forward of the pump.*

With or without air conditioning, the standard ratio on the base L35 engine was 3.31, and on the L34 and L78 engine it was 3.55. The performance ratio was 3.73, and it was available for all three engines. The 2.73 was a special order option on the L35 engine. Special options on the L34 and L78 engines included 3.07 and 4.10 ratios. Economy ratios of 3.07 for the L35 engine and 3.31 for the others were also optional.

Four different transmissions were used in 1970. The L34 engine in the SS 396 used part number 8626794, code CD, and the L78 and L89 engines used part number 8626795, code CE. The transmission in the base LS5 SS 454 package was listed as part number 8626656, code CR, and the LS6 used part number 8626659 and was coded CS and CY.

The car's VIN was stamped on the transmission in two places. The Flint and Oshawa plants stamped the transmission on the edge of the bell housing on the left-hand side; the other plants used the same pad as before. Both locations were stamped in the same manner as described for 1968.

For the cooling lines—inlet part number 3967775, code GI, and outlet part number 3967776, code GJ—the codes appeared in red on white tape. The code location and the line route were the same as in 1969.

Throttle control was handled by a system of switches and wires. A 30 degree gloss-black bracket, part number 3972676, was mounted to the back of the accelerator pedal and support. This bracket supported the throttle control switch, part number 1233031, with a single ¼×½ in. screw.

This sytem was also used on a few late-model 1969 SS 396s with the 402 ci engine. Parts were different, though, and the bracket was secured to the pedal with two bolts instead of a bolt and pin. The switch was smaller in 1969, and the wiring harness was supported to the heater-defroster assembly under the dash with a single clip. This clip was not used in 1970 models.

**1969 Throttle Control Part Numbers**
Bracket     3930796
Switch      1993424

Also, all 1970 transmissions were equipped with a Transmission Controlled Spark system, a form of emission control that eliminated the vacuum advance in lower gears. The switch, part number 6462286, was engaged with the pressure of the transmission oil. In high gear the switch would disengage and allow the vacuum advance to operate. If a car is stalling out or lacks performance in high gear, the switch could be defective.

Only a 3.31 rear end gear ratio was available with the automatic transmission with all engines; no optional ratios were offered except with the LS6, where 4.10 gears were available.

Two types of Turbo Hydra-matic transmissions were available as optional equipment in the 1971 Chevelle SS. The L65 and L48 350 ci engines used the smaller Turbo 350 unit, RPO M38, coded

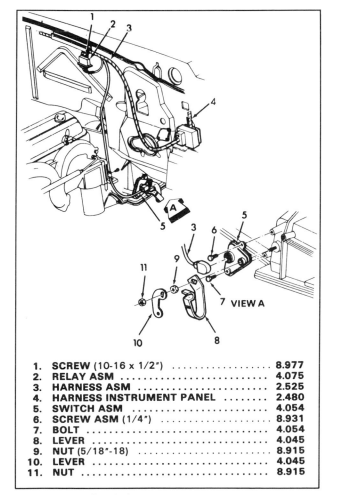

| 1. | SCREW (10-16 x 1/2") | 8.977 |
|----|----------------------|-------|
| 2. | RELAY ASM | 4.075 |
| 3. | HARNESS ASM | 2.525 |
| 4. | HARNESS INSTRUMENT PANEL | 2.480 |
| 5. | SWITCH ASM | 4.054 |
| 6. | SCREW ASM (1/4") | 8.931 |
| 7. | BOLT | 4.054 |
| 8. | LEVER | 4.045 |
| 9. | NUT (5/18"-18) | 8.915 |
| 10. | LEVER | 4.045 |
| 11. | NUT | 8.915 |

*1970-72 neutral switch.*

*This switch controlled the downshift and was mounted to the accelerator pedal with a bracket.*

HW and listed as part number 6261841, for both engines. The code was stamped on the right-hand side of the pan. These transmissions also used a smaller 11.75 in. diameter torque converter.

The other Turbo Hydra-matic transmission was the Turbo 400 used only on the big-blocks—LS3, LS5 and LS6. Three transmissions were used: LS3 used part number 8627259, LS5 used part number 8627260, and LS6 part number 8627264. Codes were the same as in 1970 except that the L78 code was dropped.

The car's VIN was stamped on a pad on the right-hand side of the case near the front except for SSs built at the Oshawa plant, which used the edge of the bell housing on the left-hand side. The stamp format was the same as in previous years.

A special cross-member, part number 3967773, was set back 6 in. farther than normal with the M40 transmission. An insulator pad, part number 9774451, was placed on each end of the support. Special retainers, part number 3967773, were used to hold the member. All Monte Carlos with automatic transmission employed this support and will interchange.

The Turbo 350 used the production member but was set back farther. No pads were used with the SS 350s.

Transmissions remained the same in 1972, but the transmission used with the LS6 engine was canceled. Also, the VIN on the Turbo 350 transmission was located only on a pad on the right-hand side of the case. However, the M40 transmission used two locations, either on the right-hand side just above the oil pan or on a pad on the left-hand side. The cooling lines were identical to those in 1971, but no code tape was used.

Gear ratios for the big-blocks were a carbon copy of those in 1970. The L65 engine came standard with a 2.56 ratio with or without air conditioning. The L48 engine was standard with 2.73 gears with or without air conditioning. Both engines were optional with a 3.31 gear with the RPO YD1 trailer.

## Three-speed Manual Transmission Shift Levers

### 1964–1965

No floor shift lever was available in the Malibu SS in 1964. All manual transmissions were shifted by a "three-on-a-tree" column shifter. A chrome lever, part number 383836, with a black plastic knob, part number 3790368, was used with all interiors.

The same part numbers were used again unchanged in 1965. During the last part of the year a chrome floor-mounted lever became available. This used a solid white shift knob with no engraved shift pattern. Also, no console was offered with this shifter.

### 1966–1967

Both of the manual transmissions offered in 1966 used a floor-mounted chrome shift lever, but each lever was different. The Warner transmission used a lever with part number 384545, and the Saginaw unit used lever part number 384346. Both levers came with the same plain black shift knob, part number 384377.

The shift lever was listed as part number 3903081 in 1967, and the knob, part number 3904035, was white with a black engraved shift pattern.

The 1966 shifters used a plain black rubber boot, part number 3842926, and a chrome retainer, part number 3842927; the latter was held in place with Phillips-head screws.

However, in 1967 a unique bezel, part number 3903960, was placed over the shift boot in the floor.

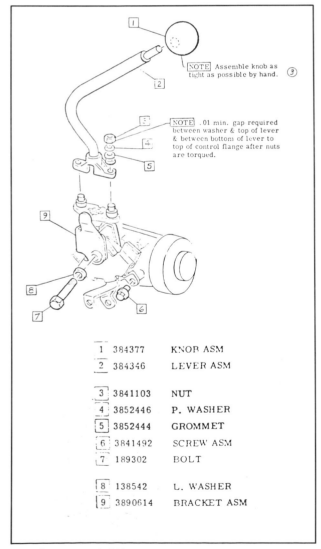

NOTE Assemble knob as tight as possible by hand. ③

NOTE .01 min. gap required between washer & top of lever & between bottom of lever to top of control flange after nuts are torqued.

| 1 | 384377 | KNOB ASM |
| 2 | 384346 | LEVER ASM |
| 3 | 3841103 | NUT |
| 4 | 3852446 | P. WASHER |
| 5 | 3852444 | GROMMET |
| 6 | 3841492 | SCREW ASM |
| 7 | 189302 | BOLT |
| 8 | 138542 | L. WASHER |
| 9 | 3890614 | BRACKET ASM |

*1966 three-speed shifter.*

This bezel was mounted over the shift lever and secured with four Phillips-head screws to a special retainer, part number 3903962. A special boot, part number 3903961, was also used. For correctness this bezel must be mounted over the carpet. Four holes should be pierced into the carpet for the mounting screws. This bezel was chrome and accented with flat-black paint.

### 1968-1969

Floor-mounted chrome shift lever part number 392422 was still standard in the 1968 SS 396 but was redesigned and was not interchangeable with earlier models. This lever attached with two 16 thread ⅜×1 in. tap screws.

The knob was also redesigned and was now in two parts. The lower half was brightly plated and listed as part number 3920218. This section was used with all manual shift levers. The top half was listed as part number 3920217. It was black plastic with the shift pattern engraved in white.

The shift boot was listed as part number 3926743 and was held in place with a flat-black retainer, part number 3926745. This retainer featured four fingers that held the carpet in place and also provided mounting points for the bright bezel, part number 3926747. The exact same parts were used again in 1969.

Unlike previous years 1968 offered the console, RPO D55, with the three-speed transmission in the SS 396. Although the console was available in other Chevelles with the heavy-duty three-speed transmission in 1966-67, it was not listed as optional with the SS 396 models. When the console was used, a solid chrome knob with no shift pattern was used in both 1968 and 1969.

The upper and lower knob halves used the same part numbers in 1969, but the lever was listed as part number 3922526. When the Muncie transmission was used, the lever was listed as part number 3973864 and the same knob was installed.

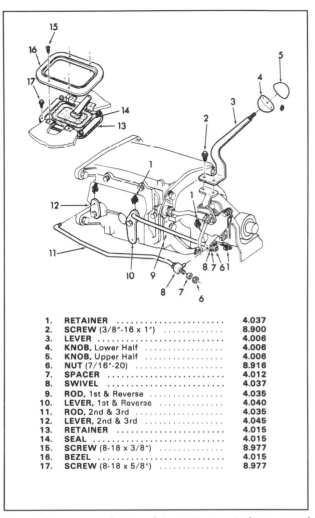

| | | |
|---|---|---|
| 1. | RETAINER | 4.037 |
| 2. | SCREW (3/8"-16 x 1") | 8.900 |
| 3. | LEVER | 4.006 |
| 4. | KNOB, Lower Half | 4.006 |
| 5. | KNOB, Upper Half | 4.006 |
| 6. | NUT (7/16"-20) | 8.916 |
| 7. | SPACER | 4.012 |
| 8. | SWIVEL | 4.037 |
| 9. | ROD, 1st & Reverse | 4.035 |
| 10. | LEVER, 1st & Reverse | 4.040 |
| 11. | ROD, 2nd & 3rd | 4.035 |
| 12. | LEVER, 2nd & 3rd | 4.045 |
| 13. | RETAINER | 4.015 |
| 14. | SEAL | 4.015 |
| 15. | SCREW (8-18 x 3/8") | 8.977 |
| 16. | BEZEL | 4.015 |
| 17. | SCREW (8-18 x 5/8") | 8.977 |

*The shifter was redesigned in 1968. (1970 three-speed version shown here.)*

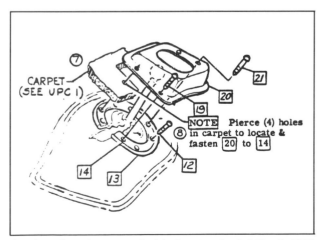

*A unique bezel was used with the standard shifter in 1967.*

*Replacement boot without the console for 1968-72.*

## 1970-1972

No three-speed manual SSs were built in 1970. The 1971 SS 350 with the L65 engine was standard with a column-mounted shift lever. This was listed as part number 3958445 with a black plastic knob, part number 3990592. The lever was held with a single pin in the steering column.

Standard on the SS 350 with the L48 engine and optional, as RPO M11, on the L65 version in 1972 only was a floor-mounted lever. This was not the heavy-duty version. A round one-piece black plastic shift knob with the shift pattern inlaid in white was used with this shifter.

Standard on the SS package with the LS3 engine was the heavy-duty three-speed shifter, part number 3973864. This transmission was also available for the first two months of production on the SS 350 with the L48 engine. A different lever, part number 3973865, was used.

However, both levers came with the same knob: a one-piece black knob, part number 3992554, with the shift pattern engraved into it. This knob was shaped like and had the same feel as the knobs on the instrument panel. The shift pattern was printed on an insert that was glued to the top of the knob. This knob will not interchange with earlier models, as it used ⅜ in. thread, whereas the knobs on earlier cars used $\frac{5}{16}$ in. thread.

Only the SS with the LS3 engine was available with the heavy-duty three-speed transmission in 1972, and this combination was standard. The lever's part number was listed as 3973864; this was the same lever that was used with the four-speed transmission. The knob was listed as part number 3992554. All other shifters were the same as in 1971. A console was available both years with the heavy-duty three-speed only, and a solid chrome knob was used.

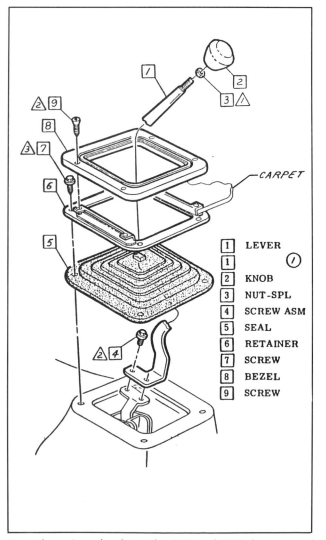

| | |
|---|---|
| 1 | LEVER |
| 1 | |
| 2 | KNOB |
| 3 | NUT-SPL |
| 4 | SCREW ASM |
| 5 | SEAL |
| 6 | RETAINER |
| 7 | SCREW |
| 8 | BEZEL |
| 9 | SCREW |

*Note the unique knob on the 1971 and 1972 three-speed heavy-duty shift lever.*

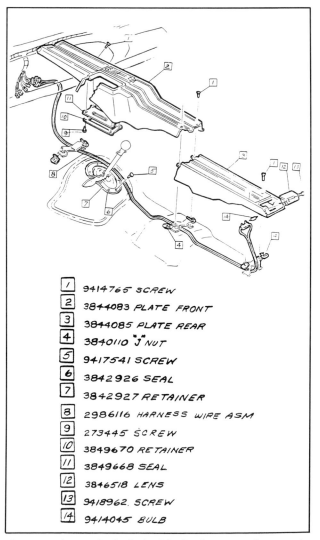

| | |
|---|---|
| 1 | 9414765 SCREW |
| 2 | 3844083 PLATE FRONT |
| 3 | 3844085 PLATE REAR |
| 4 | 3840110 "J" NUT |
| 5 | 9417541 SCREW |
| 6 | 3842926 SEAL |
| 7 | 3842927 RETAINER |
| 8 | 2986116 HARNESS WIRE ASM |
| 9 | 273445 SCREW |
| 10 | 3849670 RETAINER |
| 11 | 3849668 SEAL |
| 12 | 3846518 LENS |
| 13 | 9418962 SCREW |
| 14 | 9414045 BULB |

*The console was included with the four-speed transmission in 1964 and 1965.*

## Four-speed Manual Transmission Shift Levers

### 1964-1965

All Malibu SSs came with a console in between the seats, which housed a chrome shift lever. Listed as part number 3853137 in both 1964 and 1965, this lever was unique to the SS and had less arc than the lever used in other models. Like all four-speed shifters this lever featured a spring-loaded gate to prevent accidentally shifting into reverse.

A chrome ball knob, part number 3845895, was also used exclusively. Any other type of knob is incorrect. The shift pattern was part of the console front panel and positioned just right of the shifter opening. For more information on the console, see Chapter 8.

### 1966-1967

Both the M20 and M21 transmissions used the same lever and knob in 1966 as in 1965, but a console was not included as part of the option. A rubber shift boot, part number 3842926, was secured with retainer part number 3842927 and Phillips-head screws.

The lever was redesigned in 1967. Listed as part number 3903077, it was bent over more than in 1966. This lever was used in all Chevelles with a four-speed transmission and no console. The knob was a solid white ball, part number 3857524, with a black inlaid shift pattern.

When the console was ordered, the 1966 shifter was used with a solid chrome knob. The boot and retainer were identical to those used in 1966, including the part numbers.

### 1968-1969

The shifter's mount was restyled for 1968 and was not interchangeable with that on earlier cars. Three shift levers were offered. The M20 transmission without bucket seats used the three-speed

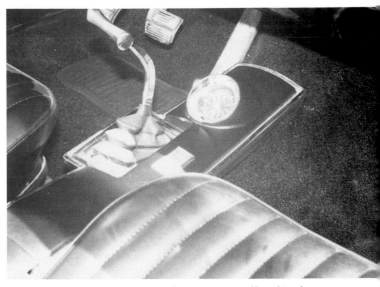

*This shift is incorrect; a T-handle was never offered in the Chevelle.*

shifter, part number 3922522; the M21 and M22 transmission used part number 3922523; and both transmissions with bucket seats used part number 3922524. The lever with bench seats was angled back more for better grip.

Knobs were of a two-piece design; the lower half was part number 3920217, and the top half was part number 3920216. The top half was black plastic with the shift pattern engraved in white. The bezel, seal and retainer were the same parts as used on the three-speed.

When the console, D55, was ordered, lever part number 3922524 was used with a solid chrome knob having no shift pattern. The shift lever should also be cast with the name Muncie in it. The Hurst shifter so commonly seen was never originally installed in the Chevelle, as it was on the GTO and

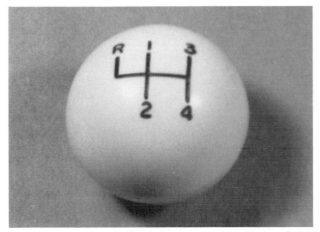

*A one-piece white ball knob was used in 1966 and 1967 when no console was ordered.*

*A 1966-67 replacement boot.*

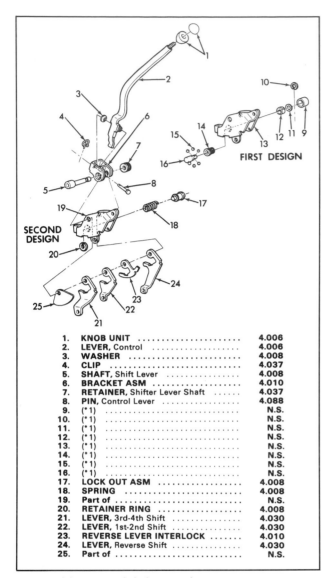

| 1. | KNOB UNIT | 4.006 |
|---|---|---|
| 2. | LEVER, Control | 4.006 |
| 3. | WASHER | 4.008 |
| 4. | CLIP | 4.037 |
| 5. | SHAFT, Shift Lever | 4.008 |
| 6. | BRACKET ASM | 4.010 |
| 7. | RETAINER, Shifter Lever Shaft | 4.037 |
| 8. | PIN, Control Lever | 4.088 |
| 9. | (*1) | N.S. |
| 10. | (*1) | N.S. |
| 11. | (*1) | N.S. |
| 12. | (*1) | N.S. |
| 13. | (*1) | N.S. |
| 14. | (*1) | N.S. |
| 15. | (*1) | N.S. |
| 16. | (*1) | N.S. |
| 17. | LOCK OUT ASM | 4.008 |
| 18. | SPRING | 4.008 |
| 19. | Part of | N.S. |
| 20. | RETAINER RING | 4.008 |
| 21. | LEVER, 3rd-4th Shift | 4.030 |
| 22. | LEVER, 1st-2nd Shift | 4.030 |
| 23. | REVERSE LEVER INTERLOCK | 4.010 |
| 24. | LEVER, Reverse Shift | 4.030 |
| 25. | Part of | N.S. |

*A typical four-speed shift control setup.*

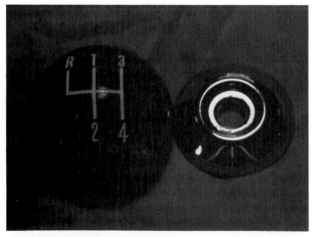

*The shift knob consisted of two separate parts for 1968-70, and the lower half was chrome.*

442s. Although the Hurst shifter provides for better shifting control, it is incorrect.

Parts were the same for 1969 except that shift lever part number 3922523 was dropped and shift lever part number 3922522 took its place. The bucket seat lever remained the same.

### 1970-1972

Levers were the same in 1970, 1971 and 1972: cars without bucket seats used part number 3973865, and cars with bucket seats used part number 3973864. Cars with consoles used part number 3973866 in 1971 and 1972, except the SS

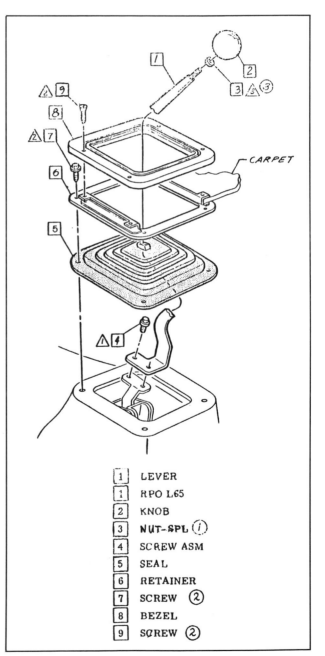

| 1 | LEVER |
|---|---|
| 1 | RPO L65 |
| 2 | KNOB |
| 3 | NUT-SPL (1) |
| 4 | SCREW ASM |
| 5 | SEAL |
| 6 | RETAINER |
| 7 | SCREW (2) |
| 8 | BEZEL |
| 9 | SCREW (2) |

*The 1971 and 1972 version of the four-speed shifter.*

350, which used part number 3973867. The 1970 and early 1971 models used part number 3973865, except the SS 350 in 1971.

The shift boot, retainer and chrome bezel without the console were the same as those used in 1968-69. Unique parts were used with the console in 1971 and 1972; see Chapter 8 for more details.

Knobs in 1970 were the same as in 1969, including part numbers. In 1971 one-piece black ball knobs, part number 3992307, with an engraved shift pattern in white were used. When the console was ordered, part number 3992308 was used. Both knobs came with a spacer nut between the knob and the shifter.

## Automatic Transmission Shift Levers

### 1964-1965

Like the four-speed transmission the Powerglide automatic option included a console in both 1964 and 1965. The shift lever, part number 3843285, used a single stock design with the Lockout feature in the black knob. The SS was not available with a column-shifted automatic transmission either year.

A rod, part number 3843287, connected the shift lever to the transmission control lever, part number 3851336. This lever was also secured to the underside base of the shift lever, with a bolt, washer, clip and pair of bushings. These were covered with a black rubber boot, part number 3843288, secured with J-nuts.

The dial indicator was mounted in the console and featured a light green background with white letters.

### 1966-1967

The shift lever was still mounted on the floor for most 1966 SS 396s and was now listed as part

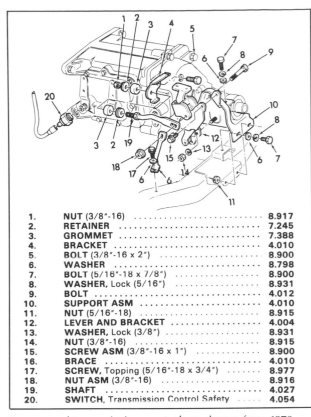

| | | | |
|---|---|---|---|
| 1. | NUT (3/8"-16) | ........................ | 8.917 |
| 2. | RETAINER | ........................ | 7.245 |
| 3. | GROMMET | ........................ | 7.388 |
| 4. | BRACKET | ........................ | 4.010 |
| 5. | BOLT (3/8"-16 x 2") | ........................ | 8.900 |
| 6. | WASHER | ........................ | 8.798 |
| 7. | BOLT (5/16"-18 x 7/8") | ........................ | 8.900 |
| 8. | WASHER, Lock (5/16") | ........................ | 8.931 |
| 9. | BOLT | ........................ | 4.012 |
| 10. | SUPPORT ASM | ........................ | 4.010 |
| 11. | NUT (5/16"-18) | ........................ | 8.915 |
| 12. | LEVER AND BRACKET | ........................ | 4.004 |
| 13. | WASHER, Lock (3/8") | ........................ | 8.931 |
| 14. | NUT (3/8"-16) | ........................ | 8.915 |
| 15. | SCREW ASM (3/8"-16 x 1") | ........................ | 8.900 |
| 16. | BRACE | ........................ | 4.010 |
| 17. | SCREW, Topping (5/16"-18 x 3/4") | ........ | 8.977 |
| 18. | NUT ASM (3/8"-16) | ........................ | 8.916 |
| 19. | SHAFT | ........................ | 4.027 |
| 20. | SWITCH, Transmission Control Safety | ...... | 4.054 |

*Four-speed transmission controls as shown from 1970.*

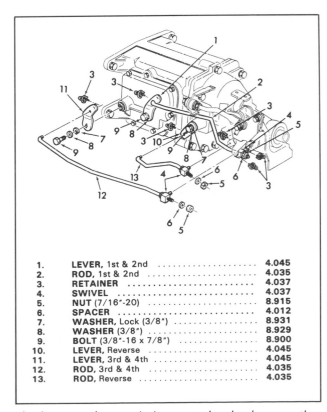

| | | | |
|---|---|---|---|
| 1. | LEVER, 1st & 2nd | ........................ | 4.045 |
| 2. | ROD, 1st & 2nd | ........................ | 4.035 |
| 3. | RETAINER | ........................ | 4.037 |
| 4. | SWIVEL | ........................ | 4.037 |
| 5. | NUT (7/16"-20) | ........................ | 8.915 |
| 6. | SPACER | ........................ | 4.012 |
| 7. | WASHER, Lock (3/8") | ........................ | 8.931 |
| 8. | WASHER (3/8") | ........................ | 8.929 |
| 9. | BOLT (3/8"-16 x 7/8") | ........................ | 8.900 |
| 10. | LEVER, Reverse | ........................ | 4.045 |
| 11. | LEVER, 3rd & 4th | ........................ | 4.045 |
| 12. | ROD, 3rd & 4th | ........................ | 4.035 |
| 13. | ROD, Reverse | ........................ | 4.035 |

*The four-speed transmission control rods, shown as they were used from 1970-73.*

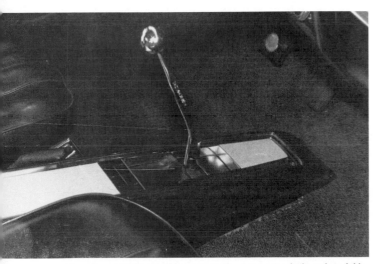

*The Hurst shifter is incorrect; the Muncie shifter should be used.*

number 3880851. Although this type of shifter was not standard, the sale sheets were written so that it sounded like a mandatory option. However, a few column-mounted shift levers were sold in the SS 396. A chrome lever with a black knob was used in this case.

The shift lever was column mounted in 1967 unless the optional console, D55, was ordered. A chrome lever with a plastic knob molded in a color that matched the interior was used. The dial indicator was light blue with white lettering and mounted in the center of the instrument panel just below the speedometer. A flat-red indicator hand showed the position of the transmission.

The M40 Turbo Hydra-matic transmission used a different dial with a quadrant pattern of P-R-N-D-L2-L1 with the same blue background and white letters.

No SS 396s were built with a column shift and bucket seats. When bucket seats were ordered, a console with a floor-shifted lever was included.

### 1968-1969

Both the M35 and M40 automatic transmission used the same column-mounted shift lever, part number 3928319. Its plastic knob was finished in the same color as the interior except with the parchment interior, when it was gloss-black.

The indicator cluster, part numbers 6480609-M35 and 6480610-M40, was located in the center of the instrument panel just in front of the steering column. The lens was clear and the letters on the cluster assembly were white.

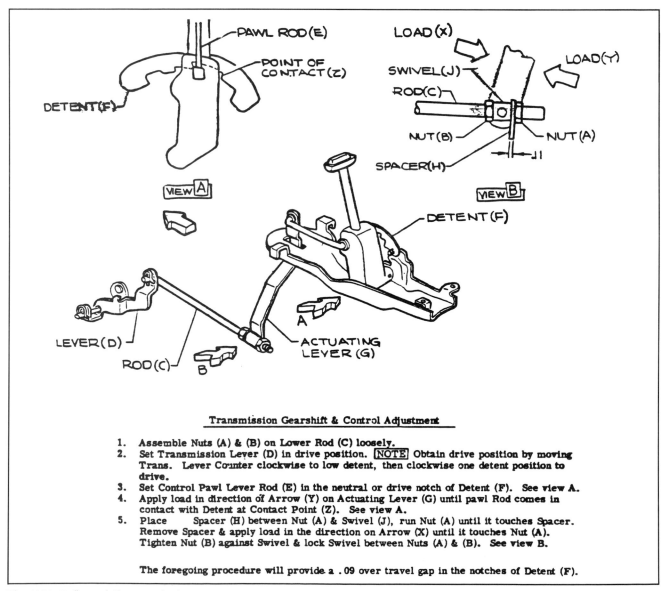

**Transmission Gearshift & Control Adjustment**

1. Assemble Nuts (A) & (B) on Lower Rod (C) loosely.
2. Set Transmission Lever (D) in drive position. NOTE Obtain drive position by moving Trans. Lever Counter clockwise to low detent, then clockwise one detent position to drive.
3. Set Control Pawl Lever Rod (E) in the neutral or drive notch of Detent (F). See view A.
4. Apply load in direction of Arrow (Y) on Actuating Lever (G) until pawl Rod comes in contact with Detent at Contact Point (Z). See view A.
5. Place Spacer (H) between Nut (A) & Swivel (J), run Nut (A) until it touches Spacer. Remove Spacer & apply load in the direction on Arrow (X) until it touches Nut (A). Tighten Nut (B) against Swivel & lock Swivel between Nuts (A) & (B). See view B.

The foregoing procedure will provide a .09 over travel gap in the notches of Detent (F).

*The 1966-67 floor shift control adjustment.*

The lever was changed to part number 3939741 in 1969. An unusual option for 1969 only was the Sports shifter, RPO M08. This shifter, part number 3958494, was mounted in a console in the floor. It looked much like the regular floor hoop but was a rachet type. The indicator was mounted in the instrument cluster, which was listed as part number 6482223.

A green lens, part number 3961594, with green lettering that read Sport Shift was used instead of the dial indicator. A black plastic plate was placed under the lens. A retainer, part number 3921415, held all the components to the outer trim panel, part number 3926729.

Bucket seats and the console options were mandatory with the M08 option. Available in 1969 only, this option was produced on fewer than 100 cars, mainly because it was canceled on June 23, 1969.

### 1970-1972

The standard shift lever, part number 3939741, was mounted on the column in 1970. A black plastic knob, part number 3973042, was installed. Although production Chevelles used a knob that was color keyed to the interior, the SS used only a black knob.

The dial indicator was housed in the center just below the speedometer. A black face with white letters and a flat-red hand was used all three years, from 1970 to 1972. The lens was clear and covered the gauge assembly.

The lever was changed to part number 9428373, and a soft-feel black vinyl knob, part number 14049351, was used in both 1971 and 1972. The floor shifter was the same in 1970-72 as in 1969. The Sports shifter option was canceled for 1970.

### Rear Axle

### 1964-1965

The rear axle was identified by the rear end cover and the code on the axle tubes. The smaller axle used a ten bolt cover, and the larger axle used a twelve-bolt cover. The ten-bolt axle was offered exclusively in 1964; both axles were offered in 1965.

The ratio was identified by the code stamped on either side of the tube adjacent to the differential carrier. This code consisted of two letters followed by the date of production and a letter indicating the plant (B for Buffalo, G for Gear & Axle or W for Warren).

All 1964 Malibu SSs used an axle with the smaller 8.125 in. diameter ring gears with thirty-seven teeth. Two ratios were available: the standard 3.08 or the optional special-purpose 3.36. The overdrive transmission came with 3.70 gears only. The L30 and L74 engines were standard with the 3.08 ratio.

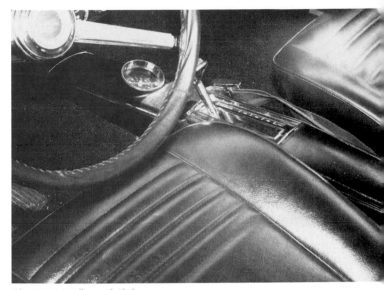

*The 1966-67 floor shift lever.*

Pinion gears were changed to create the different ratios. The standard pinion used twelve teeth, the 3.36 eleven, and the 3.07 ten. When Positraction, RPO G80, was ordered, two pinions with dual disc clutches were used.

The plate was listed as part number 3830740 and was manufactured by Dana. The preceding ratios were available with the G80 option.

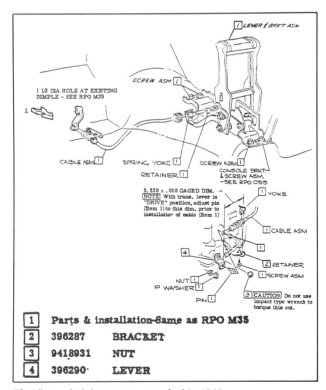

*The floor shift lever was restyled in 1968.*

## 1964 Rear Axle Ratio Codes

| Code | Axle Type | Ratio | Accessories |
|------|-----------|-------|-------------|
| LA† | Standard | 3.08 | Standard Gears |
| ZC | Standard | 3.08 | w/Metallic Brakes |
| LG* | Positraction | 3.08 | |
| ZE | Positraction | 3.08 | w/Metallic Brakes |
| LB‡ | Standard | 3.36 | Optional |
| LH§ | Positraction | 3.36 | |
| ZD | Standard | 3.36 | w/Metallic Brakes |
| ZF | Positraction | 3.36 | w/Metallic Brakes |
| ZJ | Standard | 3.70 | Standard w/Over-drive |
| ZK | Positraction | 3.70 | w/Overdrive only |
| ZL | Standard | 3.70 | w/Metallic Brakes and Overdrive only |
| ZM | Positraction | 3.70 | w/Metallic Brakes and Overdrive only |

†–Codes YA, and ZA also used
*–Codes YG, and ZG also used
‡–Codes YB and ZB also used
§–Codes YH and ZH also used
Pos.–Positraction Rear Axle

The ten-bolt axle with an 8.125 in. ring gear returned for 1965, joined by a larger twelve-bolt axle with 8.874 in. diameter ring gears. The larger axle was standard on SSs with the L30, L74 or L79 engine, along with the L37 396 ci engine, which came with the 3.31 ratio as standard equipment.

The standard ratios for the L30 engine were 3.07 with manual and 2.73 with automatic transmissions. The L74 and L79 engines both used the 3.31 gears with manual transmission; the L74 engine with automatic used a ratio of 3.07. A ratio of 3.73 was optional with all engines and used the rear end with a larger ring gear. All ratios were available with the Positraction axle option.

Available ratios with the ten-bolt axle were juggled around some. The L77 engine was standard with 3.36 gears, and a 3.70 ratio was optional. The two-barrel base V-8 used the same ratios and axle as in 1964.

Although all 8.125 in. rings used thirty-seven teeth and the same pinions as in 1964, the 8.875 in. ring used different combinations.

## 1965 Rear Axle Ring and Pinion Gear Tooth Combinations

| Ratio | Ring | Pinion |
|-------|------|--------|
| 2.73 | 41 | 15 |
| 3.07 | 43 | 14 |
| 3.31 | 43 | 13 |
| 3.73 | 41 | 11 |

### 1966-1967

All SS 396s used the twelve-bolt axle with the 8.875 in. ring gear. The standard ratio with the base L35 engine was 3.31, and with the L34 engine a 3.73 gear ratio was used. The L78 engine option used a

## 1965 Rear Axle Ratio Codes

| Code | Axle Type | Ratio | Accessories |
|------|-----------|-------|-------------|
| CA | Standard | 3.08 | Standard 283 ci |
| CE | Positraction | 3.08 | |
| CL | Standard | 3.08 | w/Metallic Brakes |
| CM | Positraction | 3.08 | w/Metallic Brakes |
| CB | Standard | 3.36 | Standard L77 |
| CG | Positraction | 3.36 | |
| CP | Standard | 3.36 | w/Metallic Brakes |
| CQ | Positraction | 3.36 | w/Metallic Brakes |
| CX | Standard | 3.07 | Standard L30 w/Man. Trans. and L74 w/Powerglide |
| CD | Positraction | 3.07 | |
| CJ | Standard | 3.07 | w/Metallic Brakes |
| CK | Positraction | 3.07 | w/Metallic Brakes |
| GB | Standard | 2.73 | Standard 130 w/Powerglide |
| GC | Positraction | 2.73 | |
| GD | Standard | 2.73 | w/Metallic Brakes |
| GE | Positraction | 2.73 | w/Metallic Brakes |
| CW | Standard | 3.31 | Standard L79 |
| CF | Positraction | 3.31 | |
| CN | Standard | 3.31 | w/Metallic Brakes |
| CM | Positraction | 3.31 | w/Metallic Brakes |
| CC | Standard | 3.73 | |
| CI | Positraction | 3.73 | |
| CT | Standard | 3.73 | w/Metallic Brakes |
| CU | Standard | 3.73 | w/Metallic Brakes |
| GA | Positraction | 3.31 | Standard Z16 Package |

3.73 ratio, but Positraction was mandatory. Powerglide-equipped cars used the same ratios as the manual-equipped cars. Air-conditioned cars used a 3.07 ratio only with all engines in both 1966 and 1967.

Unlike earlier years 1966 saw many different ratio options available. With the L35 engine, performance options were 3.73 and 4.10, and 3.55 gears were a special order item. The L34 engine was optional with a 4.10 gear as the performance option. Highway gears of 3.31 and 3.55 were also available for the L34 engine.

When the M21 close-ratio transmission was ordered, ratios of 3.31, 3.55, 4.10, 4.56 and 4.88 could be ordered. The last three were mandatory with the Positraction axle, and the ratios of 4.56 and 4.88 were dealer installed. All five ratios were also optional on the L78 engine option. Positraction, option G80, was available with all ratios.

Ratios were readjusted in 1967. The standard ratios with the Powerglide transmission were 3.07 with the L35 engine and 3.31 with the L34 engine. The 3.31 gears were also listed as a performance option on the base L35 engine. A performance ratio of 3.55 was used on the L34 engine with the Powerglide transmission. Special order options included ratios of 3.73 and 4.10 for both engines without air conditioning. The 3.55 gears were also available as a special order with the L35 engine.

The standard ratios for the Turbo Hydramatic transmission were 2.73 with the L35 engine and 3.07 with the L34 powerplant. Performance gear ratios were also available with this transmission. A ratio of 3.07 was listed for the L35 car without air conditioning. The L34 cars used 3.31 as the optional ratio. This ratio was also a special order option for the L35 car without air conditioning.

New for 1967 were economy ratios for all engines and all transmissions. The Powerglide-equipped cars with the L35 engine used 2.73 as the economy ratio. With the L34 engine the economy ratio was 3.07. No economy ratio was available for the Turbo 400 with the L35 engine, but a 2.73 economy ratio was listed for the L34 powerplant.

Standard ratios for the manual transmission were the same in 1967 as in 1966, but the performance ratios were changed. Economy ratios were also added.

## 1966 Rear Axle Ratio Codes

| Code | Axle Type | Ratio | Accessories |
|------|-----------|-------|-------------|
| KI | Standard | 2.73 | Powerglide |
| CX | Standard | 3.07 | Powerglide w/A.C. |
| CW | Standard | 3.31 | |
| CF | Positraction | 3.31 | |
| CN | Standard | 3.31 | w/Metallic Brakes |
| CO | Positraction | 3.31 | w/Metallic Brakes |
| KJ | Standard | 3.55 | |
| KF | Standard | 3.55 | w/Metallic Brakes |
| KH | Positraction | 3.55 | |
| KJ | Positraction | 3.55 | w/Metallic Brakes |
| CC | Standard | 3.73 | |
| CT | Standard | 3.73 | w/Metallic Brakes |
| CI | Positraction | 3.73 | |
| CU | Positraction | 3.73 | w/Metallic Brakes |
| KL | Positraction | 4.10 | w/Metallic Brakes |
| KK | Positraction | 4.10 | |
| KN | Positraction | 4.56 | w/Metallic Brakes |
| KM | Positraction | 4.56 | Close-Ratio 4-Speed |
| KP | Positraction | 4.88 | w/Metallic Brakes |
| KO | Positraction | 4.88 | Close-Ratio 4-Speed |

Note: Ratios 2.73 and 3.07 were considered economy gears. They were added late in the year and are available only with Powerglide and the base 325 hp engine.

Ratios 4.56 and 4.88 were available with a close ratio (RPO M21) four-speed manual transmission only. They are rare and were used usally with racing applications.

## 1967 Rear Axle Ratios
L34, L78*

| | |
|---|---|
| Economy | 3.31 |
| Standard | 3.55 |
| Performance | 3.73 |
| Special order | 4.10 |

L35

| | |
|---|---|
| Economy | 3.07 |
| Standard | 3.31 |
| Performance | 3.55 |
| Special order | 3.73, 4.10 |

*Required Positraction

When the M21 close-ratio transmission was ordered, the L34 ratios were available along with a special order ratio of 3.07 and dealer-installed options of 4.56 and 4.88 with Positraction.

## 1967 Rear Axle Ratio Codes

| Code | Axle Type | Ratio | Accessories |
|------|-----------|-------|-------------|
| CH | Positraction | 2.73 | Turbo Hydra-Matic only |
| CX | Standard | 3.07 | Standard w/Powerglide |
| CJ | Standard | 3.07 | w/Metallic Brakes |
| CD | Positraction | 3.07 | |
| CK | Positraction | 3.07 | w/Metallic Brakes |
| CW | Standard | 3.31 | Standard w/All Manual Tran. except 375 hp |
| CN | Standard | 3.31 | w/Metallic Brakes |
| CF | Positraction | 3.31 | |
| CO | Positraction | 3.31 | w/Metallic Brakes |
| KJ | Standard | 3.55 | |
| KH | Standard | 3.55 | w/Metallic Brakes |
| KF | Positraction | 3.55 | |
| KG | Positraction | 3.55 | w/Metallic Brakes |
| CC | Standard | 3.73 | |
| CT | Standard | 3.73 | w/Metallic Brakes |
| CI | Positraction | 3.73 | Standard w/L78 (375 hp) |
| CU | Positraction | 3.73 | w/Metallic Brakes |
| KL | Positraction | 4.10 | w/Metallic Brakes |
| KK | Positraction | 4.10 | |
| KM | Positraction | 4.56 | |
| KN | Positraction | 4.56 | w/Metallic Brakes |
| KO | Positraction | 4.88 | |
| KP | Positraction | 4.88 | w/Metallic Brakes |

### 1968-1969

Axle codes became confusing in 1968 with the introduction of the 2.73 and 3.55 gears in the smaller ten-bolt axle, along with the same ratio in the larger twelve-bolt axle. Just remember, the only axle used on the SS 396 was the twelve-bolt unit. You will also notice that some ratios have more than one code. It is believed that not all plants used the same identification code.

Ratios, both standard and optional, were identical to those in 1967, except that the 2.56 economy ratio on the L35 engine with Turbo Hydra-matic transmission was added for 1968 only.

Additional codes for the axles were dropped for 1969, as were the ratios for the Powerglide automatic and the economy ratio of 2.56. Standard ratios were also revised. All cars with an optional

## 1968 Rear Axle Codes

| Code | Type | Ratio | Accessories |
|------|------|-------|-------------|
| KD | Standard | 2.73 | Std.: Turbo Hydra-Matic w/base V-8<br>Econ.: Powerglide base w/Turbo Hydra-Matic L34 |
| CX<br>CY | Standard | 3.07 | Std.: w/A.C.<br>Perf.: w/base V-8, no A.C. and Turbo Hydra-Matic<br>Econ.: L34 w/Powerglide<br>Special Option: L34 4-Speed |
| CD<br>KX | Positraction | 3.07 | Like CX but w/Positraction rear |
| KZ | Standard | 3.31 | Std.: Base V-8 w/Manual and L34 w/Powerglide<br>Econ.: L34 w/Manual<br>Perf.: Base V-8 w/Powerglide and L34 w/Turbo Hydra-Matic; n/a w/A.C. |
| CF<br>KY | Positraction | 3.31 | Same applications as CW but w/Positraction axle |
| KF<br>K2 | Standard | 3.55 | Std.: L34 w/Manual<br>Perf.: Base V-8 and L34 w/Powerglide<br>Special Option: Base V-8 w/Powerglide; n/a w/Turbo Hydra-Matic |
| KF<br>K3 | Positraction | 3.55 | Same applications as above but w/Positraction axle;<br>Standard axle w/L78 |
| CC<br>K4<br>CU | Standard | 3.73 | Special ratio w/Base engine and L34 w/Powerglide<br>Perf.: L34 w/Manual;<br>n/a w/A.C. or Turbo Hydra-Matic |
| CI<br>K5 | Positraction | 3.73 | Same applications as above but w/Positraction axle |
| KK<br>K6 | Positraction | 4.10 | Special applications only on base and L34;<br>Perf.: L78 engines |
| KM<br>K7 | Positraction | 4.56 | Special applications only: Close-ratio 4-Speed is mandatory; n/a w/any<br>other transmissions |
| KO<br>K8 | Positraction | 4.88 | |

Note: 4.56 and 4.88 are dealer-installed items
All performance ratios are not applicable w/A.C. or automatic transmissions
Key: Std.: Standard; Econ.: Economy; Perf.: Performance (package); Base V-8: 325 hp 396 ci

---

four-speed transmission included 3.55 gears; this same ratio was also standard with the three-speed manual with the L34 engine. The L35 with the three-speed manual used 3.31 gears as standard equipment.

Turbo 400 equipped cars used the same ratios as cars with air conditioning. The L78 and L72 engines used the same ratios as the L34 engine, but Positraction was required. Several ratios were optional.

## 1969 Optional Rear Axle Ratios

| L35 | Standard & Turbo<br>Hydra-matic 400 | |
|-----|-----|-----|
| | Economy | 3.07 |
| | Performance | 3.55*, 3.73† |
| | Special order | 2.73‡ |
| | | 3.73*†, 4.10*† |
| | M20 four-speed | |
| | Economy | 3.31 |
| | Performance | 3.73† |
| | Special order | 3.07, 4.10† |
| L34, L78, L72 | All transmissions | |

| Economy | 3.31 |
|---------|------|
| Performance | 3.73† |
| Special order | 3.07‡, 4.10† |

*With standard three-speed manual only.
†Required Positraction.
‡Not with the standard three-speed manual.

Dealer-installed ratios of 4.56 and 4.88 were still available with the optional engines and M21 close-ratio transmission only. Positraction was mandatory on both ratios and optional on all other ratios.

## 1969 Rear Axle Ratio Codes

| Code | Axle Type | Ratio |
|------|-----------|-------|
| KD | Standard | 2.73 |
| FI | Positraction | 2.73 |
| CX | Standard | 3.07 |
| CD | Positraction | 3.07 |
| CW | Standard | 3.31 |
| CF | Positraction | 3.31 |
| KJ | Standard | 3.35 |
| KF | Positraction | 3.35 |

## 1969 Rear Axle Ratio Codes

| Code | Axle Type | Ratio |
|------|-----------|-------|
| CC | Standard | 3.73 |
| CI | Positraction | 3.73 |
| KK | Positraction | 4.10 |
| KM | Positraction | 4.56* |
| KO | Positraction | 4.88* |

*Dealer Installed

## 1970-1972

Only one set of gears was available from the factory in 1970. The standard ratio of 3.31 was used with both manual and automatic transmissions and with or without air conditioning.

In 1971 the big-block cars used the same 3.31 standard ratio. However, the LS6 cars could be ordered with a 4.10 Positraction rear end as a performance option, RPO ZQ9. Positraction was also optional with the standard 3.31 gears, but the 4.10 gears were not available with the LS3 engine.

The only Chevelle SS to use a ten-bolt rear end was one equipped with the L65 engine and manual transmission. All others used the twelve-bolt axle.

The standard ratio for 1971 Chevelle SSs with manual transmission was 3.31, with no optional ratio. The L48, L65 and LS3 with the Turbo Hydramatic used a 2.73 ratio, with 3.31 as part of the optional YD1 trailer package.

The 1972 ratios were a carbon copy of the 1971 ratios except that the 4.10 gears were no longer available as an option. Positraction was available for all ratios all three years, from 1970 to 1972.

For detailing purposes all axle assemblies should be painted gloss-black enamel in two even light coats. Positraction differentials were often marked at the factory with the letter *P* in yellow paint.

## 1970 Rear Axle Ratio Codes

| Code | Axle Type | Ratio | Accessories |
|------|-----------|-------|-------------|
| CCW | Standard | 3.31 | — |
| CCF | Positraction | 3.31 | — |
| CRU | Standard | 3.31 | — |
| CRV | Positraction | 3.31 | — |

## 1970 Rear Axle Ratio Codes

| Code | Axle Type | Ratio | Accessories |
|------|-----------|-------|-------------|
| CKK | Positraction | 4.10 | Performance; |
| CRW | | | Dealer Installed |

## 1971 Axle Ratio Codes

| Code | Axle Type | Ratio | Accessories |
|------|-----------|-------|-------------|
| GG | Standard | 3.36 | Standard L65 w/Manual |
| GI | Positraction | 3.36 | w/Manual only |
| GA | Standard | 2.56 | Standard L65 w/Automatic |
| GB | Positraction | 2.56 | w/Automatic only |
| CW | Standard | 3.31 | Standard w/3-Speed Manual L48 and LS3 |
| CF | Positraction | 3.31 | Optional on above |
| RU | Standard | 3.31 | Standard 4-Speed Manual w/all 454s |
| RV | Positraction | 3.31 | Optional on above |
| GC | Standard | 2.73 | Standard w/Automatic except L65 and 454 |
| GD | Positraction | 2.73 | Optional on above |
| KD | Standard | 2.73 | |
| CH | Positraction | 2.73 | |
| GH | Standard | 2.73 | |
| RW | Positraction | 4.10 | Performance option w/454 V-8s |

## 1972 Rear Axle Ratio Codes

| Code | Axle Type | Ratio |
|------|-----------|-------|
| GD | Positraction | 2.73 |
| GF | Standard | 3.08 |
| GH | Positraction | 2.73 |
| GC | Standard | 2.73 |
| GG | Standard | 3.36 |
| GI | Positraction | 3.36 |
| CW | Standard | 3.31 |
| RU | Standard | 3.31 |
| RV | Positraction | 3.31 |
| GH | Standard | 2.73 |
| GN | Standard | 3.08 |

*Chapter 4*

# Frame and Suspension

### Frame

#### 1964-1972

From 1964 to 1967 all wheelbases were 115 in. From 1968 to 1972 two wheelbases were used: all coupes and convertibles had a 112 in. wheelbase, and the El Camino pickup sedan wheelbase was measured at 116 in.

All Chevelles used the same basic type of frame all nine years: an all-welded perimeter frame with front and rear cross-members, and a rear axle control member. The coupe used C-shaped center sections, and the convertible and pickup used boxed construction.

Contrary to popular belief the 1965 Z16 option did not use the convertible frame but came with a specially manufactured frame, part number 3872801, with boxed construction just for this option. Extra body mounts were also installed. The illusive Z16 convertible used frame part number 3864505.

### Front Suspension

#### 1964-1972

Chevelle used the GM independent front suspension consisting of upper and lower control arms with ball joints, coil springs, shock absorbers

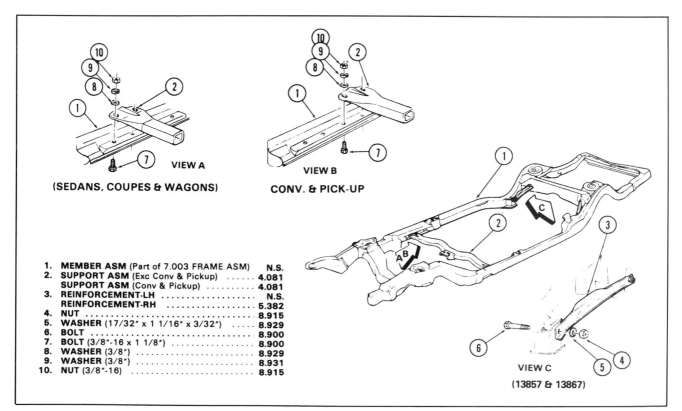

| | | |
|---|---|---|
| 1. | **MEMBER ASM** (Part of 7.003 FRAME ASM) | **N.S.** |
| 2. | **SUPPORT ASM** (Exc Conv & Pickup) | **4.081** |
| | **SUPPORT ASM** (Conv & Pickup) | **4.081** |
| 3. | **REINFORCEMENT-LH** | **N.S.** |
| | **REINFORCEMENT-RH** | **5.382** |
| 4. | **NUT** | **8.915** |
| 5. | **WASHER** (17/32" x 1 1/16" x 3/32") | **8.929** |
| 6. | **BOLT** | **8.900** |
| 7. | **BOLT** (3/8"-16 x 1 1/8") | **8.900** |
| 8. | **WASHER** (3/8") | **8.929** |
| 9. | **WASHER** (3/8") | **8.931** |
| 10. | **NUT** (3/8"-16) | **8.915** |

VIEW A
(SEDANS, COUPES & WAGONS)

VIEW B
CONV. & PICK-UP

VIEW C
(13857 & 13867)

*Typical Chevelle SS 396 and SS 454 frame.*

and steering knuckles that were spherically jointed at each wheel.

Upper control arms were basically the same from 1964 to 1972, but three different sets were used. From 1964 to 1969 all Chevelles used part numbers 382714-LH and 382715-RH. All 1970 models and some 1971 models used part numbers 3932545-LH and 3932546-RH. All SSs built after the fourth week in April 1971 used part numbers 6263615-LH and 6263616-RH, which were considered heavy-duty items. These were also installed on all El Caminos with or without the SS equipment and will interchange.

When buying replacement arms be sure the upper ball joint is riveted into place like the original. Many rebuilt arms do not have this feature and would be incorrect. The Chevrolet replacement arms, part numbers 3974217-LH and 39977062-RH, come with the riveted ball joints but without a shaft or a bushing kit.

Either the aftermarket urethane bushing—for better wear and drivability—or the original-type rubber bushings, part number 3849412, could be installed. However, the aftermarket bushings would be incorrect. If your car is a daily driver the aftermarket bushing could be used, but if you are going for awards at shows stick with the original type.

Except for the Z16 option all 1964–66 SSs used the production Chevelle lower control arms. The 1965 Z16 option used a specially modified arm to hold the Impala steering knuckle.

| | | |
|---|---|---|
| 1. | STUD UNIT | 6.174 |
| 2. | BOLT | 6.172 |
| 3. | SHIM | 6.178 |
| 4. | ARM | 6.168 |
| 5. | SHAFT UNIT | 6.164 |
| 6. | WASHER, Lock (7/16") | 8.931 |
| 7. | NUT (7/16"-14) | 8.915 |
| 8. | NUT (3/8-24) | 8.915 |
| 9. | FITTING | 8.984 |
| 10. | RIVET (1/4") | 8.967 |
| 11. | RETAINER | 7.389 |
| 12. | STUD UNIT | 6.164 |
| 13. | ARM | 6.168 |
| 14. | GROMMET | 7.388 |
| 15. | BUMPER | 6.176 |
| 16. | NUT (1/2"-20) | 8.917 |
| 17. | NUT (9/16"-18) | 8.917 |
| 18. | PIN (1/8" x 1") | 8.938 |
| 19. | NUT (3/8"-16) | 8.915 |
| 20. | KNUCKLE | 6.020 |
| 21. | DRUM ASSEMBLY | 5.809 |
| 22. | BUMPER ASSEMBLY | 6.176 |
| 23. | ARM | 6.168 |
| 24. | SPACER | 7.240 |
| 25. | BOLT (5/16"-18 x 7/8") | 8.900 |
| 26. | ABSORBER UNIT | 7.345 |
| 27. | BOLT | 7.240 |
| 28. | BOLT (5/16"-18 x 1 1/8") | 8.900 |
| 29. | BRACKET | 7.242 |
| 30. | BUSHING | 7.243 |
| 31. | SHAFT | 7.241 |
| 32. | NUT (1/2"-13) | 8.915 |
| 33. | WASHER, Lock (1/2") | 8.931 |
| 34. | BOLT (1/2"-13 x 3 3/4") | 8.900 |
| 35. | ARM | 6.168 |

GM A-body front suspension.

## 1964-1966 Front Suspension Control Arm Part Numbers

Production

| | |
|---|---|
| LH | 3852319 |
| RH | 3852320 |

Z16

| | |
|---|---|
| LH | 3874689 |
| RH | 3874690 |

The arms were redesigned in 1967, and the SS series now used special lower arms with larger cutouts for the shock absorbers. Listed as part numbers 3898223-LH and 3898224-RH, they will interchange with earlier models but would be incorrect because of the larger-diameter hole. However, control is improved with the larger shocks, so you may want to use them on a daily driver but not on a show car.

Part numbers were changed again in 1968 and 1970. Note that the RPO F41 arms were identical to those used on all Chevelle wagons; even the part number was the same.

## 1968-1972 Front Suspension Control Arm Part Numbers

1968-69

| | |
|---|---|
| LH | 3931453 |
| RH | 3931454 |

1970-72 SS & F41

| | |
|---|---|
| LH | 3990509 |
| RH | 3990510 |

Several different knuckles were used on the 1964 Malibu SS. The latest, replacement part number 3881524, has the correct ⅝ in. anchor hole. These knuckles can also be used in 1965 vehicles, but not on the Z16 cars.

The Z16 option used specially modified cast-steel knuckles to accommodate the Impala brakes. The original part numbers, listed as 3872943-LH and 3872944-RH, also included the drum assembly.

The steering knuckles in 1966 were standard production units and used the same part number as in 1965: 3881524.

The steering knuckles were redesigned in 1967. Two different parts were used, one with drums brakes and one with optional disc brakes. This continued through 1968.

Disc brakes were part of the SS package from 1969 to 1972, and only the disc brake knuckles were used. The 1971 and 1972 Heavy Chevy was standard with drum brakes; disc brakes were optional.

Since many different part numbers were used for steering knuckles on models built after 1967, the issue can be simplified using these:

## 1967-1972 Front Suspension Knuckle Part Numbers

| | |
|---|---|
| Drum brakes | 9799305 |
| Disc brakes | 478171 |

Both the frame and the suspension components should be painted 60 degree gloss-black for detailing and show quality.

### Front Shock Absorbers
#### 1964-1972

Without the optional RPO F40 suspension, front shocks were the Delco twist type, part number 3186918, in 1964-65. When the optional suspension was ordered, station wagon shocks, part number 3178155, were used. These part numbers were continued in 1966 and 1967.

Special suspension was standard on the 1968 SS 396. The shocks, part number 3192824, featured heavy-duty valving with a higher calibration. These same shocks were unchanged in 1969 and were used in the standard and F41 suspension.

All 1970-72 SSs used the station wagon front shock absorbers, part number 3192822. All shocks were Delco parts. For detailing, they should be painted medium dove-gray for those before 1970. On 1971 and 1972 models they should be painted 30 percent gloss black. Any other brand or color of shock is incorrect.

### Stabilizer Bar
#### 1964-1965

Except for use with the 1965 Z16 package, the standard stabilizer bar in 1964 and early 1965 was 0.812 in. in diameter and was listed as part number 381953. This was changed in the second week of February 1965. Cars built after the code date 02B used part number 392082; the diameter was the same, however. No rear bar was available in 1964.

The 1965 Z16 package included a specially manufactured bar listed as part number 3872808. It measured 1.06 in. in diameter. Special bushings, part number 3872809, were also used with this bar.

A 1.06 in. diameter rear bar, part number 3872281, was also included in the Z16 package. It bolted between the lower control arms. Shims part number 385967 were used as required to align the bar.

#### 1966-1969

The standard bar in 1966 and early 1967 models was the production bar of 0.812 in. diameter. This proved unstable for the SS 396, and a larger 0.937 in. bar was made standard in 1967 models built after code date 12A. Listed as part number 397705, this bar was optional till it was made standard. Owing to the larger bar's better handling and stability, it should be used.

In 1968 the part number of the standard bar was changed to 398411 but the diameter was the same as before. This bar was continued over into 1969 as the standard unit. Even though the diameter was the same this bar will not interchange with earlier frames.

A 1.25 in. diameter front bar was also optional, listed as part number 402544 in the F41 special

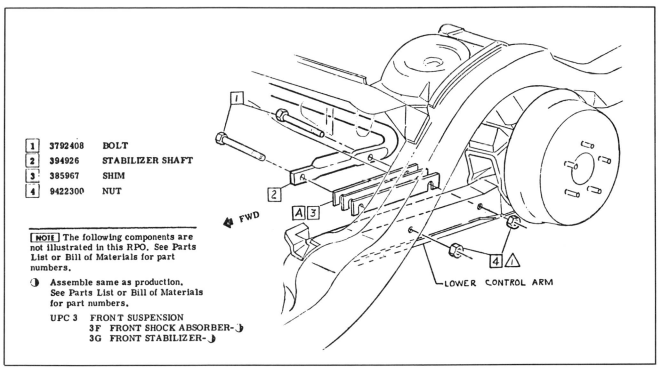

| | | |
|---|---|---|
| 1 | 3792408 | BOLT |
| 2 | 394926 | STABILIZER SHAFT |
| 3 | 385967 | SHIM |
| 4 | 9422300 | NUT |

**NOTE** The following components are not illustrated in this RPO. See Parts List or Bill of Materials for part numbers.

◐ Assemble same as production. See Parts List or Bill of Materials for part numbers.

UPC 3 FRONT SUSPENSION
 3F FRONT SHOCK ABSORBER-◐
 3G FRONT STABILIZER-◐

FWD

LOWER CONTROL ARM

*Rear sway bar mount.*

performance suspension package. Bushings were listed as part number 396420. A 0.875 in. diameter rear bar, part number 394926, was also included in this package. It was mounted like the 1965 bar used on the Z16 package.

### 1970-1972

The optional F41 suspension became standard equipment on all SS packages from 1970 to 1972. Parts and part numbers were identical to those used in 1969.

Note that the front bar is the same one used on the Monte Carlo Custom model. When at the salvage yard, be sure to pick up the brackets, part number 3994334, to mount the bar on your Chevelle. The bushings are listed as part number 388294 and can be obtained from Chevrolet.

For detail purposes the bar should be painted with gloss-black to match the rest of the suspension. The mounting links, however, should be left their natural color.

## Front Springs

### 1964-1972

Coil springs were used all nine years, from 1964 to 1972. Rates depended on the type of body, engine, transmission and options on the car. Until 1969 springs were selected in pairs. After that springs were selected with a computer according to the weight of the car. Weight can be affected by the addition or deletion of optional equipment.

### 1964 Malibu SS Front Coil Springs (V-8)

| Application | Code | Part Number | Rate |
|---|---|---|---|
| Coupe | GP | 3856585 | 290 |
| Convertible | AH | 3843588 | 290 |
| Coupe w/C60 | GQ | 3856586 | 290 |
| Coupe w/327 | GX | 3859074 | 290 |
| Convertible w/327 | AJ | 3843589 | 290# |
| Coupe w/327 and C60 | GW | 3859075 | 290# |
| Convertible w/327 and C60 | AL | 3849723 | 290# |

All springs have a wire diameter of .598 in. except those with #, which have a .619-in. wire diameter.

### 1964 Malibu SS F40 Front Coil Springs (V-8)

| Application | Code | Part Number | Rate |
|---|---|---|---|
| Coupe | GS | 3856588 | 290 |
| Convertible or Coupe w/C60 | AU | 3851077 | 290 |
| Convertible w/C60 | GT | 3856589 | 290 |
| Coupe w/327 | AN | 3850965 | 320 |
| Convertible w/327 or Coupe w/327 and C60 | AP | 3850966 | 320 |
| Convertible w/327 and C60 | AQ | 3850967 | 320 |

### 1965 Malibu SS Front Coil Springs (V-8)

| Application | Code | Part Number | Rate |
|---|---|---|---|
| Coupe | AH | 3866286 | 290 |
| Convertible or Coupe w/C60 | AM | 3866287 | 290 |
| Convertible w 327 | AN | 3866288 | 290 |
| Coupe w/C60 | AR | 3866290 | 290 |
| Convertible w/60 or Coupe w/327 and C60 | AS | 3866291 | 290 |
| Convertible w/327 and C60 | AT | 3866292 | 290 |
| 396 Coupe and Convertible | AY | 3866296 | 320 |

### 1965 Malibu SS F40 Front Coil Springs (V-8)

| Application | Code | Part Number | Rate |
|---|---|---|---|
| All Styles | GT | 3856589 | 290 |
| All w/327 | AO | 3850967 | 320 |
| Coupe w/C60 | GZ | 3859077 | 320 |
| Convertible w/C60 or All 327 w/C60 | AY | 3866296 | 320 |

### 1965 Malibu SS RPO G67 Super Lift Shocks Front Coil Springs

| Application | Code | Part Number | Rate |
|---|---|---|---|
| Coupe | GD | 3872205 | 290 |
| Convertible and all w/327 | AF | 3866285 | 290 |
| All w/C60 and 327 w/C60 | GF | 3872207 | 290 |
| Z16 Convertible only | AY | 3866296 | 320 |

### 1966 SS 396 Front Coil Springs (V-8)

| Application | Code | Part Number | Rate |
|---|---|---|---|
| Coupe | AJ | 3857692 | 320 |
| Convertible | GR | 3850966 | 320 |
| All styles w/C60 | AQ | 3850967 | 320 |
| All styles w/F40 | GK | 3895817 | 320 |
| All styles w/F40 and C60 | AB | 3890620 | 320 |

### 1967 SS 396 Front Coil Springs (V-8)

| Application | Code | Part Number | Rate |
|---|---|---|---|
| Coupe | AA | 3856589 | 320 |
| Convertible | AQ | 3850967 | 320 |
| All styles w/C60 | GJ | 3895816 | 320 |
| All styles w/F40 | AB | 3890630 | 320 |
| All styles w/F40 and C60 | AC | 3870475 | 320 |

All 1970-72 Chevelles with the SS package used the heavy-duty springs with a deflection rate of 435 lb/in. regardless of the engine size. However, some springs had a thicker 0.679 in. wire diameter, instead of the more common 0.659 in. diameter. The thicker-diameter springs were not used on cars with the 350 engines; they were found on optionally loaded 454s and Monte Carlos.

Springs were identified at the factory by a code on a piece of tape attached to one of the coils. The letters were black and the tape was red for the front springs.

### Rear Suspension

#### 1964-1972

Like the front suspension the rear suspension wavered little in design, using the same four-link system through the 1964-72 run.

The upper control arms were shorter than the lower control arms and attached to the cross-member of the frame and to an eye on the differential housing with $\frac{1}{2}$-13×3$\frac{7}{8}$ in. bolts and nuts. The 1964-66 cars used the standard Chevelle arms. Part numbers were listed as 3863925 in 1964 and 3869854 in 1965. The Z16 option used the same arm.

The 1966 SS used the 1965 production upper arms, but beginning in 1967 the SS used a special arm on the left-hand side. Listed as part number 3869853, it was added in the fifth week of January 1967, so early models did not use it. The right-hand side upper arm was listed as part number 3869854 all year.

The upper arms were redesigned in 1968 and were listed as part numbers 9790978-RH and 9790979-LH. These were shorter and flared out more at the ends; they will not interchange with earlier models. The production Chevelle arm, part number 9790978, was used on both sides beginning in 1969.

The longer lower control arms were attached to the side of the frame with welded-on brackets and the outer ends of the axle housing. Except for the Z16 option all SSs up to 1968 used the production Chevelle arms.

### 1964-1968 Rear Suspension Lower Control Arm Part Numbers

| | |
|---|---|
| 1964 | 9773163 |
| 1965-66 | 3869856 |
| 1967 | 3910950 |
| 1968 | 9794177 |

The Z16 option used special arms, part number 388725, with two holes drilled in each one to support the rear stabilizer bar. They will not correctly interchange with production arms because of the mounting holes.

The 1969 SS 396 without the F41 suspension used the 1968 arm; with the F41 suspension, part

## 1968 SS 396 Front and Rear Coil Springs

| Body Style | Front Code | Part Number | Rate | Rear Code | Part Number | Rate |
|---|---|---|---|---|---|---|
| | | | **Standard** | | | |
| 13837/67 | AD | 3923383 | 320 | BH | 3893388 | 130 |
| 13837/67(1) | AE | 3923384 | 320 | Same as above | | |
| 13380 | Same as AD above | | | BN | 3935710 | 130 |
| 13380(1) | Same as AE above | | | Same as above | | |
| | | | **Heavy Duty F40** | | | |
| 13837/67 | GK | 3926993 | 390 | OJ | 3926999 | 160 |
| 13837/67(1) | GL | 3926994 | 390 | Same as above | | |
| 13880 | Same as GK above | | | OF | 3924405 | 160 |
| 13880(1) | Same as above | | | Same as above | | |

(1)-with C60 Air Conditioning

## Computer Selected Coil Springs for 1969 Chevelle SS 396

| Front Springs Selective Weight | Code | Part Number | Rate | Rear Springs Selective Weight | Code | Part Number | Rate |
|---|---|---|---|---|---|---|---|
| 0–264 | GW | 3952818 | 320 | 0–130 | BL | 3952827 | 130 |
| 265–326 | GX | 3952819 | 320 | 131+ | BM | 3952828 | 130 |
| 327–372 | GY | 3952820 | 320 | See Code BM | | | |
| 373–456 | GZ | 3952821 | 320 | | | | |
| 456+ | AA | 3952822 | 320 | | | | |
| | | | **Pickup** | | | | |
| Same as above | | | | All | BR | 3952831 | 130 |
| | | | **Heavy Duty F40 and F41** | | | | |
| 0–304 | AB | 3952823 | 390 | All | BT | 3952833 | 160 |
| 305–422 | AC | 3952824 | 390 | See Code BT | | | |
| 423+ | AD | 3952825 | 390 | | | | |
| | | | **Pickup w/F40 or F41** | | | | |
| Same as above | | | | All | BX | 3952834 | 160 |

## Computer Selected Coil Springs for 1970 Chevelle SS 396/454

| Front Springs Selective Weight | Code | Part Number | Rate | Rear Springs Selective Weight | Code | Part Number | Rate |
|---|---|---|---|---|---|---|---|
| 0–968 | GA | 3960655 | 435 | All | OQ | 3960652 | 160 |
| 969–1045 | GB | 3960665 | 435 | | | | |
| 1046+ | GC | 3960686 | 435 | | | | |

## Computer Selected Coil Springs for 1971–72 Chevelle SS

| Front Springs Selective Weight | Code | Part Number | Rate | Rear Springs Selective Weight | Code | Part Number | Rate |
|---|---|---|---|---|---|---|---|
| 0–968 | GB | 3960665 | 435 | 0–620 | OQ | 3960652 | 160 |
| 969–1045 | GC | 3960686 | 435 | 621+ | OG# | 3987799 | 160 |
| | | | | 621+ | OH | 3987800 | 160 |
| 1046+ | GP | 3987798 | 435 | See Codes OG and OH above | | | |
| | | | **Pickup** | | | | |
| 0–890 | AB | 3952823 | 390 | All | OZ | 3974701 | 160 |
| 891–1020 | GB | 3960665 | 435 | | | | |
| 1020+ | AC | 3952824 | 390 | See Code OZ | | | |

## 1969 SS 396 Spring Weight Selection

| RPO # | Item | Front | Rear |
|---|---|---|---|
| A31 | Power windows | 11 | 13 |
| A31 | Power windows (Pickup) | 6 | 4 |
| A51 | Bucket seats | 11 | 10 |
| A93 | Power door locks | 5 | 3 |
| B37 | Floor mats (300) | 7 | 5 |
| B37 | Floor mats (Pickup) | 5 | 2 |
| C08 | Vinyl top | 2 | 5 |
| C08 | Vinyl top (Pickup) | 0 | 3 |
| C60 | Air conditioning | 101 | 7 |
| D55 | Console (manual trans.) | 7 | 4 |
| D55 | Console (automatic trans.) | 12 | 4 |
| J52 | Power disc brakes | 10 | 2 |
| L34 | 350 hp 396 ci V-8 | 194 | 46 |
| L35 | 325 hp 396 ci V-8 | 196 | 46 |
| L78 | 375 hp 396 ci V-8 | 179 | 44 |
| L89 | 375 hp 396 ci V-8 | 124 | 44 |
| M20 | 4-speed | 13 | 5 |
| M40 | TH 400 automatic | 23 | 9 |
| MC1 | Heavy Duty 3-speed | 16 | 3 |
| N10 | Dual Exhaust (Pickup and L78) | 3 | 29 |
| N40 | Power steering | 30 | 0 |

## 1969 SS 396 Spring Weight Selection

| RPO # | Item | Front | Rear |
|---|---|---|---|
| T60 | Heavy Duty Battery | 18 | -3 |
| U57 | Tape player | 9 | 3 |
| U57/ U79 | Stereo tape player | 12 | 4 |
| U63 | AM radio | 6 | 2 |
| U69 | AM/FM radio | 6 | 3 |
| U79 | Stereo | 7 | 2 |
| V01 | Heavy Duty Radiator | 7 | -1 |

number 3937877 was used. Like the 1965 Z16 arm, this one had provisions for the rear sway bar. This arm was used on all SSs from 1970 to 1972. Regular production Chevelle arms will not interchange onto the SS without modification. Be sure that the holes are clean and free of rough edges, as a dirty, rough hole could indicate a production arm drilled to support the bar, possibly identifying a faked SS car.

It is essential that the bolt head be installed so that it is next to the bar, for maximum strength and for correctness.

The 1965 L37, L74 and L79 engines used a pair of frame suspension supports, part numbers 3869875-LH and 3869876-RH, to tie the suspen-

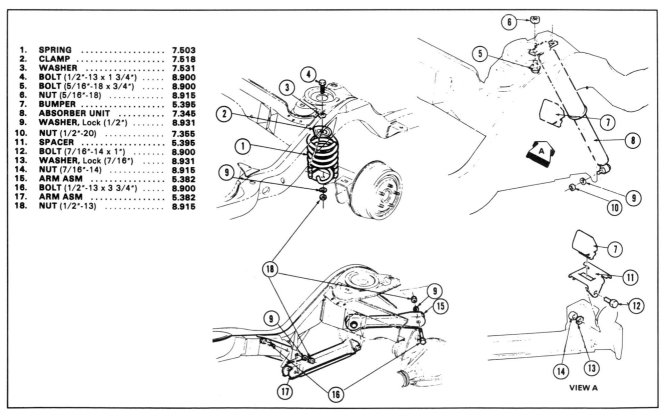

| | | |
|---|---|---|
| 1. | SPRING | 7.503 |
| 2. | CLAMP | 7.518 |
| 3. | WASHER | 7.531 |
| 4. | BOLT (1/2"-13 x 1 3/4") | 8.900 |
| 5. | BOLT (5/16"-18 x 3/4") | 8.900 |
| 6. | NUT (5/16"-18) | 8.915 |
| 7. | BUMPER | 5.395 |
| 8. | ABSORBER UNIT | 7.345 |
| 9. | WASHER, Lock (1/2") | 8.931 |
| 10. | NUT (1/2"-20) | 7.355 |
| 11. | SPACER | 5.395 |
| 12. | BOLT (7/16"-14 x 1") | 8.900 |
| 13. | WASHER, Lock (7/16") | 8.931 |
| 14. | NUT (7/16"-14) | 8.915 |
| 15. | ARM ASM | 5.382 |
| 16. | BOLT (1/2"-13 x 3 3/4") | 8.900 |
| 17. | ARM ASM | 5.382 |
| 18. | NUT (1/2"-13) | 8.915 |

*Chevelle rear suspension details.*

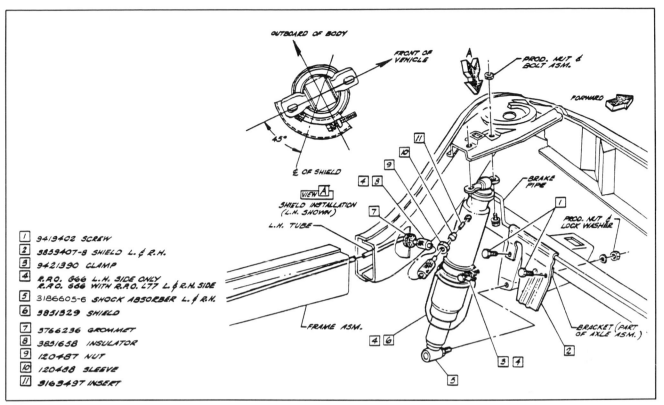

OUTBOARD OF BODY

FRONT OF VEHICLE

45°

℄ OF SHIELD

VIEW A

SHIELD INSTALLATION
(L.H. SHOWN)

L.H. TUBE

PROD. NUT 6 BOLT ASM.

FORWARD

BRAKE PIPE

PROD. NUT 2 LOCK WASHER

FRAME ASM.

BRACKET (PART OF AXLE ASM.)

| 1 | 9419402 | SCREW |
|---|---|---|
| 2 | 3859407-8 | SHIELD L. & R.H. |
| 3 | 9421390 | CLAMP |
| 4 | R.P.O. G66 L.H. SIDE ONLY R.P.O. G66 WITH R.P.O. L77 L. & R.H. SIDE | |
| 5 | 3186605-6 | SHOCK ABSORBER L. & R.H. |
| 6 | 3851329 | SHIELD |
| 7 | 5766236 | GROMMET |
| 8 | 3851658 | INSULATOR |
| 9 | 120487 | NUT |
| 10 | 120488 | SLEEVE |
| 11 | 3163497 | INSERT |

*1964-65 air shocks mounting.*

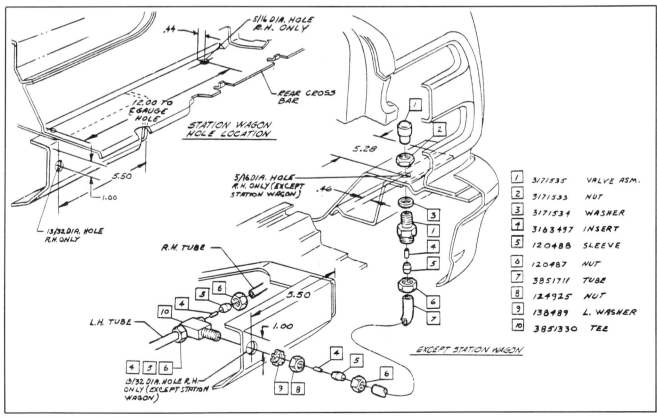

5/16 DIA. HOLE R.H. ONLY

.44

REAR CROSS BAR

12.00 TO ℄ GAUGE HOLE

STATION WAGON HOLE LOCATION

5.50

1.00

13/32 DIA. HOLE R.H. ONLY

5/16 DIA. HOLE R.H. ONLY (EXCEPT STATION WAGON)

.46

5.28

R.H. TUBE

5.50

1.00

L.H. TUBE

13/32 DIA. HOLE R.H. ONLY (EXCEPT STATION WAGON)

| 1 | 3171535 | VALVE ASM. |
|---|---|---|
| 2 | 3171533 | NUT |
| 3 | 3171534 | WASHER |
| 4 | 3163497 | INSERT |
| 5 | 120488 | SLEEVE |
| 6 | 120487 | NUT |
| 7 | 3851711 | TUBE |
| 8 | 124925 | NUT |
| 9 | 138489 | L. WASHER |
| 10 | 3851330 | TEE |

EXCEPT STATION WAGON

*1964 air inlet location for air lift rear shocks.*

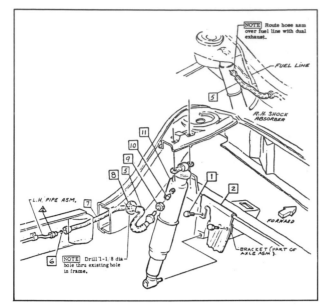

*1967 air shocks. These were typical for 1968-72 applications.*

sion points together. Attached to the upper and lower control arm mounting points with the production nut and space washer, part number 2436165, it solidified the suspension considerably, eliminating most axle tie-up.

The same support part numbers were used on the 1966 SS.

The supports were restyled in 1967 and listed as part numbers 3909669-LH and 3909670-RH. They attached in the same way as in 1965.

The supports were again redesigned in 1968 for the new frame and were listed as part numbers 3918061-LH and 3918061-RH. Attachment was the same, but instead of the production bolt a 17-32×1 1/16 in. bolt was used at the bracket. For this reason these supports are not interchangeable with those on earlier frames.

These supports were unchanged until 1972 and were used on all big-block-equipped cars. The small-block SS 350s did not have these supports. If a 1971 or 1972 SS 350 has these supports it is incorrect.

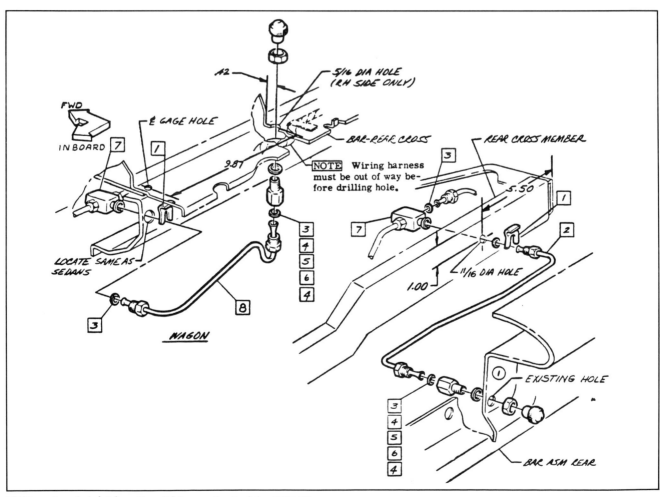

*1967 center air inlet location. This was typical for 1968-72 applications.*

## Rear Shock Absorbers
### 1964-1972

Delco rear shocks were installed all nine years, from 1964 to 1972. Until 1966 the SS used the production Chevelle shocks. With the introduction of the 396 ci engine in 1966, shocks with higher-calibrated valving were used. At the beginning of production the station wagon shocks, part number 3186920, were used, but these were replaced with part number 3192430 after build date 11B 65.

Part number 3192430 was used until 1972 when it was replaced with part number 4949840 for cars with the L48 and L65 engines. Part number 4949841 was used with the LS3 and LS5 powerplants. All shock absorbers should be painted to match the front shocks.

Air shocks were standard equipment on the El Camino all nine years and optional equipment, as RPO G66, from 1964 to 1969. Both systems were similar in design and consisted of two special shocks and tubing that allowed the driver to use compressed air to alter the ride.

Early El Caminos, up to 1968, had the air inlet valve installed on the rear shelf behind the passenger seat. Later models, 1968-72, like the cars, had the inlet valve in the rear bumper. The following charts and part numbers included 1964-69 cars and 1968-72 El Caminos.

## Rear Springs
### 1964-1972

Coil springs were used from 1964 to 1972 and were selected like the front springs. They were identified at the factory by a yellow tape with black letters wrapped around one of the coils.

### 1964 Malibu SS Rear Coil Springs (V-8)

| Application | Code | Part Number | Rate |
|---|---|---|---|
| Coupe | BS | 3856268 | 115 |
| Convertible | BU | 3856590 | 115 |

### 1964 Malibu SS Rear Coil Springs (V-8)

| Application | Code | Part Number | Rate |
|---|---|---|---|
| Coupe w/327 | BW | 3857643 | 115 |
| Convertible w/327 | BY | 3859078 | 115 |
| With F40 and all 327s | BK | 3851067 | 130 |
| Convertible w/F40 | BD | 3843674 | 130 |
| Coupe w/F40 | BK | 3851067 | 130 |

### 1965 Malibu SS Rear Coil Springs (V-8)

| Application | Code | Part Number | Rate |
|---|---|---|---|
| Coupe w/ or w/o C60 | BB | 3866298 | 115 |
| Convertible w/o C60 | BJ | 3866259 | 115 |
| w/C60 | BL | 3866276 | 115 |
| Coupe w/ or w/o C60 | BC | 3866299 | 115 |
| 327 Convertible w/ or w/o C60 | BL | 3866276 | 115 |
| Coupe w/F40 w/ or w/o 327 | BV | 3856591 | 130 |
| Convertible w/F40 w/ or w/o 327 | BK | 3851067 | 130 |
| w/Z16 | BY | 3870488 | 120 |

## Standard Steering Gears
### 1964-1965

A manual Saginaw steering gearbox with a 24:1 ratio was standard. The part number was listed as 5679270 for both 1964 and 1965 except with the Z16 package, which used a special gearbox (see the RPO N40 Power Steering Gearboxes section later in this chapter for details).

The steering box should be painted gloss-black except for the side cover and lower end plug, which should have a natural aluminum appearance.

### 1966-1967

The gearbox for 1966 was identical to that used in 1965, including the part number. In 1967

## 1964-1972 Chevelle Air Shocks

| Year | Shocks | Hose | T-Connector | Pipe Assembly | Valve |
|---|---|---|---|---|---|
| 1964 | 3186605 LH | n/a | 3851330 | 3851322 LH | 3171535* |
|  | 3186606 RH | n/a |  | 3851323 RH |  |
| 1965 | See 1964 | 3863550 | 3863935 | 3863553 LH | 3863540† |
|  | Special clamp part number 9421390 on shock | | | 3863554 RH | |
|  | and sheild part number 3861040 needed with Z-16 | | | | |
| 1966 | 3186502 LH | 3863550 | 3863935 | See 1965 | See 1965 |
| 1967 | 3186503 RH | | | | |
| 1968 | 3186577 LH | 3920631 | 3863546 | 3920633 LH | See 1965 |
|  | 3186578 RH | | | 3920634 RH | |
| 1968-69 Pickup | 3197583 LH | 3920631 | 3863935 | 3931465 LH | See 1965 |
|  | 3197584 RH | | | 3924407 RH | |
| 1970-72 Pickup | 3197337 LH | 3920631 | 3863935 | See 1968 | See 1965 |
|  | 3197338 RH | | | | |

*–Valve is located on RH side of rear bumper
†–Valve located in center of bumper

## 1966 SS 396 Rear Coil Springs (V-8)

| Application | Code | Part Number | Rate |
|---|---|---|---|
| Coupe w/ or w/o C60 | OI | 3895821 | 130 |
| Convertible w/ or w/o C60 | OM | 3895822 | 130 |
| Coupe w/F40 w/ or w/o C60 | OT | 3895825 | 130 |
| Convertible w/F40 w/ or w/o C60 | OV | 3895826 | 130 |

## 1967 SS 396 Rear Coil Springs (V-8)

| Application | Code | Part Number | Rate |
|---|---|---|---|
| Coupe | BH | 3893388 | 130 |
| Convertible | BV | 3908799 | 130 |
| With C60 | | Same as standard | |
| Coupe w/F40 | BZ | 3893396 | 130 |
| Convertible w/F40 | BP | 3893397 | 130 |
| F40 with C60 | | Same as above | |

part number 5699254 was used, although the ratio was the same.

A heavy-duty steering flange—part number 5692597, 5699177 in 1967—was used on the steering shaft. This flange was used only on vehicles with the 396 ci engine. It should be painted gloss-black.

### 1968-1972

Not much changed in 1968-72. The standard ratio was still 24:1 for all five years. The finish was the same as in previous years.

### 1968-1972 Standard Steering Gear Part Numbers

| Year | Steering Gearbox | Heavy-duty Flange |
|---|---|---|
| 1968 | 5699254 | 5698634 |
| 1969-70 | 7802333 | 5698634 |
| 1971 | 7809557 | 7807052 |
| 1972 | 7814142; 7813496* | 7807052 |

*After build date 11 B on the data plate.

1. **RING**, Steering Gear Housing End(*10,12) ............... 6.824
2. **PLUG**, Steering Gear Housing End .... 6.824
3. **SEAL**, Steering Gear Housing End Cover "O" Ring(*10,12) ................ 6.825
4. **RING**, Steering Gear Power Cylinder Piston(*5,13) ................. 6.579
5. **SEAL**, Piston Ring Back Up "O" Ring (2 7/16" ID)(*5,13) ................. 6.579
6. **PLUG**, Piston End(*5) ........... 6.586
7. **SCREW**, W/Lockwasher, Worming Bearing(*5) ..................... 6.586
8. **CLAMP**, Ball Return Guide(*5) ....... 6.843
9. **GUIDE**, Ball Return(*5) ........... 6.842
10. **BALL**, Gear Worm(*5) ............ 6.844
11. **RACK & PISTON**, Steering Gear(*5) .. 6.586
12. **NUT**, Lash Adjuster(*7,12) ......... 6.822
13. **COVER ASM**, Housing Guide(*7) ..... 6.807
14. **SEAL**, Housing Side Cover(*7,8,11,12) . 6.809
15. **GEAR**, Pitman Shaft(*8) .......... N.S.
16. **SEAT**, Steering Gear Housing Hose(*6) . 6.673
17. **VALVE**, Housing(*6,14) .......... 6.673
18. **SPRING**, Housing Check Valve(*6,14) . 6.673
19. **CONNECTOR**, Hose Fitting to Hsg (9/32" ID x 31/32" OD)(*6,14) ....... 6.673
20. **RACE**, Thrust Bearing(*9) .......... 6.835
21. **BEARING**, Lower Thrust(*9) ........ N.S.
22. **RACE**, Thrust Bearing(*9) .......... 6.835
23. **WORM**, Steering(*5) ............ N.S.
24. **SEAL**, Stub Shaft(*1,4,12) ........ N.S.
25. **SHAFT**, Steering Gear Pitman(*1) .... 6.850
26. **BEARING**, Needle (1 3/4" OD)(*6) .... 6.786
27. **SEAL**, Pitman Shaft Oil(*6,15) ....... 6.855
28. **WASHER**, Pitman Shaft Seal Back-Up . 6.855
29. **SEAL**, Pitman Shaft Oil (Double Lip)(*6,12,15) ................... 6.855
30. **WASHER**, Pitman Shaft Seal Back-Up(*6,12,15) ............... 6.855
31. **RING**, Retaining(*6,12,15) ......... 6.856
32. **WASHER**, Pitman Arm (7/8") ....... 6.861
33. **NUT**, Pitman Arm (7/8"-14) ....... 6.861
34. **SEAL**, Spool(*1,4,12) ............ N.S.
35. **BODY**, Valve(*1) .............. N.S.
36. **BOLT**, Flange to Shaft Coupling ...... 6.525
37. **SEAL**, Hydraulic Valve ........... 6.552
38. **SPRING**, Spool Valve ............ 6.552
39. **SEAL**, Valve Body(*1,4,12) ........ N.S.
40. **RING**, Valve Body(*1,4,12) ........ N.S.
41. **RETAINER**, Adj Bearing(*2,9) ....... 6.835
42. **SPACER**, Thrust Bearing(*2,9) ...... N.S.
43. **RACE**, Thrust Bearing(*2,9) ........ 6.835
44. **BEARING**, Valve Asm(*2,9) ........ 6.835
45. **RACE**, Thrust Bearing(*2,9) ........ 6.835
46. **SEAL**, Adj Plug Seal(*2,3,12) ....... 6.840
47. **CLAMP**, Ball Return(*2) .......... 6.843
48. **BEARING**, Upper End Plug Stud Shaft(*2) ................... 6.826
49. **SEAL**, Eng Plug Steel Shaft Oil(*2,3,12) . N.S.
50. **SEAL**, Steel Shaft(*2,3,12) ........ 6.840
51. **RING**, Retaining(*2,3,12) ......... 6.840
52. **NUT**, Adjusting (2 1/4"-20) ........ 6.832
53. **COUPLING**, Steering Shaft ......... 6.525
54. **HOUSING**, Steering Gear(*6) ....... 6.803
55. **BOLT**, Housing Side Cover(*5,6,7,8,11,12,15) ........... 6.809

1959 THRU 1971

*Power steering gearbox.*

To identify the gearbox look for the build date on a pad stamped on the inboard side of the box near the top. The code was simple: the number of the day of the year followed by the last digit of the year.

Remember, this is the build date, and the year may not agree with the model year of the car. For example, a code that reads 121 9 would indicate that the box was built on the 121st day of the year 1969, or May 1, 1969, and was used on the 1969 models. However, a box with the code 334 9 would have been built on the 334th day of the year 1969, or November 30, 1969, making it used on a 1970 model.

## RPO N40 Power Steering Gearboxes

### 1964-1965

Optional power-assisted steering decreased the steering gear ratio to 17.5:1. It also decreased the number of turns of the steering wheel from lock to lock: with RPO N40 the number was 3.98 turns; without N40 it was 5.48. The part numbers were listed as 5692398 in 1964 and 5696113 in 1965 for all production Chevelles.

A wider spiral worm shaft, which quickened the ratio to 15:1, was used in the gearbox with the Z16 option. The shaft has no replacement part number, but the gearbox was listed as part number 5616015. Only 3.5 turns of the steering wheel were required from lock to lock with this gearbox.

### 1966-1969

The only power steering ratio available for 1966-69 was the 17.5:1.

### 1966-1969 RPO N40 Power Steering Gearbox Part Numbers

| 1966 | 5696113 |
| 1967-68 | 7801584 |
| 1969 | 7806671 |

### 1970-1972

The coupe and the convertible used a new variable-ratio gearbox for 1970. It was listed as part number 7811176, featured ratios of 16:1 on center and 12.4:1 and only took 2.9 turns of the wheel from lock to lock.

The El Camino was not equipped with the variable-ratio gearbox and instead used part number 7811175 with a 17.5:1 ratio. It required 3.98 turns of the wheel from lock to lock.

The variable-ratio gearbox was used on all body styles and was listed as part number 7811949 for 1971 and 1972. The ratios were revised to 18.5 on center and 12.4:1.

Power steering gearboxes are recognizable by their long cylindrical design with a provision for the fluid hoses on the nose. The natural aluminum end cap was smooth with no adjusting nut. The case should be painted gloss-black, the end caps

left natural. The build date code and location were the same as for the manual units.

## Power Steering Hydraulic Hoses

### 1964-1972

### 1964-1972 Power Steering Hydraulic Hose Part Numbers

| Year | Pressure | Return | End Pipe Assembly |
|---|---|---|---|
| 1964 | 5691968 | 5683933 | 5692268 |
| 1965 | | | |
| Z16 only | 5691968 | 3853200 | 3874659 |
| Except Z16 | 5691968 | 3853200 | 5692268 |
| 1966-67 | 3880584 | 3874658 | 3874659 |
| 1968 | 3928204 | 3786228 | 3928207 |
| 1969 | 3964567 | 3874695 | 3874659 |
| 1970 | 3972651 | 3874695 | 3874659 |
| 1971-72 | | | |
| LS3, LS5 & LS6 only | 3994399 | 3874695 | 3874659 |
| LS65 & L48 only | 7811621 | 3905115 | 3874659 |

## Power Steering Pumps and Pulleys

### 1964-1965

Only one pump, part number 5693781, was used in 1964 with all V-8 engines. It was mounted with a V-shaped bracket and a rear brace. The pump and its brackets should be painted gloss-black, with the fill cap having a natural appearance.

A total of three different pumps were used in 1965. Most V-8s used part number 5693560, and the L79 engine used part number 5696221. Both pumps used the same mounting brackets and a single-groove pulley.

The third pump in 1965 was listed as part number 5696016 and was unique in design. The pump itself was shaped like a canteen with an elbow on top. A flexible black hose, part number 3874656, routed from the elbow to a separate reservoir, part number 3823695, mounted in a bracket on the left hand side of the radiator support wall and front fender. Tower clamps were used on both ends of the hose. A special mounting bracket, part number 3873845, and rear brace, part number 3873846, were used to mount the pump. A larger pump pulley, part number 3873847, was also used. The pump, brackets, brace, reservoir and pulley should all be painted gloss-black; the reservoir cap, part number 3823695, should have a natural metal appearance. This setup was used only with the 396 ci engine.

### 1966-1968

Two pumps were installed in early 1966. The base L35 engine used part number 5696635, and the other engines part number 5696636. However, beginning in the third week of November 1967 all

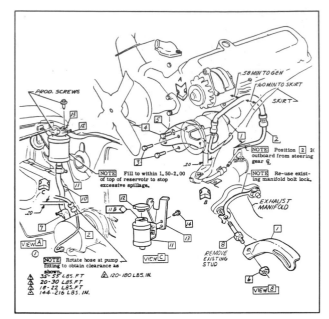

*1967 power steering pump and reservoir. These were typical for 1966-68 applications.*

engines used the later pump. Two different pulleys were also employed: the L35 engine used part number 3873847, and the other engines part number 3860457. Both were single-groove units.

The pump design was the same from 1966 to 1968 and was similar to that used on the 1965 L37 engine. As a matter of fact, all pump system components except the pump itself used the same part numbers in 1966, although slightly different clamps, part number 9414923, must be used on the reservoir hose for correctness.

Pump part number 5698077 was visually different for 1967 with the elbow extension on the side of the housing instead of the top. For this reason it will not interchange with earlier designs. The mounting brackets were redesigned, and the front bracket, part number 3873845, was flat with five holes drilled in it. A rear brace, part number 3878286, with an adjusting slot in it was also used. A special stud, part number 3923299, was installed in the exhaust manifold to mount the brace.

The reservoir bracket, part number 3893373, featured a slot that hooked over a bolt up under the left front fender. The gloss-black fluid reservoir was now listed as part number 3900185, and the cap, part number 5695670, had a natural finish. All 396 ci engines used the same single-groove pulley, listed as part number 3873847. The pump, pulley and mounting accessories should be painted gloss-black.

The pump was listed as part number 7803404 for 1968. Mounting was identical to that in 1967. Two different pulleys were available: the L78 engine used part number 3873847, and the other

| | | |
|---|---|---|
| 1. | **SHAFT**, Steering Oil Pump Drive | 6.614 |
| 2. | **KEY**, Pully to Shaft | 6.655 |
| 3. | **SEAL**, Steering Oil Pump Shaft | 6.617 |
| 4. | **SEAL**, Reservoir O-Ring | 6.635 |
| 5. | **HOUSING ASM**, Steering Oil Pump | 6.608 |
| 6. | **SEAL**, Pump End & Pressure Plate O-Ring | 6.609 |
| 7. | **PIN**, Pump Ring Dowel | 6.608 |
| 8. | **PLATE**, Thrust | 6.612 |
| 9. | **CAP**, Filler | 6.635 |
| 10. | **VALVE ASM**, Flow Control | 6.624 |
| 11. | **SPRING**, Flow Control | 6.612 |
| 12. | **SEAL**, Union to Pump Hsg O-Ring | 6.674 |
| 13. | **ROTOR KIT**, Pump (Incl #14 & 15) | N.S. |
| 14. | **RING**, Shaft Retainer | N.S. |
| 15. | **VANE KIT**, Rotor (Incl #12 & 15) | 6.610 |
| 16. | **RING KIT**, Pump Rotor (Incl #12 & 14) | 6.610 |
| 17. | **PLATE**, Pressure | 6.612 |
| 18. | **SPRING**, Pressure Plate | 6.612 |
| 19. | **PLATE**, Pump Hsg End | 6.609 |
| 20. | **RING**, End Plate Retaining | 6.609 |
| 21. | **SEAL**, Reservoir | 6.635 |
| 22. | **RESERVOIR ASM**, Steering Oil Pump | 6.635 |
| 23. | **BOLT** (3/8"-16 x 3/4") | 8.900 |
| 24. | **SEAL**, Fitting | 6.674 |
| 25. | **FITTING**, W/Orifice | 6.673 |

*1969-72 power steering pump.*

engines used part number 3925537. Both pulleys were single-groove units.

A reservoir mounting bracket was now included with the reservoir, part number 3928205. The cap was the same as in 1967. A preformed hose, part number 3781439, connected the reservoir to the pump, and tower clamps were used at both ends of the hose. The finish for each component should be the same as in previous years.

**1969-1972**

The reservoir and pump were combined into one unit, part number 780670, in 1969. The pump was cradled in two brackets: the lower bracket was part number 3946017 and the outside bracket was part number 3846016. Each bracket was secured to the pump with two ⅜ in. bolts. The outside bracket was bolted to a support, part number 3946017, mounted on the exhaust manifold.

Three pulleys were offered: two single-groove units used without air conditioning and one dual-groove unit used with air conditioning. The single-groove pulleys were listed as part numbers 3941105 with the L78 or COPO 427 engine and 3770509 with the L35 and L34 engines. Because the air-conditioning compressor was now mounted on the left-hand side of the engine, a dual-groove pulley, part number 3941107, had to be used with it.

A special pump, part number 7808283, was required with the variable-ratio steering in 1970. This system was installed in all coupes and convertibles with power steering. A straight-ratio pump, part number 7808282, was used on the El Camino.

Only one bracket, part number 3967422, was used to mount the pump to the engine. A brace, part number 3967420, on the inward side of the pump helped secure the pump.

Without air conditioning, a single-groove pulley was installed: the base L34 and LS5 engines used part number 3770509, and all other engine options used part number 3941105. When air conditioning was selected, a dual-groove pulley, part number 3941107, was used for all engines.

The 1971-72 pump was identical to the 1970 variable-ratio unit and was used on all body styles with power steering. Early SS 350s in 1971 used part number 7806371; the change occurred at the start of the fourth week in October 1970. In 1972 the part number was changed to 7813397 for all engines all year.

Mounting for the big-block cars in 1971 and 1972 was identical to that in 1970. The small-block cars used two mounting brackets: a cradle type, part number 3941102, on the inward side and an adjustable bracket, part number 3941103, on the outward side. The outer bracket was secured to a support brace, part number 3959558, with a ⅜×1 in. bolt. For correctness the bolt head must face toward the firewall. This same setup was used on all Chevrolet cars with power steering and a small-block engine from 1969 on, and all parts were interchangeable.

All engines used the same single-groove pulley, listed as part number 3770509, unless air conditioning was ordered; then a double-groove pulley, part number 3941107, was used both years. Except for the natural filler cap, all components should be painted gloss-black.

## Power Steering Belts

### 1964-1968

The power steering belt was in the same position from 1964 to 1968. It always rode in the outermost pulley on the crankshaft, whether or not air conditioning was used. All 396 ci belts were 49.5 in. in length. The 1964 and 1965 V-8 belts were 41.5 in. in length. All belts were ⅜ in. wide.

### Original Power Steering Belt Part Numbers

| | |
|---|---|
| 1964–65 all | 3847706 |
| January 1965 on | 3877478 |
| 1965 Z–16 | 3791043 |
| 1966 L78 | 3791043 |

### Original Power Steering Belt Part Numbers

| | |
|---|---|
| 1967 | 3909819 |
| 1968 | 3925530 |

### 1969-1972

From 1969 to 1972, without air conditioning, the power steering belt rode in the groove of the first pulley, next to the engine. When air conditioning was selected, the belt rode in the middle groove of the crankshaft pulley and in the outer groove of the pump pulley.

### 1969-1972 Power Steering Belts

| Year | Engine | Part Number | Dimensions |
|---|---|---|---|
| 1969 | L34, L35 | 3849258; 3946019* | 41.5×⅜; 42.5×⅜* |
| | L78 | 3946020 | 40×¹⁵⁄₃₂ |
| 1970 | L35, LS3 | 3849258 | 41.5×⅜ |
| | L78, LS6 | 3946020 | 41×¹⁵⁄₃₂ |
| 1971-72 | LS3, LS5 | 3986190 | 41×⅜ |
| | LS6 | 3946020† | 41×¹⁵⁄₃₂ |
| | L65, L48 | 3988721 | 36×⅜ |

*With automatic transmission or C60.
†In 1971 only.

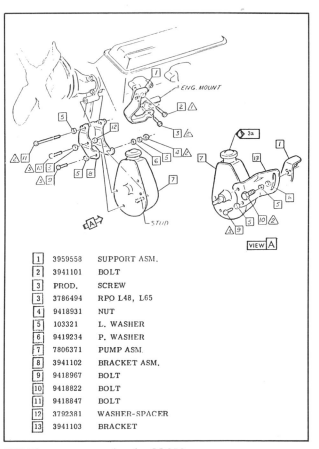

| | | |
|---|---|---|
| 1 | 3959558 | SUPPORT ASM. |
| 2 | 3941101 | BOLT |
| 3 | PROD. | SCREW |
| 3 | 3786494 | RPO L48, L65 |
| 4 | 9418931 | NUT |
| 5 | 103321 | L. WASHER |
| 6 | 9419234 | P. WASHER |
| 7 | 7806371 | PUMP ASM. |
| 8 | 3941102 | BRACKET ASM. |
| 9 | 9418967 | BOLT |
| 10 | 9418822 | BOLT |
| 11 | 9418847 | BOLT |
| 12 | 3792381 | WASHER-SPACER |
| 13 | 3941103 | BRACKET |

*1971-72 pump mounting for SS 350s.*

# Chapter 5

# Wheels, Wheel Covers and Tires

*There were a number of small changes on the styling of the Z16 which separated it from its standard Super Sport brothers. There were only 201 of the model produced that lone 1965 production year and one of the real designators of the breed was a set of these nifty simulated magnesium wheel covers. Phil Kunz/Bill Holder*

*Rally wheels made their first appearance in 1967. This center cap is incorrect, and the wheel is painted red, which is also incorrect.*

## Wheels

### 1964–1965

The standard 14×5 in. stamped steel wheel was the only wheel available for the 1964 Malibu SS. All plants used part number 3838461, except Fremont, which used part number 395178 only. Both wheels used five lug nuts, part number 358501. Wheels and nuts should be painted gloss-black enamel.

Three wheels were used in 1965: two measured 14×5 in. and were stamped J; the other was 1 in. wider. Again the Fremont plant used a different part number, 3872276, and the other plants used part number 3869447. Both wheels were 5 in. wide.

The Z16 option used 14×6 in. stamped steel wheels, which were listed as part number 3872813 and were stamped JK. These wheels were offered exclusively with the Z16 option. All wheels were painted with DuPont gloss-black enamel.

### 1966–1968

The standard 14×6 in. steel wheel, part number 3871919, code JK, was the only available wheel in 1966. With the standard dog-dish hubcaps the wheel was painted the same color as the lower

*The center cap was restyled in 1968. The wheel was basically the same.*

portion of the body. If the full wheel cover was ordered, the wheel was painted gloss-black. Paint should be enamel for correctness.

The standard wheel for 1967 was identical but used part number 1373846.

Slotted Rally wheels made their first appearance in 1967. Measuring the same as the standard wheels, they had five slots cut into them for better airflow. They were painted argent—DuPont 9692L, Ditzler DQE-8568, Rinshed Mason AT114—in a 60 degree gloss finish.

Rally wheels were part of the disc brake option, RPO J52, and were not available as a separate option. Each wheel was outlined by a bright trim ring, part number 3901317, and a center hub, part number 3901710, in the center. The center hub also housed a small cap that was cast with the label Chevrolet Motor Division Disc Brakes in capital letters. In the center of the cap was the bow-tie emblem.

A total of four different standard wheels were used in 1968. At the beginning of production, part number 161894 was used at all plants except Framingham and Fremont, which used part number 8871919. After build date 01D 1968 these part numbers were changed: the Framingham and Fremont plants used part number 9792552, and the other plants used part number 9789878.

Two different wheels with an offset of 0.88 in. were used with disc brakes. Be sure the wheels have this offset and are 14×6 in. wide. These were available solely on the SS 396.

Rally wheels—replacements were stamped XB—became an option, RPO ZJ7, and were available with all braking systems. The center hubcap, part number 3925800, was restyled. It was longer with a ribbed pattern on the outer radius. The name Chevrolet Motor Division was cast into a circle on the cap. All wheels should be painted according to 1967 directions. The original trim ring, part number 3921105, had four mounting clips. Replacements and reproductions usually have more, which makes for easier installation but is incorrect.

### 1969-1970

All 1969 SS 396s came with only one type of wheel. Commonly referred to as an SS wheel or Sports wheel, it was listed as part number 3956744, measured 14×7 in. and was stamped JJ. It featured a five-spoke design, looking similar to a Magnum 500 wheel. The outer rim and spokes were painted argent, and the inset was painted 60 degree gloss-black.

### 1969-1970 Wheel Paint Codes

| | Ditzler | Rinshed Mason | DuPont |
|---|---|---|---|
| Argent | DQE-8568 | AT114 | 9692L |
| Gloss-black | 9000 | A-946 | 99L |

*These original 1969 SS wheels were the only available wheels with the SS 396 in 1969 and 1970.*

A bright trim ring, part number 3956775, and center hub, part number 3956770, were also used with this wheel. In the center of the hub was a Mylar-covered identification emblem with a black background and the letters *SS* in white. Each wheel also used five chrome-plated lug nuts, part number 399683, and a tire valve extension listed as part number 9417745.

No wheel option was available with the SS 396; although Rally wheels were available on the Chevelle line, they would be incorrect for the SS 396. However, Chevelles designated as COPO cars were available with 15×7 in. Rally wheels only. The replacement part number is listed as 3997899 and the wheel is stamped DZ. The center hub was the same as that used with Rally wheels in 1968. The trim ring, part number 3901708, should have an outside diameter of 16.625 in.

*The striking sport wheels really set off the overall look of the 1969 SS Chevelle. No longer was the engine's cubic inch number identified on the front fender as on the 1968 model. As would be the case for a number of the following models, the cubic inch number was carried under the SS designator on the front fender. Phil Kunz/Bill Holder*

*A center cap retainer was used with 1969 and early 1970 SS packages.*

Early 1970 SS wheels were identical to those used in 1969, including part numbers. In late October 1969 the wheel and center hub were redesigned. The wheel was now listed as part number 3975671, and the center cover as part number 3983323. The center cover design was distinguished by the elimination of the retainer and the use of a snap-in center cap. Late-model 1970 SSs with the 1969 style wheels are incorrect. The ring,

*Even though high performance was fading away for the 1971 Chevelle Super Sport, Chevy was still working hard to keep the looks of performance going. The flashy five-spoked wheels still spoke of speed and style. The mag-style wheels had a grey finish, and white-lettered tires were also featured. Phil Kunz/Bill Holder*

valve extension and lug nuts were the same for both wheels.

### 1971-1972

Special wheels were again part of every SS package in both 1971 and 1972. They were listed as part number 3983045 both years, except for those installed at the Canadian plant, which used part number 3983044 for early 1971 models, then used the same part number as the American plants did for later models.

The specially styled wheels measured 15×7 in. and were painted dark gray—Ditzler DQE-32961, Rinshed Mason 71B16, DuPont 9901L. These wheels were commonly called Z28 wheels, as they were also used on the Camaro. A bright trim ring, part number 394523, and a center hub with a blue bow-tie center, part number 3989478, were used both years.

## Wheel Covers

### 1964-1965

The standard wheel covers for 1964 consisted of four separate parts: a full wheel disc, part number 3841602; a tri-spinner ornament, part number 3840974; a ribbed hub, part number 3841192, with a plastic insert with a red SS logo; and a reinforcement, part number 3840976, on the back of the disc. All components were held together with six hex-head screws.

Simulated wire wheel covers, RPO PO2, part number 3839767, were the only optional covers available for the Malibu SS. The wire basket appeared to be attached to the outer rim with eight

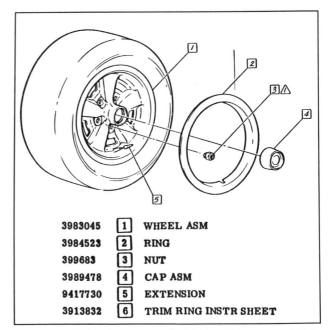

| | | |
|---|---|---|
| 3983045 | 1 | WHEEL ASM |
| 3984523 | 2 | RING |
| 399683 | 3 | NUT |
| 3989478 | 4 | CAP ASM |
| 9417730 | 5 | EXTENSION |
| 3913832 | 6 | TRIM RING INSTR SHEET |

*Styled steel wheels were used with the SS in 1971 and 1972.*

small clips. The center cap used a star-burst design with a bow-tie symbol in the center on a black background. The double S logo was not used with the PO2 option. The covers were also available as dealer-installed equipment.

Wheel covers could also be deleted, as RPO P43, for credit, exposing the wheel. This option was mainly for those who were going racing or were going to install custom wheels. Unless you can document this option, a car without wheel covers would be incorrect.

For 1965, instead of sharing the Impala's wheel cover, as it did in 1964, the SS received its

own wheel covers. Each cover consisted of three parts: a louvered disc, part number 3860240; a tri-spinner-look hub, part number 3860243; and a rear reinforcement, part number 3860244. All the parts were bound together with four screws.

The simulated wire wheel covers were identical and carried the same part number. The standard wheel covers could be deleted again this year. Simulated mag wheel covers, part number 3872360, were standard with the Z16 option. They were also available as a dealer-installed option beginning in December 1965; they were not available as a factory option.

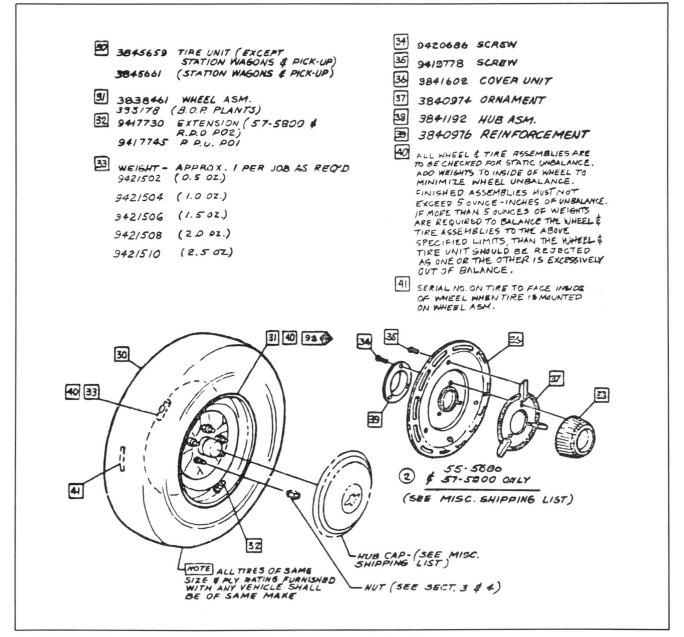

*1964 SS full wheel covers.*

## 1966-1968

The standard hubcap for the beginning of 1966 was the dog-dish type, part number 3875038, that was used on all Chevelles. Cars constructed after build date 11C used a full wheel cover, part number 3875040; before that this cover was optional. The full wheel covers used a black insert with a small white bow-tie symbol in the center.

The simulated wire wheel cover, PO2, and the simulated mag wheel—now available as a factory option, RPO N96—were unchanged. Both were also available as dealer options.

The dog-dish-style hubcap was standard on all 1967 SS 396s. Listed as part number 3890678, it was recognizable by the black bow-tie symbol in the center of the cap.

Full wheel covers, RPO PO1, part number 3893340, were optional. These featured an insert with a black background and the letters *SS* in white. Full wheel covers from other 1967 Chevelles will interchange if the identification insert is changed.

The simulated wire wheel covers, part number 3908760, were restyled for 1967 and were not cor-

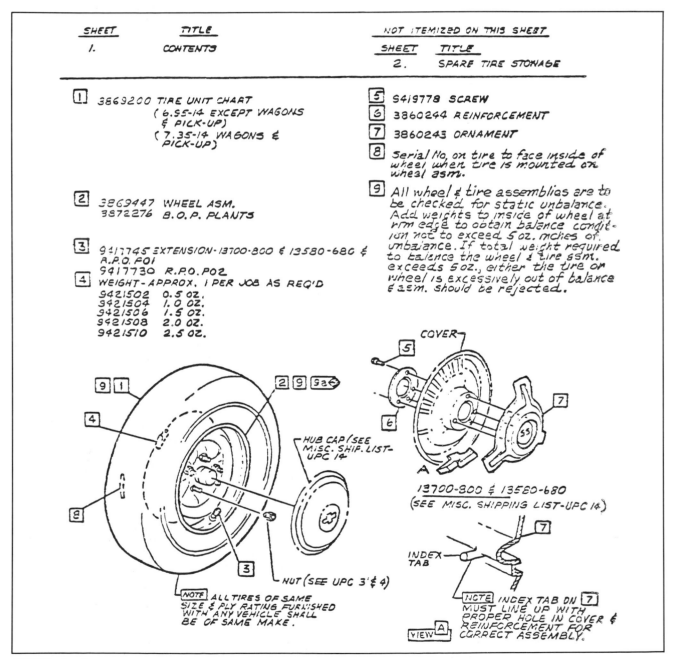

*1965 SS wheel covers.*

rectly interchangeable with earlier models. Wire spokes ran all the way to the edge of the rim, and more spokes were used. A small center cap in the middle of the basket featured a bow-tie symbol, and the name Chevrolet Motor Division in capital letters was cast into it.

Hubcap part number 3916432 was standard in 1968 and was similar to that used the year before. Full wheel covers, PO1, part number 3920602, were available. The center identification cap read SS 396 in white lettering. Other Chevelle full wheel covers will interchange, but the center cap, part number 3920604, must be replaced.

The 1968 wire wheel cover was identical to the 1967 version but was now listed as RPO N95. The simulated mag wheel, N96, continued and was listed as part number 3903085; this cover was restyled in 1967 and was unchanged for 1968. Another simulated mag wheel cover, RPO PA2, part number 3918079, was also available. It featured six sections painted flat-black with chrome outlining strips and a bright center cap with the name Chevrolet Motor Division in black. Simulated lug nuts were also bright.

Tire valve extensions had to be used with the optional wheel covers.

### 1966-1968 Tire Extension Part Numbers

| | |
|---|---|
| PO1 & N95 | 9417730 |
| N96 | 9417745 |
| PA2 | 9417466 |

All of the above covers were available as dealer-installed options as well as factory options, except PA2, which was available only from the factory. The year 1968 was the last for wheel covers being available with the SS. From 1969 to 1972 styled wheels were part of the package.

## Original Tires

### 1964-1965

The standard tires were 6.5×14 tubeless blackwalls for 1964 and 6.95×14 blackwalls for 1965. Both tires were made by Firestone. The Z16 option used 7.75 Gold Stripe Firestones only.

A common option both years was whitewall tires, RPO P67, in the same size as the standard tires. The following tires were also optional.

*1965 wheel cover. Note the correct inlay of red in the lettering.*

### 1966-1967

Only two tires were used on the SS 396 in 1966. The standard tire was a 7.75×14 Red Line. Tubeless four-ply nylon whitewall tires in the same size were a no-cost option. Both of these tires were used exclusively on the SS and were not available on any other Chevelle.

Cars with the base engine used the same tires in 1967 as in 1966. With the optional engines, F70×14 four-ply Red Line tires were standard. Whitewall tires, of the same size, RPO PW7, were optional. The F70 tires were not available with the 325 hp engine.

### 1968-1969

The coupe and convertible both used F70×14 Red Line tires with all engines in 1968. The El

*The trunk for the redesigned '68 Chevelle Super Sport was spacious and functional. And you still got a regular spare! The color was standard grey with a mat covering the bottom of the floor. Phil Kunz/Bill Holder*

### 1964-1965 Optional Original Tire Sizes

| RPO | 1964 | Description | 1965 |
|---|---|---|---|
| P57 | 7×14 | 4 ply rayon blackwall | 7.35×14 |
| P58 | 7×14 | 4 ply rayon whitewall | 7.35×14 |
| P60 | 7.5×14 | 4 ply nylon blackwall | 7.75×14 |
| P61 | 7.5×14 | 4 ply nylon whitewall | 7.75×14 |
| P62 | 7.5×14 | 4 ply rayon whitewall | 7.75×14 |
| P63 | 7.5×14 | 6 ply rayon blackwall | NA |
| P65 | 7.5×14 | 4 ply rayon blackwall | 7.75×14 |
| T14 | NA | 8 ply rayon blackwall | 7.75×14 |

Camino used slightly wider G70×14 tires. Both tires were also available with whitewalls.

White-letter tires were standard in 1969, and Sizes were the same as in 1968. Whitewall and red-stripe tires in the same sizes were optional. Many different brands of tires were used, the most common being Goodyear, Goodrich, Firestone and Uniroyal.

**1970-1972**

Either Goodyear Polyglas or Firestone Wide Oval tires were standard in 1970. Both tires were F70×14 ply. The El Camino used G70×14 white-letter tires.

The standard tires for 1971 and 1972 were Firestone Wide 60 Ovals and Goodyear Polyglas GTs. Both tires were F70×15 except on the El Camino, which used G60×15s. These are the most commonly seen tires, but other brands were occasionally used.

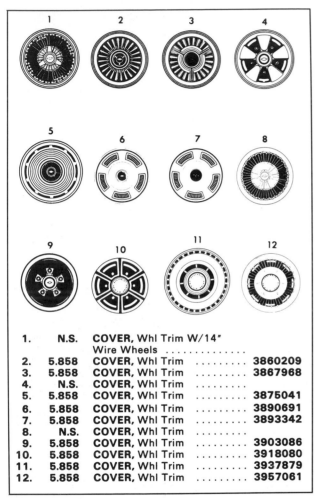

| | | | |
|---|---|---|---|
| 1. | N.S. | COVER, Whl Trim W/14" Wire Wheels ............. | |
| 2. | 5.858 | COVER, Whl Trim ........ | 3860209 |
| 3. | 5.858 | COVER, Whl Trim ........ | 3867968 |
| 4. | N.S. | COVER, Whl Trim | |
| 5. | 5.858 | COVER, Whl Trim ........ | 3875041 |
| 6. | 5.858 | COVER, Whl Trim ........ | 3890691 |
| 7. | 5.858 | COVER, Whl Trim ........ | 3893342 |
| 8. | N.S. | COVER, Whl Trim ........ | |
| 9. | 5.858 | COVER, Whl Trim ........ | 3903086 |
| 10. | 5.858 | COVER, Whl Trim ........ | 3918080 |
| 11. | 5.858 | COVER, Whl Trim ........ | 3937879 |
| 12. | 5.858 | COVER, Whl Trim ........ | 3957061 |

*Available wheel covers. Number 3 was the standard 1965 cover, yet the insert is incorrect. Number 4 was N96 in 1966. Number 5 was the standard wheel cover for late 1966 models. Number 7 was the full wheel cover option in 1967. Number 9 was N96 in 1967 and 1968. Number 8 was the wire wheel cover in 1967 and 1968. Number 10 was listed as option PA2 in 1968.*

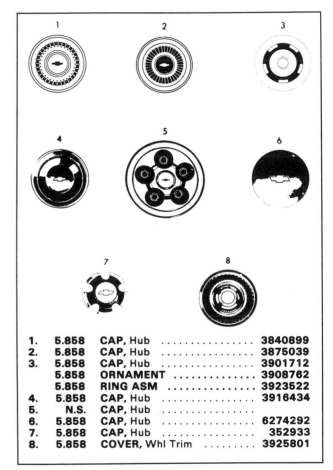

| | | | |
|---|---|---|---|
| 1. | 5.858 | CAP, Hub ................ | 3840899 |
| 2. | 5.858 | CAP, Hub ................ | 3875039 |
| 3. | 5.858 | CAP, Hub ................ | 3901712 |
| | 5.858 | ORNAMENT ............. | 3908762 |
| | 5.858 | RING ASM .............. | 3923522 |
| 4. | 5.858 | CAP, Hub ................ | 3916434 |
| 5. | N.S. | CAP, Hub ................ | |
| 6. | 5.858 | CAP, Hub ................ | 6274292 |
| 7. | 5.858 | CAP, Hub ................ | 352933 |
| 8. | 5.858 | COVER, Whl Trim ........ | 3925801 |

*Standard hub caps included number 2 for early 1966 models, number 1 in 1967 and number 4 in 1968. Options were the 1967 rally center cap, number 3, and the 1968 rally wheel center cap, number 8. Number 7 was the standard wheel cap on the Heavy Chevy models.*

# Chapter 6

# Brakes

## Drum Brakes

### 1964-1965

A single-reservoir master cylinder—part number 5465094, 5463779 after May 8, 1968—with a 1 in. diameter piston was used in both 1964 and 1965. When power brakes, RPO J50, were ordered, mas-ter cylinder part number 5464900 was used. A vacuum chamber was also included with this option. Both master cylinders were built by Delco Moraine. However, cylinders manufactured by Bendix were optional. The standard cylinder was listed as part number 3845275, and the power unit as part number 3843669.

The master cylinders should be painted 60 degree gloss-black, the lid should be gold cadmium and the bail should be natural metal in appearance. The vacuum chamber should also have a gold cadmium finish.

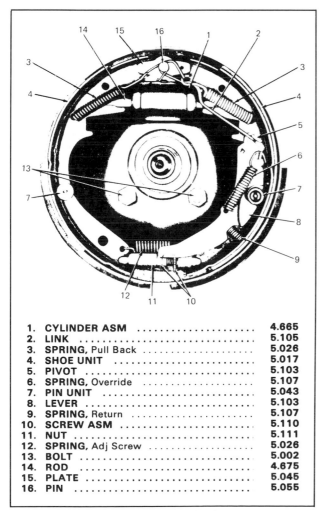

| 1. CYLINDER ASM | 4.665 |
| 2. LINK | 5.105 |
| 3. SPRING, Pull Back | 5.026 |
| 4. SHOE UNIT | 5.017 |
| 5. PIVOT | 5.103 |
| 6. SPRING, Override | 5.107 |
| 7. PIN UNIT | 5.043 |
| 8. LEVER | 5.103 |
| 9. SPRING, Return | 5.107 |
| 10. SCREW ASM | 5.110 |
| 11. NUT | 5.111 |
| 12. SPRING, Adj Screw | 5.026 |
| 13. BOLT | 5.002 |
| 14. ROD | 4.675 |
| 15. PLATE | 5.045 |
| 16. PIN | 5.055 |

*Detail view of self-adjusting drum brakes.*

*A single-reservoir master cylinder was standard in 1964-67.*

A black rubber hose, part number 3711021, was routed from the vacuum chamber to a T-fitting, part number 3868857, in the rear of the intake manifold. The hose was supported by a clip, part number 3843300, that attached to the left-hand spark plug wire retainer.

When air conditioning or automatic transmission was ordered, fitting part number 3868858 was used. And when both air conditioning and automatic transmission were selected, fitting part number 3868859 with three provisions was used. These parts were identical in 1964 and 1965.

The drums were nonfinned and 9.5 in. in diameter except with the 1965 Z16 package, which used Impala 11 in. diameter drums. Replacement part numbers for the Z16 are 3872326 front and 3985944 rear. Drums from 1965-68 Impalas will work. They should be painted dark cast-iron-gray for the original look or gloss-black for detail.

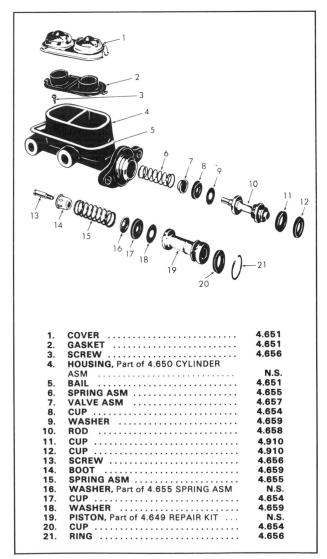

| | | |
|---|---|---|
| 1. | COVER | 4.651 |
| 2. | GASKET | 4.651 |
| 3. | SCREW | 4.656 |
| 4. | HOUSING, Part of 4.650 CYLINDER ASM | N.S. |
| 5. | BAIL | 4.651 |
| 6. | SPRING ASM | 4.655 |
| 7. | VALVE ASM | 4.657 |
| 8. | CUP | 4.654 |
| 9. | WASHER | 4.659 |
| 10. | ROD | 4.658 |
| 11. | CUP | 4.910 |
| 12. | CUP | 4.910 |
| 13. | SCREW | 4.656 |
| 14. | BOOT | 4.659 |
| 15. | SPRING ASM | 4.655 |
| 16. | WASHER, Part of 4.655 SPRING ASM | N.S. |
| 17. | CUP | 4.654 |
| 18. | WASHER | 4.659 |
| 19. | PISTON, Part of 4.649 REPAIR KIT | N.S. |
| 20. | CUP | 4.654 |
| 21. | RING | 4.656 |

*1967-72 dual-reservoir master cylinder.*

## 1966-1968

The master cylinder for the 1966 SS 396 was identical to that in 1965. The vacuum chamber was also the same. The vacuum hose was listed as part number 3874295; it was held with a support, part number 3876944, at the rear of the engine. A white check valve was used in the vacuum chamber.

Owing to federally mandated safety regulations, a dual-reservoir master cylinder, part number 5452475, was standard in the 1967 Chevelle. Only the Delco Moraine unit was available.

The power brake booster chamber was also changed in 1967. Either a Delco Moraine built chamber, part number 5460709, or a Bendix-built chamber, part number 3908757, was used. The Bendix was slightly larger in diameter. These part numbers were also used with the original master cylinder.

A hose, part number 3715073, was routed to a natural metal pipe assembly, part number 3909606, which connected to a natural brass fitting (see Drum Brakes, 1964-1965, for part numbers). The pipe was supported with a clamp that mounted to the rear left-hand carburetor bolt. The original clamp was part of the pipe assembly.

The brake drums were identical in 1966 and 1967 and were the same as in previous years, measuring 9.5 in. in diameter. The master cylinder, lid, bail, vacuum chamber and drums should be finished according to the directions in 1964 and 1965.

The master cylinder used in 1968 was identical to the one used in 1967. The SS 396 with power brakes employed a special vacuum chamber: the Delco unit was listed as part number 5468981, and the Bendix unit as part number 3934077. Care must be taken that the correct chamber is installed, as those used on other Chevelles will not interchange.

The vacuum hose was now listed as part number 3928216 and was routed the same as in 1967. Two pipe assemblies were available: the L78 engine used part number 3921929, and the other engines used part number 3921927.

Brake drums still measured 9.5 in. in diameter but were now finned for better cooling. All 1968 Chevelles were supposed to be equipped with these drums, but a few early models at some plants came off the assembly line with the 1967 drums.

Drums should be finished in dark cast-iron-gray, for the original look. Master cylinders should be painted gloss-black. The cover and vacuum chambers should be gold cadmium.

## Disc Brakes

### 1967-1968

A special dual-bail master cylinder, part number 5435800, was installed in 1967. Vacuum assistance was required with all disc brake applications, so a gold cadmium vacuum chamber was used. Also, a special metering valve, part number 3905525, was used to balance pressure between the wheels. It was attached to a bracket, part number 3912539, with a single ⁵⁄₁₆-18×½ bolt. The bracket was mounted to the base of the master cylinder using existing hardware. The valve and bracket should be painted gloss-black. The master cylinder should be painted the same as the production unit.

Production junction block part number 3921043 was used with disc brakes. Front brake line part number 3922503 was routed from the rear of the side of the metering valve to the top forward port of the junction block. Production lines were also used at the front wheels, but a high-pressure hose, part number 3904943, was used between the line and the caliper.

Rotors were 11 in. in diameter. Bendix calipers used four 2.167 in. diameter pistons each. Most

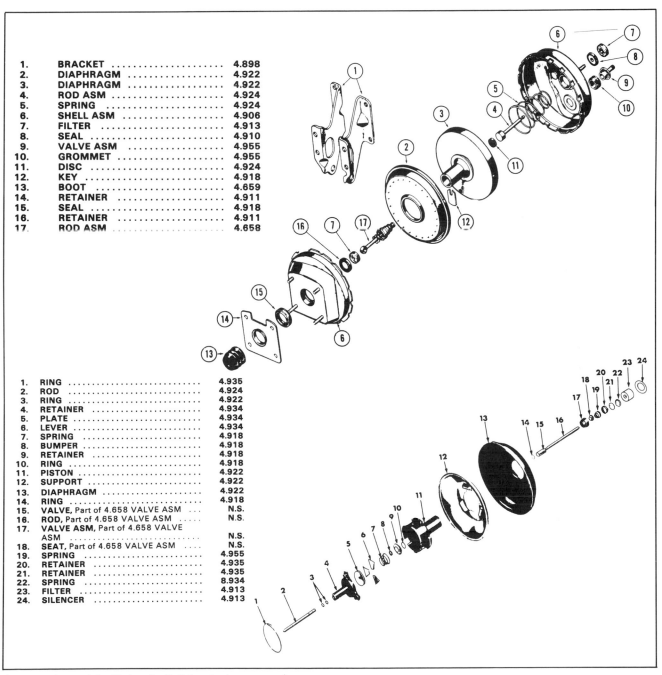

| 1.  | BRACKET   | 4.898 |
| 2.  | DIAPHRAGM | 4.922 |
| 3.  | DIAPHRAGM | 4.922 |
| 4.  | ROD ASM   | 4.924 |
| 5.  | SPRING    | 4.924 |
| 6.  | SHELL ASM | 4.906 |
| 7.  | FILTER    | 4.913 |
| 8.  | SEAL      | 4.910 |
| 9.  | VALVE ASM | 4.955 |
| 10. | GROMMET   | 4.955 |
| 11. | DISC      | 4.924 |
| 12. | KEY       | 4.918 |
| 13. | BOOT      | 4.659 |
| 14. | RETAINER  | 4.911 |
| 15. | SEAL      | 4.918 |
| 16. | RETAINER  | 4.911 |
| 17. | ROD ASM   | 4.658 |

| 1.  | RING                                | 4.935 |
| 2.  | ROD                                 | 4.924 |
| 3.  | RING                                | 4.922 |
| 4.  | RETAINER                            | 4.934 |
| 5.  | PLATE                               | 4.934 |
| 6.  | LEVER                               | 4.934 |
| 7.  | SPRING                              | 4.918 |
| 8.  | BUMPER                              | 4.918 |
| 9.  | RETAINER                            | 4.918 |
| 10. | RING                                | 4.918 |
| 11. | PISTON                              | 4.922 |
| 12. | SUPPORT                             | 4.922 |
| 13. | DIAPHRAGM                           | 4.922 |
| 14. | RING                                | 4.918 |
| 15. | VALVE, Part of 4.658 VALVE ASM      | N.S.  |
| 16. | ROD, Part of 4.658 VALVE ASM        | N.S.  |
| 17. | VALVE ASM, Part of 4.658 VALVE ASM  | N.S.  |
| 18. | SEAT, Part of 4.658 VALVE ASM       | N.S.  |
| 19. | SPRING                              | 4.955 |
| 20. | RETAINER                            | 4.935 |
| 21. | RETAINER                            | 4.935 |
| 22. | SPRING                              | 8.934 |
| 23. | FILTER                              | 4.913 |
| 24. | SILENCER                            | 4.913 |

*A comparison of the Delco-built (Moraine) vacuum chamber and the Bendix unit.*

*Twin-bail master cylinder on a 1967 Chevelle. Note that the data plate in the background should be painted flat-black.*

replacement calipers use the single-piston design, but this would be an incorrect application. Original brake pads were made out of asbestos, but this material is being replaced for health reasons. Substitutions would therefore be accepted, but be sure the replacements, no matter what the lining is, are riveted like the originals and not bonded. The caliper housing should have a natural cast-iron finish.

Note that the pipe, part numbers 1382794-LH and 1382795-RH, that connected the brake hose to the caliper had two different sized ends. The larger ½-20 thread nut attached to the caliper, and the 7/16-24 thread end routed to the hose. Always use a back-up wrench on the hose fitting to prevent distortion of the support bracket, part numbers

131724-LH and 1381725-RH, when installing the caliper line.

The disc brake system for 1968 was nearly identical to that used for 1967. Master cylinder part number 5463779 and the metering valve were the same. The front brake line was rerouted and used hose part number 3923311. The four-cylinder caliper remained unchanged.

### 1969-1972

Power front disc brakes were part of the SS 396 package in 1969. The master cylinder was built by Delco and was listed as part number 5468168. The cylinder assembly should be painted gloss-black, the cover should be gold cadmium and the twin retainers should be natural metal.

The metering valve and bracket were the same parts as in 1968. The front brake line was listed as part number 3923311 and should be routed behind the booster chamber, which should be plated with gold cadmium.

Vacuum hose part number 3715073 was routed from the white check valve in the chamber to a pipe assembly—part number 3921927, except 3921929 with the L78 and COPO engines—that was attached to a fitting in the intake manifold. A bracket that attached to the carburetor stud supported the pipe assembly. Three different fittings were used.

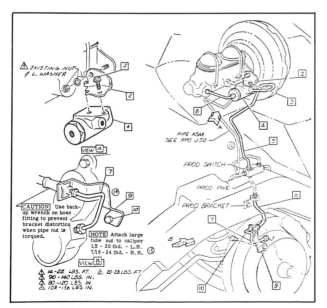

*1967 disc brakes.*

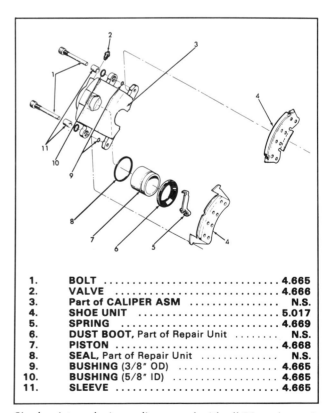

| 1. | BOLT | 4.665 |
|----|------|-------|
| 2. | VALVE | 4.666 |
| 3. | Part of CALIPER ASM | N.S. |
| 4. | SHOE UNIT | 5.017 |
| 5. | SPRING | 4.669 |
| 6. | DUST BOOT, Part of Repair Unit | N.S. |
| 7. | PISTON | 4.668 |
| 8. | SEAL, Part of Repair Unit | N.S. |
| 9. | BUSHING (3/8" OD) | 4.665 |
| 10. | BUSHING (5/8" ID) | 4.665 |
| 11. | SLEEVE | 4.665 |

*Single-piston-design caliper used with all SS packages in 1969-72.*

## 1969 Disc Brake Fitting Part Numbers

| | |
|---|---|
| Brakes only | 3905370 |
| Brakes & automatic or C60 | 3905372 |
| Brakes & automatic & C60 | 3905374 |

The calipers were redesigned and used only one 2.9375 in. diameter piston. Replacement part numbers are listed as 5472161-LH and 5472162-RH and are built by Delco. High-pressure braided 11.375 in. OD brake hose, part number 1230992, was supported with a bracket, part numbers 1230991-LH and 1230990-RH, and a clip where it connected to the master cylinder line. Brake pads were still riveted together.

The master cylinder in 1970 was listed as part number 5470263, and the cover was wider and more squared. The master cylinder should have a natural cast-iron finish, the cover should be plated gold cadmium and the single bail should be natural metal.

The vacuum booster chamber was the same unit in 1970 as in 1969 with the same gold finish. Vacuum hoses were also identical.

The master cylinder was listed as part number 541659 in 1971 and 1972. The body should have a natural cast-iron finish, the cover should be gold cadmium and the bail should be natural metal. The vacuum booster chamber was listed as part number 5472704 for both years. Only the Delco unit was used. The vacuum hose was listed as part number 3733157 with all applications. Vacuum was drawn from the base of the carburetor with all engines except the LS6 unit, which as in earlier years drew air from the intake manifold.

The 400 Turbo-Jet and LS5 454 engines used pipe part number 3989307, which was routed to a fitting, part number 145476, in the base of the carburetor. This pipe also featured a support with a notch in it, which secured it to the rear of the intake manifold. For correctness the support must face toward the front of the car.

The Turbo-Fire 350s used pipe part number 3995679 with the four-barrel carburetor and pipe part number 3989024 with the two-barrel. These pipes were routed to the same fitting as above in the base of the carburetor. Both pipes were supported by the spark plug wire tower.

## Metallic Brakes

### 1964-1965

Listed as RPO J65, metallic brakes used a special Delco master cylinder with a piston diameter

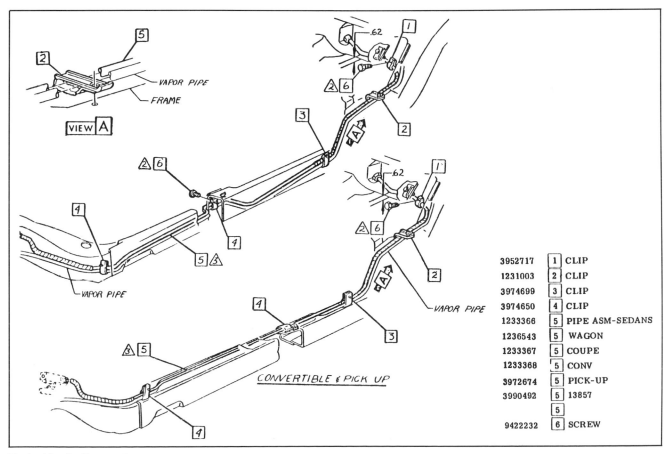

| | | |
|---|---|---|
| 3952717 | 1 | CLIP |
| 1231003 | 2 | CLIP |
| 3974699 | 3 | CLIP |
| 3974650 | 4 | CLIP |
| 1233366 | 5 | PIPE ASM-SEDANS |
| 1236543 | 5 | WAGON |
| 1233367 | 5 | COUPE |
| 1233368 | 5 | CONV |
| 3972674 | 5 | PICK-UP |
| 3990492 | 5 | 13857 |
| | 5 | |
| 9422232 | 6 | SCREW |

*Typical brake line route.*

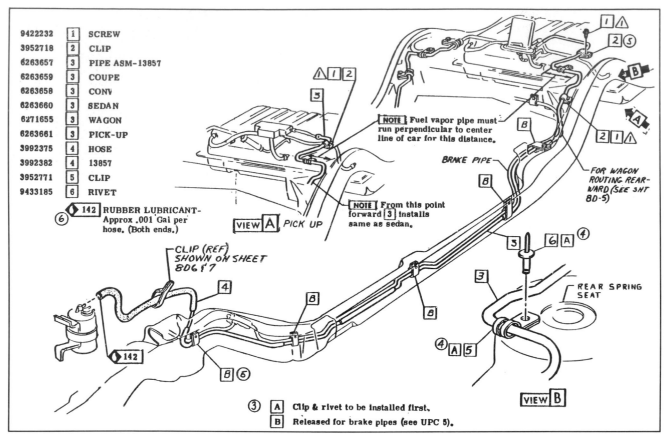

| 9422232 | 1 | SCREW |
| 3952718 | 2 | CLIP |
| 6263657 | 3 | PIPE ASM-13857 |
| 6263659 | 3 | COUPE |
| 6263658 | 3 | CONV |
| 6263660 | 3 | SEDAN |
| 6271655 | 3 | WAGON |
| 6263661 | 3 | PICK-UP |
| 3992375 | 4 | HOSE |
| 3992382 | 4 | 13857 |
| 3952771 | 5 | CLIP |
| 9433185 | 6 | RIVET |
| 6 | ◆142 | RUBBER LUBRICANT—Approx .001 Gal per hose. (Both ends.) |

NOTE Fuel vapor pipe must run perpendicular to center line of car for this distance.

BRAKE PIPE

FOR WAGON ROUTING REARWARD (SEE SHT 8D-5)

NOTE From this point forward 3 installs same as sedan.

VIEW A PICK UP

CLIP (REF) SHOWN ON SHEET 8D6 & 7

REAR SPRING SEAT

3 | A | Clip & rivet to be installed first.
   | B | Released for brake pipes (see UPC 5).

VIEW B

In 1971-72 and on all 1970 California cars, the brake line was routed along with the EEC hose.

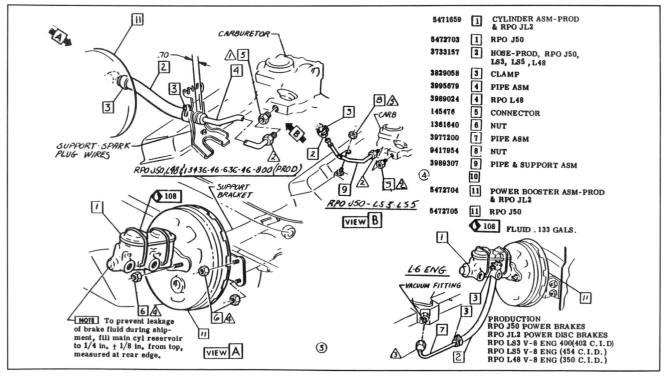

CARBURETOR

SUPPORT-SPARK PLUG WIRES

RPO J50,L48 &13436-46-636-46-800 (PROD)

SUPPORT BRACKET

RPO J50-LS3-LS5

VIEW B

| 5471659 | 1 | CYLINDER ASM-PROD & RPO JL2 |
| 5472703 | 1 | RPO J50 |
| 3733157 | 2 | HOSE-PROD, RPO J50, LS3, LS5, L48 |
| 3829058 | 3 | CLAMP |
| 3995679 | 4 | PIPE ASM |
| 3989024 | 4 | RPO L48 |
| 145476 | 5 | CONNECTOR |
| 1361640 | 6 | NUT |
| 3977200 | 7 | PIPE ASM |
| 9417954 | 8 | NUT |
| 3989307 | 9 | PIPE & SUPPORT ASM |
|  | 10 | |
| 5472704 | 11 | POWER BOOSTER ASM-PROD & RPO JL2 |
| 5472705 | 11 | RPO J50 |
| ◆108 | | FLUID .133 GALS. |

NOTE To prevent leakage of brake fluid during shipment, fill main cyl reservoir to 1/4 in. ± 1/8 in. from top, measured at rear edge.

VIEW A

L-6 ENG
VACUUM FITTING

PRODUCTION
RPO J50 POWER BRAKES
RPO JL2 POWER DISC BRAKES
RPO LS3 V-8 ENG 400(402 C.I.D)
RPO LS5 V-8 ENG (454 C.I.D.)
RPO L48 V-8 ENG (350 C.I.D.)

Note the different vacuum hose routes in 1972.

of 0.875 in. This option was available with both the standard axle and Positraction, G80, axle. Power brakes were also available with the metallic linings.

The front and rear brake shoes each had six primary and ten secondary segments. Original segments were welded to the shoes; most replacements are bonded, and this would be incorrect.

### 1966-1968

The metallic brakes used in 1966 were identical to the 1964-65 components. In 1967 a dual master cylinder was used. Metallic brakes were available with or without the Positraction axle and with all gear ratios. Power assist, J50, was also available both years.

Shoes were restyled for 1967. The segments were wider and thicker than before. Also, only three primary and five secondary segments were provided for each front and rear shoe. Again the segments were welded into place and not bonded.

Brake drums were originally left their natural color. The drums for metallic brakes were identified by a white dash of paint.

It is uncertain whether or not any 1968 SS 396s were built with metallic brakes. The option was canceled in December 1967, and most SS buyers opted for the disc brakes, as they stopped better and were less noisy. If any metallic brake cars were built they would have used the same parts as in 1967.

*Various pedals were used in the Chevelle. Clockwise from upper left are the: 1966 parking brake cover; brake pedal cover for models with automatic transmission and power brakes; accelerator pedal for 1964-67; accelerator pedal for 1968-72; and the pedal used both for models with standard brakes and for the clutch.*

## Brake Pedals

### 1964-1965

Two different brake pedals were used in 1964: part number 3843931 with manual transmissions

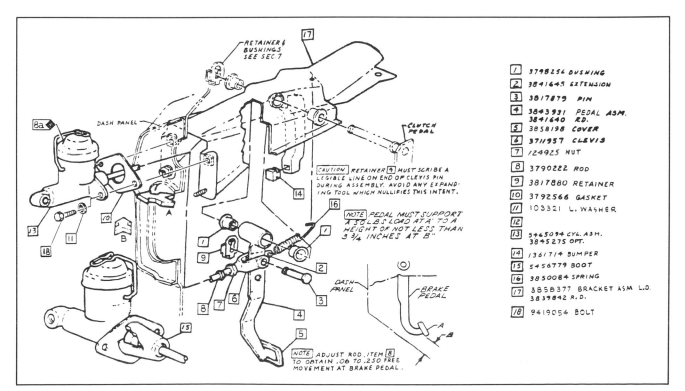

*The brake pedal was identical from 1964 to 1967. The 1964 standard pedal is shown.*

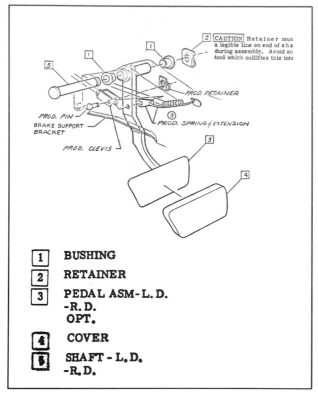

| | |
|---|---|
| **1** | BUSHING |
| **2** | RETAINER |
| **3** | PEDAL ASM-L. D. |
| | -R. D. |
| | OPT. |
| **4** | COVER |
| **5** | SHAFT - L.D. |
| | -R. D. |

*A wider pedal was used with automatic transmissions.*

and part number 3843935 with the Powerglide. These same pedals were used again unchanged in 1965.

Both pedal assemblies should be painted 60 degree gloss-black. The paint part numbers are Ditzler DL-9248, Rinshed Mason 400 and DuPont 88L. The DuPont product is acrylic lacquer; the others are standard lacquer, which was the original paint. Covers were listed as part numbers 3858198 for the manual pedal and 3858199 with

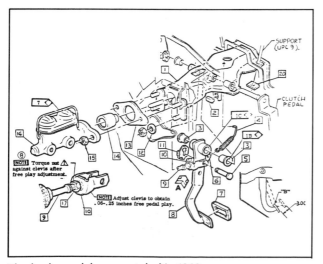

*The brake pedal was restyled in 1968.*

the automatic. No chrome trim was used on either cover.

### 1966-1967

The manual pedal assembly was the same in both 1966 and 1967 and was identical to the part used in 1964-65. The pedal assembly used with the automatic transmission was listed as part number 3900525 for both 1966 and 1967.

Covers for nondisc brakes were identical to those installed in 1964-65 and used the same part numbers. Again no trim plates were used. Disc-brake-optioned cars used the same pedal with a different cover, part numbers 3934000 with manual transmission and 3934002 with both automatics. Both covers featured a chrome circle trim in the center with the words *disc brakes* cast into it.

### 1968-1972

The brake pedal was redesigned in 1968 and will not interchange with earlier models. Part number 3934055 was used until the second week of March 1968 when part number 3937889 took its place. The pedal used with an automatic transmission was also redesigned and was listed as part number 3937893 all year.

Manual-equipped cars used pedal assembly part number 3937889, and cars with the Turbo Hydra-matic used part number 3937893 in 1969. No further changes were made, and these pedals were used on all 1970-72 Chevelles. Only the disc brake covers were used; part numbers were the same as in earlier years.

Note that the pedal assembly should be painted 30 degree gloss-black instead of 60 degree gloss-black as in the years before. The correct paint part numbers for the 1968-72 cars are Ditzler 9387, Rinshed Mason 170B40 and DuPont 99L. No 60 degree gloss finish was used in the interior past 1968.

The same brake return spring, part number 3850084, and bushings, part number 3798256, were used all nine years, from 1964 to 1972, with all pedal assemblies. Mounting was also the same. When nonpower drum brakes were used, the brake pin, part numbers 3817879 from 1964 to 1967 and 1379621 from 1968 to 1972, was installed in the upper hole. If power brakes or disc brakes were ordered, the pin was installed through the lower hole in the pedal arm.

## Parking Brake

### 1964-1965

A ratchet type of parking brake assembly, part numbers 3846501 in 1964 and 3071191 in 1965, was used both years and was mounted under the instrument panel on the left-hand side. A black ribbed cover, part number 1363585, was imprinted with the word *park* in white letters.

The brake was released by a black plastic T-handle with the words *brake release* in white letters on it. The 1964 handle used smaller letters than the 1965 version. A few 1965s used the 1964 handle and lever. The lever assembly should be painted gloss-black (see the 1964-65 brake pedals section earlier in this chapter for paint part numbers).

To correctly install the parking brake it must be in the 2 in. applied position. The front cable, 44.5 in. overall length, part number 3847980, and equalizer, part number 6256437, should be positioned approximately 3.7 in. from the transmission extension seal housing. Next the inside nut is tightened so that the cable tension measures 80 lb at a point 2.5 in. in front of the transmission crossmember. Then the inside nut is held in place while the outside nut is tightened to 80-120 lb-in. of torque. (This information was taken from the 1964 assembly manual.)

The center cable was 100 in. in length and used part number 3854125 both years. The guides were listed as part number 1361845. A connector, part number 537485, and a retainer, part number 518213, attached the center cable to the rear cable.

### 1966-1967

The Chevelle used the same parking brake in 1966 as in 1965. All other parts were also the same, but the installation procedure was revised and the cable tension should be only 35 lb. The locking nut

torque was also revised to 35-45 lb-in. No brake warning lamp was available.

The lever assembly was listed as part number 3908775 in 1967, although it was the same as the 1966 unit and installed the same way with the same cables. However, with the introduction of the Turbo Hydra-matic 400 transmission a shorter center cable and a longer front cable had to be used.

A brake warning lamp, part number 9417863, was added into the instrument panel as standard equipment for all 1967 Chevelles. Late-model 1966s may have used this warning lamp.

### 1968-1969

The lever assembly was redesigned in 1968 and was listed as part number 3949154. The pedal cover, part number 1370792, was like that in 1967 and resembled the brake and clutch covers; it was plain with no trim and without the word *park* embossed into it. The lever assembly should be painted 30 degree gloss-black.

The front cable was the same, part number 3925045, with all transmissions. The center cable was dependent on the body style and type of transmission ordered.

### 1968-1969 Parking Brake Center Cable Part Numbers

Coupe & convertible

| | |
|---|---|
| Manual | 3934839 |
| Powerglide | 3925051 |
| Turbo Hydra-matic | 3925055 |

Pickup (El Camino)

| | |
|---|---|
| Manual | 3934838 |
| Powerglide | 3925049 |
| Turbo Hydra-matic | 3925053 |

No changes were made in 1969.

*Standard parking brake cover for 1964-67.*

*Correct 1967-72 parking brake cover. Note that no trim was used.*

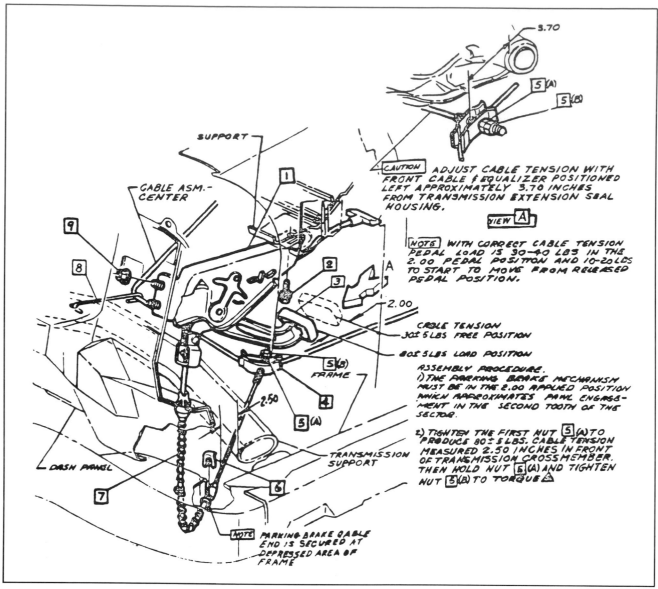

*Parking brake assembly.*

## 1970-1972

The lever assembly was listed as part number 3960783 from 1970 to 1972. The cover was identical to that in 1968-69 and used no trim plate. The lever assembly should be painted 30 degree gloss-black. The release rod, part number 3960791, should have a natural metal appearance; it was attached to the parking lever by a clip, part number 3890698. The T-handle, part number 3960789, was black plastic with the words *brake release* inlaid in white.

Front cable part number 3987896 was installed in all cars except those with the automatic transmission, which used part number 3925057. The center cables were dependent on the body style and type of transmission used.

## 1970-1972 Parking Brake Center Cable Part Numbers

| | |
|---|---|
| Coupe & convertible | |
|   Manual | 3934839 |
|   Turbo Hydra-matic 400 automatic | |
|     only | 3925055 |
|   Turbo Hydra-matic 350 automatic, | |
|     & standard three-speed manual | |
|     w/350 ci | 3925051 |
| Pickup (El Camino) | |
|   Manual | 3934838 |
|   Turbo Hydra-matic 400 only | 3925053 |
|   Turbo Hydra-matic 350, | |
|     & standard three-speed manual | |
|     w/350 ci | 3925049 |

# Chapter 7

# Sheet Metal and Exterior Trim

## Exterior Color

### 1964-1972

The color of the original paint was coded on the data plate. Lacquer finish was used all nine years, from 1964 to 1972.

## Hoods

### 1964-1965

No special hood was used on the Malibu SS in either 1964 or 1965, but each hood was different and will not interchange. The standard Chevelle hood, part number 3854195, was used in 1964. All Chevelle hoods will interchange. The El Camino hood will need to have holes drilled in it for the center crown molding.

The 1965 hood, part number 3860112, was the standard Malibu hood. The 300 series hood will not interchange, as the predrilled holes will not line up with the Malibu moldings.

Both hoods were trimmed with a chrome crown molding, a front header molding and the name Chevrolet spelled out in block letters.

## 1964 Exterior Colors

| RPO/Code | Color Name | Ditzler | Rinshed-Mason | DuPont |
|---|---|---|---|---|
| 900 | Tuxedo Black | DDL-9300 | A-946 | 88-L |
| 905 | Meadow Green | DDL-43264 | A-1613 | 4532-L |
| 908 | Bahama Green | DDL-43263 | A-1614 | 4534-L |
| 912 | Silver Blue | DDL-12546 | A-1481 | 4250-L |
| 916 | Daytona Blue | DDL-12696 | A-1539 | 4395-L |
| 918 | Azure Aqua | DDL-12525 | A-1476 | 4253-L |
| 919 | Lagoon Aqua | DDL-12848 | A-1611 | 4529-L |
| 920 | Almond Fawn | DDL-22392 | A-1610 | 4527-L |
| 922 | Ember Red | DDL-71336 | A-1538 | 4387-L |
| 932 | Saddle Tan | DDL-22269 | A-1537 | 4392-L |
| 936 | Ermine White | DDL-8259 | A-1199 | 4024-L |
| 938 | Desert Beige | DDL-22391 | A-1609 | 4526-L |
| 940 | Satin Silver | DDL-32173 | A-1477 | 4247-L |
| 943 | Goldwood Yellow | DDL-81450 | A-1612 | 4530-L |
| 948 | Palomar Red | DDL-50633 | A-1536 | 4389-L |

### Two-Tone Combinations

| | |
|---|---|
| 952 | 908/905 |
| 954 | 936/905 |
| 959 | 936/912 |
| 960 | 916/912 |
| 965 | 936/919 |
| 971 | 938/932 |
| 975 | 938/922 |
| 982 | 916/940 |
| 988 | 918/936 |
| 993 | 938/948 |
| 995 | 940/948 |

For color names and paint codes, see above chart.

## 1965 Exterior Colors

| RPO/Code | Color Name | Ditzler | Rinshed-Mason | DuPont |
|---|---|---|---|---|
| AA | Tuxedo Black | DDL-9300 | A-946 | 88 |
| CC | Ermine White | DDL-8259 | A-1199 | 4024-L |
| DD | Mist Blue | DDL-13042 | A-1720 | 4630-L |
| EE | Danube Blue | DDL-13002 | A-1721 | 4631-L |
| HH | Willow Green | DDL-43391 | A-1716 | 4633-L |
| JJ | Cypress Green | DDL-43390 | A-1717 | 4634-L |
| KK | Artesian Turquoise | DDL-43364 | A-1718 | 4628-L |
| LL | Tahitian Turquoise | DDL-13003 | A-1719 | 4629-L |
| NN | Madeira Maroon | DDL-50700 | A-1711 | 4624-L |
| PP | Evening Orchid | DDL-50693 | A-1722 | 4632-L |
| RR | Regal Red | DDL-71472 | A-1712 | 4625-L |
| SS | Sierra Tan | DDL-22553 | A-1713 | 4626-L |
| VV | Cameo Beige | DDL-22270 | A-1530 | 4401-L |
| WW | Glacier Gray | DDL-32461 | A-1710 | 4623-L |
| YY | Crocus Yellow | DDL-81500 | A-1715 | 4620-L |

Two-tone code is a combination of the above codes. Example: WA would be Glacier Gray with Tuxedo Black upper section.

## 1966 Exterior Colors

| RPO/Code | Color Name | Ditzler | Rinshed-Mason | DuPont |
|---|---|---|---|---|
| AA | Tuxedo Black | DDL-9300 | A-946 | 88 |
| CC | Ermine White | DDL-8259 | A-1199 | 4024-L |
| DD | Mist Blue | DDL-13042 | A-1720 | 4630-L |
| EE | Danube Blue | DDL-13002 | A-1721 | 4631-L |
| FF | Marina Blue | | | 4704-L |
| HH | Willow Green | DDL-43391 | A-1716 | 4633-L |
| KK | Artesian Turquoise | DDL-43364 | A-1718 | 4628-L |
| LL | Tahitian Turquoise | DDL-13003 | A-1719 | 4629-L |
| MM | Aztec Bronze | | | 4707 LM |
| NN | Madeira Maroon | DDL-50700 | A-1711 | 4624-L |
| RR | Regal Red | DDL-71472 | A-1712 | 4625-L |
| TT | Sandalwood Tan | | | 4625-LH |
| VV | Cameo Beige | DDL-22270 | A-1530 | 4401-L |
| WW | Chateau Slate | DDL-32461 | A-1710 | 4623-L |
| YY | Lemonwood Yellow | DDL-81500 | A-1715 | 4620-L |

Two-tone code is a combination of the above codes.

## 1967 Exterior Colors

| RPO/Code | Color Name | Ditzler | Rinshed-Mason | DuPont |
|---|---|---|---|---|
| AA | Tuxedo Black | 9300 | A-946 | 88 |
| CC | Ermine White | 8259 | A-1199 | 4024-L |
| DD | Nantucket Blue | 13349 | A-1899 | 4815-L |
| EE | Deepwater Blue | 13346 | A-1900 | 4817-L |
| FF | Marina Blue | 13364 | A-1920 | 4850-L |
| GG | Granada Gold | 22818 | A-1919 | 4825-L |
| HH | Mountain Green | 43651 | A-1901 | 4816-L |
| KK | Emerald Turquoise | 43661 | A-1903 | 4818-L |
| LL | Tahoe Turquoise | 43659 | A-1904 | 4824-L |
| MM | Royal Plum | 50717 | A-1905 | 4832-L |
| NN | Madeira Maroon | 50700 | A-1711M | 4624-LH |
| RR | Bolero Red | 71583 | A-1907R | 4822-LH |
| SS | Sierra Fawn | 22813 | A-1908 | 4826-L |
| TT | Capri Cream | 81578 | A-1909 | 4819-L |
| YY | Butternut Yellow | 81500 | A-1715 | 4620-L |

Two-tone code is a combination of the above codes.

## 1968 Exterior Colors

| RPO/Code | Color Name | Ditzler | Rinshed-Mason | DuPont |
|---|---|---|---|---|
| AA | Tuxedo Black | 9300 | A-946 | 88L |
| CC | Ermine White | 8259 | A-1199 | 4024-L |
| DD | Grotto Blue | 13512 | A-1985 | 4829-L |
| EE | Fathom Blue | 13513 | A-1992 | 4899-L |
| FF | Island Teal | 13514 | A-1994 | 4901-L |
| GG | Ash Gold | 22942 | A-1988 | 4896-L |
| HH | Grecian Green | | | 4902-L |
| KK | Tripoli Turquoise | 13517 | A-1993 | 4900-L |
| LL | Teal Blue | 13516 | A-1986 | 4893-L |
| NN | Cordovan Maroon | 50775 | A-199F | 4915-LH |
| PP | Seafrost Green | 43774 | A-1989 | 4897-L |
| RR | Matador Red | 71634 | A-1997F | 4948-LH |
| TT | Palomino Ivory | 81617 | A-1987 | 4895-L |
| VV | Sequoia Green | 43773 | A-1990 | 4898-L |
| YY | Butternut Yellow | 81500 | A-1715 | 4620-L |

## 1969 Exterior Colors

| RPO/Code | Color Name | Ditzler | Rinshed-Mason | DuPont |
|---|---|---|---|---|
| 10 | Tuxedo Black | 9300 | A-946 | 88L |
| 50 | Dover White | 2058 | A-2080 | 5033-L |
| 69 | Cortez Silver | 2059 | A-2108 | 5032-L |
| 52 | Garnet Red | 2076 | A-2099R | 5009-LH |
| 67 | Burgundy Maroon | 50700 | A-2107M | 5063-LH |
| 65 | Olympic Gold | 2082 | A-2160D | 5010-L |
| 40 | Butternut Yellow | 81500 | A-1715 | 5036-L |
| 63 | Champagne | 22813 | A-2105 | 5064-L |
| 61 | Burnished Brown | 2081 | A-2104 | 5011-L |
| 59 | Frost Lime | 2080 | A-2103 | 5012-L |
| 57 | Fathom Green | 2079 | A-2102 | 5013-L |
| 55 | Azure Turquoise | 2078 | A-2101 | 5014-L |
| 53 | Glacier Blue | 2077 | A-2100 | 5015-L |
| 51 | Dusk Blue | 2075 | A-2098 | 5016-L |
| 71 | LeMans Blue | 2083 | A-2109 | 5030-L |
| *72 | Hugger Orange | 2084 | A-211R | 5021-LM |
| *76 | Daytona Yellow | 2094 | A-2119 | 5026-LM |

*-Special order only with SS396 package on Malibu line. Not available on 300 Deluxe or El Camino line.

## 1970 Exterior Colors

| RPO/Code | Color Name | Ditzler | Rinshed-Mason | DuPont |
|---|---|---|---|---|
| 19 | Tuxedo Black | 8631 | A-1802 | 5040L |
| 14 | Cortez Silver | 2059 | A-2108 | 5032L |
| 34 | Misty Turquoise | 2168 | A-2265 | 5119L |
| 10 | Classic White | 8631 | A-1802 | 5040L |
| 28 | Fathom Blue | 2166 | A-2264 | 5124L |
| 75 | Cranberry Red | 2189 | A-2278F | 5118LH |
| 25 | Astro Blue | 2165 | A-2261 | 5123L |
| 50 | Gobi Beige | 2175 | A-2270D | 5121L |
| 48 | Forest Green | 2173 | A-2269 | 5116L |
| 45 | Green Mist | 2171 | A-2268 | 5122L |
| 58 | Autumn Gold | 2179 | A-2272 | 5117L |
| 63 | Desert Sand | 2183 | A-2275 | 5125L |
| 55 | Champagne Gold | 2178 | A-2271D | 5120L |
| 78 | Black Cherry | 50700 | A-2107M | 5063LH |
| 17 | Shadow Gray | 32604 | A-1910 | 5113L |

See stripes for two tones

## 1971 Exterior Colors

| RPO/Code | Color Name | Ditzler | Rinshed-Mason | DuPont |
|---|---|---|---|---|
| 11 | Antique White | 2058 | A-2080 | 5338L |
| 13 | Nevada Silver | 2327 | A-2438 | 5276L |
| 19 | Tuxedo Black | 9300 | A-946 | 99L |
| 24 | Ascot Blue | 2328 | A-2439 | 5270L |
| 26 | Mulsanne Blue | 2213 | A-2482 | 5295L |
| 42 | Cottonwood Green | 2333 | A-2444G | 5274L |
| 43 | Lime Green | 2334 | A-2445D | 5322LH |
| 52 | Sunflower Yellow | 2338 | A-2422 | 5283LH |
| 53 | Placer Gold | 2339 | A-2449F | 5280LH |
| 61 | Sandalwood | 2181 | A-2273 | 5325L |
| 62 | Burnt Orange | 2340 | A-2451G | 5281LH |
| 67 | Classic Copper | 23215 | A-2276G | 5323LH |
| 75 | Cranberry Red | 2189 | A-2278F | 5339LH |
| 78 | Rosewood Met. | 2350 | A-2461 | 5275L |

See stripes for two tones

## 1972 Exterior Colors

| RPO/Code | Color Name | Ditzler | Rinshed-Mason | DuPont |
|---|---|---|---|---|
| 11 | Antique White | 2058 | A-2080 | 5338L |
| 14 | Pewter Silver | 2429 | A-2541 | 5426L |
| 24 | Ascot Blue | 2328 | A-2439 | 5270L |
| 26 | Mulsanne Blue | 2213 | A-2482 | 5295L |
| 36 | Spring Green | 2433 | A-2546D | 5436L |
| 43 | Gulf Green | 2435 | A-2548 | 5428L |
| 48 | Sequoia Green | 2439 | A-2552 | 5429L |
| 50 | Covert Tan | 2441 | A-2554 | 5431L |
| 54 | Placer Gold | 2339 | A-2578F | 5469L |
| 56 | Cream Yellow | 2444 | A-2558G | 5443L |
| 57 | Golden Brown | 2445 | A-2559 | 5439L |
| 63 | Mohave Gold | 2448 | A-2562D | 5434L |
| 65 | Orange Flame | 2450 | A-2564D | 5435L |
| 68 | Midnight Bronze | 2451 | A-2565 | 5430L |
| 75 | Cranberry Red | 2189 | A-2278F | 5339LH |

See stripes for two tones

### 1964-1965 Hood Molding Part Numbers

| Molding | 1964 | 1965 |
|---|---|---|
| Crown | 3837454 | 3860111 |
| Header | 3838493 | 3859710 |

Underhood insulation was included as standard equipment both years, except on the 1964 convertible. The 1964 hood used four pieces, part number 3839672, and the 1965 hood only three, part number 3862383. The undersides of all hoods should be painted 30 degree gloss-black.

### 1966-1967

Two different hoods were available in 1966. Most cars used the Malibu hood, part number 3874746; however, near the end of the production run this was replaced with part number 3896559. The later hood featured two rectangular cutouts for the nonfunctional air vents. The undersides of both hoods should be painted 30 degree gloss-black.

The fake air vents consisted of two parts: a base, part numbers 3891431-LH and 3891432-RH,

and a flat-black-accented insert, part number 3891430, which was used on either side. The base was secured to the hood with eight nuts. Cars built after October 1965 used two space washers, part number 3891488, on the outer side of the vent bases and seal part number 3891488. Before that, a 58 in. long seal, part number 3891433, was used. This came on the standard Malibu hood.

Both hoods used the same chrome header molding, part number 3874586. However, the crown molding was different for each hood. The first design used part number 3874587, and the second design used part number 3887580; they are not interchangeable.

Insulation was also different. The first-style hood used three pieces, part number 3877233, glued into place. The second-style hood used a one-piece insulator, part number 3891425, in between the vent openings.

Only one hood, part number 3897504, was used all year on the 1967 SS. Nonfunctional air

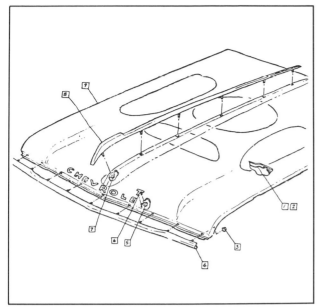

1964 Malibu hood.

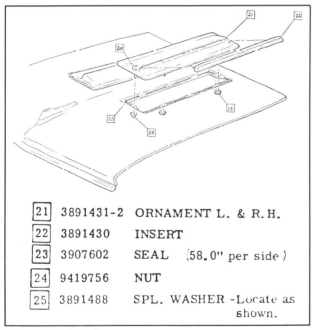

| 21 | 3891431-2 | ORNAMENT L. & R.H. |
| 22 | 3891430 | INSERT |
| 23 | 3907602 | SEAL (58.0" per side) |
| 24 | 9419756 | NUT |
| 25 | 3891488 | SPL. WASHER -Locate as shown. |

1966 SS 396 hood.

The Chevelle Super Sport design was continually changing through the years, as can be seen from this line-up. From front to rear, the model years are 1969, 1967, 1966 and 1965. Phil Kunz/Bill Holder

The Chevelle Super Sport for 1964, the first of the breed, was aimed at the youth market and was right on the money. The Super Sport equipment included the all-vinyl interior, floor console, and front bucket seats. The slab-side styling of the '64 Super Sport was extremely popular with the buying public. Phil Kunz/Bill Holder

Body changes were the name of the game for the Chevelle Super Sport during the 1960s. The line-up displayed here shows the changes from the body styles of (left to right) 1965, 1966, 1967 and 1969. Phil Kunz/Bill Holder

*Although the Z16 got a majority of the publicity for the 1965 Super Sport, most of the models were the less muscular models such as this machine carrying the smallest 327 powerplant. The model sported slightly revised sheet metal from the previous year. Phil Kunz/Bill Holder*

vents were again part of the decor. The bases were molded in as part of the hood, and the inserts, part number 3897500, were restyled and accented with flat-black paint. A special two-part seal, part numbers 3897552 for the sides and 3897550 for the ends, were also used with this hood.

The Chevelle nameplate, part number 3893924, was positioned on the left-hand corner of the hood. A header molding, part number 3887559, was secured to the front edge of the hood with nine barrel nuts.

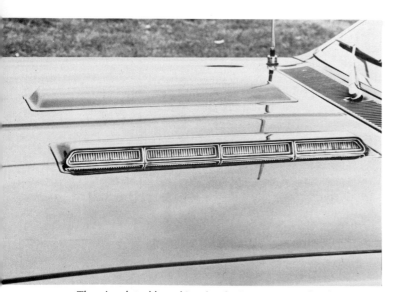

*The simulated hood intake design was new for the 1966 SS and reflected a considerable change from the 1965 model. The Super Sport coupes featured a new roof line and the classy black-out grille. There was no doubt that this was a Super Sport with the SS-cubic inch emblem on the front quarter and the Super Sport scripting on the rear fender. Phil Kunz/Bill Holder*

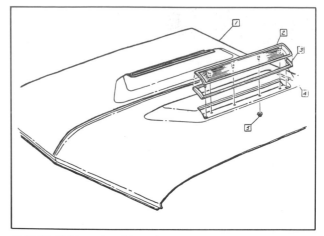

*1967 SS 396 hood and hood vents.*

Hood insulation was listed as part number 3887555. Each piece should be cemented into place using approximately 2.5 ounces of glue. The underside of the hood should be painted 30 degree gloss-black.

**1968–1969**

A special twin-dome hood was used in both 1968 and 1969. The 1968 SS 396 began production with part number 3915452. Hinges were redesigned in mid November 1968, and a different hood, part number 3940660, was used. The later hood was installed till March 1969 and was replaced with part number 3940632.

The hood grille vents, part numbers 3915489-LH and 3915490-RH, were the same for all hoods and both years and were accented with flat-black. The best way to paint the grilles is to use flat-black—DuPont 4428L, Ditzler 9317 or Rinshed Mason 168C41. Then take a lint-free cloth soaked,

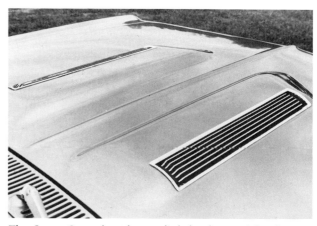

*The Super Sport hood was slightly changed for the 1967 model with the six horizontal slabs on each vent. There were also other changes made in the body design. Sales for the year totaled slightly more than 4,000 Super Sports sold for the model year. Phil Kunz/Bill Holder*

The 1969 Super Sport featured minor cleaning up from the previous year. The hood again featured the twin protrusions with the slotted vents near the front. SS identification was still carried in the grille, front quarters and on the rear. The SS hardware could also be acquired with the El Camino SS 396. Phil Kunz/Bill Holder

but not dripping, with thinner and gently wipe the paint off the outer edges. When the paint is fully dried, buff the vents with a high-quality chrome wax to revive the brilliance of the chrome. Use wax sparingly to avoid its dripping down on the painted surface, which will ruin the finish.

The hood insulator, part number 39174111, was separated into four parts and glued into the indentations under the hood. It was used both

Hood grille.

years but was not included on the 300 based car. The portion of the cowl visible under the hood from the passenger compartment should be painted 30 degree gloss-black, as should the underside of the hood.

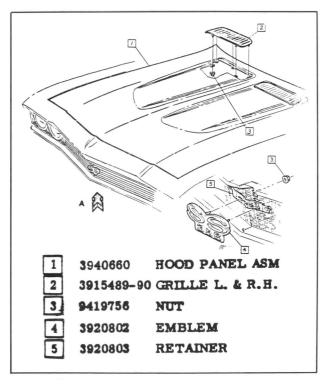

| 1 | 3940660 | HOOD PANEL ASM |
| 2 | 3915489-90 | GRILLE L. & R.H. |
| 3 | 9419756 | NUT |
| 4 | 3920802 | EMBLEM |
| 5 | 3920803 | RETAINER |

1968-69 SS 396 hood.

The RPO ZL2 was one of the extremely popular options that could be ordered with a '70 Super Sport. The device was functional, being vacuum operated, and it opened the flap when the accelerator was punched to the floor. There was a solid connection between the hood and top of the air cleaner assuring that cool air was provided to the carburetor. Phil Kunz/Bill Holder

## 1970-1972

A center domed hood was used from 1970 to 1972 as standard equipment with all SS packages. The 1970 hood was listed as part number 3965949, 3987022 after build date 03D 1970. Neither hood had provisions for the hold-down pins.

The standard hood for 1971 and 1972 was listed as part number 3996936. This hood differed from the 1970 standard hood, as it featured provisions for the hold-down pins, which were now standard equipment. For this reason a 1971 or 1972 hood will not interchange on a 1970 SS without cowl induction, as hood hold-down pins were not available on non-cowl-induction hoods in 1970.

Two 0.625 in. diameter holes must be drilled into the top of the radiator support wall to accommodate the pins, part number 3975338, which were secured in place with two ½ in. nut and washer combinations. Two chrome discs, part number 3975340, and rubber gaskets, part number 3975339, were used on the hood and attached with four ⅝ in. number 10 Phillips-head screws. A pair of cables, part number 3975342, were attached to the support wall with a ½ in. number 8 Phillips-head screw. Cotter pins, part number 3975341, were fastened to the other end of the cable and were used to retain the hood. This setup applied to the cowl induction hood as well.

Many Chevelle fans consider the 1970 Super Sport to be the best of the breed. Under the hood, there was the 454 ci powerplant with a maximum horsepower (in the LS-6) of 450. The body was also completely redesigned from the previous year, a design that would be extremely popular and carried on for several more years. Phil Kunz/Bill Holder

Cowl induction hood, ZL2, available in 1970-72.

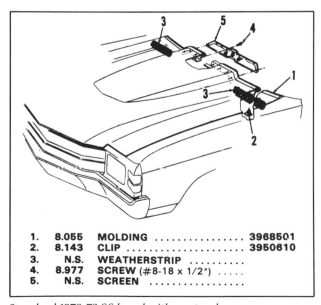

| | | | |
|---|---|---|---|
| 1. | 8.055 | MOLDING | 3968501 |
| 2. | 8.143 | CLIP | 3950610 |
| 3. | N.S. | WEATHERSTRIP | |
| 4. | 8.977 | SCREW (#8-18 x 1/2") | |
| 5. | N.S. | SCREEN | |

Standard 1970-72 SS hood with center dome screen.

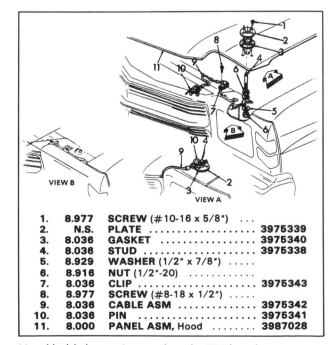

| | | | |
|---|---|---|---|
| 1. | 8.977 | SCREW (#10-16 x 5/8") | |
| 2. | N.S. | PLATE | 3975339 |
| 3. | 8.036 | GASKET | 3975340 |
| 4. | 8.036 | STUD | 3975338 |
| 5. | 8.929 | WASHER (1/2" x 7/8") | |
| 6. | 8.916 | NUT (1/2"-20) | |
| 7. | 8.036 | CLIP | 3975343 |
| 8. | 8.977 | SCREW (#8-18 x 1/2") | |
| 9. | 8.036 | CABLE ASM | 3975342 |
| 10. | 8.036 | PIN | 3975341 |
| 11. | 8.000 | PANEL ASM, Hood | 3987028 |

Hood hold-down pins used on the ZL2 hood.

A flat-black screen, part number 3972919, was used all three years to fill in the back of the dome of the standard SS hoods. It was held with eight ½ in. number 8 Phillips-head screws.

Cowl induction, RPO ZL2, used a different hood with a slot cut out of the dome for the option. The 1970 models used two different hoods: part number 3365951 was used till March 1970 when part number 3987028 took its place, and the latter was used till 1972. All hoods had provisions for hold-down pins.

Bright molding part number 3968501 was used with all hoods—both ZL2 versions and the standard dome units—all three years, as was the cowl-to-hood seal, part number 3968561, on either side of the dome.

With the ZL2 option, Cowl Induction emblems were placed on the sides of the dome. Original emblems were two separate parts: Cowl, part number 3968567, and Induction, part number 3968568. Both were attached with glue but featured locating studs that were positioned in five predrilled holes on each side of the dome.

To install the correct emblems be sure the hood is free of wax and is thoroughly dry. The temperature of the hood should be between 70 and 90 degrees Fahrenheit for ideal bonding. First wipe the dome area with mineral spirits and dry completely after cleaning. Next peel the protective backing from the emblem and locate it into place. Then press the emblem into place. A small ink roller with a rubber face works great for this (you can obtain ink rollers from art supply stores.) Roll the roller over the emblem using moderate pressure. Too much pressure can distort the emblem; not enough pressure, and the bond will not be strong enough. Roll the emblem six to eight times to ensure a good bond.

Early 1970 hoods used insulator part number 3972914, and the later hoods all used part number 3987034. The undersides of all hoods should be painted 30 degree gloss-black.

## Hinges, Hood Latch and Catch

### 1964-1967

Hinge assemblies were similar in design from 1964 to 1967, but the 1964 hinges, part numbers 3825827-LH and 3825828-RH, were shorter than

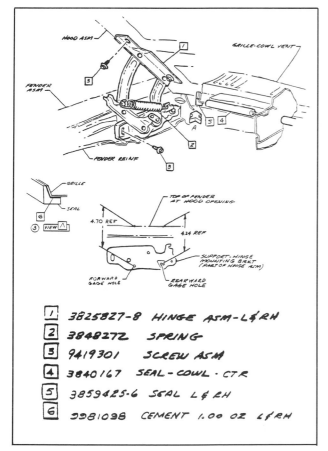

*Typical hood hinge. A 1964 unit is shown.*

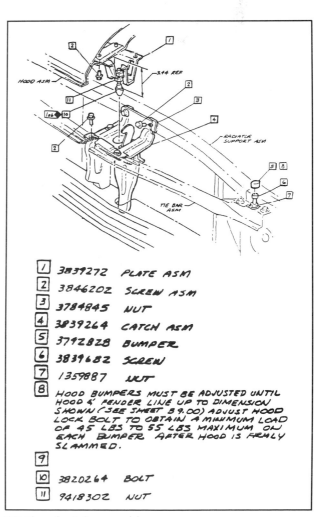

*1964 hood catch assembly.*

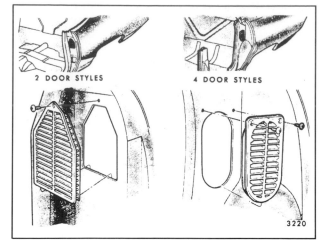

*Pillar-mounted pressure relief valves.*

the others. The 1966 springs were the same as the 1965 units. In 1967 three sets of hinges were used. Replacement hinges are listed as part numbers 3910667-LH and 3910668-RH; these can be used on all 1965-67 Chevelles correctly, but they will not fit the 1964 hood.

The above hinge assemblies should have a natural metal appearance to be correct. If the replacements are painted black an acceptable alternative is to have them plated with silver cadmium to produce the look of a natural metal.

Catch and latch assemblies were different each year and will not interchange. The catch support was also different.

### 1964-1967 Catch and Latch Part Numbers

| Part | 1964 | 1965 | 1966 | 1967 |
|---|---|---|---|---|
| Catch assembly | 3839264 | 3863280 | 3874579 | 3887540 |
| Latch plate | 3839272 | 3858087 | 3877226 | 3891447 |
| Latch bolt | 3820264 | 3863466 | 3863466 | 3863466 |
| Support | 3854135 | 3858089 | 3874572 | 3891445 |

The catch assembly should have the same appearance as the hinges. The latch plate should be painted flat-black, as should the support assembly.

### 1968-1969

It is important to match the 1968 and 1969 hoods to the correct hinges. All hinge assemblies were black cadmium, except those on the first style used on the first hood design, which were natural. All hinge springs should have a natural metal appearance and should not be painted.

### 1968-1972 Hood and Hinge Part Numbers

| Hood | Hinges |
|---|---|
| 3915452 | 3910679-LH* |
| | 3910680-RH* |
| 3940660 | 3926829-LH |

### 1968-1972 Hood and Hinge Part Numbers

| Hood | Hinges |
|---|---|
| | 3926830-RH |
| 3940632 | 3949201-LH |
| | 3949202-RH |

*Should have a natural finish.

The hood latch was redesigned in 1968. The release was located under the front header panel just above the grille. The catch assembly was listed as part number 3910669 and was bolted to support part number 3910674, which was mounted to the radiator support wall. Two striker plates were used: part number 3910673 till January 1968, then part number 3942129. Both plates used the same bolt, part number 3810669, which was now slipped into a natural metal retainer, part number 3857884, which held the spring part number 3857882, in place. This spring was needed to pop the hood open when the latch was released.

Owing to the difficulty in opening the hood, the release mechanism was moved under the front bumper on the left-hand side in 1969. Parts were given new numbers and attached in much the same way as in 1968. The catch is not interchangeable because of the release lever location.

### 1969 Catch and Latch Part Numbers

| | |
|---|---|
| Catch assembly | 3938181 |
| Striker plate | 3947953 |
| Spring | 3947929 |
| Retainer | 3947931 |
| Bolt | 3947952 |

The catch assembly, spring and bolt should be finished in black cadmium. The retainer and plate should have a natural finish. This applies to both 1968 and 1969 components.

### 1970-1972

The same set of hinges, part numbers 3976675-LH and 3976676-RH, was used from 1970 to 1972 without change. The hood spring was listed as part number 3864680 all three years. The hinges were black cadmium, and the springs should have a natural metal appearance.

A spring-loaded handle with a black-rubber-tipped end located under the front bumper just left of the center was used to open the hood. The catch was listed as part number 3975406 all three years.

The striker plate, part number 3963342, was redesigned. The spring, part number 3938019, was placed in a natural metal seat, part number 3767846; the retainer, part number 3947931, was still used. The bolt, part number 3963344, was, as in previous years, secured with a nut.

### Grilles

### 1964-1965

Two grilles were available in 1964. Early models used part number 3830720, and cars con-

108

structed after build date 10 B 63 used part number 3854130. The first-style grille was mounted with Phillips-head screws except at the top, where it was riveted. The second-style grille was secured with rivets only. Both grilles were brightly plated.

The extensions also included the headlamp bezels, listed as part numbers 3830723-LH and 3830724-RH. Each one was mounted with four Phillips-head screws. The extensions should have the same finish as the center grille.

A special flat-satin-black grille, part number 3875757, was used on the Malibu SS models. The center crossbar was left bright, with lower black accents. It was mounted using only rivets. An emblem, part number 3875758, with a blue bow tie and black accents was used in the center of the grille. The original emblem was secured by tabs on the back of it, and these tabs should be bent to a 45 degree angle after the emblem is installed.

The extensions in 1965, as in 1964, included the headlamp bezels and were mounted the same. Like the main grille the extensions, part numbers 3871305-LH and 3871306-RH, were accented in black. Regular Chevelle or Malibu extensions carried a different part number and will not correctly interchange.

## 1966-1967

The 1966 grille consisted of three parts: a main center section, part number 3891429, and two side extensions, part numbers 3891427-LH and 3891428-RH. All three were used on the SS only and were finished in 0 degree satin-black. Regular Chevelles carried a different set of part numbers.

The grille was mounted with rivets, the extensions with Phillips-head screws. The headlamp bezels, part numbers 3874589-LH and 3874590-RH, were riveted to the extensions.

In the center of the main grille assembly an SS 396 emblem, part number 3891434, was mounted with two barrel nuts. The letters should be inlaid in white.

The grille was redesigned for 1967. The extensions no longer supported the headlamp bezels. Both the extensions and the main grille section were accented with 0 degree satin-black paint. Part numbers were listed as follows: main grille, 3892182; left-hand extension, 3893977; right-hand extension, 3893978. The regular Chevelle grille used a different part number and will not interchange.

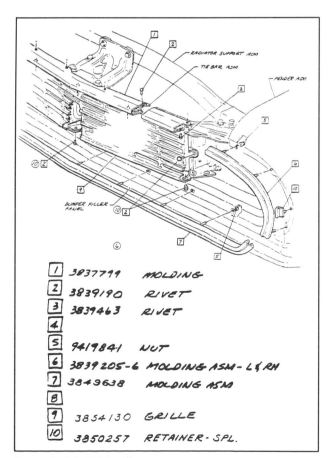

| | | |
|---|---|---|
| 1 | 3937779 | MOLDING |
| 2 | 3839190 | RIVET |
| 3 | 3839463 | RIVET |
| 4 | | |
| 5 | 9419841 | NUT |
| 6 | 3839205-6 | MOLDING ASM-L & RH |
| 7 | 3849638 | MOLDING ASM |
| 8 | | |
| 9 | 3854130 | GRILLE |
| 10 | 3850257 | RETAINER-SPL. |

*Second-style 1964 grille.*

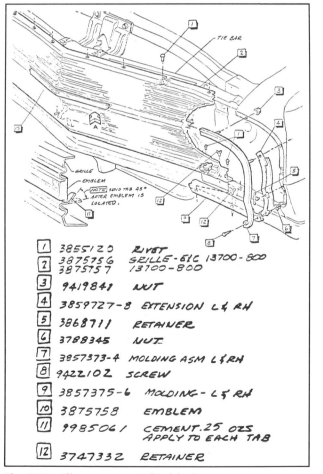

| | | |
|---|---|---|
| 1 | 3855120 | RIVET |
| 2 | 3875756 | GRILLE-EIC 13700-800 |
| | 3875757 | 13700-800 |
| 3 | 9419841 | NUT |
| 4 | 3859727-8 | EXTENSION L & RH |
| 5 | 3868711 | RETAINER |
| 6 | 3788345 | NUT |
| 7 | 3857373-4 | MOLDING ASM L & RH |
| 8 | 9422102 | SCREW |
| 9 | 3857375-6 | MOLDING-L & RH |
| 10 | 3875758 | EMBLEM |
| 11 | 9985061 | CEMENT.25 OZS APPLY TO EACH TAB |
| 12 | 3747332 | RETAINER |

*The 1965 grille was accented in black.*

109

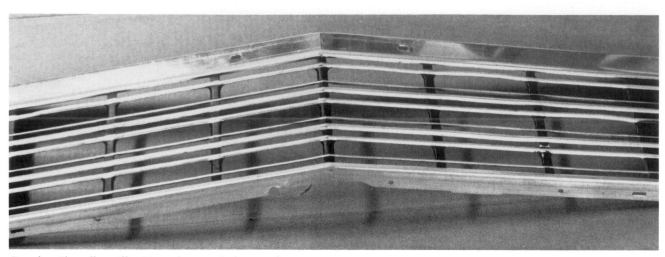

*Regular Chevelle grille. Note the two holes on the top, which make this unit incorrect for a 1967 SS 396. Also note that the thinner bars were blacked out.*

Once again the main grille was riveted into place, but the extensions were mounted uniquely. The extensions featured studs on the back and were secured with a nut. Phillips-head screws were employed along with push-in white plastic nuts. On the bottom of the outward side of the extension a bolt was used for more support.

### 1968-1969

An anodized aluminum grille was used again in 1968 with a fine crosshatched insert, which was blacked out with 0 degree satin-black paint. The extensions used the same pattern and were also blacked out.

Two different extensions were used. Earlier units (those built before build date 10 A 67) used a one-piece design while later models used an exten-

sion with a lower section, part number 3926805-6 LH/RH, that was riveted in place. Lower sections should also be painted 0 degree gloss black.

### 1968-1969 Grille Original Part Numbers

Main grille        3917465
Extension
    LH            3917421; 3926803*
    RH            3917422; 3926804*
    *From September 1, 1967, on.

The extensions were secured with three different sizes of Phillips-head screws. The main grille section was riveted into place on the header and support assemblies. Again the regular Chevelle used different part numbers, but unlike the 1967 grille it can be modified to work.

The grille was redesigned in 1969 and was now made from plastic. Two different main grille sec-

*The year 1967 was a year with little change in the engine compartment for the Super Sport, but sizeable changes in the body style. Outside, the SS 396 featured a black-out grille with the SS 396 tag and other appearance options. The production total for the SS 396 was slightly over 63,000. Phil Kunz/Bill Holder*

*There was no confusing the 1968 Super Sport with any of the previous or succeeding SS machines. It had a unique design with a sweeping color line over the front of the hood, down the front of the front fender and then straight back to the wheelwell. The SS emblem was located directly in the center of the vertically slatted grille. Phil Kunz/Bill Holder*

110

tions were used. The Malibu-based SS 396s and all El Camino SS 396s used part number 3938180, and the 300 based models used part number 3938106. The Malibu grille had holes drilled for the center chrome molding, part number 3938199. The 300 grille did not use this molding and had no provisions for it. A Malibu grille on a 300 car would be incorrect.

Special extensions, part numbers 3938191-LH and 3938192-RH, were used with the 300 Deluxe series car. However, they were used only until build date 12B 68 when they were replaced with the Malibu units, part numbers 3938111-LH and 3938112-RH. The Malibu-based cars and El Caminos used the later units all year. The 300 Deluxe extensions had no chrome center molding, as the Malibu units did. This chrome was blacked out when the Malibu extensions were used with the 300 based cars.

The regular production Chevelle grille and extensions were used with the above exceptions and were painted 0 degree satin-black. An SS 396 emblem, part number 3942781, with long studs was installed in the center of the grille. A natural metal retainer, part number 3942762, provided support. The grille and the extensions were mounted with Phillips-head screws and plastic backing nuts.

### 1970-1972

The regular production Chevelle grille, part number 3956117, was used on the 1970 SSs. For the classic SS look the grille was painted 0 degree satin-black.

### 1970 Grille Paint Part Numbers

| | |
|---|---|
| Ditzler | 9358 |
| Rinshed Mason | 171B90 |
| DuPont | 9895L |

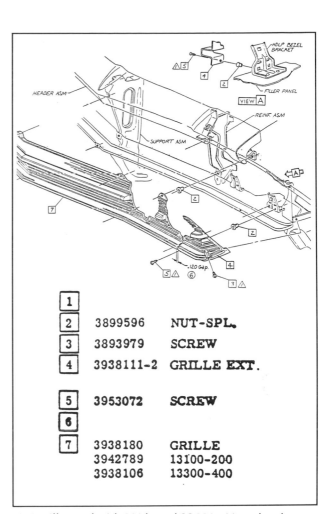

| | | |
|---|---|---|
| 1 | | |
| 2 | 3899596 | NUT-SPL. |
| 3 | 3893979 | SCREW |
| 4 | 3938111-2 | GRILLE EXT. |
| 5 | 3953072 | SCREW |
| 6 | | |
| 7 | 3938180 | GRILLE |
| | 3942789 | 13100-200 |
| | 3938106 | 13300-400 |

*1969 grille used with 300 based SS 396s. Note the absence of a center molding.*

*The 1969 Super Sport looked a lot like its brother from the previous year, but there were some distinct differences. The blacked-out grille and black stripe across the rear gave the model a race car look. Phil Kunz/Bill Holder*

*Sweeping lines for 1970 were the keynote of this one-year design for the Chevelle Super Sport. SS equipment was available only on convertibles and coupes that model year and consisted of the unique hood design, the black-out grille, wheelhouse moldings, various SS emblems, and bright exhaust extensions. The popular five-spoke wheels carried the SS designation on the center mount. It was one sharp machine and is generating increasing interest among collectors in the 1990s. Phil Kunz/Bill Holder*

The middle bar of the grille was painted the same color as the body. Bright trim traced the outlines of the grille halves, making them appear to be twin units.

A black-outlined SS emblem, part number 3958564, with white inlaid letters was positioned in the center of the middle bar. A natural retainer, part number 3972988, was used behind the grille. The grille was mounted using 18 thread ½ in. number 8 Phillips-head screws, along with plastic push nuts for extra support.

*There were real differences in the front end SS treatment from 1970. Gone were the dual headlights with the parking lamps now rolling around to replace the outer headlight. A single horizontal bar crossed the blackout grille, and the large SS letters were centered. Hood pins were also included in two locations at the front of the hood. Phil Kunz/Bill Holder*

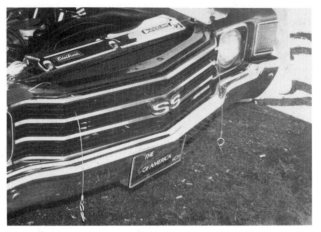

*Note the incorrect use of the two chrome moldings in the center. This would indicate a regular Chevelle grille and is incorrect for the SS.*

| | | |
|---|---|---|
| 1. | **SCREW** (1/4"-14 x 5/8") | 8.977 |
| 2. | **BAR ASM,** Frt Fender Tie | 1.267 |
| 3. | **BRACKET ASM,** Rad Grille | 1.267 |
| 4. | **NUT "U"** (1/4"-14) | 8.921 |
| 5. | **PANEL ASM,** Rad Grille to Frt Bpr Filler | 1.287 |
| 6. | **LAMP ASM** (Inner) | 2.725 |
| 7. | **LAMP ASM** (Outer) | 2.725 |
| 8. | **SPRING,** Headlamp Lens, Sealed Beam Retaining | 2.737 |
| 9. | **LAMP ASM,** Park | 2.575 |
| 10. | **BUMPER,** Backing Lamp Bumper | 7.800 |
| 11. | **SCREW** (#10-24 x 1/2") | 8.913 |
| 12. | **SCREW** (#8-18 x 1/2") | 8.131 |
| 13. | **EXTENSION,** Frt Fdr | 8.131 |
| 14. | **BUMPER,** Frt | 7.800 |
| 15. | **LAMP ASM,** Frt Fdr Marker | 2.575 |
| 16. | **NUT "U"** (#8-18) | 8.921 |
| 17. | **BEZEL ASM,** Headlamp | 2.728 |
| 18. | **MOLDING,** Extension | 8.132 |
| 19. | **BOLT** (7/16"-14 x 1 1/8") | 8.900 |
| 20. | **NUT** (7/16"-14) | 8.915 |
| 21. | **WASHER,** Lock (7/16") | 8.931 |
| 22. | **WASHER** | 8.929 |
| 23. | **BRACE ASM,** Front Face Bar | 7.836 |
| 24. | **BOLT** (1/2"-13 x 1 1/4") | 8.900 |
| 25. | **WASHER,** Frt & Rr (1/2" x 1 1/4" x 1/8") | 7.865 |
| 26. | **BOLT** (7/16"-14 x 1") | 8.900 |
| 27. | **BOLT** (7/16"-14 x 1") | 8.903 |
| 28. | **BOLT** (1/3"- 20 x 5/8") | 8.900 |
| 29. | **BUMPER,** Front | 7.800 |
| 30. | **BRACKET,** License | 7.800 |
| 31. | **NUT,** Spring (1/4"-14) | 7.800 |
| 32. | **BAR,** Front | 7.831 |
| 33. | **NUT** (1/4"-20) | 8.917 |
| 34. | **NUT** (1/2"-13) | 8.915 |
| 35. | **BRACKET,** Front Face Bar | 7.869 |
| 36. | **WASHER,** Rr Face Bar Reinf to Bumper Serr Tooth | 7.865 |
| 37. | **PAD,** Jack | 8.820 |
| 38. | **BRACKET,** Jack Rad | 8.820 |
| 39. | **SCREW** (#8-18 x 3/4") | 8.977 |
| 40. | **BRACKET,** Extension | 8.153 |
| 41. | **NUT "U"** (1/4"-14) | 8.921 |
| 42. | **SCREW** (#8-18 x 1/2") | 8.977 |
| 43. | **GRILLE,** Radiator | 1.266 |
| 44. | **SUPPORT ASM,** Hood Lock Catch | 8.080 |
| 45. | **NUT** (1/4"-20) | 8.915 |
| 46. | **SCREW ASM,** Headlamp Asm & Mldg Attach (1/4"-20 x 3/8") | 2.729 |
| 47. | **NUT,** Bezel at Upr End, Pnl Compt, Cluster Upr | 9.744 |
| 48. | **SCREW,** Rad Supt, Rad Fan Shroud, Rad Grille (5/16-18 x3/4) | 1.276 |

*1970 grille and accessories.*

The production grille, part number 3982409, was used again in 1971. It resembled the 1970 unit but featured fewer vertical bars. A bright center bar, part number 3982431, divided the grille horizontally. This molding was used on all three tiers of the grille and will interchange. The part number or source identification must appear on the bottom face of the molding for correctness. As before, the insert of the grille should be painted 0 degree satin-black. The center bar should be left bright.

As in 1970, a small Chevelle name block—part number 3975396, 3987072 after May 1970—was used in the lower section of the grille on the left-hand side. El Caminos used a different block—part number 5979918, 3987056 after May 1970—that read Chevrolet. Both name blocks were mounted with two barrel nuts. The center SS emblem was identical to that used in 1970.

All SS packages in 1972 came with a special grille, part number 6261924, which had no holes drilled in the center crossbar for the center molding. This molding was used on all Chevelles but was incorrect for the SS packages. For this reason a standard Malibu grille will not interchange.

The above grille was painted 0 degree satin-black, including the two center bars. An SS emblem,

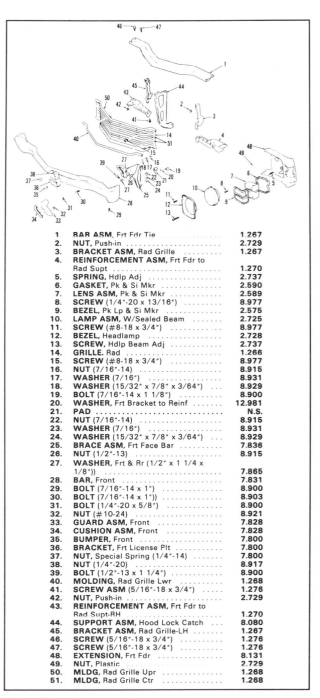

| | | |
|---|---|---|
| 1. | BAR ASM, Frt Fdr Tie | 1.267 |
| 2. | NUT, Push-in | 2.729 |
| 3. | BRACKET ASM, Rad Grille | 1.267 |
| 4. | REINFORCEMENT ASM, Frt Fdr to Rad Supt | 1.270 |
| 5. | SPRING, Hdlp Adj | 2.737 |
| 6. | GASKET, Pk & Si Mkr | 2.590 |
| 7. | LENS ASM, Pk & Si Mkr | 2.589 |
| 8. | SCREW (1/4"-20 x 13/16") | 8.977 |
| 9. | BEZEL, Pk Lp & Si Mkr | 2.575 |
| 10. | LAMP ASM, W/Sealed Beam | 2.725 |
| 11. | SCREW (#8-18 x 3/4") | 8.977 |
| 12. | BEZEL, Headlamp | 2.728 |
| 13. | SCREW, Hdlp Beam Adj | 2.737 |
| 14. | GRILLE, Rad | 1.266 |
| 15. | SCREW (#8-18 x 3/4") | 8.977 |
| 16. | NUT (7/16"-14) | 8.915 |
| 17. | WASHER (7/16") | 8.931 |
| 18. | WASHER (15/32" x 7/8" x 3/64") | 8.929 |
| 19. | BOLT (7/16"-14 x 1 1/8") | 8.900 |
| 20. | WASHER, Frt Bracket to Reinf | 12.981 |
| 21. | PAD | N.S. |
| 22. | NUT (7/16"-14) | 8.915 |
| 23. | WASHER (7/16") | 8.931 |
| 24. | WASHER (15/32" x 7/8" x 3/64") | 8.929 |
| 25. | BRACE, Frt Face Bar | 7.836 |
| 26. | NUT (1/2"-13) | 8.915 |
| 27. | WASHER, Frt & Rr (1/2" x 1 1/4" x 1/8") | 7.865 |
| 28. | BAR, Front | 7.831 |
| 29. | BOLT (7/16"-14 x 1") | 8.900 |
| 30. | BOLT (7/16"-14 x 1") | 8.903 |
| 31. | BOLT (1/4"-20 x 5/8") | 8.900 |
| 32. | NUT (#10-24) | 8.921 |
| 33. | GUARD ASM, Front | 7.828 |
| 34. | CUSHION ASM, Front | 7.828 |
| 35. | BUMPER, Front | 7.800 |
| 36. | BRACKET, Frt License Plt | 7.800 |
| 37. | NUT, Special Spring (1/4"-14) | 7.800 |
| 38. | NUT (1/4"-20) | 8.917 |
| 39. | BOLT (1/2"-13 x 1 1/4") | 8.900 |
| 40. | MOLDING, Rad Grille Lwr | 1.268 |
| 41. | SCREW ASM (5/16"-18 x 3/4") | 1.276 |
| 42. | NUT, Push-in | 2.729 |
| 43. | REINFORCEMENT ASM, Frt Fdr to Rad Supt-RH | 1.270 |
| 44. | SUPPORT ASM, Hood Lock Catch | 8.080 |
| 45. | BRACKET ASM, Rad Grille-LH | 1.267 |
| 46. | SCREW (5/16"-18 x 3/4") | 1.276 |
| 47. | SCREW (5/16"-18 x 3/4") | 1.276 |
| 48. | EXTENSION, Frt Fdr | 8.131 |
| 49. | NUT, Plastic | 2.729 |
| 50. | MLDG, Rad Grille Upr | 1.268 |
| 51. | MLDG, Rad Grille Ctr | 1.268 |

*1972 grille and accessories.*

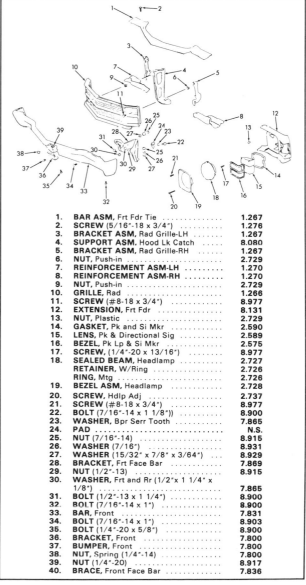

| | | |
|---|---|---|
| 1. | BAR ASM, Frt Fdr Tie | 1.267 |
| 2. | SCREW (5/16"-18 x 3/4") | 1.276 |
| 3. | BRACKET ASM, Rad Grille-LH | 1.267 |
| 4. | SUPPORT ASM, Hood Lk Catch | 8.080 |
| 5. | BRACKET ASM, Rad Grille-RH | 1.267 |
| 6. | NUT, Push-in | 2.729 |
| 7. | REINFORCEMENT ASM-LH | 1.270 |
| 8. | REINFORCEMENT ASM-RH | 1.270 |
| 9. | NUT, Push-in | 2.729 |
| 10. | GRILLE, Rad | 1.266 |
| 11. | SCREW (#8-18 x 3/4") | 8.977 |
| 12. | EXTENSION, Frt Fdr | 8.131 |
| 13. | NUT, Plastic | 2.729 |
| 14. | GASKET, Pk and Si Mkr | 2.590 |
| 15. | LENS, Pk & Directional Sig | 2.589 |
| 16. | BEZEL, Pk Lp & Si Mkr | 2.575 |
| 17. | SCREW, (1/4"-20 x 13/16") | 8.977 |
| 18. | SEALED BEAM, Headlamp | 2.727 |
| | RETAINER, W/Ring | 2.726 |
| | RING, Mtg | 2.726 |
| 19. | BEZEL ASM, Headlamp | 2.728 |
| 20. | SCREW, Hdlp Adj | 2.737 |
| 21. | SCREW (#8-18 x 3/4") | 8.977 |
| 22. | BOLT (7/16"-14 x 1 1/8") | 8.900 |
| 23. | WASHER, Bpr Serr Tooth | 7.865 |
| 24. | PAD | N.S. |
| 25. | NUT (7/16"-14) | 8.915 |
| 26. | WASHER (7/16") | 8.931 |
| 27. | WASHER (15/32" x 7/8" x 3/64") | 8.929 |
| 28. | BRACKET, Frt Face Bar | 7.869 |
| 29. | NUT (1/2"-13) | 8.915 |
| 30. | WASHER, Frt and Rr (1/2" x 1 1/4" x 1/8") | 7.865 |
| 31. | BOLT (1/2"-13 x 1 1/4") | 8.900 |
| 32. | BOLT (7/16"-14 x 1") | 8.900 |
| 33. | BAR, Front | 7.831 |
| 34. | BOLT (7/16"-14 x 1") | 8.903 |
| 35. | BOLT (1/4"-20 x 5/8") | 8.900 |
| 36. | BRACKET, Front | 7.800 |
| 37. | BUMPER, Front | 7.800 |
| 38. | NUT, Spring (1/4"-14) | 7.800 |
| 39. | NUT (1/4"-20) | 8.917 |
| 40. | BRACE, Front Face Bar | 7.836 |

*1971 grille and bumper.*

| | | | |
|---|---|---|---|
| 1. | 12.940 | PANEL, Outer | 8761648 |
| 2. | 12.941 | PANEL, Rear Inner Front Upper | 7671562 |
| 3. | 12.981 | PANEL, Rear Compartment | |
| 4. | N.S. | BAR ASM, Rear Cross | |
| 5. | N.S. | BAR ASM, Rear Cross Front | 9809167 |
| 6. | 8.977 | SCREW | |
| 7. | N.S. | PANEL | |
| 8. | 8.977 | SCREW (8-18 x 3/8") | |
| 9. | 10.571 | PLATE, Lock Striker Upr | 4849938 |
| 10. | N.S. | PLATE, Lock Striker Rear | |
| 11. | 12.237 | SPACER, Lock Striker | 4800021 |
| 12. | 12.237 | STRIKER | |
| 13. | N.S. | SCREW | |
| 14. | N.S. | COVER | |
| 15. | 12.184 | BOLT | 7740373 |
| 16. | 8.929 | WASHER (3/8" X 1" X 3/32") | |
| 17. | 12.203 | CABLE | 7732274 |
| 18. | 12.179 | PANEL ASM, Outer | 9862702 |
| 19. | 8.977 | SCREW (8-18 x 3/8") | |
| 20. | 10.474 | SCREW | 1708768 |
| 21. | 12.195 | PLATE | 8731353 |
| 22. | 12.242 | SCREW | 4422699 |
| 23. | N.S. | HANDLE | |
| 24. | 12.249 | ESCUTCHEON | 4409003 |
| 25. | 12.242 | LOCK ASM | 7741883 |
| 26. | 12.242 | ROD, -RH | 7725971 |
| | 12.242 | ROD, -LH | 7726253 |
| 27. | N.S. | LOCK ASM | |
| | 12.242 | LOCK ASM | 7733778 |
| 28. | 8.977 | SCREW | |
| 29. | 12.197 | GATE ASM | 9862703 |
| 30. | 8.970 | PLUG, Black Plastic (5/16") | |
| 31. | 10.571 | WASHER | 4469196 |
| 32. | 12.203 | SPRING | |
| 33. | 12.184 | BOLT | 7740374 |
| 34. | 10.463 | BOLT | 9438916 |
| 35. | 12.186 | PIN | 9712980 |
| 36. | 12.184 | STRAP, Hinge Gate Side | 9719758 |
| | N.S. | STRAP, Hinge Gate Side | |
| 37. | N.S. | STRAP, Hinge Body Side | 9712976 |
| | 12.184 | STRAP, Hinge Body Side | 9712977 |
| 38. | N.S. | PANEL, Rear Inner | |
| | 12.941 | PANEL, Rear Inner | 7671537 |
| 39. | 12.941 | PANEL, Rear Inner Front Upper | 7671563 |
| 40. | 12.981 | EXTENSION, Pan to Outer Panel Filler Front | 7723600 |
| 41. | 12.981 | FILLER, Pan to Qtr Panel | 9814156 |
| | 12.981 | FILLER, Pan to Qtr Panel | 9814157 |
| 42. | 12.940 | PANEL, Outer | 8761649 |
| 43. | 12.944 | PANEL, Wheelhouse Outer | 9815030 |
| 44. | 12.944 | PANEL, Wheelhouse | 9814166 |
| | N.S. | PANEL, Wheelhouse | |
| 45. | 12.941 | PANEL, Rear Qtr Inner Front | 7787061 |
| | 12.941 | PANEL, Rear Qtr Inner Front | 7787062 |

*1968-72 pickup rear section sheet metal.*

| | | | |
|---|---|---|---|
| 1. | 8.917 | NUT (7/16"-14) | |
| 2. | 7.865 | SPACER | 3895100 |
| 3. | 8.900 | BOLT (7/16"-14 x 1") | |
| 4. | 8.931 | WASHER (15/32" x 1 1/4") | |
| 5. | 8.923 | NUT (7/16"-14) | |
| 6. | N.S. | REINFORCEMENT | |
| 7. | 9.831 | WASHER (7/16") | |
| 8. | 8.900 | BOLT (7/16"-14 x 1 1/4") | |
| 9. | 8.900 | BOLT (7/16"-14 x 7/8") | |
| 10. | 7.800 | BUMPER | 3938600 |
| 11. | 7.800 | NUT | 559547 |
| 12. | 8.915 | NUT (7/16"-14) | |
| 13. | 8.913 | SCREW (10-24 x 1/2") | |
| 14. | 8.903 | BOLT (7/16"-14 x 1") | |
| 15. | 7.800 | BUMPER | 3841098 |
| 16. | N.S. | REFLECTOR | |
| 17. | 8.929 | WASHER (15/32") | |
| 18. | 7.831 | BAR | 3935692 |
| 19. | 7.865 | PAD | 3922841 |
| 20. | N.S. | BRACE-LH | |
| | N.S. | BRACE-RH | |
| 21. | 7.865 | WASHER | 1362249 |
| 22. | 8.915 | NUT (1/2"-13) | |
| 23. | N.S. | BRACE-LH | |
| | N.S. | BRACE-RH | |
| | N.S. | BRACKET ASM-LH | |
| | 7.869 | BRACKET ASM-RH | 3922836 |

*1969-71 pickup rear bumper.*

part number 6264838, was placed in the center, and a natural retainer, part number 6264839, was also used. The Chevelle name block was not used with this package either.

## Moldings and Emblems

### 1964-1965

Bright wheelhouse moldings were standard in both 1964 and 1965 but were not interchangeable.

### 1964-1965 Wheelhouse Molding Part Numbers

| Part | 1964 | 1965 |
|------|------|------|
| Front | | |
| LH | 3843029 | 3860133 |
| RH | 3843030 | 3860134 |
| Rear | | |
| LH | 3852957 | 3871622 |
| RH | 3852958 | 3871623 |

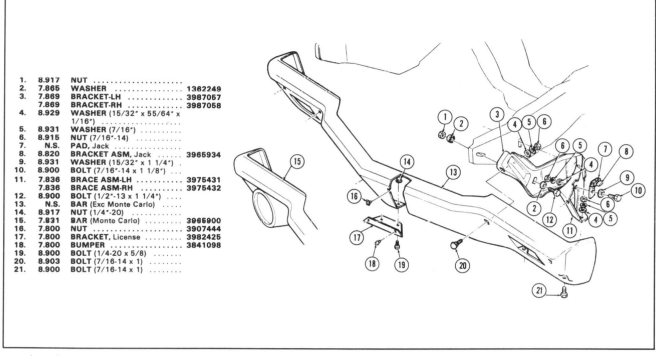

| | | | |
|---|------|------|------|
| 1. | 8.917 | NUT | |
| 2. | 7.865 | WASHER | 1362249 |
| 3. | 7.869 | BRACKET-LH | 3987057 |
| | 7.869 | BRACKET-RH | 3987058 |
| 4. | 8.929 | WASHER (15/32" x 55/64" x 1/16") | |
| 5. | 8.931 | WASHER (7/16") | |
| 6. | 8.915 | NUT (7/16"-14) | |
| 7. | N.S. | PAD, Jack | |
| 8. | 8.820 | BRACKET ASM, Jack | 3965934 |
| 9. | 8.931 | WASHER (15/32" x 1 1/4") | |
| 10. | 8.900 | BOLT (7/16"-14 x 1 1/8") | |
| 11. | 7.836 | BRACE ASM-LH | 3975431 |
| | 7.836 | BRACE ASM-RH | 3975432 |
| 12. | 8.900 | BOLT (1/2"-13 x 1 1/4") | |
| 13. | N.S. | BAR (Exc Monte Carlo) | |
| 14. | 8.917 | NUT (1/4"-20) | |
| 15. | 7.831 | BAR (Monte Carlo) | 3965900 |
| 16. | 7.800 | NUT | 3907444 |
| 17. | 7.800 | BRACKET, License | 3982425 |
| 18. | 7.800 | BUMPER | 3841098 |
| 19. | 8.900 | BOLT (1/4-20 x 5/8) | |
| 20. | 8.903 | BOLT (7/16-14 x 1) | |
| 21. | 8.900 | BOLT (7/16-14 x 1) | |

*1970 front bumper.*

| | | | |
|---|------|------|------|
| 1. | 8.900 | BOLT (1/2"-13 x 1 1/4") | |
| 2. | 7.865 | WASHER | 1362249 |
| 3. | 8.931 | WASHER | |
| 4. | 8.931 | WASHER (7/16") | |
| 5. | 8.915 | NUT (7/16"-14) | |
| 6. | 7.869 | BRACKET-LH | 3982423 |
| | 7.869 | BRACKET-RH | 3982424 |
| 7. | N.S. | PAD | |
| 8. | 8.931 | WASHER (15/32" x 1 1/4") | |
| 9. | 8.900 | BOLT (7/16"-14 x 1 1/8") | |
| 10. | 8.820 | BRACKET ASM | 3965934 |
| 11. | 7.836 | BRACE ASM-LH | 3982441 |
| | 7.836 | BRACE ASM-RH | 3982442 |
| 12. | 8.915 | NUT (1/2"-13) | |
| 13. | 8.900 | BOLT (7/16"-14 x 1") | |
| 14. | 8.903 | BOLT (7/16"-14 x 1") | |
| 15. | 8.900 | BOLT (1/4"-14 x 5/8") | |
| 16. | 7.800 | BRACKET | 3982425 |
| 17. | 7.800 | BUMPER | 3841098 |
| 18. | 7.800 | NUT | 3907444 |
| 19. | 8.917 | NUT (1/4"-20) | |
| 20. | 7.831 | BAR | 3982398 |

*1971-72 front bumper.*

*Here is a look at the correct moldings and emblems for the 1964 Malibu SS. This also shows the correct wheel covers.* Chevrolet

A thin bright molding traced the upper contours of the body in 1964. These were eliminated for 1965, and no bodyside moldings were used.

### 1964 Body Contour Molding Part Numbers
Front fender
| | |
|---|---|
| LH | 3841947 |
| RH | 3841948 |
| Doors | 3841950 |

Rear fender
| | |
|---|---|
| LH | 3841951 |
| RH | 3841952 |

Anodized aluminum rocker sill moldings, part numbers 3843557-LH and 3843558-RH, were used in 1964 as standard equipment. End caps, part numbers 3843559-LH and 3843560-RH, were used with the sill moldings. The end cap was secured to a retainer, part number 3838003, that was bolted to the body with tap screws. The molding was slid into place over the retainer and then held there with a small bolt at each end and in the middle.

*Rear end view of a 1965 SS. Note the correct moldings. However, the center section of the deck lid is blacked out; it should be the same color as the body.*

The retainer was identical for 1965, but the moldings were now listed as part numbers 3860181-LH and 3860182-RH, and the pattern was changed to a ribbed texture. The end caps were integrated into the moldings. Mounting was the same as in 1964.

The rear deck and cove moldings were different each year. A ribbed anodized aluminum rear cove molding was used on all SSs and Malibus in 1964. Bright trim moldings, part numbers 3853435 for the upper piece and 3853436 for the lower piece, were placed on the deck lid.

In 1965 two thinner ribbed trim moldings, part numbers 3871641 for the upper piece and 3871642 for the lower piece, framed the center of the deck lid. A bright upper molding, part number 3871639, and a bright lower molding, part number 3871640, were placed across the the deck lid, as before. Also, special black-accented moldings were used on all cars except those painted Tuxedo Black, which had silver-accented moldings. The center section of the rear deck cove area framed by the moldings was left the color of the car.

The Z16 used a special blacked-out cove molding that covered the lower half of the deck lid and was trimmed with chrome strips.

The following brightwork installed by Chevrolet was unique to the Chevelle and will not interchange with that on other GM A-bodies.

### 1964-1965 Chevrolet-installed Brightwork Part Numbers

| | 1964 | 1965 |
|---|---|---|
| Hood | | |
| Front | 3838493 | 3859710 |
| Center | 3837434 | 3860111 |
| Headlight | | |
| LH | 3839205 | 3857373 |
| RH | 3839206 | 3857374 |

## 1964-1965 Chevrolet-installed Brightwork Part Numbers

|                      | 1964    | 1965    |
|----------------------|---------|---------|
| Front filler Bumper  | 3849638 | NA      |
| Front                | 3830727 | 3856906 |
| Rear                 | 3383799 | 385843  |

The following brightwork was installed by Fisher Body Company and is interchangeable with that on all other GM A-bodies—Pontiac LeMans, Buick Skylark and Oldsmobile Cutlass. It was the same both years.

## 1964-1965 Fisher Body Installed Brightwork Part Numbers

Windshield
| | |
|---|---|
| Upper | |
|   LH | 4430503 |
|   RH | 4430502 |
| Side | |
|   LH | 4430501 |
|   RH | 4430500 |
| Lower | 4430558 |

Drip rails
| | |
|---|---|
| A-pillar | |
|   LH | 4456264 |
|   RH | 4456263 |
|   (1) LII | 4456266 |
|   (1) RH | 4456265 |
| Roof | |
|   LH | 4456073 |
|   RH | 4456072 |
| Escutcheon | 4456067 |
| C-pillar | |
|   LH | 4456075 |
|   RH | 4456074 |

Door trim
| | |
|---|---|
| LH | 4453603 |
| RH | 4453602 |
| (1) LH | 4453605 |
| (1) RH | 4453604 |

Quarter trim
| | |
|---|---|
| LH | 4482525 |
| RH | 4482524 |
| (1) LH | 4483675 |
| (1) RH | 4483674 |

Quarter window
| | |
|---|---|
| 1964 reveal | |
|   LH | 4496256 |
|   RH | 4411688 |
| 1965 reveal | |
|   LH | 4496258 |
|   RH | 4496257 |

Rear window
| | |
|---|---|
| Upper | |
|   LH | 4430553 |
|   RH | 4430552 |
| Sides | |
|   LH | 4430545 |
|   RH | 4430544 |

| Lower | 4430549 |
|---|---|

(1)-Convertible

SSs had Chevrolet spelled out across the front of the hood both years. In 1965 the letters were spaced out farther. Also used both years was the

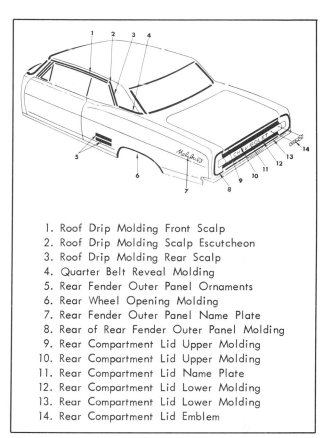

1. Roof Drip Molding Front Scalp
2. Roof Drip Molding Scalp Escutcheon
3. Roof Drip Molding Rear Scalp
4. Quarter Belt Reveal Molding
5. Rear Fender Outer Panel Ornaments
6. Rear Wheel Opening Molding
7. Rear Fender Outer Panel Name Plate
8. Rear of Rear Fender Outer Panel Molding
9. Rear Compartment Lid Upper Molding
10. Rear Compartment Lid Upper Molding
11. Rear Compartment Lid Name Plate
12. Rear Compartment Lid Lower Molding
13. Rear Compartment Lid Lower Molding
14. Rear Compartment Lid Emblem

*Three quarter view of the 1965 SS. The side moldings, number 5, were never used on the production car.*

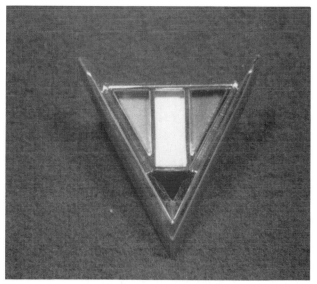

*This emblem signified a V-8 engine in 1964.*

The Super Sport identification of the 1964 model was boldly carried on the rear flanks of the Malibu SS. There was only marginal performance, though, available from the Super Sport this initial year with Motor Trend testing the model in the quarter mile at 17.5 seconds at slightly over 80 mph. It would be a far cry from the 14-second cars that would come along later in the decade. Phil Kunz/Bill Holder

The rear deck emblem looked like this in 1965 except with the Z16 option, which used a special emblem.

Malibu SS script on the rear quarters, with a circle around the red-filled SS letters.

The Chevelle nameplate, part number 3849498, was placed on the forward section of each front fenders on all 1964 Chevelles. A chrome *V* with red, white and blue insets, part number 3840317, was used to indicate a V-8 engine. It was positioned on the rear section of the front fenders.

In 1965 the nameplate was eliminated and the engine size was identified by a call-out badge, part numbers 3863852 for the 283 ci and 3863853 for the 327 ci. Under this was a flying flag emblem, part number 3840318, which indicated a V-8 engine.

Across the deck lid in 1964, Chevrolet was spelled out. On the right-hand side of the end panel was a circle emblem with red letters like that on the quarter panels. In 1965 the Chevrolet name was spelled across the cove of the deck lid, and to the

right was a plaque that read Malibu SS; the original had the letters *SS* in red.

The 1965 Z16 option used special emblems. The Malibu script, part number 4477687, was re-

There were slight but significant changes to the Z16 design as compared to the standard Super Sport. The most noticeable change was the moving of the Malibu SS emblems to the front fenders. Also, a portion of the rear deck was blacked out. Finally, an SS 396 tag was mounted on the vertical part of the rear deck. Phil Kunz/Bill Holder

The engine designations for the 1965 Chevelle Super Sport were carried far forward on the front fender with the triangular emblem highlighted by the racing-style flag. The L79 was the top 327 ci powerplant that model year with an impressive 350 horses available. It carried some of the same components as the 365 hp version of the 327 used the previous year in the Corvette. Phil Kunz/Bill Holder

positioned to the rear section of the front fenders. A 396 Turbo-Jet flag emblem, part number 3871057, replaced the call-out and V-8 identification emblems. On the rear the Chevrolet name was eliminated and a special Malibu SS 396 plaque was placed on the upper half of the deck lid on the right-hand side.

**1966-1967**

Bright wheelwell moldings were standard in both 1966 and 1967. Each year used a different set of part numbers. Both years the moldings were installed with chrome Phillips-head screws. The moldings will not interchange, as the 1967 pieces were wider.

### 1966-1967 Wheelwell Molding Part Numbers

| Part | 1966 | 1967 |
|---|---|---|
| Front | | |
| LH | 3874573 | 3893991 |
| RH | 3874574 | 3893992 |
| Rear | | |
| LH | 3884033 | 4229718 |
| RH | 3884034 | 4229719 |

*The top of the line Super Sport model for 1966 was coined the SS 396. The Super Sport identification was scripted on the rear quarter along with the SS 396 on the rear deck. Although the Super Sport was just a little longer and wider than the 1965 model, it certainly portrayed a much sleeker look. The chassis was updated with stronger springs, advanced shocks, and a larger stabilizer bar. Phil Kunz/Bill Holder*

*The 1967 Chevelle SS incorporated an attractive black-out grille carrying the SS 396 designation in the center. Other SS identifiers were located on the dash and on the steering wheel. The final SS medallion was located in the middle of the black-out rear deck panel. Phil Kunz/Bill Holder*

*With the range of muscular powerplants available with the 1966 Super Sport, the model really came into its own during this model year. The no-frills appearance of the Super Sport was exactly the right look for the time and a look that truly performance-minded drivers really liked a lot. It would be a trend that would be copied by others in the years to follow. Phil Kunz/Bill Holder*

## 1966–1967 Chevrolet-installed Bright Molding Part Numbers

| Part | 1966 | 1967 |
|---|---|---|
| Hood | | |
| Front | 3874586 | 3887559 |
| Crown | 3874587* | NA |
| Filler | | |
| Center | 3876413 | NA |
| LH | 3878485 | NA |
| RH | 3878486 | NA |
| Rocker sill | | |
| LH | 3873753 | 3893965 |
| RH | 3873754 | 3893966 |
| Door edge* | | |
| LH | 3880961 | NA |
| RH | 3880962 | NA |
| Rear deck | | |
| Upper | 4227108 | 4229434 |
| Lower | 4227108 | 4229432 |
| Bumpers | | |
| Front | 3869723 | 3884920 |
| Rear | 3869756 | 3895146 |

*Optional.

Special ribbed molding was used in 1966 on the rockersill, and it extended to the rear of the quarter panel. The extension was used solely on the SS 396. Both the rockersill and extensions were accented with 0 degree gloss black paint in the valleys of the ribs.

Optional bumper guards were different each year and are not interchangeable. The 1966 guards were solid brightmetal. The 1967 units were redesigned and featured a black rubber insert. Also in 1967 a special rear bumper, part number 3897502, had to be used with rear bumper guards. This bumper is recognizable by the two holes in the top for the guards' mounting bolts. In 1966 the production rear bumper was used.

## 1966–1967 Bumper Guard Part Numbers

| Part | 1966 | 1967 |
|---|---|---|
| Front guards | | |
| LH | 3874593 | 3895109 |
| RH | 3874594 | 3895110 |

*An emblem like this was used on the front fenders of all 1966 and 1967 SS 396s. It was also used with the 1965 Z16s.*

## 1966–1967 Bumper Guard Part Numbers

| Part | 1966 | 1967 |
|---|---|---|
| Rear guards | | |
| LH | 3874595 | 3895111 |
| RH | 3874596 | 3895112 |
| Rubber inserts | | |
| Front | NA | 3895168 |
| Rear | NA | 3895190 |
| Mounting clamps | | |
| Front | | |
| LH | 3860563 | 3895191 |
| RH | 3860564 | 3895192 |
| Rear | 3877824 | 3895185 |

## 1966–1967 Fisher Body Molding Part Numbers

| Windshield | |
|---|---|
| Upper | |
| LH | 4541649 |
| RH | 4541648 |
| Side | |
| LH | 4541651 |
| RH | 4541650 |
| Lower | 4430558 |
| Finish pillar | |
| Coupe | |
| LH | 4543091 |
| RH | 4543090 |
| Convertible | |
| LH | 4543093 |
| RH | 4543092 |
| Roof drip rails | |
| LH | 4547734 |
| RH | 4547733 |
| Door trim | |
| Coupe | |
| LH | 7580770 |

*The 1967 SS Chevelle featured a sleek new design that carried a black-out strip on the rear deck with horizontal lines through the rear lights. The Super Sports for 1967 also carried the shiny metal wheelhouse moldings and color-keyed body strips on the sides of the cars. Phil Kunz/Bill Holder*

## 1966-1967 Fisher Body Molding Part Numbers

|  |  |
|---|---|
| RH | 7580770 |
| Convertible |  |
| LH | 7580769 |
| RH | 7580768 |
| Quarter trim |  |
| Coupe |  |
| LH | 7580594 |
| RH | 7580593 |
| Convertible |  |
| LH | 4541661 |
| RH | 4541660 |
| Back glass |  |
| Upper |  |
| LH | 7580181 |
| RH | 7580180 |
| Lower |  |
| LH | 7581671 |
| RH | 7581670 |

An SS 396 emblem was used both years in the center of the grille. However, the emblems are not interchangeable and used different part numbers. The 1966 emblem, part number 3891434, used two spacers, part number 3878494. In 1967 part number 3897537 used no spacers and used a natural metal retainer, part number 3897538, behind the grille. For both years the letters were inlaid in white.

The 396 Turbo-Jet flag emblem, part number 3871057, was used both years on the forward section of the front fenders. It was held with four barrel nuts. No nameplate was used on the hood in 1966, but an underlined Chevelle nameplate, part

*This rear end view is incorrect, as the center Chevelle nameplate is missing.*

*There was no doubt from any Chevelle carrying this lettering on its rear panel. The staggered lettering had the first letter in each word with a white facing. An interesting fact is that the Super Sport models listed for only $285 more than comparable Malibu convertibles and coupes. Phil Kunz/Bill Holder*

*In 1966 the rear quarter emblem was underlined.*

*Rear view of a 1967 SS 396. Note the blacked-out tail and accented chrome.*

*The 1968 Chevelle Super Sport featured a completely new design with this new rear deck treatment. Again, the SS identification was carried in the middle of the black-out rear panel. The overall vehicle was slightly shorter at 112 in. in length, but had a slightly wider stance. Phil Kunz/Bill Holder*

number 3893924, was used on the left-hand front corner in 1967.

Super Sport was spelled out on the rear quarter panels each year but was different each year. In 1966 the name was on a single line and was underlined with a chrome bar. In 1967 the nameplate was two separate units, part number 4229717, placed on two lines, and was not underlined. In 1967 the capital *S*s were inlaid in white.

The name Chevelle was underlined and placed across the body-colored rear cove panel in 1966. To the right of this emblem was an open SS 396 emblem.

In 1967 the rear panel was blacked out and the only emblem used was an SS 396 emblem, part number 4229992, which had a solid black background with white lettering. The Chevelle name did not appear on the rear of the car.

### 1968-1969

Wheelwell moldings were no longer standard equipment on the SS 396 in either 1968 or 1969.

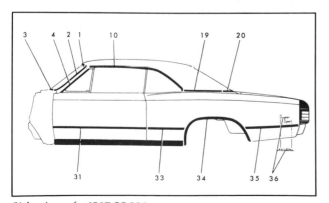

*Side view of a 1967 SS 396.*

Special side molding ran the entire length of the car tracing the lower contours in 1968.

### 1968 Side Molding Part Numbers

| | |
|---|---|
| Front header | 3920849 |
| Extension | |
|   LH | 3920845 |
|   RH | 3920846 |
| Front fender | |
|   LH | 3920153 |
|   RH | 3920154 |
| Door | |
|   LH | 7795007 |
|   RH | 7795006 |
| Rear quarter | |
|   Forward | 7795072 |
|   Forward El Camino | 7795071 |
|   Rear | 7795069 |
|   Rear El Camino | 7795070 |

Optional stick-on side molding, RPO B84, was available but was rarely ordered. The front fender molding was listed as part numbers 3945263-LH and 3945264-RH. When the optional stripes were ordered, a shorter front molding, part numbers 3945265-LH and 3945266-RH, was used. The other moldings were the same with or without the optional striping.

### 1968-1969 Optional Stick-on Side Molding Part Numbers

| | |
|---|---|
| Door | |
|   LH | 3945267 |
|   RH | 3945268 |
| Rear quarter | |
|   LH | 3945273 |
|   RH | 3945274 |
| El Camino | |
|   LH | 3945277 |
|   RH | 3945278 |

*Whether a Super Sport or not, this Chevelle scripting was carried on the back of every Chevelle. The 1969 model year was the best ever for the Chevelle with over 86,000 units sold. It has been reported that a few of the 396 engines installed in Super Sports carried the L89 aluminum head option which makes them outstanding collectables. Phil Kunz/Bill Holder*

An SS 396 emblem like the one in previous years was used in the center of the grille. Each year it was different. In 1968 it was listed as part number 3920802 and used retainer part number 3920803. In 1969 it was redesigned and used part number 3942781 and retainer part number 3942762. The lettering, as in years before, was inlaid in white.

A unique engine call-out and a turn light bezel, part numbers 3920877-LH and 3920878-RH, were placed on the forward sections of the front fenders. The bezels had a black background with white lettering that read SS 396. However, models made after build date 11C 67 used part numbers 3935901-LH and 3935902-RH, and these bezels had a painted black background with a vertical ribbed design and bright lettering that read 396 only. Both bezels were made of zinc.

In 1969 the bezel was eliminated and double S emblems, part number 3949238, were placed on the front fenders. Directly below the inlaid white letters was a 396 emblem, part number 3948030; the numbers were inlaid in red.

In the center of the blacked-out rear cove panel both years was an SS 396 emblem. No other emblem was installed in 1968. However, in 1969 an emblem that read Chevelle by Chevrolet, part number 8701218, was positioned on the right-hand side of the deck lid. A 1969 deck lid will therefore not interchange with a 1968 deck lid because of the predrilled holes for the emblem, but a 1968 deck lid can be fitted to a 1969 Chevelle.

The El Camino was available as an SS 396 model in 1968 and included special emblems. The El Camino name, part number 3920867, replaced the Chevelle script, part number 3920825, on the front header both years. In 1969 the By Chevrolet name block, part number 3942788, was not used, as it was on the cars.

### 1970-1972

Bright wheelwell moldings were standard with the El Camino only and optional on the car in 1970; in 1971 and 1972 they were standard on all. Part numbers were the same all three years.

### 1970-1972 Wheelwell Molding Part Numbers

| Front | |
|---|---|
| LH | 3965913 |
| RH | 3965914 |
| Rear | |
| LH | 8702561 |
| RH | 8702560 |
| Rear El Camino only | |
| LH | 8702999 |
| RH | 8703000 |

Rocker sill molding was listed as part numbers 3965941-LH and 3965942-RH all three years. However, this molding was not used with the El Camino. No other side moldings were standard. Stick on molding along the beltline was optional, as RPO BX4; it was installed by Fisher Body.

Chrome trim was used each year around the grille. In 1970 a three-part molding was placed around each section of the grille. The main molding was listed as part number 3958326, and the exten-

One of the most popular aspects of the 1971 Chevelle Super Sport was the rear end treatment. The biggest change was the omission of the black strip that had characterized early Super Sports. The SS emblem protruded and carried a black background. Phil Kunz/Bill Holder

Any opposition at the stop light had better heed these letters and numbers. The emblem said that under that hood beat either an LS-6 powerplant with 450 horses or the LS-5 with 360 horses. The production for the Chevelle in 1970 was a still-impressive total of 53,599 units. Some 4,475 of that number carried the LS-6 450 hp engine. Phil Kunz/Bill Holder

sions as part numbers 3958327-LH and 3958328-RH. The original molding had the part number cast into the extensions along with the letters *L* and *R* to distinguish between left and right. When the unit is installed, the part number and the letter must be on the lower surface of the molding to be correct.

In 1971 the moldings were changed to part numbers 3982431 for the center bars and 3982433-LH and 3982434-RH for the extensions. Installation was the same as before, but the extension contained a retaining tab that also must be located on the bottom molding.

An upper molding, part number 6261909, and a lower molding, part number 6261910, were used in 1972, as described earlier. The SS did not include a center molding.

Emblems were nearly the same all three years. In the center of the grille was a double S emblem. The part numbers were listed as 3968564 in 1970 and 6264838 in 1971-72. The retainer was the same all three years, part number 6264839, which was a 1970 production retainer. It should have a natural appearance.

The side emblems are where most mistakes occur in restoration. In 1970 the two S emblems, part number 3949238, were placed on the front fenders. Below these was the engine call-out badge: 396, part number 3948030, and 454, part number 3975410, were used. In 1971 and 1972 the double letters were installed, but the only engine call-out used was the 454. The El Camino carried a nameplate, part number 3972937, above the SS badges on the fender.

At the rear of the car a rubber insert with white embossed SS identification on the right-hand side was placed into the bumper of the 1970 Chevelle. In 1971 and 1972 a special rear bumper, part

Rear view of a 1970 SS showing the position of the rubber bumper insert.

1970 rear bumper rubber insert. Note the correct embossed white lettering and border.

The Chevelle Super Sport was becoming less of a muscle car in 1972. It looked about the same on the outside, but the power was lacking under the hood. The SS tags were still carried on the front quarters and the design was little changed from the 1971 version. Phil Kunz/Bill Holder

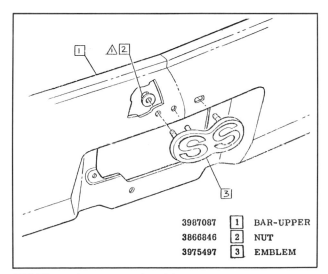

| 3987087 | 1 | BAR-UPPER |
| 3866846 | 2 | NUT |
| 3975497 | 3 | EMBLEM |

1971-72 rear bumper and emblem.

number 3987087, with three cutouts was used to mount the rear bumper emblem, part number 3975497.

In 1970 the pickup used the two S emblems, and under them was the engine call-out. The center portion of the tailgate was divided by two chrome molding strips. This section was not blacked out in 1970.

For 1971 and 1972 the center portion of the tailgate on the pickup was blacked out in 30 degree gloss-black. The double S emblems were used alone unless the 454 ci was ordered; then the 454 name-plate was placed under them.

### Standard Outside Mirror

**1964-1965**

No outside mirror was standard in either 1964 or 1965. A non-remote-control left-hand mirror was part of the comfort and convenience package, RPO Z01; part number 3821956 was used both years. A dealer-installed mirror was also available. A right-hand-mounted mirror was not offered with this mirror.

Two 0.141 in. diameter holes had to be drilled into the left-hand door in 1964. The mirror was mounted with a flat-black bracket, part number 3825896, and two screws, part number 9421495. This was changed in November 1964: holes were no

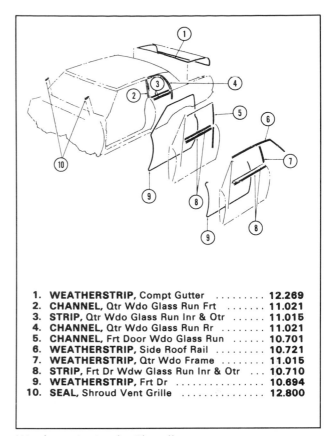

| 1. | WEATHERSTRIP, Compt Gutter | 12.269 |
| 2. | CHANNEL, Qtr Wdo Glass Run Frt | 11.021 |
| 3. | STRIP, Qtr Wdo Glass Run Inr & Otr | 11.015 |
| 4. | CHANNEL, Qtr Wdo Glass Run Rr | 11.021 |
| 5. | CHANNEL, Frt Door Wdo Glass Run | 10.701 |
| 6. | WEATHERSTRIP, Side Roof Rail | 10.721 |
| 7. | WEATHERSTRIP, Qtr Wdo Frame | 11.015 |
| 8. | STRIP, Frt Dr Wdw Glass Run Inr & Otr | 10.694 |
| 9. | WEATHERSTRIP, Frt Dr | 10.694 |
| 10. | SEAL, Shroud Vent Grille | 12.800 |

*Weather stripping for Chevelle coupes.*

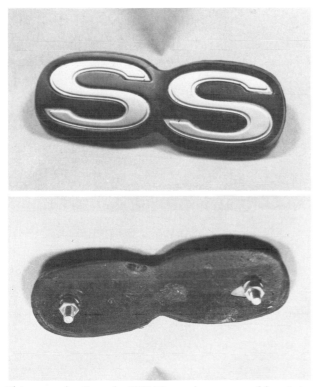

*This reproduction of a 1971-72 rear bumper emblem is incorrect; it does not have the third positioning stud, as the original unit did.*

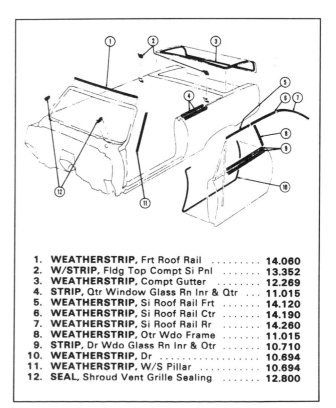

| 1. | WEATHERSTRIP, Frt Roof Rail | 14.060 |
| 2. | W/STRIP, Fldg Top Compt Si Pnl | 13.352 |
| 3. | WEATHERSTRIP, Compt Gutter | 12.269 |
| 4. | STRIP, Qtr Window Glass Rn Inr & Qtr | 11.015 |
| 5. | WEATHERSTRIP, Si Roof Rail Frt | 14.120 |
| 6. | WEATHERSTRIP, Si Roof Rail Ctr | 14.190 |
| 7. | WEATHERSTRIP, Si Roof Rail Rr | 14.260 |
| 8. | WEATHERSTRIP, Otr Wdo Frame | 11.015 |
| 9. | STRIP, Dr Wdo Glass Rn Inr & Otr | 10.710 |
| 10. | WEATHERSTRIP, Dr | 10.694 |
| 11. | WEATHERSTRIP, W/S Pillar | 10.694 |
| 12. | SEAL, Shroud Vent Grille Sealing | 12.800 |

*Weather stripping for the Chevelle convertible.*

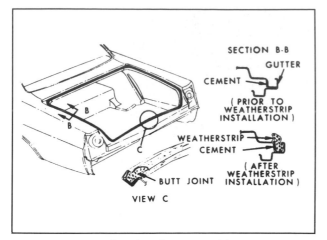

*Inner quarter panel sealing for convertibles.*

longer drilled and two self-drilling screws, part number 9423324, were installed. These screws must be used for correctness. The mirror was mounted to the bracket with a chrome Phillips-head screw both years.

**1966-1968**

A left-hand-door-mounted side mirror, part number 3874240, was standard equipment in 1966. The bow-tie mirror was slightly restyled: the bow tie and its mounting hardware were no longer inlaid in red. Part numbers were as follows:

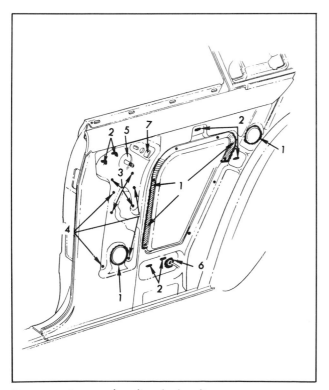

*Inner quarter panel sealing for hardtops.*

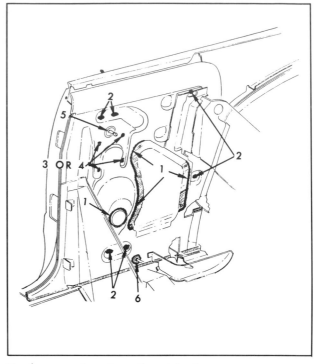

*Trunk compartment weather stripping.*

**1966 Bow-Tie Mirror Mounting Hardware Part Numbers**

| | |
|---|---|
| Gasket | 3874250 |
| Bracket | 3874252 |
| Screws & lock washers | 9421495 |
| Screw to attach mirror to bracket | 3821961 |

A few bow-tie mirrors were installed on the 1967 SSs but only in the first eight days of production, so no SS 396 with a build date of 08B 66 or later should have bow-tie mirrors. After that a

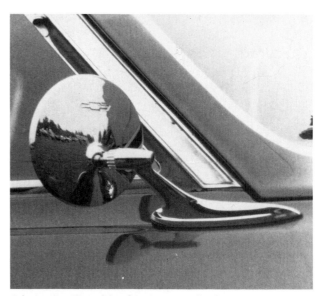

*A bow-tie mirror like this was standard in 1966.*

plain round-head mirror, part number 3909197, was used as standard equipment.

The 1968 standard mirror was identical to the second-style mirror used in 1967, including the part number. Mounting hardware was also identical and used the same part numbers as the mounting hardware for the 1966 bow-tie mirror.

For all three years a right-hand-mounted mirror was available as a dealer-installed option. It matched the driver's-side mirror, including the 1966 bow-tie mirror, in design.

### 1969–1972

The standard outside mirror, part number 3914753, was redesigned in 1969. The base was wider and the head was rectangular in shape. The mirror was mounted with a bracket, part number 3953067, which was held to the door with two 16×⅝ in. number 10 Phillips-head screws, part number 9421495. The mirror was held to the bracket with a chrome Phillips-head screw.

The 1970 standard mirror—part number 3965921, 3957200 for the El Camino—was similar to the 1969 unit. It used a different bracket, part number 3965931. Phillips-head screws, part number 9414723, with a rounded head secured the bracket. A black rubber gasket, part number 3965929, was placed between the mirror base and the bracket. The mirror was secured to the bracket as before with a single screw.

A driver's-door-mounted remote control side mirror, part number 3950761, was standard equipment for 1971 and 1972 with the SS package.

1969-70 standard mirror.

A round-head mirror like this was used in 1967 and 1968 as standard equipment.

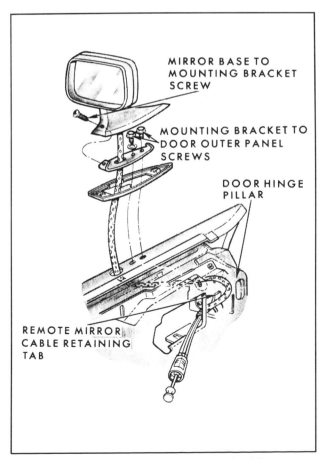

MIRROR BASE TO MOUNTING BRACKET SCREW

MOUNTING BRACKET TO DOOR OUTER PANEL SCREWS

DOOR HINGE PILLAR

REMOTE MIRROR CABLE RETAINING TAB

A remote control driver's mirror was standard for 1971-72.

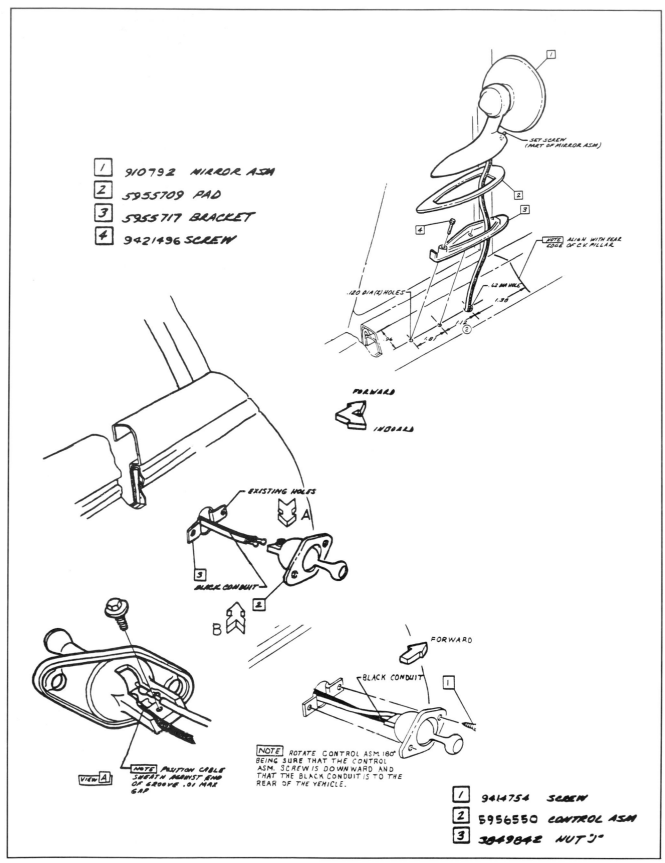

1  910792  MIRROR ASM
2  5955709  PAD
3  5955717  BRACKET
4  9421496  SCREW

SET SCREW (PART OF MIRROR ASM)

NOTE ALIGN WITH REAR EDGE OF C.V. PILLAR

.120 DIA (2) HOLES

.62 DIA HOLE

1.38

FORWARD

INBOARD

EXISTING HOLES

A

BLACK CONDUIT

B

FORWARD

BLACK CONDUIT

VIEW A

NOTE POSITION CABLE SHEATH AGAINST END OF GROOVE .01 MAX GAP

NOTE ROTATE CONTROL ASM 180° BEING SURE THAT THE CONTROL ASM. SCREW IS DOWNWARD AND THAT THE BLACK CONDUIT IS TO THE REAR OF THE VEHICLE.

1  9414754  SCREW
2  5956550  CONTROL ASM
3  3849842  NUT "J"

*1964-65 remote control side mirror.*

128

It was mounted much the same way as the standard 1970 mirror.

## 1971-1972 Remote Control Mirror
## Mounting Hardware Part Numbers

| | |
|---|---|
| Gasket | 3921835 |
| Phillips-head screws | 9414723 |
| Washers for screws | 3769610 |
| Screw to mount mirror to bracket | 9796652 |

The escutcheon plate, part number 3945996, was mounted in the upper section of the door panel and secured with two Phillips-head screws. The adjustment cable was mounted to the escutcheon plate with a setscrew, part number 9400827.

All three years a dealer-installed matching right-hand mirror, part number 3965922, was available. The 1971 and 1972 passenger's-side mirror was not remote control.

### Remote Control Outside Mirror

#### 1964-1965

In 1964 a left-hand-door-mounted remote control mirror was available as part of the comfort and convenience option, RPO Z13, or as a dealer-installed option. The mirror was listed as part number 910472, superseded by part number 910792 in February 1964. A black pad, part number 5955709, was used between the mirror's base and the bracket, part number 5955717. The bracket was secured with two hex-head screws, part number 9421496. The mirror was mounted to the bracket with a setscrew.

The escutcheon plate was combined with the control assembly. It was listed as part number 5956550—part number 5955670 was used with the first-style mirror—and was mounted in the door panel. When part number 5956550 is used, the control assembly must be rotated 180 degrees so that the black cable faces the rear of the car.

A dealer-installed mirror was also available as a single unit or as part of a matched set with a non-remote-control mirror on the passenger's door.

The 1965 mirror was identical to the second-style mirror and controls in every way including part numbers.

#### 1966-1967

Early 1966 models used the same mirror as in 1965 and a control assembly, part number 5958039, that looked similar to the 1964-65 part but was not rotated. The black cable should still face the rear of the car. The cables were held to the rear of the control with a small black retainer, part number 5957967. The control was mounted to the door panel with Phillips-head screws and J-nuts. A plate, part number 5956894, covered up the screws.

Late 1966 models, constructed after build date 03A 66, and all 1967 models used a different mir-

A chrome hook inside rearview mirror was used in all SSs except the 300-based cars in 1969. The 300-based cars used a mirror painted silver. The plastic cover on the mirror matched the interior trim.

ror, part number 5958039, with a control at the end of the cable. The escutcheon plate, part number 3891496, was round in shape and mounted to the door panel with an existing retainer in the door.

The mirror used a small, uniquely shaped bracket, part number 3899859, and a gasket, part number 3899860, instead of a pad. It was mounted to the bracket with a Phillips-head screw on the rear of its base.

A measure of the popularity of the Super Sport can be denoted from the fact that almost half of the Chevelles sold in 1964 were the Super Sport models. Some 76,860 of the Super Sport convertibles and Sport Coupes were produced that first model year. The fact that the '64 didn't carry a bigger powerplant probably kept it from being as popular as the later SS versions. Phil Kunz/Bill Holder

*The SS convertible for 1965 took the nice design of 1964 and made it even better. The model carried practically no chrome and had an extremely clean look about it. The '65 model also had a much lower stance than the previous model. There were also subtle changes in the interior that featured a new instrument panel design. Some 81,812, or over half the total Chevelles built that year, were Super Sports. Phil Kunz/Bill Holder*

A right-hand mirror was available as a dealer-installed option in both 1966 and 1967. It matched the driver's-side mirror in design but was not remote control.

### 1968-1972

The 1968 remote control mirror, now RPO D33, looked nothing like the standard unit. Listed as part number 3921832, it used a rectangular head. However, a few early models, till the second week in September 1967, used the 1967 remote round-head side mirror.

A two-piece bracket was used to install the mirror. A single Phillips-head screw mounted the main bracket to the door. The mirror was attached to the smaller bracket with a chrome Phillips-head screw. A black rubber gasket, part number 3921835, was also placed between the mirror's base and the door.

A rectangular escutcheon plate, part number 3921834, was installed on the driver's door panel with two Phillips-head screws. The control cable was connected to the plate with a setscrew, part number 9400827.

A remote control side mirror was still optional in 1969 and 1970. It used the same part number, 3950761, both years and was similar in design to the 1968 unit. In fact, the gasket was identical.

The mounting bracket was redesigned and grafted into one part. It was held to the door with two Phillips-head screws and washers. The escutcheon plate was similar to the 1968 version but was listed as part number 3945996. The control cable was mounted the same as before.

For 1971 and 1972 the above mirrors were standard equipment with the SS package. How-ever, custom bullet mirrors, RPO D35, were also available for these two years. With the SS package the driver's-side mirror was remote control and was listed as part number 9878201. The body of this mirror was painted to match the color of the car. This option is not well known and is fairly rare. It was available only as a factory-installed option.

A right-hand-mounted nonremote side mirror was available as a dealer-installed option from 1968 to 1972. It matched the left-hand mirror in design, including the custom bullet mirror.

### 1968-1972 Right-hand Nonremote Side Mirror Part Numbers
| | |
|---|---|
| 1968 | 3914754 |
| 1969-72 | 3965922 |
| 1971-72 custom | 9878202 |

## Folding Top

### 1964-1965

A counterbalanced manual convertible top was standard with all SSs in both 1964 and 1965. However, it is believed that the exclusive Z16 convertible—only one was built—was equipped with a power top. A white top was standard; black tops, RPO CO5AA, or beige tops, RPO CO5AB, were optional both years. The boot matched the top's color.

Owing to the folding top, certain parts must be changed. Sun visors were shorter to clear the top lock mechanisms. They used part numbers 4484804-LH and 4484803-RH, and both were painted gloss-black. The chrome hook was listed as part number 5716613. Also changed were the rear seat armrests. Weather stripping was listed as follows:

### 1964-1965 Folding Top Weather Stripping Part Numbers
| | |
|---|---|
| Center header | 4406207 |
| Pillar post | |
|   LH | 4409037 |
|   RH | 4409036 |
| Side roof rail | |
|   Front | |
|     LH | 4407737 |
|     RH | 4407736 |
|   Center | |
|     LH | 4477662 |
|     RH | 4477661 |
|   Rear | |
|     LH | 4477665 |
|     RH | 4477664 |

The power top, RPO CO6, was optional. The switch was placed in a natural metal housing up under the instrument panel on the driver's side. An escutcheon plate was mounted on the underside of the instrument panel on the driver's side, to the left of the steering column, and held with two Phillips-head screws. Part numbers were listed as the same both years.

## 1964-1965 Power Top Component Part Numbers

| | |
|---|---|
| Switch | 3840095 |
| Housing | 3840097 |
| Escutcheon | 3840096 |

The wiring route was changed in 1965. Whereas the 1964 unit was routed to the starter solenoid, the 1965 unit drew power from the horn relay.

The hydraulic pump and motor were listed as part number 7595117 and mounted on rubber grommets to the pan both years. The mounting package was listed as part number 3698109. Early 1964 models used a steel shield; late 1964s—the change probably occurred in October 1963—and all 1965s used a black cardboard shield. The lift cylinders, part number 4407818, are interchangeable with all GM A-bodies.

The top assembly, motor and metal shield should be painted gloss-black.

### 1966-1967

Folding top color choices were the same in 1966 as in 1965, but they were now up to the customer and were available with all exterior colors. In 1967 color choices were black, white and blue. The manual top was still standard both years.

The roof rail locks, part numbers 7590746-LH and 7590745-RH, were painted gloss-black. The

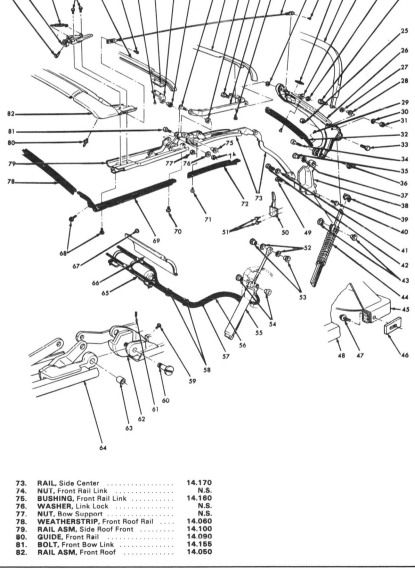

| No. | Part | Group |
|---|---|---|
| 1. | HOOK, Roof Rail | 14.080 |
| 2. | LOCK, Roof Rail Handle | 14.080 |
| 3. | SPRING, Lock Handle Return | 14.080 |
| 4. | SCREW, Roof Rail Lock | 14.080 |
| 5. | BOW, Top Front | 14.130 |
| 6. | SCREW, Hold Down Cable | N.S. |
| 7. | SCREW, Front Bow to Support | 14.155 |
| 8. | SPACER, Front Bow | 14.130 |
| 9. | SUPPORT, Front Bow | 14.140 |
| 10. | BUSHING, Front Bow to Link | 14.160 |
| 11. | BOLT, Control Link | 14.155 |
| 12. | BOW, Top Center | 14.215 |
| 13. | WASHER, Control Link | 14.162 |
| 14. | BOLT, Control Link | 14.155 |
| 15. | LINK ASM, Roof Rail Control | 14.140 |
| 16. | SCREW, Center Bow to Support | 14.215 |
| 17. | CABLE, Trim Hold Down | 14.102 |
| 18. | WASHER, Rear Rail Spring | 14.162 |
| 19. | SCREW, Hold Down Cable | N.S. |
| 20. | STRIP, Rear Rail Filler | 14.260 |
| 21. | BOW, Top Rear | 14.340 |
| 22. | BUSHING, Rear Rail Control Link | 14.160 |
| 23. | NUT, Rear Rail Control Link | N.S. |
| 24. | BOLT, Rear Bow to Rear Rail | 14.155 |
| 25. | NUT, Lift to Rear Rail | 14.157 |
| 26. | RAIL ASM, Side Roof Rear | 14.170 |
| 27. | WASHER, Rear Rail | 14.162 |
| 28. | BUSHING, Rear Rail | 14.160 |
| 29. | FASTENER, Rear Rail W/Strip | 14.260 |
| 30. | WASHER, Rear Rail Lock | N.S. |
| 31. | NUT, Rear Rail | 14.157 |
| 32. | WEATHERSTRIP, Side Rear Rail | 14.260 |
| 33. | BOLT, Lift to Rear Rail | 14.478 |
| 34. | BOLT, Male Hinge | 14.155 |
| 35. | BUSHING, Male Hinge | 14.160 |
| 36. | NUT, Male Hinge | 14.157 |
| 37. | WASHER, Male Hinge | 14.162 |
| 38. | HINGE, Male | 14.310 |
| 39. | SPACER, Top Life Guide | 14.475 |
| 40. | BOLT, Male Hinge to Lift | 14.155 |
| 41. | WASHER, Center Rail to Male Hinge | N.S. |
| 42. | BOLT, Center Rail to Male Hinge | 14.155 |
| 43. | BUSHING, Male Hinge to Lift | 14.160 |
| 44. | LIFT ASM, Counter Balance | 14.475 |
| 45. | BAG, Top Compartment | 13.450 |
| 46. | FILLER, Panel | 12.946 |
| 47. | SCREW | N.S. |
| 48. | STICK, Trim | 12.946 |
| 49. | BOLT, Male Hinge to Lift | 14.155 |
| 50. | CATCH ASM, Center Rail | 14.310 |
| 51. | SCREW, Center Rail Catch | N.S. |
| 52. | WASHER, Rear Rail to Lift | 14.162 |
| 53. | BUSHING, Rear Rail to Lift | 14.160 |
| 54. | BUSHING, Male Hinge to Lift | 14.160 |
| 55. | LIFT ASM, Top | 14.475 |
| 56. | HOSE, Pump to Lift Bottom | 14.472 |
| 57. | HOSE, Pump to Lift Top | 14.472 |
| 58. | CLIP, Hose | N.S. |
| 59. | SCREW, Roof Rail Stop | 14.155 |
| 60. | BOLT, Front to Center Rail | 14.155 |
| 61. | SCREW, Center Rail | 14.155 |
| 62. | RAIL ASM, Side Center | 14.170 |
| 63. | BUSHING, Front to Center Rail | 14.160 |
| 64. | RAIL ASM, Side Roof Front | 14.100 |
| 65. | MOTOR ASM | 14.481 |
| 66. | SHIELD, Motor | N.S. |
| 67. | SCREW | N.S. |
| 68. | SCREW, W/Strip to Rail | N.S. |
| 69. | WEATHERSTRIP, Roof Rail Side | 14.120 |
| 70. | SCREW, Weatherstrip to Rail | N.S. |
| 71. | SCREW, Weatherstrip to Rail | N.S. |
| 72. | WEATHERSTRIP, Side Rail | 14.190 |
| 73. | RAIL, Side Center | 14.170 |
| 74. | NUT, Front Rail Link | N.S. |
| 75. | BUSHING, Front Rail Link | 14.160 |
| 76. | WASHER, Link Lock | N.S. |
| 77. | NUT, Bow Support | N.S. |
| 78. | WEATHERSTRIP, Front Roof Rail | 14.060 |
| 79. | RAIL ASM, Side Roof Front | 14.100 |
| 80. | GUIDE, Front Rail | 14.090 |
| 81. | BOLT, Front Bow Link | 14.155 |
| 82. | RAIL ASM, Front Roof | 14.050 |

*1964-67 convertible frame.*

hook used the same part number as before. Also the same as in 1965 were the power top pump motor and lift cylinders. Weather stripping was listed as follows:

### 1966-1967 Folding Top Weather Stripping Part Numbers

| | | |
|---|---|---|
| Center header | 7615002 | |
| Pillar post | | |
|    LH | 7615144 | |
|    RH | 7615143 | |
| Side roof rail | | |
|   Front | | |
|     LH | 4548206 | |
|     RH | 4548205 | |
|   Center | | |
|     LH | 4548206 | |
|     RH | 4548205 | |
|   Rear | | |
|     LH | 4548208 | |
|     RH | 4548207 | |

The power top switch was located in the same place and used the same parts in 1966 as in 1964-65. In 1967 the switch was changed to part number 3897314—part number 3906118 was also used. All other components remained the same. The circuit breaker was listed as part number 4849847 in 1967 and mounted on the firewall.

### 1968-1972

Till 1971 a counterbalanced manual folding top was standard. From 1971 on a power top was standard. Color choices for 1968 were the same as in 1967. For 1969-72 white was standard and black was the only other choice.

The roof rail locks were listed as part numbers 7742777-LH and 7742776-RH. The chrome hook was the same part as in previous years. Sun visor supports, part numbers 4548357-LH and 4548356-RH, were chrome. As in years before,

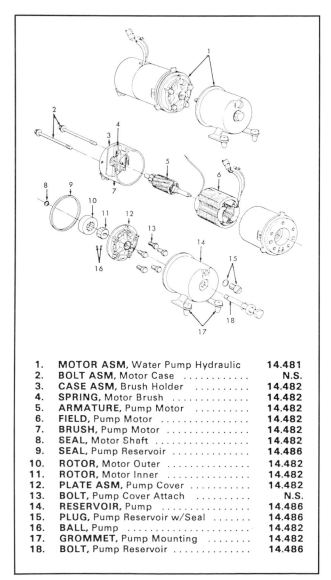

| | | | |
|---|---|---|---|
| 1. | **MOTOR ASM,** Water Pump Hydraulic | 14.481 |
| 2. | **BOLT ASM,** Motor Case . . . . . . . . . . . . | N.S. |
| 3. | **CASE ASM,** Brush Holder . . . . . . . . . | 14.482 |
| 4. | **SPRING,** Motor Brush . . . . . . . . . . . . | 14.482 |
| 5. | **ARMATURE,** Pump Motor . . . . . . . . . | 14.482 |
| 6. | **FIELD,** Pump Motor . . . . . . . . . . . . . . | 14.482 |
| 7. | **BRUSH,** Pump Motor . . . . . . . . . . . . . | 14.482 |
| 8. | **SEAL,** Motor Shaft . . . . . . . . . . . . . . | 14.482 |
| 9. | **SEAL,** Pump Reservoir . . . . . . . . . . . | 14.486 |
| 10. | **ROTOR,** Motor Outer . . . . . . . . . . . | 14.482 |
| 11. | **ROTOR,** Motor Inner . . . . . . . . . . . . | 14.482 |
| 12. | **PLATE ASM,** Pump Cover . . . . . . . . | 14.482 |
| 13. | **BOLT,** Pump Cover Attach . . . . . . . . | N.S. |
| 14. | **RESERVOIR,** Pump . . . . . . . . . . . . | 14.486 |
| 15. | **PLUG,** Pump Reservoir w/Seal . . . . . . | 14.486 |
| 16. | **BALL,** Pump . . . . . . . . . . . . . . . . . | 14.482 |
| 17. | **GROMMET,** Pump Mounting . . . . . . . | 14.482 |
| 18. | **BOLT,** Pump Reservoir . . . . . . . . . . . | 14.486 |

*Power top motor.*

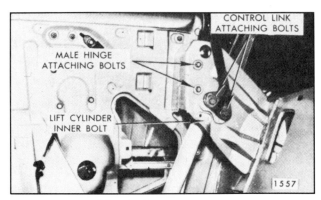

*1964-65 GM top lift cylinders.*

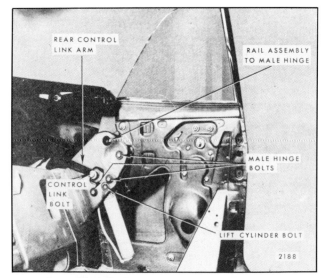

*1966-67 top lift cylinders.*

shorter sun visors were used. Weather stripping was the same from 1968 to 1972 except as noted in the following chart:

## 1968-1972 Folding Top Weather Stripping Part Numbers

| | |
|---|---|
| Center header | 7726803 |
| Pillar post | |
| 1968-69 300 w/wing windows | |
| LH | 7726961 |
| RH | 7726960 |
| 1969-72 | |
| LH | 9823139 |
| RH | 9823138 |
| Side roof rail | |
| Front | |
| 1968-69 300 w/wing windows | |
| LH | 7783477 |
| RH | 7783476 |
| 1969-72 | |
| LH | 8715373 |
| RH | 8715372 |
| Center | |
| LH | 7783479 |
| RH | 7783478 |
| Rear | |
| LH | 8796921 |
| RH | 8796920 |

The motor was listed as part number 7710923, 5044586 in 1971-72, and was mounted on four ½ in. rubber grommets, part number 3698109, to the pan behind the rear seat. The lift cylinders were the same from 1968 to 1972 and were listed as part number 9812594.

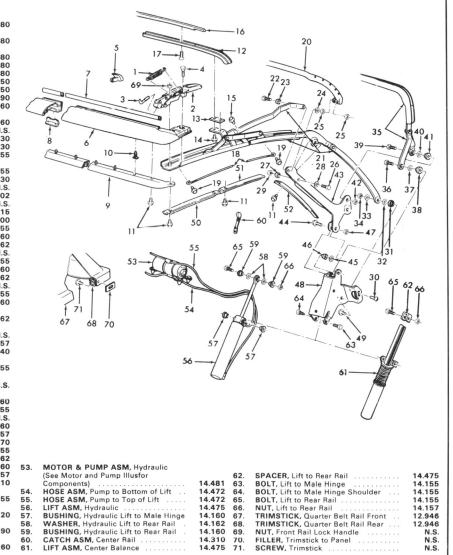

| No. | Description | Ref |
|---|---|---|
| 1. | SPRING, Frt Rf Rail Lock Hdle Return (Comp of Item 2) | 14.080 |
| 2. | LOCK & HANDLE ASM, Front Roof Rail (Incl Item 1-3) | 14.080 |
| 3. | HOOK, Front Roof Rail Lock Handle (Comp of Item 2) | 14.080 |
| 4. | BOLT, Front Roof Rail Handle & Lock | 14.080 |
| 5. | STRIKER, Lock | 14.080 |
| 6. | RAIL ASM, Front Roof | 14.050 |
| 7. | LACE, Front Roof Rail | 14.650 |
| 8. | SPACER, Front Roof Rail Center | 14.090 |
| 9. | WEATHERSTRIP ASM, Front Roof Rail | 14.060 |
| 10. | FASTENER, Front Roof Rail Weatherstrip | 14.060 |
| 11. | SCREW, Roof Rail W/Strip to Rail | N.S. |
| 12. | BOW ASM, Front | 14.130 |
| 13. | SPACER, Front Bow | 14.130 |
| 14. | SCREW, Front Bow to Rail | 14.155 |
| 15. | SCREW, Side Roof Front Rail Hinge Set | 14.155 |
| 16. | RETAINER, Front Bow Material | 14.130 |
| 17. | SCREW, Front Bow Material Retainer | N.S. |
| 18. | CABLE ASM, Material Hold Down | 14.102 |
| 19. | SCREW, Material Hold Down Cable | N.S. |
| 20. | BOW ASM, Center | 14.215 |
| 21. | RAIL ASM, Side Roof Front & Center | 14.100 |
| 22. | BOLT, Control Link to Rear Rail | 14.155 |
| 23. | BUSHING, Control Link to Rear Rail | 14.160 |
| 24. | WASHER, Control Link to Rear Rail | 14.162 |
| 25. | NUT, Control Link to Rear Rail | N.S. |
| 26. | BOLT, Center Rail to Rear Rail | 14.155 |
| 27. | BUSHING, Center Rail to Rear Rail | 14.160 |
| 28. | WASHER, Center Rail to Rear Rail | 14.162 |
| 29. | NUT, Center Rail to Rear Rail | N.S. |
| 30. | BOLT, Center Rail to Male Hinge | 14.155 |
| 31. | BUSHING, Center Rail to Male Hinge | 14.160 |
| 32. | WASHER, Center Rail to Male Hinge Spring | 14.162 |
| 33. | WASHER, Center Rail to Male Hinge Flat | N.S. |
| 34. | NUT, Center Rail to Male Hinge | 14.157 |
| 35. | BOW ASM, Rear | 14.340 |
| 36. | BOLT, Rear Bow Control Link to Male Hinge | 14.155 |
| 37. | WASHER, Rear Bow Control Link to Male Hinge | N.S. |
| 38. | BUSHING, Rear Bow Control Link to Male Hinge | 14.160 |
| 39. | BOLT, Rear Bow to Rear Rail | 14.155 |
| 40. | WASHER, Rear Bow to Rear Rail | N.S. |
| 41. | BUSHING, Rear Bow to Rear Rail | 14.160 |
| 42. | NUT, Rear Bow to Rear Rail | 14.157 |
| 43. | RAIL ASM, Side Roof Rear | 14.170 |
| 44. | BOLT, Rear Rail to Male Hinge | 14.155 |
| 45. | WASHER, Rear Rail to Male Hinge | 14.162 |
| 46. | BUSHING, Rear Rail to Male Hinge | 14.160 |
| 47. | NUT, Rear Rail to Male Hinge | 14.157 |
| 48. | HINGE ASM, Male | 14.310 |
| 49. | BOLT, Male Hinge to Mounting Support | 14.155 |
| 50. | WEATHERSTRIP ASM, Side Roof Rail Front | 14.120 |
| 51. | WEATHERSTRIP ASM, Side Roof Rail Center | 14.190 |
| 52. | WEATHERSTRIP ASM, Side Roof Rail Rear | 14.260 |
| 53. | MOTOR & PUMP ASM, Hydraulic (See Motor and Pump Illus for Components) | 14.481 |
| 54. | HOSE ASM, Pump to Bottom of Lift | 14.472 |
| 55. | HOSE ASM, Pump to Top of Lift | 14.472 |
| 56. | LIFT ASM, Hydraulic | 14.475 |
| 57. | BUSHING, Hydraulic Lift to Male Hinge | 14.160 |
| 58. | WASHER, Hydraulic Lift to Rear Rail | 14.162 |
| 59. | BUSHING, Hydraulic Lift to Rear Rail | 14.160 |
| 60. | CATCH ASM, Center Rail | 14.310 |
| 61. | LIFT ASM, Center Balance | 14.475 |
| 62. | SPACER, Lift to Rear Rail | 14.475 |
| 63. | BOLT, Lift to Male Hinge | 14.155 |
| 64. | BOLT, Lift to Male Hinge Shoulder | 14.155 |
| 65. | BOLT, Lift to Rear Rail | 14.155 |
| 66. | NUT, Lift to Rear Rail | 14.157 |
| 67. | TRIMSTICK, Quarter Belt Rail Front | 12.946 |
| 68. | TRIMSTICK, Quarter Belt Rail Rear | 12.946 |
| 69. | NUT, Front Rail Lock Handle | N.S. |
| 70. | FILLER, Trimstick to Panel | N.S. |
| 71. | SCREW, Trimstick | N.S. |

*1968-72 folding top frame.*

The power top switch for 1968 was in the same location as in 1967 and used the same parts. However, the escutcheon plate was not used. For 1969 the switch was placed in the instrument carrier to the right of the tachometer housing. In 1970–72 the switch, part number 3973645, was located in a bezel, part number 3973641, to the right of the radio, between the radio and the cigarette lighter.

## Vinyl Top

### 1964–1972

No vinyl top was available in 1964; the option, RPO C08, was added to the line-up sometime after the first of January 1965. Although it was not listed as part of the option package, most Z16s came with a black vinyl roof; black was the only available color.

When this option was ordered, special moldings were added at the quarter belt reveal. Three pieces were used in 1965: the right-hand molding, part number 4437501; the center molding, part number 4440332; and the left-hand molding, part number 4437502. These were also used with two-tone colors.

A choice of black or beige was available for 1966 and 1967. A two-part four-piece molding was used both years.

### 1966–1967 Vinyl Top Molding Part Numbers
Inner
| | |
|---|---|
| LH | 7589293 |
| RH | 7589292 |

Outer
| | |
|---|---|
| LH | 7589525 |
| RH | 7589524 |

Black and white were the only choices available in 1968. In 1969 a total of five colors were available. Choices depended on exterior colors.

### 1969 Vinyl Top Colors

| Top | Exterior |
|---|---|
| Black | All colors |
| Parchment (white) | All colors |
| Dark blue | Dover White, Cortez Silver, Dusk Blue, Glacier Blue & Lemans Blue |

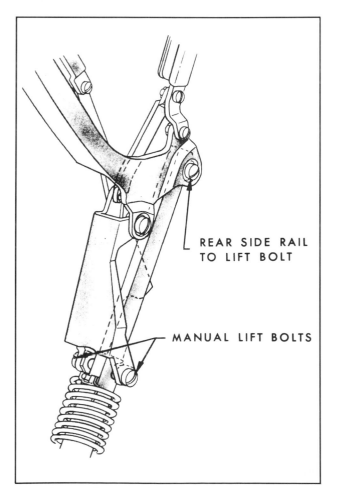

*1964-70 manual top attachment.*

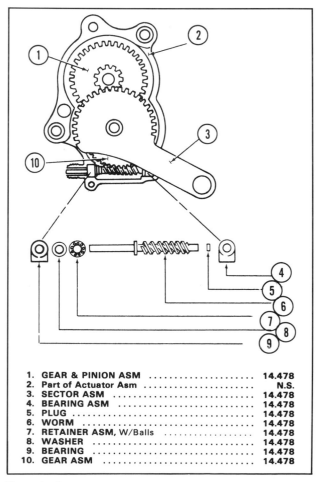

| | | |
|---|---|---|
| 1. | GEAR & PINION ASM | 14.478 |
| 2. | Part of Actuator Asm | N.S. |
| 3. | SECTOR ASM | 14.478 |
| 4. | BEARING ASM | 14.478 |
| 5. | PLUG | 14.478 |
| 6. | WORM | 14.478 |
| 7. | RETAINER ASM, W/Balls | 14.478 |
| 8. | WASHER | 14.478 |
| 9. | BEARING | 14.478 |
| 10. | GEAR ASM | 14.478 |

*Top actuator.*

## 1969 Vinyl Top Colors

| Top | Exterior |
|---|---|
| Dark brown | Olympic Gold, Butternut Yellow, Champagne & Burnished Brown |
| Midnight green | Tuxedo Black, Dover White, Fathom Green & Frost Lime |

Five colors were again offered in 1970, but the choices were revised.

## 1970 Vinyl Top Colors

| Top | Exterior |
|---|---|
| Black | All colors |
| White | All colors |
| Dark blue | Cortez Silver, Classic White, Astro Blue & Fathom Blue |
| Dark green | Classic White, Green Mist & Forest Green |
| Dark gold | Champagne Gold, Autumn Gold & Gobi Beige |

For 1971 five choices were again available.

## 1971 Vinyl Top Colors

| Top | Exterior |
|---|---|
| Black | All colors |
| Dark blue | Tuxedo Black, Nevada Silver, Antique White, Ascot Blue & Malsane Blue |
| Dark brown | Classic Copper, Burnt Orange, Rosewood Metallic, Sandalwood & Antique White |

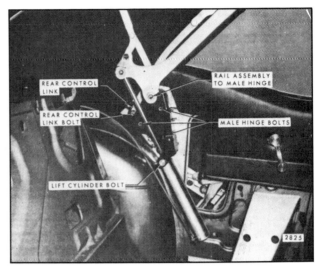

*1970-72 power top lift cylinders.*

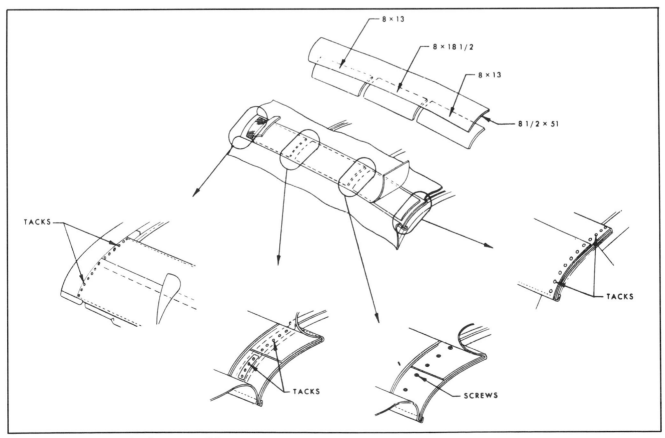

*GM A-body stay pads for the convertible top.*

## 1971 Vinyl Top Colors

| Top | Exterior |
|---|---|
| Dark green | Tuxedo Black, Lime Green, Cottonwood Green, Antique Green & Antique White |
| White | All colors |

Vinyl roof colors were again revised in 1972.

## 1972 Vinyl Top Colors

| Top | Exterior |
|---|---|
| Black | All colors |
| White | All colors |
| Medium green | Antique White, Pewter Silver, Gulf Green & Sequoia Green |
| Medium tan | Antique White, Mohave Gold & Midnight Bronze |

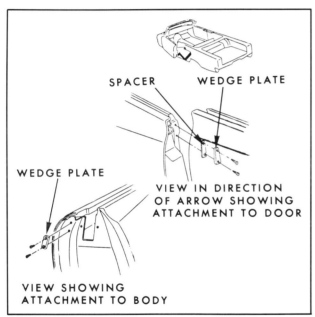

SPACER   WEDGE PLATE

WEDGE PLATE

VIEW IN DIRECTION OF ARROW SHOWING ATTACHMENT TO DOOR

VIEW SHOWING ATTACHMENT TO BODY

*Wedge plates used with the convertible.*

*The vinyl top was also available on the pickup.*

Light covert — Antique White, Sequoia Green, Covert Tan, Placer Gold, Cream Yellow, Golden Brown, Mohave Gold, Orange Flame & Midnight Bronze

Quarter belt moldings were listed as follows:

## 1968-1972 Vinyl Top Quarter Belt Molding Part Numbers

1968-69
Front
| | |
|---|---|
| LH | 7739443 |
| RH | 7739442 |

Rear
| | |
|---|---|
| LH | 7746859 |
| RH | 7746858 |

1970-72
Front
| | |
|---|---|
| LH | 8788125 |
| RH | 8788124 |

Rear
| | |
|---|---|
| LH | 9811346 |
| RH | 9811345 |

The original color of the vinyl top, or whether your car originally was built with a vinyl top, can be determined by the data plate (see Chapter 1).

## Sport Stripes

### 1964-1967

No optional or standard sport stripes were available for the Chevelle from 1964 to 1966.

### 1967 Standard SS Decal Stripes

| Decal Location | Part Number Black | White |
|---|---|---|
| **Front Fender** | | |
| Forward Section | 3913623-LH | 3913625-LH |
| | 3913624-RH | 3913626-RH |
| Rear Section | 3913631-LH | 3913633-LH |
| | 3913632-RH | 3913634-RH |
| Doors | 3913639 | 3913640 |
| **Rear Fender** | | |
| Forward Section | 3913647-LH | 3913649-LH |
| | 3913648-RH | 3913650-RH |
| Rear Section | 3913655-LH | 3913657-LH |
| | 3913656-RH | 3913658-RH |
| | **Dark Blue** | **Red** |
| **Front Fender** | | |
| Forward Section | 3913627-LH | 3913629-LH |
| | 3913628-RH | 3913630-RH |
| Rear Section | 3913635-LH | 3913637-LH |
| | 3913636-RH | 3913638-RH |
| Doors | 3913641 | 3913642 |
| **Rear Fender** | | |
| Forward Section | 3913651-LH | 3913653-LH |
| | 3913652-RH | 3913654-RH |
| Rear Section | 3913659-LH | 3913661-LH |
| | 3913660-RH | 3913662-RH |

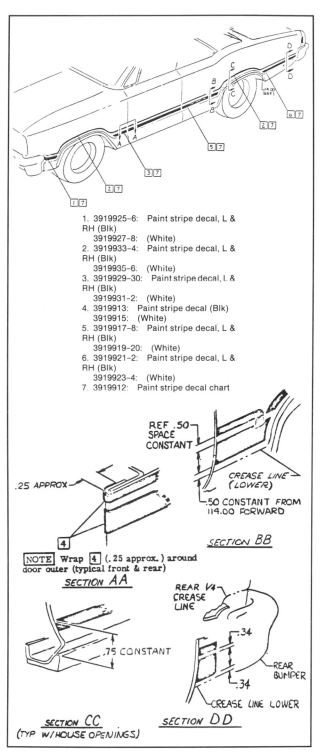

1. 3919925-6:  Paint stripe decal, L & RH (Blk)
   3919927-8:  (White)
2. 3919933-4:  Paint stripe decal, L & RH (Blk)
   3919935-6:  (White)
3. 3919929-30:  Paint stripe decal, L & RH (Blk)
   3919931-2:  (White)
4. 3919913:  Paint stripe decal (Blk)
   3919915:  (White)
5. 3919917-8:  Paint stripe decal, L & RH (Blk)
   3919919-20:  (White)
6. 3919921-2:  Paint stripe decal, L & RH (Blk)
   3919923-4:  (White)
7. 3919912:  Paint stripe decal chart

*Detail of optional 1967 stripes.*

*An example of the standard stripes in 1968 and 1969. The side lamp bezels were never released on production cars. Full wheel covers were listed as option PO1 in 1968 only.* Chevrolet

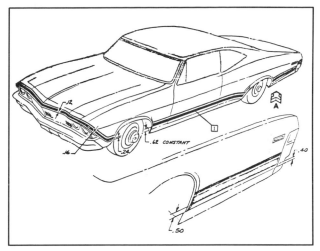

*The optional stripes in 1968 were available in black, white or red and were tape stripes.*

## 1967 Optional SS Decal Stripes

| Decal Location | Part Number Black | White |
|---|---|---|
| **Front Fender** | | |
| Forward Section | 3919925 LH | 3919927 LH |
| | 3919926 RH | 3919928 RH |
| **Wheel House Opening** | | |
| | 3919933 LH | 3919935 LH |
| | 3919934 RH | 3919936 RH |
| Rearward Section | 3919929 LH | 3919931 LH |
| | 3919930 RH | 3919932 RH |
| **Door** | 3919913 | 3919914 |
| **Rear Fender** | | |
| Forward Section | 3919917 LH | 3919919 LH |
| | 3919918 RH | 3919920 RH |
| Rearward Section | 3919921 LH | 3919923 LH |
| | 3919922 RH | 3919924 RH |

Although early factory promo shots show a 1966 SS with side pinstriping, this detailing was never released for the SS 396 model.

In 1967 a tape stripe manufactured by 3M was standard on the SS series. It consisted of two thin stripes—the bottom stripe being slightly wider—that spanned the entire length of the car. The stripes were located 0.5 in. above the lower body creaseline. A constant 0.3 in. gap should run between the two lines. Four colors were available: black, and white, dark blue and red.

Optional stripes, RPO D96, were also available. Like the standard stripes, these too were tape decals manufactured by 3M. They looked similar to the standard stripes except that the top stripe wrapped around the wheelhouse openings.

For the stripes to fit correctly, a 0.5 in. gap must separate the bottom stripe and the lower creaseline on the car from the front to 114 in. backward. At this point the gap must increase to 0.75 in. and then it must narrow to 0.34 in. at the rear of the car.

Two different colors were available: black and white. Both were offered on all exterior colors except Tuxedo Black, which used white stripes only, and Ermine White, which used black stripes only.

### 1968-1969

Two thin pinstripes were placed 0.9 in. under the beltline of the car as the standard stripe in both 1968 and 1969. They were painted on and not decals. The top stripe had a constant thickness of

### 1968 RPO D96 Stripe Color Availability Chart

| Exterior Color | | | Interior Trim Color | | | |
|---|---|---|---|---|---|---|
| | Black | Teal | Blue | Red | Gold | Parchment |
| | | | Stripe Color | | | |
| Tuxedo Black | Red | White | White | Red | White | Red |
| Fathom Blue | White | White | White | n/a | n/a | White |
| Grecian Green | Black | n/a | n/a | n/a | n/a | Black |
| Cordovan Maroon | White | n/a | n/a | White | n/a | White |
| Palomino Ivory | Black | Black | n/a | n/a | Black | Black |
| Ermine White | Black | Black | Black | Black | Black | Red |
| Island Teal | Black | White | White | n/a | n/a | White |
| Tripoli Turquoise | Black | n/a | n/a | n/a | n/a | Black |
| Seafrost Green | Black | n/a | n/a | n/a | n/a | Black |
| Sequoia Green | White | n/a | n/a | n/a | White | White |
| Grotto Blue | White | n/a | n/a | n/a | n/a | White |
| Ash Gold | Black | n/a | n/a | n/a | Black | Black |
| Teal Blue | Black | White | White | n/a | n/a | White |
| Matador Red | White | n/a | n/a | White | n/a | White |
| Butternut Yellow | Black | n/a | n/a | n/a | Black | Black |

| Paint part numbers | DuPont |
|---|---|
| Black | 99L |
| Red | 4688LH |
| White | 4024L |

*The optional stripes were revised in 1969. They were not available on the pickup. (The vertical lines just in front of the rear wheel are from the old negative.)* Chevrolet

138

0.06 in. and the lower stripe was wider at 0.1 in. A 0.16 in. space separated the two stripes.

The stripes pinpointed at each end. To apply the paint correctly, start the decrease at 9 in. from the front end. Start decreasing at 4.75 in. from the rear of the car, and leave a 0.75 in. gap from the end of the stripe to the tail of the car. The stripes were available in either white or black. They could also be deleted.

The black lower body paint, which was not used on dark colors, was removed when the optional stripes, D96, were ordered on cars built after December 1, 1967. However, early models used the black paint along with the stripes.

The stripes were available in three colors: black, red and white. Choice was dependent on the exterior and interior colors of the car. The stripes were tape decals manufactured by 3M. For correctness certain specifications must be adhered to.

A 0.62 in. constant gap was found between the lower stripe and the lower body contour line from the rear of the front wheel opening to the front of the rear wheel opening on all body styles. From the rear of the rear wheel opening to the end of the stripe, the cars continued with the 0.62 in. gap, but the pickup started with a 0.5 in. gap and narrowed to a 0.4 in. gap at the end.

At the front of the front wheel opening was a gap of 0.24 in. This narrowed to 0.16 in. as the stripe traced up the fender at the mid beltline. Across the front header the gap should be only 0.12 in. between the bottom line and the front edge of the car.

The optional stripes were restyled in 1969 and were originally painted on, not tape. They were routed along the side of the car 0.12 in. above the beltline like the standard stripes. They consisted of two thin 0.12 in. wide pinstripes around a wider 0.66 in. center stripe. A gap of 0.12 in. separated each pair of stripes.

Like the standard stripes, the optional stripes pinpointed at each end; the 0.12 in. gap remained constant. To be applied correctly, the stripes should start decreasing 12.25 in. from the front end, stopping 0.55 in. from the edge of the fender, and at 29.2 in. from the rear end, stopping 1 in. from the peak edge of the quarter panel.

The stripes were available in a variety of colors dependent on the exterior and interior colors of the car. They were not available on the El Camino; nor were the standard stripes either year.

Near the end of the model run in 1969, twin hood and deck stripes became available as a special order. They were similar to the the 1970-72

The rear of the 1970 Chevelle Super Sport was a completely new style. The tail lights were rectangular in shape with horizontal lines across the glass and the SS emblem highlighted in the rear black-out strip in white letters. The twin stripes running the length of the hood and outlined with pinstriping really set off this Super Sport. Phil Kunz/Bill Holder

The rear-end treatment of the 1971 Chevelle Super Sport showed considerable bumper differences with the four-light treatment. The SS emblem on the rear bumper was centered and quite prominent. The popular striping that had been introduced earlier was continued in the 1971 Super Sport. Phil Kunz/Bill Holder

1969 optional stripes.

139

stripes, but different dimensions were used. A standard production Chevelle hood was also offered, and not the twin-dome unit.

### 1969 Twin Hood and Deck Stripe Specifications (in Inches)

| Dimension | Hood | Deck Lid |
|---|---|---|
| Width | | |
|   Main stripe | 10.7 | 10.64 |
|   Pinstripe | 0.25 | 0.3 |
|   Space between stripes | 0.3 | 0.25 |
| Distance from end of stripe to edge of panel | | |
|   Main stripe | 1.55 | 1.38 |
|   Pinstripe | 1 | 0.8 |
| Overall Centering Dimensions | | |
|   Outward from centerline | 1.8 | 1.68 |
|   Inward from outer hood crease | 2.3 | |

The hood stripes were painted over both ends of the panel. The deck stripes *do not* extend past the edge of the deck lid. Only two colors were available: gloss-black and white.

### 1969 Sport Stripe Paint Part Numbers

| Color | DuPont | Ditzler | Rinshed Mason |
|---|---|---|---|
| Black | 88L | 9266 | 169C41 |
| White | 5033L | 2058 | A-2080 |

### 1970-1972

No standard stripes were available with the SS package from 1970 to 1972. The twin hood and deck stripes, RPO D88, were optional all three years for both the cars and the truck. With the pickup only, the hood stripes were used. These stripes were standard with the cowl induction option, ZL2.

Note that the 1970 SSs used two different sets of dimensions, and for originality the proper specifications must be employed. The dimensions were changed in the first week of April 1970. Cars with a build date before 04 A 70 should use the first set of dimensions, and those with a later build date should use the second set. All 1971 and 1972 SSs used the second set of dimensions unchanged. Reproduction stencils are usually the 1971-72 type and would be incorrect for the early 1970 cars, but you can make your own by following the guidelines given here.

### 1970 SS Twin Hood-Deck Stripes Specifications

| Width: | Early Design | Second Design |
|---|---|---|
| Main Stripe | | |
|   Hood | 10.64 | 9.63 |
|   Deck | 10.64 | 9.63 |
| Pin Stripe | | |
|   Hood | .30 | .30 |
|   Deck | .30 | .30 |
| Gap between hood/deck | .28 | .28 |
| **Length (Stops from edge of panel)** | | |
| Main Stripe | | |
|   Hood | 1.53 | 1.53 |
|   Deck | 1.38 | 1.38 |
| Pin Stripe | | |
|   Hood | .95 | .95 |
|   Deck | .80 | .80 |
| **Overall Centering Dimensions** | | |
| Outward from centerline | | |
|   Hood | 1.77 | 1.66 |
|   Deck | 1.68 | 1.68 |
| Inward from hood outer crease | | |
|   Hood | 2.28 | 2.28 |

Note: The stripes on the hood continue over the rear edge of the hood and disappear into the bright molding. The stripes on the deck lid *do* extend over for another 2 in. on the coupe and 1.09-in. on the convertible. On coupes with a vinyl top (C08), the stripes should end at the lid opening.

*Twin stripes were part of the cowl induction package and could not be deleted.* Chevrolet

_Chapter 8_

# Interior

## Interior Trim Codes

### 1964-1972

The interior trim color was fairly simple in the sense that it was uniform, except for the white interiors. In 1964 the carpet, kick panel, instrument panel and mid portion of the steering wheel were red, and the seats, door panels, console base and headliner were white. In 1965 the red was replaced with black, RPO 792, or aqua, RPO 796, in the same places.

With parchment—white, ivory—interiors the instrument panel, carpet, console base and seatbelts were black, and the headliner, seats and door panels were white. However, in 1971 and 1972 the headliner was black.

Except for 1964 and 1965, when bucket seats were standard, each year had two available styles of seating: a standard bench or optional Stratobuckets. However, some interior colors, like turquoise in 1970, were not available with bucket seats.

Vinyl seating was standard from 1964 to 1968; in 1969 the cloth-and-vinyl interior was made standard, with all-vinyl as optional. All bucket seats were covered in vinyl; no cloth-and-vinyl bucket seats were offered in the Chevelle. The SS pickup was standard with vinyl bench seating.

Degrees of gloss in interior paint were also changed. All 1964-67 cars used 60 degree gloss, whereas the 1968-72 cars used a 30 degree gloss finish. These two variations must be used to match the original gloss and color.

## Instrument Panel

### 1964-1965

The instrument panel was similar in 1964 and 1965. The glove compartments were made of black cardboard and held together with twelve staples both years but were slightly different each year. In 1964 a filler panel, part number 3852907, had to be used between the compartment assembly and the door's edge. In 1965 the compartment, part number 3862694, did not use this filler strip.

Placed across the top of the 1964 glove compartment door was a chrome-plated plastic identification plate that read Malibu SS with black and red lettering—the SS was inlaid in red on the original plate. This same style of identification was used

## 1964 Interior Refinish Colors

| Body Code | Color Name | Gloss | Paint Manufacturer's Part Number | | |
| | | | DuPont | Rinshed-Mason | Ditzler |
|---|---|---|---|---|---|
| 714 | Black | 60 | 88-L | 400 | DL-9248 |
| | | 0 | 4428-L | | DIA-9317 |
| 722 | Dark Aqua | 60 | 9012-L | | DL-12534 |
| | | 0 | 4429-L | 63B23 | DIA-12753 |
| 741 | Dark Blue | 60 | 96221 | | DL-12923 |
| | | 0 | 4430-L | 63B22 | DIA-12754 |
| 710 | Med. Saddle | 60 | 9015-L | 62C82 | DL-22162 |
| | Dark Saddle | 0 | 4436-L | 63B83 | DIA-22306 |
| 770 | Med. Fawn | 60 | 4527-L | 64082 | DL-22454 |
| | | 0 | 4436-L | 63B83 | DIA-22306 |
| 786 | Med. Red | 60 | 9016-L | 62151 | DL-71276 |
| | Dark Red | 0 | 4431-LH | 64T62M | DIA-50637 |
| 729 | White | 60 | 4024-L | 62V91 | DL-8259 |
| | Med. Red | 60 | 9016-L | 62151 | DL-71276 |
| | Dark Red | 0 | 4431-LH | 64T62M | DIA-50637 |

## 1965 Interior Refinish Colors

| Body Code | Color Name | Gloss | DuPont | Rinshed-Mason | Ditzler |
|---|---|---|---|---|---|
| 714 | Black | 60 | 88-L | A-946 | DL-9248 |
| | | 0 | 4428-L | | DIA-9317 |
| 741 | Med. Blue | 60 | 4630-L | 65V22 | DL-13006 |
| | Dark Blue | 0 | 9194-L | | DIA-13010 |
| 710 | Med. Saddle | 60 | 4626-L | 65B83 | DL-22570 |
| | Dark Saddle | 0 | 9199-L | | DIA-22534 |
| 786 | Med. Red | 60 | 9183-L | 65B53 | DL-71747 |
| | Dark Red | 0 | 9201-L | | DIA-71486 |
| 770 | Med. Fawn | 60 | 9171-L | 65B84 | DL-22571 |
| | Dark Fawn | 0 | 9202-L | | DIA-22568 |
| 799 | Med. Slate | 60 | 4623-L | 65B14 | DL-32469 |
| | Dark Slate | 0 | 9196-L | | DIA-32467 |
| 792 | White | 60 | 4024-L | 62V91 | DL-8259 |
| | Black | 60 | 88-L | A-946 | DL-9248 |
| | | 0 | 4428-L | | DIA-9317 |
| 796 | White | 60 | 4024-L | 62V91 | DL-8259 |
| | Med. Turquoise | 60 | 4628-L | 65B31 | DL-43400 |
| | Dark Turquoise | 0 | 9197-L | | DIA-43398 |

Above: **Paint Manufacturer's Part Number**

## 1966 Interior Refinish Colors

| Body Code | Color Name | Gloss | DuPont | Rinshed-Mason | Ditzler |
|---|---|---|---|---|---|
| 709/712 | Light Fawn | 60 | 9170 L | | DL-22569 |
| | Dark Fawn | 0 | 9202-L | | DIA-22568 |
| 776 | Dark Turquoise | 60 | 9273-LH | 66B31 | DL-71474 |
| | | 0 | 9287-LH | 66B35 | DIA43532 |
| 732/731 | Med. Bright Blue | 60 | 9271 LH | 67024 | 13223 |
| | Dark Bright Blue | 0 | 9286-LH | 66B28 | 13217 |
| 729# | Dark Blue | 60 | 9268-LH | 66B21 | DL-13222 |
| | | 0 | 9284-LH | 66B27 | DIA-13216 |
| 761/763 & 798/797 | Black | 60 | 88 | 400-A-946 | DL-9248 |
| | | 0 | 4428-L | | DIA-9317 |
| 787/790 | Med. Bronze | 60 | 9276 LH | | |
| | Dark Bronze | 0 | 9290 LH | | |
| 747/750 | Red | 60 | 9183-LM | 65B53R | DL-71474 |
| | | 0 | 9201-LM | 65B55M | DIA-22533 |

Above: **Paint Manufacturer's Part Number**

#-Cancelled at end of December 1965

## 1967 Interior Refinish Colors

| Body Code | Color Name | Gloss | DuPont | Rinshed-Mason | Ditzler |
|---|---|---|---|---|---|
| 782/783 | Med. Gold | 60 | 9390-L | 67B78 | 22839 |
| | Dark Gold | 0 | 9378-L | 67B77 | 22822 |
| 723 | Med. Bright Blue | 60 | 9387-L | 67024 | 13223 |
| | Dark Bright Blue | 0 | 9286-LH | 66B28 | 13217 |
| 728/729 | Dark Blue | 60 | 9395-L | 67B29 | 13383 |
| | | 0 | 9373-L | 67B28 | 13365 |
| 759/761 | Black | 60 | 88 | A-946 | 9248 |
| | | 0 | 4428-L | | 9317 |
| 775/776 | Turquoise | 60 | 9399-LH | 67B38 | 43680 |
| | | 0 | 9374-LH | 67B31 | 13366 |
| 746 | Maroon | 60 | 9389-LM | 67B61M | 50752 |
| | | 0 | 9293-L | 66B64M | 50729 |
| 747 | Red | 60 | 9366-LM | 67B54R | 71591 |
| | Dark Red | 0 | 9201-LM | 65B55M | 71486 |

Above: **Paint Manufacturer's Part Number**

## 1968 Interior Refinish Colors

| Body Code | Color Name | Gloss | Paint Manufacturer's Part Number | | |
| --- | --- | --- | --- | --- | --- |
| | | | DuPont | Rinshed-Mason | Ditzler |
| 765/765 | Black | 30 | 99L | A-946 | 9000 |
| & | | 0 | 4428L | 168C41 | 9317 |
| 793/794 | | | | | |
| 754/756 | Gold | 30 | 9478-L | 168B74 | 22988 |
| | Dark Gold | 0 | 9705 LH | 170B700 | 23318 |
| 759 | Red | 30 | 4688 LH | 165V51R | 71645 |
| | Dark Red | 0 | 9580 LM | 167C53R | 71643 |
| 755/757 | Teal Blue | 30 | 9467-LH | 168B29 | 13567 |
| | | 0 | 9453-LH | 168B22 | 13556 |

## 1969 Interior Refinish Colors

| Body Code | Color Name | Gloss | Paint Manufacturer's Part Number | | |
| --- | --- | --- | --- | --- | --- |
| | | | DuPont | Rinshed-Mason | Ditzler |
| 751/752 (b) | | | | | |
| 753/755 (a) | Black | 30 | 99L | A-946 | 9000 |
| & | | 0 | 4428L | 168C41 | 9317 |
| 793/794 (a) | | | | | |
| 760(c) | Medium Blue | 30 | 9585 LH | 169V21 | 13786 |
| | Dark Blue | 0 | 9578 LH | 169V22 | 13767 |
| 762/764 | | | | | |
| 765 (a) | Dark Blue | 30 | 9586 LH | 169B29 | 13789 |
| | | 0 | 9578 LH | 169V22 | 13767 |
| 760 (b) | | | | | |
| 783/784/ | Medium Green | 30 | 9591 L | 169B32 | 44008 |
| 785(a) | Dark Green | 0 | 9581 LH | 169V34 | 43994 |
| 782/795 | | | | | |
| & 796 (d) | Dark Green | 30 | 9592 LH | 169V31 | 44013 |
| | Dark Green | 0 | 9581 LH | 169V34 | 43994 |
| 779   (d) | Medium Turquoise | 30 | 9587 LH | 169V23 | 13787 |
| | Dark Turquoise | 0 | 9579 LH | 169V32 | 13768 |
| 787/788 (d) | Medium Red | 30 | 9528 LH | 168C51R | 71751 |
| | Dark Red | 0 | 9580 LM | 167C53R | 71643 |
| 770/771 (e) | Saddle | 30 | 9475 L | 168B85 | 22968 |
| | Dark Saddle | 0 | 9458 L | 168B82 | 22974 |

(a)-Malibu and El Camino only
(b)-300 only
(c)-300 and El Camino only
(d)-Malibu only
(e)-El Camino only

## 1970 Interior Refinish Colors

| Body Code | Color Name | Gloss | Paint Manufacturer's Part Number | | |
| --- | --- | --- | --- | --- | --- |
| | | | DuPont | Rinshed-Mason | Ditzler |
| 753/755/756 & | | | | | |
| 790/791 (a) | Black | 30 | 99L | A-946 | 9000 |
| | | 0 | 4428L | 168C41 | 9317 |
| 762/764/765 | Medium Blue | 30 | 9711 L | 170B26 | 13973 |
| | Dark Blue | 0 | 9712 LH | 170B27 | 13974 |
| 782/795/796 (a) | Dark Green | 30 | 9697 LH | 170B38 | 44169 |
| | | 0 | 9708 LH | 170B300 | 44173 |
| 776/777 (a) | Medium Gold | 30 | 9707 LH | 170B77 | 22316 |
| | Dark Gold | 0 | 9698 LH | 170B75 | 23308 |
| 770/771 | Saddle | 30 | 9714 L | 170B800 | 23321 |
| | | 0 | 9703 L | 170B88 | 23310 |
| 787/788 (a) | Red | 30 | 9709 LH | 170B51R | 71827 |

(a)-Not available with pickup

## 1971 Interior Refinish Colors

| Body Code | Color Name | Gloss | Paint Manufacturer's Part Number | | |
|---|---|---|---|---|---|
| | | | DuPont | Rinshed-Mason | Ditzler |
| 704/705/706 | Black | 30 | 99L | A-946 | 9000 |
| | | 0 | 4428 L | 168C41 | 9317 |
| 725/726(a) | Dark Blue | 30 | 9807 L | 171B27 | 14104 |
| | | 0 | 9818 | 171B25 | 14103 |
| 730/731/732 | Dark Jade | 30 | 9808 L | 171B38 | 44315 |
| | | 0 | 9823 | 171B36 | 44316 |
| 718/714/715 | Sandalwood | 30 | 9716 L | 170B76 | 23434 |
| | Dark Beige | 0 | 9819 | 171B85 | 23452 |
| 721/722 | Dark Saddle | 30 | 9801 L | 171B88 | 23436 |
| | | 0 | 9817 | 171B86 | 23453 |

(a)-Not available on pickup

## 1972 Interior Refinish Colors

| Body Code | Color Name | Gloss | Paint Manufacturer's Part Number | | |
|---|---|---|---|---|---|
| | | | DuPont | Rinshed-Mason | Ditzler |
| 703/704 & 743 (a) | Black | 30 | 99L | A-946 | 9000 |
| | | 0 | 4428 L | 168C41 | 9317 |
| 711/713 | Dark Green | 30 | 9911 L | 172B33 | 44508 |
| | | 0 | 9920 L | 172B31 | 44504 |
| 720 | Medium Tan | 30 | 9915 L | 172B86 | 23628 |
| | Dark Saddle | 0 | 9817 L | 171B86 | 23453 |
| 724 (a) | Dark Blue | 30 | 9818 L | 172B25 | 14103 |
| | | 0 | 9807 L | 171B27 | 14104 |
| 730/732 | Light Covert | 30 | 9912 L | 172B82 | 44509 |
| | Dark Covert | 0 | 9926 L | 172B81 | 44507 |

(a)-Not available on pickup

in 1965 but was slightly redone with a horizontal bar across the middle and all the lettering in black.

The upper portion of the instrument panel should be painted in a 0 degree gloss finish that matches the interior, and the lower portion in a 60 degree gloss finish—except with white in 1964; then the instrument panel was painted red in the same degrees of gloss.

In 1965 two white interiors were available: 796, which featured an instrument panel finished in aqua, and 792, which featured an instrument panel finished in black. These color combinations were used exclusively in the SS. The top portions of all instrument panels in 1965 should be painted 0 degree gloss in a color matching the interior trim, except as noted above, and the lower half in a 60 degree gloss of the same color.

A padded dash was optional, as RPO B70, both years, and when it was ordered, a vinyl-covered pad was placed on the top portion of the panel. This pad was molded in the same color as the instrument panel.

### 1966-1967

The instrument panel was redesigned for 1966, and the production Malibu unit, part number 3893909, was used. Cars with air conditioning used part number 3893915, which featured round cutouts on each side for the air conditioning vents.

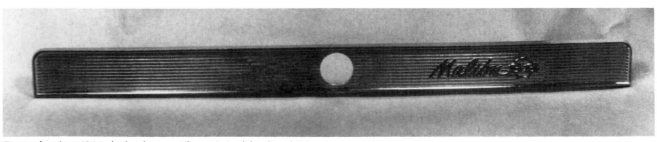

*Reproduction 1964 dash plaque. The original had red SS lettering.*

*The first year for the Chevelle Super Sport was 1964, and Chevy did it up right. The flashy interior of this '64 shows the bucket seats, console-mounted clock, SS emblem, and deluxe interior. The SS identification was also carried on the interior door panels and the glove compartment door. Phil Kunz/Bill Holder*

A vinyl pad was now standard and was molded in the same color as the instrument panel. The upper portion of the panel was painted 0 degree gloss, and the lower 60 degree gloss in both 1966 and 1967.

Special black-accented upper and lower trim plates were used in the 1966 SS. The upper plate was listed as part number 3891439 and identified the instrument controls. When air conditioning was ordered, a different trim plate, part number 3891455, was used. It featured a rectangular cutout in the center, for the center vent.

The lower plate, part number 3891437, was placed above the glove compartment door. A small plaque that read Super Sport was placed on it.

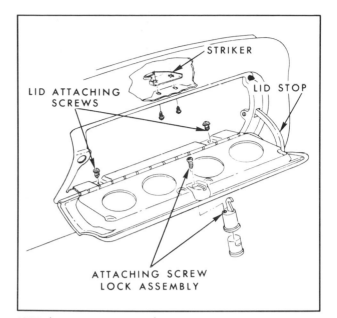

*1965 glove compartment door.*

Two glove compartments were used. The standard unit, part number 3885933, was held with twelve staples; part number 3885195 was used with air conditioning and was held with seventeen staples. Both compartments were made from black cardboard. The standard door was used with both applications.

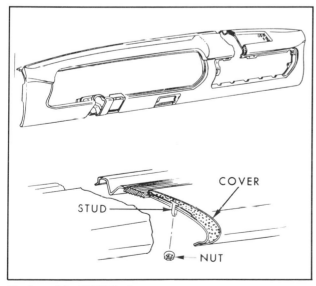

*Dash pad for 13000 Series.*

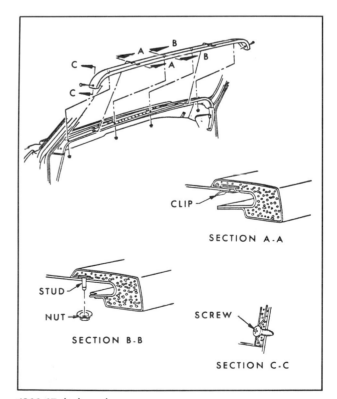

*1966-67 dash pad.*

1966 dash identification plate, top left, and shorter 1967 dash identification plate, on the right.

A lower steering column cover, part number 3876549, was bolted to the underside of the instrument panel and should be painted to match the lower portion of the panel.

The 1967 instrument panel, part number 3897579, was virtually unchanged and was painted according to the 1966 directions.

The instrument panel trim plates were revised. The upper plate was still accented in flat-black. The Malibu used a wood-grain insert, but this was incorrect for the SS model. The El Camino with the 396 ci engine used the Malibu plate, as it was not a true SS model. A plate with a rectangular cutout in the center was installed again with air conditioning and matched the standard part in color.

The lower instrument panel trim was also redesigned and used a ribbed texture with a dull aluminum finish. The SS plaque was still used but was shorter with smaller lettering than the year before.

The steering column cover, part number 3897563, was smaller owing to a redesigned steer-ing column. It should be painted in the same degree of gloss as in 1966.

### 1968-1969

The instrument panel was redesigned for the new body in 1968. The upper portion should be painted in 0 degree gloss, and the lower portion in 30 degree gloss, in a finish that matches the interior trim—except for parchment interiors, which have the panel painted black in the same degrees of

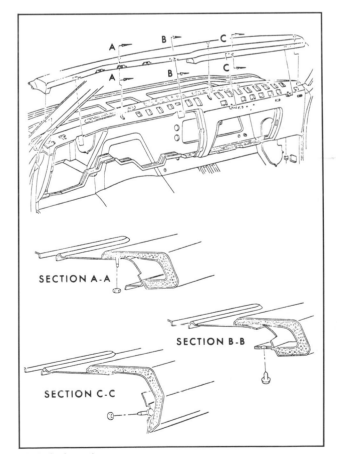

1969 dash pad.

The 1966 trim plate was accented in satin-black.

146

gloss. The same dash pad was used with or without air conditioning. It was molded in a color to match the interior—except for parchment interiors, which used a black pad.

The 1969 Malibu and 300 sport coupe (without wing windows) used the air conditioning instrument panel with all applications because of the Astro ventilation. The El Camino and 300 coupe (with wing windows) were not available with Astro ventilation. The Malibu panel was used when air conditioning was ordered, though.

Two bright air vents were placed on the lower section of the instrument panel on each side. These vents were connected to ducting that provided fresh air to the passenger compartment. A small plaque, part number 3950046, was placed to the right of the glove compartment door and read Astro Ventilation. A small Astro ventilation decal was also placed on the driver's window.

When air conditioning was ordered, the vent bezels were painted to match the lower portion of the instrument panel. In non-air-conditioned cars with Astro ventilation the bezels were chrome-plated.

A nameplate molding, part number 3922832, was placed above the glove compartment. This molding was bright and accented with 0 degree gloss satin black that read SS 396. An identification strip was also used in 1969; it too was black accented but used a different texture with a Mylar cover. Several part numbers should appear on the back of the molding, as the metal back plate was also cast for the Malibu and the Concours along with the SS.

*The cockpit for the 1965 Z16 looked like pure race car, which indeed it was. Included in the Z16 package was the 6000 rpm tach, the dash-mounted clock, the underdash controlled multiplex stereo and the 160 mph speedometer. The Z16 could well be the most collectable of all the Super Sport Chevelles. Phil Kunz/Bill Holder*

The standard glove compartment was listed as part number 9985028 in 1968 and was fastened together with twenty-four staples. In 1969 the part number was changed to 3939635, although the compartment was identical to the 1968 unit. When air conditioning was ordered, a one-piece plastic compartment, part number 3930197, was used both years. Because this compartment was mounted to the inside of the glove compartment door, a special door, part number 3930193, must be

*The interior of the 1965 Malibu Super Sport was clean and uncluttered. An upraised portion of the dash provided the driver a clear view of the instrument package. Gauges included temperature, ammeter and oil pressure gauges. Also a part of the design was an all-vinyl luxury interior and a center console. Phil Kunz/Bill Holder*

*An SS logo was located above the glove compartment door on this 1968 model. The U14 instrument package carried a series of gauges including oil pressure, ammeter and temperature in addition to a tach and a clock. Phil Kunz/Bill Holder*

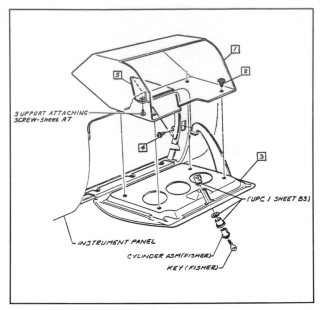

*This type of glove compartment and door must be used with air conditioning on the 1968-69 models.*

used. The compartment was mounted with four Phillips-head screws.

A large lower steering column cover—part number 3919937, 3939627 in 1969—was used both years. It should be painted the same color as the lower portion of the instrument panel.

### 1970-1972

As in 1968-69, in 1970 the upper portion of the instrument panel was painted in a 0 degree gloss finish matching the interior trim color, and the lower portion was painted in a 30 degree gloss finish of the same color—except for white interiors (ivory in 1970), which used black in the same degrees of gloss.

A vinyl-covered crash pad was still standard and should match the interior trim in color, except for white interiors, which used a black pad.

The glove compartment door panel consisted of two parts: an outer shell, part number 3957090, and an inner shell, part number 3957091. This panel was changed to part number 3991762 in the fifth week of May 1970. The later panel was flatter

| No. | Part | Group |
|---|---|---|
| 11. | PAD, Inst Panel | 14.655 |
| 12. | SCREW (#10-16 x 1/2") | 8.977 |
| 13. | SCREW | 8.977 |
| 14. | AIR CONDITION, Ctr | 9.262 |
| 15. | CONTROL ASM | 8.849 |
| 16. | SCREW (#10-24 x 3/4") | 8.900 |
| 17. | OUTLET ASM | 9.262 |
| 18. | SCREW | 8.977 |
| 19. | STRIKER | 10.268 |
| 20. | BUMPER, Stop | 10.263 |
| 21. | PANEL (*1) | 10.230 |
| 22. | SCREW | 8.977 |
| 23. | NUT ASM | 8.915 |
| 24. | DOOR, Inner | 10.261 |
| 25. | STOP, Door | 10.268 |
| 26. | SCREW (#8-18 x 3/8") | 8.977 |
| 27. | DOOR, Outer | 10.261 |
| 28. | CASE ASM | 10.266 |
| 29. | WASHER | 10.266 |
| 30. | ESCUTCHEON | 10.267 |
| 31. | OUTLET, Lower-RH | 9.262 |
| 32. | KNOB ASM | N.S. |
| 33. | SCREW (#8-32 x 3/8") | 8.900 |
| 34. | HOUSING | 9.709 |
| 35. | BEZEL | 9.709 |
| 36. | ASH TRAY ASM | 12.009 |
| 37. | SCREW (#8-18 x 1/2") | 8.977 |
| 38. | NUT (7/16"-28) | 9.650 |
| 39. | SPACER | 9.650 |
| 40. | WASHER, Special | 9.650 |
| 41. | KNOB ASM | 9.650 |
| 42. | KNOB | 9.650 |
| 43. | ROD ASM | 2.486 |
| 44. | NUT | 2.487 |
| 45. | SCREW | 8.977 |
| 46. | OUTLET, Lower-LH | 9.262 |
| 47. | SCREW (#8-18 x 7/8") | 8.977 |
| 48. | COVER | 6.518 |
| 49. | NUT (#8-18) | 8.921 |
| 50. | SWITCH ASM | 10.163 |
| 51. | SCREW (18 x 3/8") | 8.977 |
| 52. | SWITCH ASM | 2.485 |
| 53. | RECEIVER | 9.650 |
| 54. | CLUSTER | N.S. |
| 55. | SCREW ASM (8-18 x 1/2") | 9.260 |

| No. | Part | Group |
|---|---|---|
| 1. | REINFORCEMENT ASM, Lower (Part of 3977631) | N.S. |
| 2. | REINFORCEMENT ASM, LH (Part of 3977631) | N.S. |
| 3. | SCREW ASM | 8.977 |
| 4. | REINFORCEMENT ASM, Ctr | 10.230 |
| 5. | SCREW | 8.977 |
| 6. | REINFORCEMENT ASM | 10.230 |
| 7. | SCREW (#10-16 x 5/8") | 8.977 |
| 8. | RADIO BRACKET, Ctr | 9.650 |
| 9. | RADIO SPEAKER ASM, Ctr | 9.650 |
| 10. | SCREW (#8-18 x 3/8") | 8.977 |

*1970-72 dash used in the SS packages.*

148

and covered with a maintenance sticker, part number 3991751, and continued throughout 1972. This door is interchangeable with all Chevelles and Monte Carlos. It should be finished in the same color and degree of gloss as the lower portion of the instrument panel.

The steering column cover was listed as part number 3965451 from 1970 to 1972. It should be painted in the same color and degree of gloss as the lower portion of the instrument panel.

## Instrumentation
### 1964-1965

The SS series utilized special instrumentation in both 1964 and 1965; although similar, each year's version was different. The part number was listed as 6408284, 6408286 with air conditioning, in 1964, and the unit consisted of three round gauges. To the far left was a 120 mph speedometer with white lettering and a black face. In the center was a smaller round pod that held the clock, part number 3841680, with a chrome set knob. To the far right were the fuel level, oil pressure, temperature and amp gauges. Warning lamps were not used on the SS.

A tachometer was optional for all V-8s. One version was listed as part number 6412221, and V-8s with transistorized ignition used part number 6412218. When ordered, the tachometer displaced the center clock assembly. An external clock, part number 3840439, in a dull black housing was placed on top of the dash panel in the center. It was supported by a bracket, part number 3813791, and a trim plate, part number 3849510. The trim plate required a 0.8×1.4 in. rectangular cutout in the dash pad.

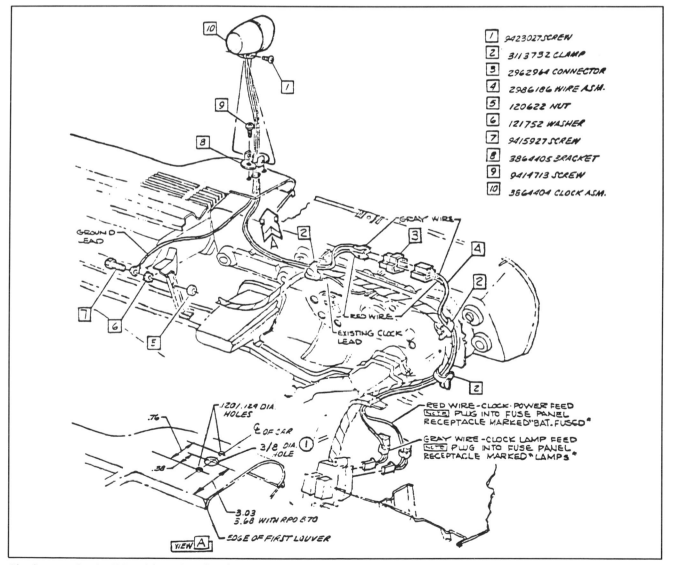

*Clock mounting in 1965 with optional tachometer.*

A pink and black wire assembly, part number 2985792, was used to connect the tachometer. The pink lead was connected to the bottom post on the tach, the black lead to the top. The other end of the black lead was connected to the negative (–) post of the ignition coil. For correctness the (black) lead should be routed through the firewall. Then, with support from a clip on the starter motor's harness, it should be routed along with the main engine harness to the coil.

The instrument panel layout was the same in 1965 as in 1964. The cluster was now listed as part number 6455199. The instrument shrouds were deeper and the insides were painted flat-black to reduce light reflections. The carrier was also restyled. It featured a smoother texture and a horizontal dividing line that was engraved with the control names. As in the year before, a different set of gauges, part number 6455445, was used with air conditioning and featured a slot for the center air vent in the carrier. Both years also supported a Chevrolet nameplate to the right of the cigarette lighter above the radio opening. When air conditioning was installed, this nameplate was deleted.

The tachometer, RPO U16, was still optional in 1965 and mounted the same as in 1964. All V-8s except the L79 and L76 350 hp 327s used part number 6411826. The L79 engine used part number 6412504, and the L76 engine part number 6412344. The L37 engine also used a different tach, listed as part number 6412218, that redlined at 6500 rpm. The Z16 package also used a 160 mph speedometer; it was similar to the Corvette part but used a silver instead of black dial center.

The wiring route was slightly revised, as the coil lead was no longer supported by the starter harness clip.

The clock was listed as part number 3864404 and was in the same location. It was mounted with bracket part number 3864405. However, no trim plate was used, and the pad was not cut out.

### 1966–1967

The 1966 SS used the standard Malibu instrumentation package, part number 6457758. It was housed in a long, rectangular unit with black faces and white lettering. The speedometer dominated the panel and was directly in front of the driver.

To the far left was the fuel gauge. Both it and the speedometer used flat-red dial hands. To the far right was the clock, part number 3874552. When the console, D55, was used, the clock was covered with plate part number 6455980, as a Rally clock was installed in the console.

Full instrumentation was optional, as RPO U14, and offered two clusters: part number 6458018 with manual transmissions and in cars with consoles and part number 6457783 with automatic transmission with the shifter on the column. The speedometer remained the same, the

fuel level and ammeter were on the left side, and the temperature and oil pressure were on the right side. All used flat-red dial hands.

The clock, part number 3892217, was moved to the top of the instrument panel in the center just in front of the speaker opening. A bracket, part number 3864405, was used to mount it. With the console this clock was eliminated.

A tachometer was also included in the instrument group or as a separate option, U16. Two different tachometers were installed, dependent on the engine. The L34 engine used part number 6412759, and the L34 and L78 engines used part number 6412816. For a short time the L78 engine used part number 6412764. All these tachometers were housed in a brightmetal case.

The correct mounting position for the tach is on the lower portion of the instrument panel next to the steering column on the right-hand side. Two holes were drilled into the panel: a 0.9375 in. diameter hole for the mounting screw and a 0.6875 in. diameter hole for the harness. A back-up plate, part number 3879588, was behind the tach for extra support.

The coil lead wire was brown, not black, and should have a two-finger copper clip that attaches to the negative side of the coil. For correctness the route should be under the carpet pad and along the wiring harness on the firewall.

A pigtail lead from the tachometer should be gray and should have a female connector that plugs into the receptacle marked Lamps on the fuse box. Another lead—pink and black—should be plugged into the receptacle marked Ign Fused.

Production Malibu gauges were used again in 1967, and except for the addition of a brake warning lamp they were identical to those used in 1966. Part numbers were listed as 6459688 production, 6459687 with the Powerglide and 6459686 with the Turbo 400. A new option, RPO U15 speed warning, was also added. It required another set of gauges, part numbers 6459692 production or with the console and 6459691 with the Powerglide. It was not available with the Turbo Hydra-matic transmission except with the console.

Optional instrumentation was still available and was identical except for the warning lamp. A total of four units were used. Gauges with the Turbo Hydra-matic transmission, M40, were available only if a console was also ordered.

### 1967 Optional Instrumentation Part Numbers

| | |
|---|---|
| Manual or console | 6459689 |
| Powerglide | 6459690 |
| Manual or console w/U15 | 6459693 |
| Powerglide w/U15 | 6459694 |

The tachometer was smaller in diameter in 1967 than in 1966 and was housed in a black case. It also supported the left-hand turn indicator. Its location was changed to the upper left-hand corner of the instrument panel, just in front of the fuel gauge. Three holes were drilled into the panel: two 0.8125 in. diameter holes for the mounting screws and a single 0.68–0.56 in diameter hole for the wire leads. A backing plate, part number 3906146, was also used.

The light blue production left-hand directional signal lead must be removed from the directional connector. A light blue lead from the tachometer was connected into a jumper wire, part number 6291386, that was inserted into the vacated cavity. The production instrument lamp lead was cut 4 in. from the socket, then was taped to the wiring harness. The removed signal lead was inserted into a connector, part number 2977864, that was connected to the jumper wire.

A total of three different tachometers were used in the 1967 SS.

### 1967 Tachometer Part Numbers
| | |
|---|---|
| Base L35 | 6468319 |
| L34 & L35 w/C60 | 6468499 |
| L78 | 6468500 |

Clock part number 3901632 was mounted on the transmission tunnel in the floor—only in cars without a console. Two 0.406 in. diameter holes were drilled in the floor to accommodate the mounting bracket, part number 3901633. A wiring harness, part number 6290685, connected the clock to the instrument harness.

For correctness a small square must be cut out of the carpet pad and a slit must be cut in the carpet to allow the wires to slip through. The above wiring harness was routed under the carpet pad and taped in place at three points.

### 1968–1969
The standard instrumentation was redesigned in 1968 but still used the production Malibu cluster assembly. Six units were offered.

### 1968 Standard Instrumentation Part Numbers
| | |
|---|---|
| Manual or w/console | 6459772 |
| Powerglide | 6480609 |
| Turbo Hydra-matic 400 | 6480610 |
| Manual or console w/U15 | 6480611 |
| Powerglide w/U15 | 6480612 |
| Turbo Hydra-matic w/U15 | 6480613 |

Two square, black-faced gauges with white lettering were angled back toward the driver. To the left of the steering column was the 120 mph speedometer with a flat-red dial indicator hand. The speedometer also housed the left turn indicator.

To the right were the warning lamps for the oil pressure, temperature and ammeter along with a small fuel level gauge. This also housed a clock, part number 3919015, which was now optional, as RPO

Optional gauge clusters in 1969. This one, part number 6482227, was used with a floor-shifted transmission.

U35. When this was not ordered, a cover, part number 6481501, was used.

Full instrumentation, U14, was again available, and six clusters were offered.

### 1968 Full Instrumentation Part Numbers
| | |
|---|---|
| Manual or w/console | 6480626 |
| Powerglide on the column | 6480627 |
| Turbo Hydra-matic on the column | 6480628 |
| Manual or console w/U15 | 6480629 |
| Powerglide w/U15 | 6480630 |
| Turbo Hydra-matic w/U15 | 6480631 |

The speedometer was identical to the production unit. In the center was a tachometer, part number 6468823, that was unusual in design. It used a vertical meter and was trimmed with a chrome bezel, part number 3918262. When installing the bezel be sure the wider side is toward the driver. The tachometer was available only as part of the instrument package; it was not available as a single option.

True dial gauges replaced the warning lamps on the right side; they surrounded a clock that was in the center. These gauges and the production units were housed in a plastic carrier, part number 6480995. The center section of the carrier was cut away to make room for the tachometer when auxiliary gauges were ordered. The carrier assembly should be finished in a 30 degree gloss that matches the instrument panel.

Three round, black-faced gauges with white lettering were used in 1969. Production Chevelle instrumentation was standard, and four cluster sets were used.

### 1969 Standard Instrumentation Part Numbers
| | |
|---|---|
| Manual or w/console | 6482218 |
| Automatic on the column | 6482221 |
| Manual or console w/U15 | 6482220 |
| Automatic on the column w/U15 | 6482226 |

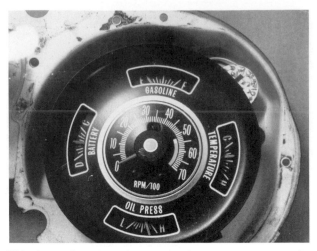

*This is a close-up of part number 6491313. Note the tachometer's redline at 5500 rpm, which would be incorrect for an L78, which should redline at 6500 rpm.*

The gauge layout was simple and clean. To the left was a 120 mph speedometer; it also contained the bright headlamps and brake warning lamps. In the center was a smaller opening that when ordered housed the clock, part number 3948956. A cover, part number 6483009, was standard. The fuel gauge was to the right and was surrounded by warning lamps for the oil pressure, temperature and battery.

Listed as option U14, full instrumentation was still available. Again four different clusters were used.

## 1969 Full Instrumentation Part Numbers

| | |
|---|---|
| Manual or w/console | 6482227 |
| Automatic on the column | 6482222 |
| Manual or console w/U15 | 6482228 |
| Automatic on the column w/U15 | 6482232 |

The cluster to the left of the steering column was identical to the production cluster. In the center was the clock. The fuel gauge on the right was replaced with a tachometer.

Two different tachometers were available: the base L35 and optional L34 engines used part number 6491313, and the L78 and COPO 427 cars used part number 6491314. The tachometer was surrounded by smaller gauges for the fuel, oil pressure, temperature and ammeter. As in 1968, the tachometer was available only as part of this instrument group.

All gauges used the same carrier, which was molded plastic painted the same color as the instrument panel in a 30 degree finish. When manual or floor-shifted automatic transmissions were used, the shift window was covered with black tape, as was the 1968 carrier assembly.

### 1970-1972

The Monte Carlo instrumentation was standard from 1970 to 1972. The layout was also the same all years. Three large round dial gauges were flanked by smaller gauges, one on the left and two on the right. Directly in the center was the 120 mph speedometer, to the left was the fuel gauge and to the far left was the warning lamp for the generator. To the right of the speedometer was a clock, part number 3973633, again standard equipment. To

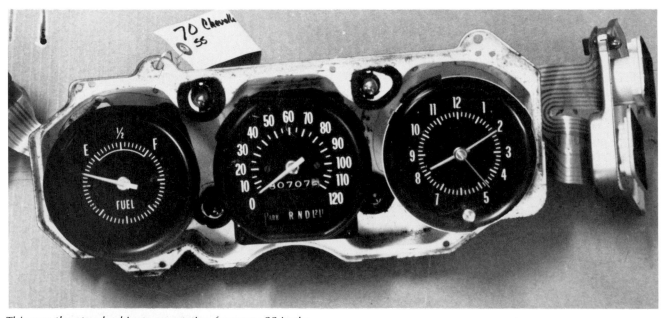

*This was the standard instrumentation for every SS in the 1970-72 model years, with warning lamps to the side of this cluster.*

the far right was the engine temperature warning lamp, and below it the oil pressure warning lamp.

## 1970-1972 Standard RPO Z15 Instrumentation Part Numbers

1970
| | |
|---|---|
| Manual or w/console | 6491957 |
| Automatic on the column | 7807851 |

1971-72
| | |
|---|---|
| Manual or w/console | 6496588 |
| Automatic on the column | 6496590 |

The optional instruments, U14, were functional and good-looking gauges. The warning lamps were replaced with operating gauges except for the oil pressure lamp, which was replaced with a red warning lamp in the tachometer. The standard warning lamp for the oil pressure was displaced by a small fuel gauge, replacement number 6431581.

The production fuel gauge was replaced with a tachometer. Several different tachometers were used each year. Part numbers were according to the size and horsepower rating of the engine.

## 1970-1972 Tachometer Part Numbers

1970
| | |
|---|---|
| L34 & LS5 | 6469985 |
| L78, L89 & LS6 | 6469983 |

1971
| | |
|---|---|
| LS6 | 5657407 |

1971-72
| | |
|---|---|
| L48 & L65 | 5657405 |
| LS3 & LS5 | 5657406 |

Unlike the standard clusters the optional gauges used a printed circuit, part number 8901487, instead of a wiring harness. This was

*A rear view reveals that this is a 1971-72 tach used with an LS-3 or LS-5 engine.*

changed in 1971, and even the standard gauges also used a printed circuit, part number 8601486.

## 1970-1972 Optional U14 Gauge Cluster Part Numbers

1970
| | |
|---|---|
| Manual or console | 8901487 |
| Automatic on the column | 6491972 |

1971-72
| | |
|---|---|
| Manual or console | 6496594 |
| Automatic on the column | 6496596 |

A black milgrained plastic carrier was used all three years. It included a shift window; when not used, this panel was blacked over with tape. This carrier was also used on the Monte Carlo. It was located under the imitation wood-grain cover.

*We can tell by the redline that this tachometer is from either an LS-3 engine or an LS-5 engine. The LS-6 redlined at 6500 rpm, and the yellow band begins at 5700 rpm.*

*This speedometer is for a car with automatic on the column and can be used correctly with a floor-shifted transmission.*

Standard clock for all 1970-72 SS packages.

## Steering Wheel

### 1964-1965

A two-tone steering wheel with a bright horn ring was standard in both 1964 and 1965. The most unusual versions were the wheels used with white interiors. In 1964 the wheel was white and red. In 1965 one was trimmed with aqua, and another one was trimmed in black.

Optional both years was a simulated wood rim steering wheel, RPO N34. Part number 9741033 was listed for both years. However, the horn caps

The instrument housing was the same for standard or optional gauges.

What's wrong with this interior? The wood-grain inserts on the carrier and the steering wheel were Monte Carlo, not Chevelle items. The accelerator pedal has a trim plate, which is incorrect. Also, this car was represented as an LS-6, and the tachometer is incorrect for that.

were changed: in 1964 part number 3845287 was used, and in 1965 the part number was listed as 3859873; both were visibly different. The horn contact was listed as part number 9741040 both years, and the wheel was mounted with Phillips-head screws and a nut and washer. The wheel also used a special mounting hub, part number 3845285 both years. Although usually seen with it, this wheel was not part of the Z16 option package.

Both the standard wheel and the optional wheel used signal canceling cam part number 382931 both years.

The cap in the center was for standard steering wheels in 1964 and 1965. The cap on the left was for the 1964 wood-rimmed steering wheel, and the cap on the right was for the 1965 wood wheel.

This is the standard 1967 steering wheel, but it is installed in a 1966 model, which is incorrect. The tachometer is also incorrect.

Standard 1968 steering wheeel. The cover is incorrect, as is the Malibu plaque; both should be SS 396 units.

1968-69 optional steering wheel.

## 1966-1967

A custom dual-spoke steering wheel with a horn ring and bright trim was standard in the 1966 SS. This wheel was molded in the color of the interior. The center horn cap read Chevelle.

The simulated wood rim steering wheel was identical to the 1965 wheel. The cap assembly was again changed and was listed as part number 3874640. It was brushed aluminum with a small bow-tie emblem in the center. All other components including the mounting hub were identical.

The standard steering wheel was redesigned for 1967. It was now a three-spoke wheel with a bright shroud and a horn button on each side. The wheel was molded in the same color as the interior. The center cap was black with the letters *SS* in white.

The optional steering wheel, N34, was also redesigned. Listed as part number 9746195, it used a three-spoke design with teardrop-shaped cutouts in each bright spoke. The rim was plastic but looked like real walnut.

The horn cap was listed as part number 3901313, and the horn contact as part number 3901330. The wheel was mounted as in previous years. The mounting hub was also redesigned and was listed as part number 3900579. As in years before, it should be painted the same color as the steering column.

## 1968-1969

The steering wheel was again restyled in 1968 with a new shroud that featured interior-color horn buttons. The shroud was the same color as the steering wheel and trimmed with black. At the top of the shroud in the center was a small SS 396 emblem part number 3925881.

The 1969 steering wheel was also restyled. Two wheels were used. All Malibu- and El Camino-based

SS 396s used a black steering wheel and shroud. The 300 based cars used a wheel molded in the same color as the interior trim—black, blue or medium green—with a black-accented shroud and horn blowing tabs. Both wheels were of the two-spoke design and featured an SS center shroud emblem.

A simulated wood rim steering wheel was optional both years, listed as part numbers 9748390 in 1968 and 3960722 in 1969. The 1967 wheel was used at the beginning of the 1968 model year, and the 1968 wheel was used at the beginning of the 1969 model year; both were identical in looks. Both wheels were mounted the same as in 1967. The 1968 mounting hub was identical to the 1967 part. The 1969 wheel used a different hub,

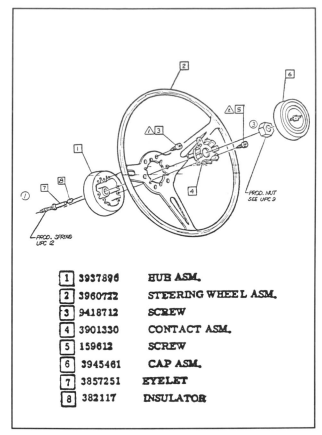

| | | |
|---|---|---|
| 1 | 3937896 | HUB ASM. |
| 2 | 3960722 | STEERING WHEEL ASM. |
| 3 | 9418712 | SCREW |
| 4 | 3901330 | CONTACT ASM. |
| 5 | 159612 | SCREW |
| 6 | 3945461 | CAP ASM. |
| 7 | 3857251 | EYELET |
| 8 | 382117 | INSULATOR |

*1967-70 optional steering wheel mounting.*

*The interior styling for the 1970 Super Sport was functional and fancy as can be seen from the interior of this SS 454. The four-spoked steering wheel told of its SS heritage on the center knob. The nifty instrument panel was unique for the Super Sport carrying a multitude of gauges and dials. Phil Kunz/Bill Holder*

part number 3937896; this smaller hub must be installed with the 1969 wheel.

Horn caps were also changed, to part number 3923667s in 1968 and 3945461 in 1969. The horn contact, part number 3901330, was the same both years. In previous years the optional wheel used the production eyelet and insulator; the 1969 wheel used special parts. The eyelet was listed as part number 3857251, and the insulator as part number 382117. Production parts will not fit.

**1970-1972**

The standard steering wheel in 1970 was a two-spoke black-plastic-covered rim with a hard plastic shroud with no rosewood insert. The shroud was attached to the wheel with four Phillips-head screws. In the center of the shroud was the double S logo.

Optional but rarely seen was the cushion grip steering wheel, RPO NK1, used in 1970 only. It featured a three-spoke design like that of the 1969 N34 wheel but used a black cushion grip instead of a wooden rim. The wheel was listed as part number 3952700, and the cap as part number 3937896. The mounting hub was part number 3937896, and the wheel was held to it with three Phillips-head screws. The horn contact was listed as part number 3937897.

In 1971 and 1972 the production steering wheel was standard, available only in black. A soft vinyl impact-resistant shroud was used. It was listed as part number 9752902, and an SS emblem was placed in the center. This shroud should not have the Chevrolet script, as other shrouds do.

Two optional steering wheels were available. Deluxe vinyl steering was RPO NK2. The wheel was listed as part number 9752131, and the shroud as part number 3992587. No SS emblem was used with this wheel.

Optional for all Chevelles was the four-spoke sport wheel, RPO NK4, listed as part numbers 458998 in 1971 and 3978125 in 1972. This same wheel was more commonly seen on the Camaro and will interchange. It was available in black only and included a black center cap, part number 3988030, that was seated in a retainer, part number 3988032, that fits snugly in the center of the wheel. In the center of the cap was a small emblem, part number 3988032, with a white background and bow-tie symbol. The SS emblem was not used on this wheel and would be incorrect.

The wheel was mounted uniquely with special parts. An insulator, part number 9740172, a receiver cup, part number 9748190, and a spring, part number 9749363, were held together with three Phillips-head screws, part number 9740173. This assembly was then placed in the wheel, and it and the wheel were secured with a nut.

A special eyelet, part number 3857251, and its insulator, part number 409190, were used along

| | | |
|---|---|---|
| 1. | **CONTACT UNIT,** W/Eylt & Spr ...... | 2.819 |
| 2. | **STEERING WHEEL** ............... | 6.513 |
| 3. | **SPRING,** Pivot ................... | 2.819 |
| 4. | **CUP,** Cap ...................... | 2.819 |
| 5. | **BUSHING,** But. Cap Adap. ......... | 2.819 |
| 6. | **SCREW** (#10-32 x 5/8") ......... | 8.913 |
| 7. | **NUT** (1/2"-20) ................. | 8.916 |
| 8. | **RETAINER,** Horn Button Cap ....... | 2.820 |
| 9. | **CAP** .......................... | 2.820 |
| 10. | **EMBLEM,** Button Cap ............. | 2.820 |

*1971-72 four-spoke sport steering wheel.*

with a canceling spring, part number 4042344. These parts must be used with the sport wheel only.

### Steering Column

#### 1964-1965

Exterior prepositions were the same in both 1964 and 1965. Only three columns were used. The standard unit, part numbers 3854381 in 1964 and 3872053 in 1965, included a bright shift lever, part number 383836 both years. The four-speed- and Powerglide-equipped cars used the same column, part numbers 384244 in 1964 and 3864545 in 1965. An extension assembly, part number 383555,

382063 in 1965, was also used with no provision for a shift lever.

A tilt column, RPO N33, was available both years. Either a four-speed manual or the Powerglide automatic was a required option. The same column—part number 5679787, 5693760 in 1965—was used with either transmission. The Malibu used a column with a bright shift lever, but this is incorrect for the SS.

The bright tilt lever, part number 3832567, and a dull black plastic knob, part number 3782965, were the same both years. The steering flange was

*The '66 Super Sport featured a redone interior with both a bench seat and the optional buckets. The SS 396 listed at only $2,776. Sales were up slightly for the Super Sport from the previous year with a total of 72,272 of both the convertibles and coupes being constructed. Phil Kunz/Bill Holder*

*As on previous models, the SS identifier on this 1969 model was carried in the middle of the steering wheel and again atop the glove compartment. This model has a bench seat, but buckets were also available. Phil Kunz/Bill Holder*

157

unique. Part number 5692962 was used in 1964. This part was also used with the Z16 package with the N33 option. All other 1965 models used part number 5692961. The directional lever was changed to part number 3782964 and used the production signal lever knob, part number 3782965, both years. The standard directional lever was listed as part number 3840903.

### 1966–1967

Four different columns were available in 1966. The standard column was used with all floor shift applications. Column shift was available with the Powerglide automatic, which used a bright lever, part number 3879746, and a black plastic knob, part number 3790368. The signal lever and the knob were identical to those in 1964–65.

The tilt-wheel—Comfortilt—option was again available, and two columns were used. Cars with floor shift used part number 5697070, and those

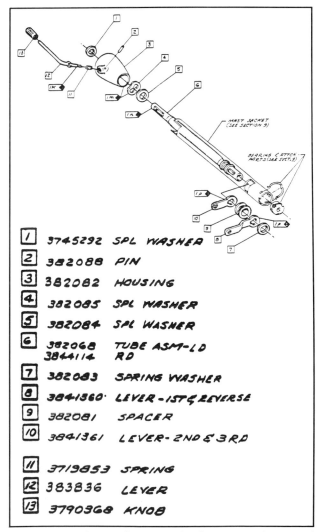

| | | |
|---|---|---|
| 1 | 3745292 | SPL WASHER |
| 2 | 382088 | PIN |
| 3 | 382082 | HOUSING |
| 4 | 382085 | SPL WASHER |
| 5 | 382084 | SPL WASHER |
| 6 | 382068 3844114 | TUBE ASM-LD RD |
| 7 | 382083 | SPRING WASHER |
| 8 | 3841860 | LEVER - 1ST & REVERSE |
| 9 | 382081 | SPACER |
| 10 | 3841361 | LEVER - 2ND & 3RD |
| 11 | 3719853 | SPRING |
| 12 | 383836 | LEVER |
| 13 | 3790368 | KNOB |

*1964-65 steering column with three-speed manual transmission.*

158

with automatic on the column part number 5697065. A special flange was required and was listed as part number 5692961 for all floor-shifted transmissions except the standard three-speed. Several column shift levers were used; the replacement part number is listed as 3884849. The tilt lever and the directional lever were the same as in previous years.

The steering column cover floor boot was listed as part number 3850999 and was used with all columns. It should be made from black plastic. Also used was a wire mast cover, part number 3886957 in 1966.

Owing to federally mandated safety regulations, the steering column was redesigned to be impact absorbent for 1967. The overall length was the same in 1966, but the outer diameter of the bowl and jacket assembly was larger.

The signal lever was listed as part number 3909580 and used a plastic knob molded in the same color as the interior. A new option, RPO K30 cruise control, was added in 1967. When it was ordered, a different signal lever, part number 6465211, was installed. This also doubled as a switch for the cruise control by pressing the end of the stalk. It used a black knob.

The canceling cam was also restyled and was now listed as part number 3900511. Four-way hazard flashers were standard. Two different column switches were available: early cars used a black knob, part number 346250, and the later models used a chrome knob, part number 398165. The change was made around build date 10A 66.

The tilt wheel was also restyled for safety. Two columns were offered, one for all floor shifts and the other for automatics on the column. The production signal lever knob was used on both columns. The tilt lever was listed as part number 3832567 and used a dull plastic knob in the same color as the interior. The column shift lever was listed as part number 3900565 and used the production knob that matched the tilt lever knob.

The tilt wheel column also used a special signal canceling cam, part number 3901609, and steering return spring part number 3900514 in 1967.

The column floor cover was restyled. It consisted of three parts: an inner cover, part number 397108; an outer cover, part number 397109; and a black plastic trim plate, part number 3897543.

The column-shifted Powerglide automatic is rare, as the sale sheets were written up so that it looked as if bucket seats and a console were mandatory options. However, it was possible to get a column-shifted automatic SS both years.

### 1968–1969

The 1968 columns were identical to the 1967 units, with only a few component changes. The signal lever was the same, and the knobs were still molded in the color of the interior except with parchment interiors—codes 793 and 794—which used a black plastic knob. The cruise control lever, part number 6465404, also used a black knob. The canceling cam was changed to part number 382116. The hazard knob was listed as part number 398165, which was chrome.

Three special tilt-wheel columns were used solely in the SS 396. Cars with floor shift used part number 7803752, and those with automatic on the column used part numbers 7803751 for the Powerglide and 7802909 for the Turbo Hydra-matic.

The automatic column shift lever was listed as part number 3928239. The tilt lever, part number 3925890, used a plastic knob that matched the interior except with parchment interiors, which used a black knob. The signal canceling cam was listed as part number 399294. This cam must be used with the Comfortilt option; the production cam will not work.

The column was restyled for 1969, as the ignition switch was moved from the instrument panel to the right-hand side of the column. The signal lever was listed as part number 3961517. The knob was still molded in the same color as the interior

trim except with Malibu- and El Camino based packages, which used a dull black knob regardless of interior color. Cruise control was available only as a dealer-installed option in 1969.

Tilt wheel, components, besides the ignition switch, were not changed much. However, the automatic with the console used a special column.

## 1969 Tilt-Wheel Column Part Numbers
| | |
|---|---|
| Automatic on the column | 7808148 |
| Automatic in the console | 7808149 |
| Manual | 7808150 |

All columns used in Malibu- or El Camino based SS 396s should be painted 30 degree gloss-black. Columns in the 300 based cars should be painted to match the interior trim: either black, blue or medium green.

## 1969 Interior Color Paint Part Numbers for 300-based Cars

| Color | DuPont | Ditzler | Rinshed Mason |
|---|---|---|---|
| Black | 88L | 926 | A-946 |
| Medium blue | 9585-LH | 13792 | 169V20 |
| Medium green | 9591-L | 44008 | 169B32 |

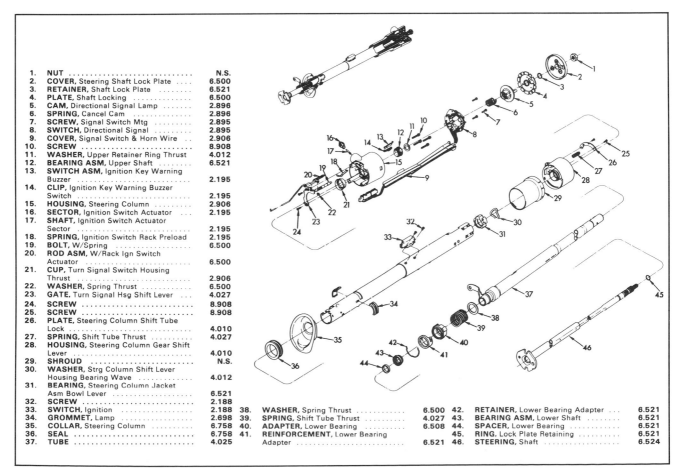

| | | |
|---|---|---|
| 1. | NUT | N.S. |
| 2. | COVER, Steering Shaft Lock Plate | 6.500 |
| 3. | RETAINER, Shaft Lock Plate | 6.521 |
| 4. | PLATE, Shaft Locking | 6.500 |
| 5. | CAM, Directional Signal Lamp | 2.896 |
| 6. | SPRING, Cancel Cam | 2.896 |
| 7. | SCREW, Signal Switch Mtg | 2.895 |
| 8. | SWITCH, Directional Signal | 2.895 |
| 9. | COVER, Signal Switch & Horn Wire | 2.906 |
| 10. | SCREW | 8.908 |
| 11. | WASHER, Upper Retainer Ring Thrust | 4.012 |
| 12. | BEARING ASM, Upper Shaft | 6.521 |
| 13. | SWITCH ASM, Ignition Key Warning Buzzer | 2.195 |
| 14. | CLIP, Ignition Key Warning Buzzer Switch | 2.195 |
| 15. | HOUSING, Steering Column | 2.906 |
| 16. | SECTOR, Ignition Switch Actuator | 2.195 |
| 17. | SHAFT, Ignition Switch Actuator Sector | 2.195 |
| 18. | SPRING, Ignition Switch Rack Preload | 2.195 |
| 19. | BOLT, W/Spring | 6.500 |
| 20. | ROD ASM, W/Rack Ign Switch Actuator | 6.500 |
| 21. | CUP, Turn Signal Switch Housing Thrust | 2.906 |
| 22. | WASHER, Spring Thrust | 6.500 |
| 23. | GATE, Turn Signal Hsg Shift Lever | 4.027 |
| 24. | SCREW | 8.908 |
| 25. | SCREW | 8.908 |
| 26. | PLATE, Steering Column Shift Tube Lock | 4.010 |
| 27. | SPRING, Shift Tube Thrust | 4.027 |
| 28. | HOUSING, Steering Column Gear Shift Lever | 4.010 |
| 29. | SHROUD | N.S. |
| 30. | WASHER, Strg Column Shift Lever Housing Bearing Wave | 4.012 |
| 31. | BEARING, Steering Column Jacket Asm Bowl Lever | 6.521 |
| 32. | SCREW | 2.188 |
| 33. | SWITCH, Ignition | 2.188 |
| 34. | GROMMET, Lamp | 2.698 |
| 35. | COLLAR, Steering Column | 6.758 |
| 36. | SEAL | 6.758 |
| 37. | TUBE | 4.025 |

| | | |
|---|---|---|
| 38. | WASHER, Spring Thrust | 6.500 |
| 39. | SPRING, Shift Tube Thrust | 4.027 |
| 40. | ADAPTER, Lower Bearing | 6.508 |
| 41. | REINFORCEMENT, Lower Bearing Adapter | 6.521 |
| 42. | RETAINER, Lower Bearing Adapter | 6.521 |
| 43. | BEARING ASM, Lower Shaft | 6.521 |
| 44. | SPACER, Lower Bearing | 6.521 |
| 45. | RING, Lock Plate Retaining | 6.521 |
| 46. | STEERING, Shaft | 6.524 |

*1969-72 standard column.*

159

## 1970-1972

No major changes were made to the steering columns in 1970. Two standard and six optional columns were now available. The automatic version was standard with a chrome shift lever and a black plastic knob. The directional signal lever was listed as part number 3961517 with a dull black plastic knob, part number 3973060.

Cruise control returned as a factory option and used stalk part number 6465627; a special wiring harness protector, part number 7806271, was installed with this option. Finger tip washers were also optional in 1970, as RPO CD3, and used a button on the end of the signal lever, part number 3973684. This option could not be used in conjunction with cruise control.

Six different columns were available during the 1970 model year. All were painted 30 degree gloss-black regardless of interior trim color. Production began with three columns.

## Early 1970 Steering Column Part Numbers

| | |
|---|---|
| Automatic on the column | 7809319 |
| Automatic on the floor | 7809320 |
| Manual | 7809321 |

Cars constructed after build date 04D 70 used three different part numbers.

## Late 1970 Steering Column Part Numbers

| | |
|---|---|
| Automatic on the column | 7811514 |
| Automatic on the floor | 7811515 |
| Manual | 7811515 |

All these columns used the same tilt lever, part number 3925890, with a black plastic knob whose part number was the same as the signal lever's. The column shift lever was listed as part number 3962727 with the standard knob.

For 1971 the signal lever and black plastic knob were changed to a soft feel to match the other knobs on the instrument panel. The hazard flasher button was in the same location but was now black

| No. | Part | Code |
|---|---|---|
| 1. | NUT | N.S. |
| 2. | COVER, Steering Shaft Lock Plate | 6.500 |
| 3. | RETAINER, Shaft Lock Plate | 6.521 |
| 4. | PLATE, Shaft Locking | 6.500 |
| 5. | CAM, Directional Signal Lamp | 2.896 |
| 6. | SPRING, Cancel Cam | 2.896 |
| 7. | SCREW, Signal Switch Mtg. | 2.895 |
| 8. | SWITCH ASM, Directional Signal | 2.895 |
| 9. | COVER, Signal Switch & Horn Wire | 2.906 |
| 10. | NUT, Upper Bearing Race Seat | 6.521 |
| 11. | SEAT, Shaft Upper Bearing | 6.521 |
| 12. | RACE, Upper Shaft Upper Bearing | 6.521 |
| 13. | SCREW | N.S. |
| 14. | SWITCH, Ignition Key Waring Buzzer | 2.195 |
| 15. | CLIP, Ignition Key Warning Buzzer Switch | 2.195 |
| 16. | HOUSING, Turn Signal and Ignition Switch | 2.906 |
| 17. | SHIELD, Tilt Lever Opening | 6.514 |
| 18. | BEARING | 6.521 |
| 19. | BOLT, Shaft Lock | 6.500 |
| 20. | SPRING, Steering Shaft | 6.500 |
| 21. | SHOE, Lock | 6.514 |
| 22. | WASHER, Ignition Switch Sector Door Shift | 2.195 |
| 23. | SHAFT, Ignition Switch Sector Door | 2.195 |
| 24. | PIN, Lock Shoe Retaining | 6.514 |
| 25. | HOUSING ASM, Strg Shaft Bearing | 2.906 |
| 26. | RETAINER, Spring | 6.514 |
| 27. | SPRING, Tilt | 6.514 |
| 28. | GUIDE, Tilt Spring | 6.514 |
| 29. | SCREW, Shaft Lock Bolt Spring | 6.500 |
| 30. | RETAINER, Ignition Switch Actuator Sector | 2.195 |
| 31. | SECTOR, Ignition Switch Actuator | 2.195 |
| 32. | PIN, Pivot | 6.514 |
| 33. | SPRING, Lock Shoe Return | 6.514 |
| 34. | SPRING, Tilt | 6.514 |
| 35. | PIN, Shoe Release Lever | 6.514 |
| 36. | LEVER, Shoe Release | 6.514 |
| 37. | BEARING, Shaft Upper | 6.521 |
| 38. | SPRING, Ignition Switch Rack Preload | 2.195 |
| 39. | RACK, Ignition Switch Actuator | 2.195 |
| 40. | ROD, Ignition Switch Actuator | 2.195 |
| 41. | SHAFT, Upper | 6.524 |
| 42. | SPHERE, Shaft Centering | 6.514 |
| 43. | SPRING, Center Sphere | 6.514 |
| 44. | SHAFT, Lower | 6.524 |
| 45. | SCREW, Housing | 6.518 |
| 46. | SUPPORT ASM, Turn Signal Housing | 6.514 |
| 47. | PIN | 6.514 |
| 48. | SCREW, Support | 6.514 |
| 49. | PLATE, Gear Shift Lever Detent | 4.027 |
| 50. | RING, Support Retainer | 4.027 |
| 51. | WASHER, Support Thrust | 4.012 |
| 52. | PLATE, Support Lock | 6.514 |
| 53. | WASHER, Support Wave | 4.012 |
| 54. | SPRING | 4.008 |
| 55. | HOUSING, Gear Shift Lever | 4.030 |
| 56. | SCREW | N.S. |
| 57. | SWITCH | 2.188 |
| 58. | JACKET | 6.518 |
| 59. | GROMMET, Lamp | 2.698 |
| 60. | REINFORCEMENT, Lower Bearing Adapter | 6.521 |
| 61. | RETAINER, Lower Bearing Adapter | 6.521 |
| 62. | COLLAR, Steering Column | 6.758 |
| 63. | SEAL, Steering Column to Dash Cover | 6.758 |
| 64. | TUBE | 4.028 |
| 65. | ADAPTER, Lower Bearing | 6.508 |
| 66. | BEARING ASM, Lower Shaft | 6.521 |
| 67. | SPACER, Lower Bearing | 6.521 |
| 68. | BOLT | 6.525 |
| 69. | FLANGE | 6.525 |
| 70. | FLANGE ASM | 6.525 |
| 71. | BOLT | 6.521 |

*1969-72 tilt steering column.*

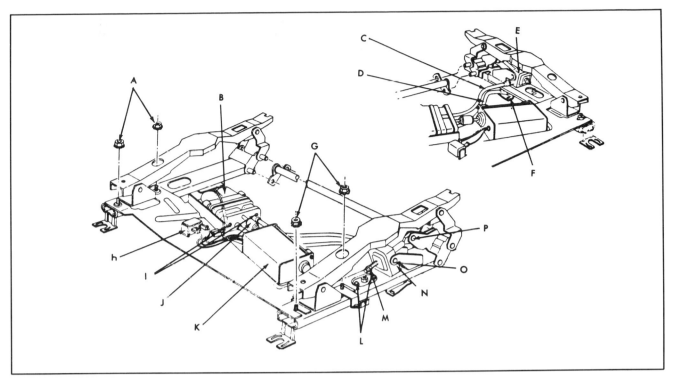

*Four-way power seat adjustment frame.*

plastic and listed as part number 411625. The finger tip washer was canceled. Cruise control, K30, continued with part number 6465256 for both 1971 and 1972. Both years used a black plastic knob.

The comfortilt steering column was still available, and a total of six columns were used with the SS packages in 1971 and 1972. All were painted 30 degree gloss-black. The tilt lever was listed as part number 3932567, 3990859 in 1972, with a black

knob. The automatic column shift lever was identical to the one employed in 1970, but a soft black vinyl shift knob was used. A cover over the column was also installed from 1970 to 1972 and was listed as part number 3990859. The following columns were available:

**1971-1972 Steering Column Part Numbers**
L65 or L48
Automatic on the column          7813111

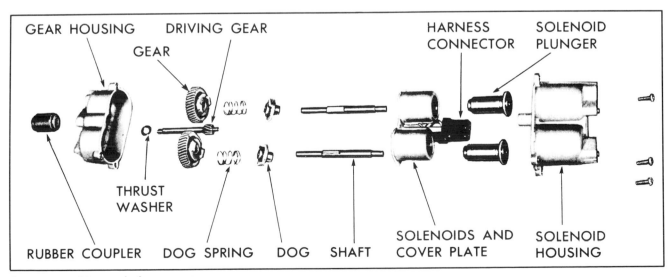

*Four-way seat transmission.*

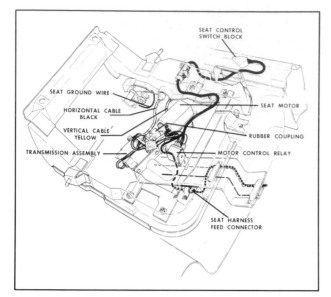

Four-way bucket seat wiring route.

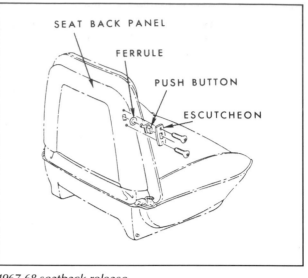

1967-68 seatback release.

### 1971-1972 Steering Column Part Numbers

| | |
|---|---|
| Automatic on the floor | 7813112 |
| Manual | 7813113 |
| LS3 | |
| Automatic on the column | 7813114 |
| Automatic on the floor | 7813115 |
| Manual | 7813116 |

### Seats

#### 1964-1965

The only seating available in both 1964 and 1965 was full-foam-cushion vinyl-covered bucket seats. The upholstery design and material were different each year.

The 1964 SS used Cadillac-grain vinyl with narrow vertical pleating. A symbol that matched ones on the front door panels were embossed into the rear seatback. Only solid-colored seating was available.

In 1965 Madrid grain was used with horizontally stitched inserts. A bow-tie symbol was embossed into the rear seatback. All seats except black ones and white ones were two-tone. The seating area was darker, then the outer edges matched the door panels in color. Two-tone seating was available exclusively on the SS model.

Chrome side trim and adjustment knobs were used both years. The seat springs and frame should be painted gloss-black.

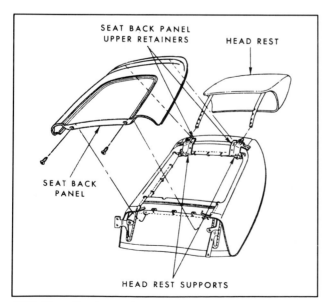

1967-68 seatback panel.

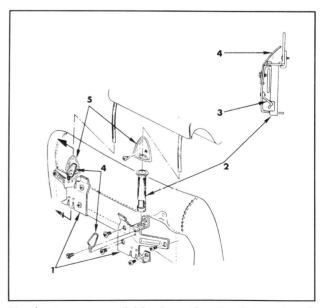

Headrests were available for either bucket or bench seating.

## 1966-1967

An all-vinyl split-back bench seat became standard equipment, with Strato-buckets optional. Wide double-stitched vertical pleats were used in the seating area. Only solid-colored seating was available in either 1966 or 1967.

Madrid-grain vinyl was still used in 1967, but the design was changed to horizontal pleating. A small rectangular button was placed in the center of each seatback. The bench seat used a two-color button, and the buckets used a solid color. Headrests were available for either type of seating, RPO A81 buckets or RPO A82 bench.

A thin chrome molding was used around the outline of the seatback on bucket seats both years. A chrome seatback release button and adjustment handle were used both years.

## 1968-1969

The all-vinyl split-back seat was still standard in 1968, and the optional bucket seats were redesigned. Seatbacks were higher and featured a one-piece hard plastic shell that covered their rears. This shell was painted the same color as the seat in a 30 degree finish. A thin chrome strip traced the outline of the shell.

The standard bench seating was cloth-and-vinyl in 1969, with all-vinyl bench or bucket seats as options. Most SS 396s were built with the all-vinyl interior.

*1969 front bucket seats. Note the buttons in the seatback.*

The Malibu and the 300 base models each used different pleating inserts for the cloth-and-vinyl bench seats. The standard Malibu and the El Camino used a wavery design with two vinyl-covered round buttons in each seatback rest. The 300 used a striped pattern with small ovals in the

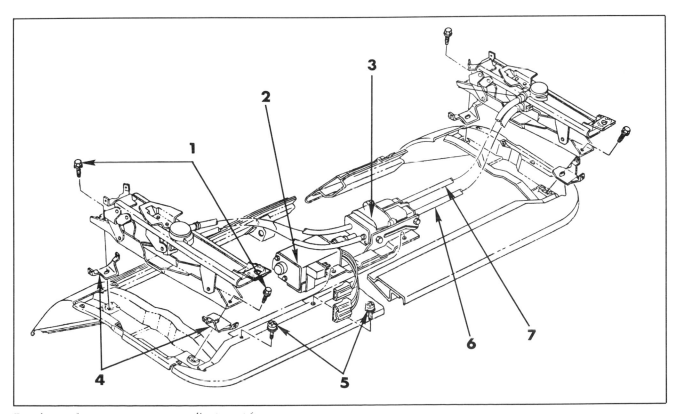

*Bench seat four-way power seat adjustment frame.*

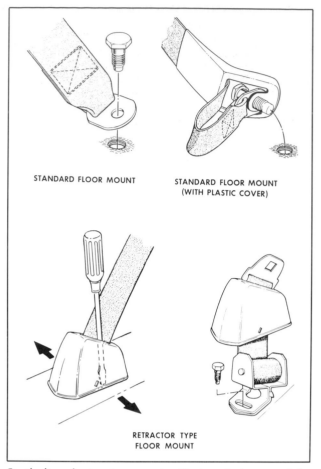

STANDARD FLOOR MOUNT

STANDARD FLOOR MOUNT
(WITH PLASTIC COVER)

RETRACTOR TYPE
FLOOR MOUNT

*Seatbelt and retractor mounts. Custom belts, top right, used a plastic cover.*

stripes and no buttons. The 300 was limited to the choice of a black, blue or medium green pleating insert or an optional all-black interior.

The foam front seat cushion in the Malibu was 1.75 in. thick, whereas in the 300 it was only 1.25 in. thick. The rear seat set was also different; the Malibu used a 0.75 in. thick foam pad, and the 300 featured a 6 ounce cotton pad. The thickness and materials must be used in the appropriate base for correctness.

Optional vinyl seating was the same for both models. It featured vertical pleating with a waffle insert strip and two vinyl-covered buttons in each back.

The 1969 bucket seatback shells were restyled and will not fit a 1968 seat. The seatback release latch was moved from the side to the top center of the shell itself. Chrome trim was again used around the shell. The shell should be painted according to 1968 directions. Headrests were now standard with all types of seating.

The SS pickup was standard beginning in 1968 with an all-vinyl bench seat. Vinyl bucket seats were optional. The interior color choice was the same as for the cars in 1968 but was limited to what was available on the Custom El Camino—the base for the SS models—thereafter.

### 1970-1972

A bench seat was standard from 1970 to 1972, as was a cloth-and-vinyl interior except with the convertible. The pattern differed slightly from that employed in 1969, but no buttons were used in the seatback.

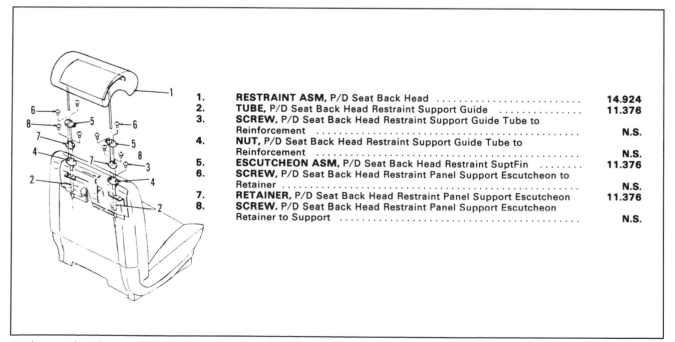

| | | |
|---|---|---|
| 1. | **RESTRAINT ASM,** P/D Seat Back Head ......................... | **14.924** |
| 2. | **TUBE,** P/D Seat Back Head Restraint Support Guide .............. | **11.376** |
| 3. | **SCREW,** P/D Seat Back Head Restraint Support Guide Tube to Reinforcement ........................................... | **N.S.** |
| 4. | **NUT,** P/D Seat Back Head Restraint Support Guide Tube to Reinforcement ........................................... | **N.S.** |
| 5. | **ESCUTCHEON ASM,** P/D Seat Back Head Restraint SuptFin ........ | **11.376** |
| 6. | **SCREW,** P/D Seat Back Head Restraint Panel Support Escutcheon to Retainer ............................................. | **N.S.** |
| 7. | **RETAINER,** P/D Seat Back Head Restraint Panel Support Escutcheon | **11.376** |
| 8. | **SCREW.** P/D Seat Back Head Restraint Panel Support Escutcheon Retainer to Support ....................................... | **N.S.** |

*Bucket seat headrests were standard from 1969 to 1972.*

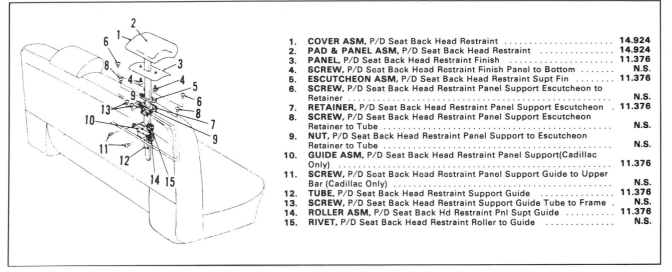

| | | |
|---|---|---|
| 1. | **COVER ASM,** P/D Seat Back Head Restraint | 14.924 |
| 2. | **PAD & PANEL ASM,** P/D Seat Back Head Restraint | 14.924 |
| 3. | **PANEL,** P/D Seat Back Head Restraint Finish | 11.376 |
| 4. | **SCREW,** P/D Seat Back Head Restraint Finish Panel to Bottom | N.S. |
| 5. | **ESCUTCHEON ASM,** P/D Seat Back Head Restraint Supt Fin | 11.376 |
| 6. | **SCREW,** P/D Seat Back Head Restraint Panel Support Escutcheon to Retainer | N.S. |
| 7. | **RETAINER,** P/D Seat Back Head Restraint Panel Support Escutcheon | 11.376 |
| 8. | **SCREW,** P/D Seat Back Head Restraint Panel Support Escutcheon Retainer to Tube | N.S. |
| 9. | **NUT,** P/D Seat Back Head Restraint Panel Support to Escutcheon Retainer to Tube | N.S. |
| 10. | **GUIDE ASM,** P/D Seat Back Head Restraint Panel Support(Cadillac Only) | 11.376 |
| 11. | **SCREW,** P/D Seat Back Head Restraint Panel Support Guide to Upper Bar (Cadillac Only) | N.S. |
| 12. | **TUBE,** P/D Seat Back Head Restraint Support Guide | 11.376 |
| 13. | **SCREW,** P/D Seat Back Head Restraint Support Guide Tube to Frame | N.S. |
| 14. | **ROLLER ASM,** P/D Seat Back Hd Restraint Pnl Supt Guide | 11.376 |
| 15. | **RIVET,** P/D Seat Back Head Restraint Roller to Guide | N.S. |

*Bench headrests were standard from 1969 to 1972.*

The all-vinyl seats still used vertical pleating, but it was narrower than in 1969. Two waffle inserts were placed on either side of the pleating. A small, long, rectangular button was placed in the center of each seatback near shoulder height.

A unique feature found on the 1970–72 Chevelle was the automatic seatback. It was available only in conjunction with power door locks. When the door was opened, the seatback automatically released.

Both 1971 and 1972 models used the same style of upholstery. The standard interior was a cloth-and-vinyl bench seat with vertical pleating in the cloth. An all-vinyl interior with elk-grain inserts was available in either bench or bucket seating. Vinyl-covered headrests were standard all three years.

## Door and Kick Panels

### 1964–1965

Neither the door or the kick panels are interchangeable, as they were different. The 1964 door panels used a vertical pleat design with a round emblem in the center. The 1965 door panels used wider horizontal pleats and a bow-tie emblem.

The kick panels are noninterchangeable because of the windlace. The vent control knobs were

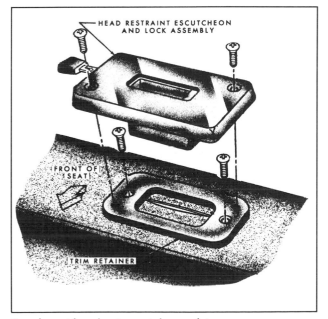

*Bench seat headrest escutcheon plate.*

*These 1970 seats show the correct design and the button in the seatback. However, they do not have headrests, which were standard equipment, so they are incorrect.*

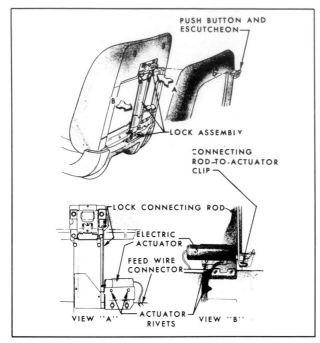

Labels in figure: PUSH BUTTON AND ESCUTCHEON, LOCK ASSEMBLY, CONNECTING ROD-TO-ACTUATOR CLIP, LOCK CONNECTING ROD, ELECTRIC ACTUATOR, FEED WIRE CONNECTOR, VIEW "A", ACTUATOR RIVETS, VIEW "B"

*Electrical seatback release.*

black plastic both years. The panels were molded in the same color as the interior trim except with white interiors, which had them molded in red in 1964 and either aqua or black in 1965.

### 1966-1967

Door panels for 1966 featured a sculptured design with upper and lower chrome trim moldings. The 1967 panel used a design of narrower horizontal pleats and only an upper chrome trim molding. Window regulator knobs were unique in 1967, as they were color keyed to match the door panels. The knob in 1966 was black for all interiors.

Kick panels are again not interchangeable. The 1966 version was nearly a carbon copy of the 1965 panel. In 1967 the kick panel was restyled, and the cable and panel were combined in one unit. The vent knob was mushroom-shaped and was chrome-plated plastic.

A special panel was available for the right-hand side. It was molded to accept the heater core for cars ordered with air conditioning. No vent control knob was used. The panel also had no provision for a vent. The left-hand panel was the pro-

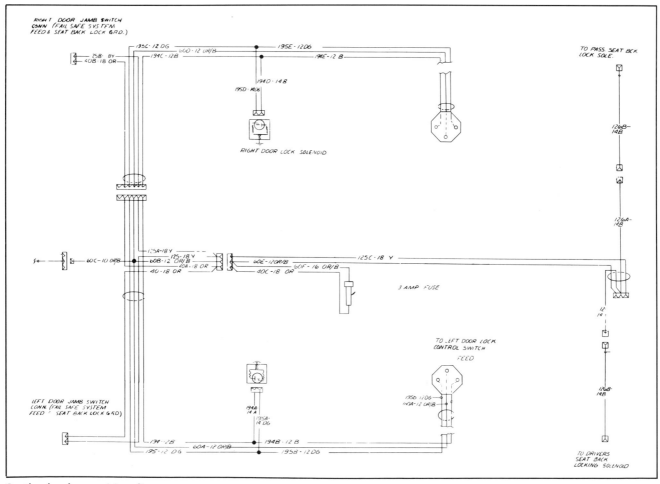

*Seatback release wiring diagram.*

duction unit. The kick panel was the same color as the instrument panel.

## 1968-1969

Door panels were again different from 1968 to 1969. The 1968 version used a straight strip of chrome molding midway down the door. In 1969 three different door panels were offered.

The Malibu- and El Camino-based packages used the same design, with a top chrome molding dipping downward in the center. The El Camino panel had a provision for the wing window, however.

The third door panel was the one used on the 300 based cars. It was completely different, and a Malibu panel will not interchange. The 300 panel

featured horizontal pleating at the bottom and rectangular sculpturing at the top. Two horizontal chrome moldings were also used at the top.

Side door emblems were installed each year. In 1968 they used a white background with red lettering for the first two months, then it was changed to a brushed metal emblem with black lettering. In 1969 they used a plate with a black background and bright lettering. However, the 300 based SS 396 did not use this plate; instead it came with a Chevelle nameplate.

The 1968 kick panel was the same design as the 1967 panel, with an integrated vent control knob. This vent was eliminated when air conditioning was ordered.

The 1969 300 pillar sedan and El Camino used the same vent as in 1968, but the Malibu-based SSs, owing to their lack of wing windows, used a twin

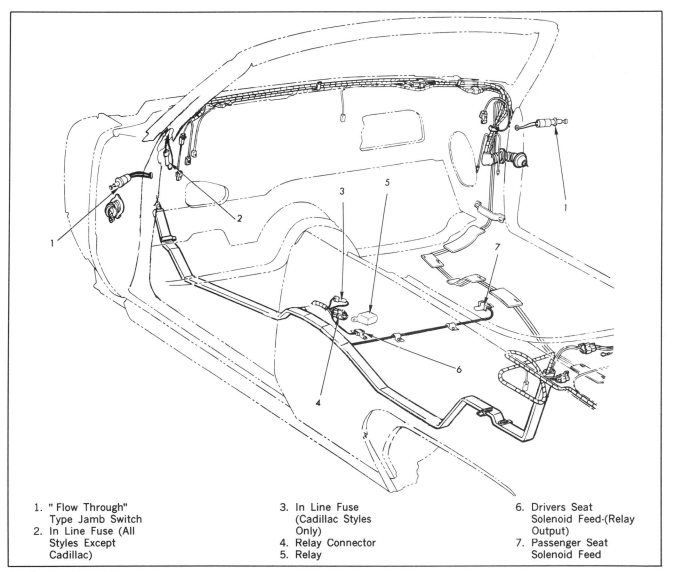

| 1. "Flow Through" Type Jamb Switch | 3. In Line Fuse (Cadillac Styles Only) | 6. Drivers Seat Solenoid Feed-(Relay Output) |
| 2. In Line Fuse (All Styles Except Cadillac) | 4. Relay Connector 5. Relay | 7. Passenger Seat Solenoid Feed |

*Seatback release wiring route.*

vent control design. The upper knob controlled the flow of air through the instrument panel ducting, and the lower knob controlled the flow of air to the vents. Both knobs were integrated into the panels.

Kick panels were molded plastic in the same color as the instrument panel. The knobs were chrome-plated plastic both years.

### 1970-1972

Door panels were identical from 1970 to 1972 and are interchangeable. An SS door emblem was placed on the upper forward section of these panels. A few SSs rolled off the assembly line with the Malibu door emblems, owing to a shortage of the SS plaques. However, unless you have validated proof to document this, a Malibu door plaque is incorrect.

All SS packages except those for the El Camino used the two-vent system all three years. The pickup used a system nearly identical to that employed in 1968. The vent knobs were chrome in 1970 and soft black in 1971 and 1972. When air conditioning was selected, the vents were eliminated.

### Rear Package Shelf

### 1964-1972

The rear package shelf was cardboard. It was painted the same color as the interior in a 0 degree finish except with parchment interiors, which had them painted the same color as the instrument panel in a flat finish.

Cars with factory-installed stereos and rear seat speakers used a slightly different panel with a weave design (1964-67) or a mesh design (1968-72). Holes were punched in the panel and covered

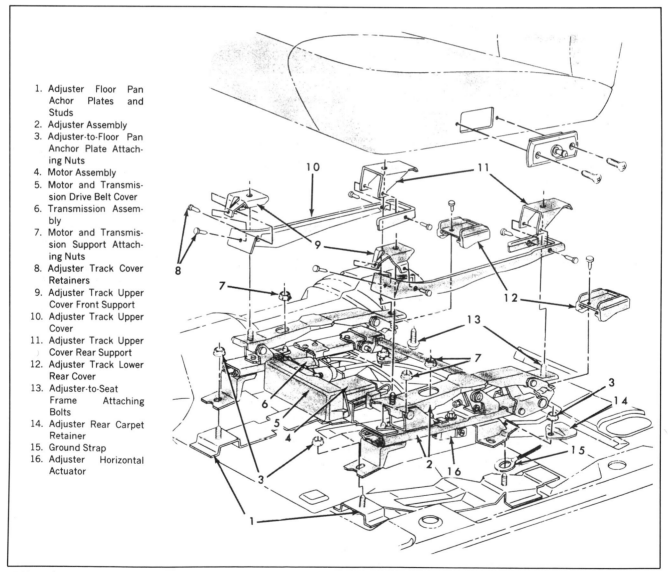

1. Adjuster Floor Pan Achor Plates and Studs
2. Adjuster Assembly
3. Adjuster-to-Floor Pan Anchor Plate Attaching Nuts
4. Motor Assembly
5. Motor and Transmission Drive Belt Cover
6. Transmission Assembly
7. Motor and Transmission Support Attaching Nuts
8. Adjuster Track Cover Retainers
9. Adjuster Track Upper Cover Front Support
10. Adjuster Track Upper Cover
11. Adjuster Track Upper Cover Rear Support
12. Adjuster Track Lower Rear Cover
13. Adjuster-to-Seat Frame Attaching Bolts
14. Adjuster Rear Carpet Retainer
15. Ground Strap
16. Adjuster Horizontal Actuator

*1969-72 four-way power seat.*

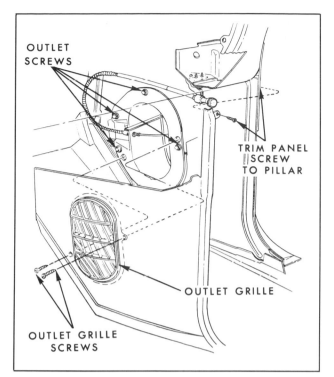

*1964-66 kick panels and standard ventilation vents.*

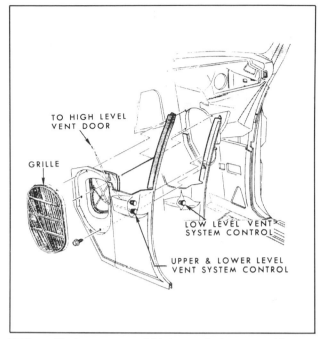

*1969 ventilation vents and kick panels for cars without a wing window.*

*1967 door panel.*

*1970-72 door panel.*

*Door panel emblems. The one on the left was used in 1969, the one to the right in all 1970-72 models.*

*These rear armrests are incorrect for the 1966-67 SS 396 because they have no ashtrays. Also, the speaker openings are incorrect.*

with a speaker grille. The speaker grilles were painted to match the rear shelf.

Cars with dealer-installed speakers or radios used the production shelf. The speaker grilles were painted to match the panel but in a 60 degree gloss finish.

Cars with the rear window defroster also used the cardboard panel. When stereo and rear defroster were ordered together, the cardboard panel was installed. Early models (1964-67) were not available with both the stereo and rear window defroster options.

## Seatbelts

### 1964-1972

Seatbelts were not standard items on early 1964 models. After January 1964, however, lap belts were standard. From 1965 to 1968 lap belts were standard equipment on all cars. From 1969 to 1972 shoulder belts were standard except in the convertible.

## Consoles

### 1964-1965

A console was included with the four-speed or Powerglide and was used solely in the Malibu SS

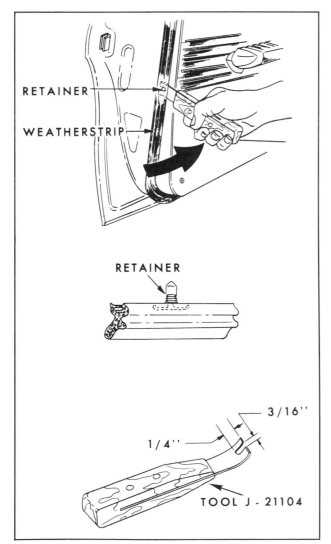

*Weather stripping removal tool.*

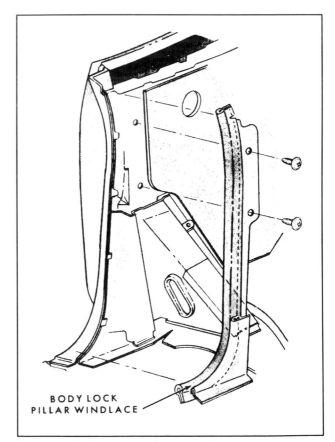

*Windlace for hardtop and convertible.*

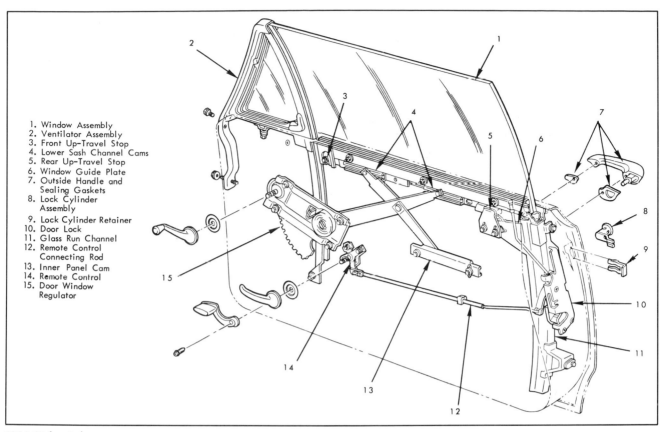

1. Window Assembly
2. Ventilator Assembly
3. Front Up-Travel Stop
4. Lower Sash Channel Cams
5. Rear Up-Travel Stop
6. Window Guide Plate
7. Outside Handle and
   Sealing Gaskets
8. Lock Cylinder
   Assembly
9. Lock Cylinder Retainer
10. Door Lock
11. Glass Run Channel
12. Remote Control
    Connecting Rod
13. Inner Panel Cam
14. Remote Control
15. Door Window
    Regulator

*1964-65 front door.*

1. Ventilator Frame Lower
   Adjusting Stud and Nut
2. Ventilator Frame Upper
   Attaching Bolt
3. Ventilator Frame to
   Inner Panel Screw
4. Ventilator to Door Inner
   Panel Attaching Screw
5. Window Front Up-Stop
6. Window Sash Channel Cam
7. Window Rear Guide
8. Glass Rear Run Channel
   Upper Bolt
9. Outside Handle Assembly
10. Lock Cylinder
11. Lock
12. Glass Rear Run Channel
    Lower Adjusting Stud
    and Nut
13. Lock to Remote Control
    Connecting Rod
14. Inner Panel Cam
15. Window Lower Stop
16. Remote Control
17. Ventilator Division Channel
    Lower Adjusting Stud
    and Nut
18. Window Regulator (Manual)
19. Window Regulator (Electric)

*1966-68 front door.*

and El Camino in both 1964 and 1965. Parts and part numbers were identical both years.

The console consisted of two trim panels. The upper trim panel was listed as part numbers 30844083 with the four-speed and 3844084 with the Powerglide. Both transmissions used the same rear trim panel, part number 3844085. They were attached to each other with two Phillips-head screws.

The four-speed shift pattern was part of the front plate. The 1964–65 Powerglide dial plate was listed as part number 3846868. A two-piece es-

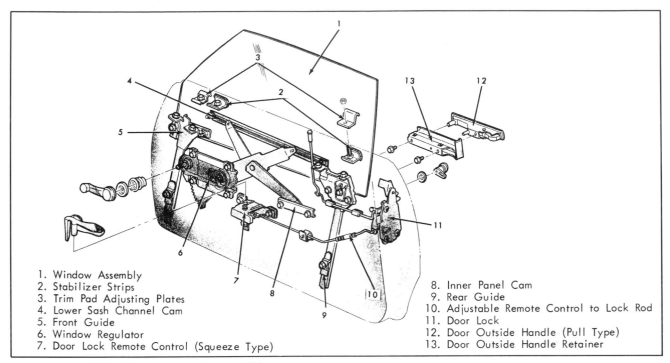

1. Window Assembly
2. Stabilizer Strips
3. Trim Pad Adjusting Plates
4. Lower Sash Channel Cam
5. Front Guide
6. Window Regulator
7. Door Lock Remote Control (Squeeze Type)
8. Inner Panel Cam
9. Rear Guide
10. Adjustable Remote Control to Lock Rod
11. Door Lock
12. Door Outside Handle (Pull Type)
13. Door Outside Handle Retainer

*1969 door for the hardtop coupe and convertible.*

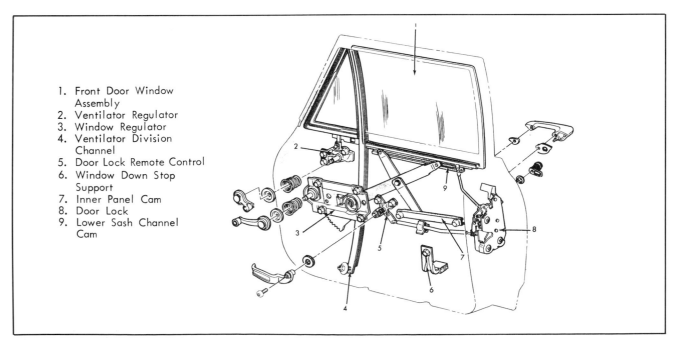

1. Front Door Window Assembly
2. Ventilator Regulator
3. Window Regulator
4. Ventilator Division Channel
5. Door Lock Remote Control
6. Window Down Stop Support
7. Inner Panel Cam
8. Door Lock
9. Lower Sash Channel Cam

*1969 door for the two-door pillar coupe.*

172

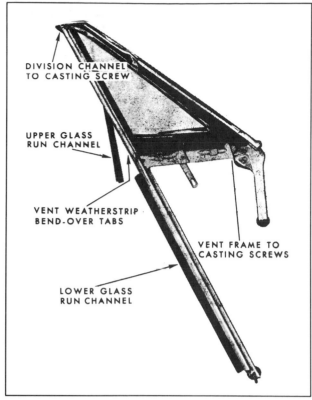

*Wing window assembly.*

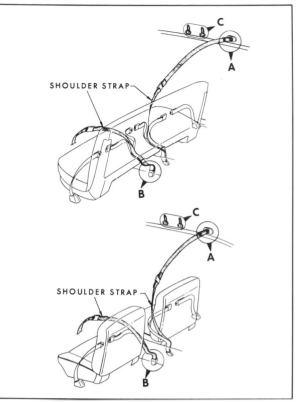

*Front shoulder belts.*

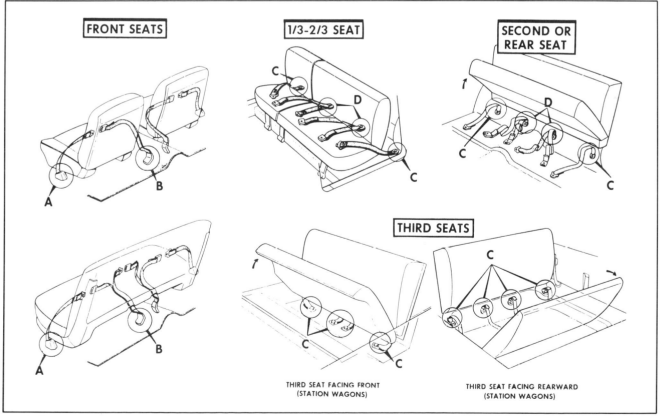

*Lap belt routing.*

cutcheon plate, part numbers 3839185-LH and 3857330-RH, was used on the automatic console. The dial assembly was bolted to the underside of the right-hand plate.

Both consoles used a courtesy light, part number 2986115, at the rear of the rear panel. This light was covered with an opaque lens, part number 3857332. The lower half of the console was

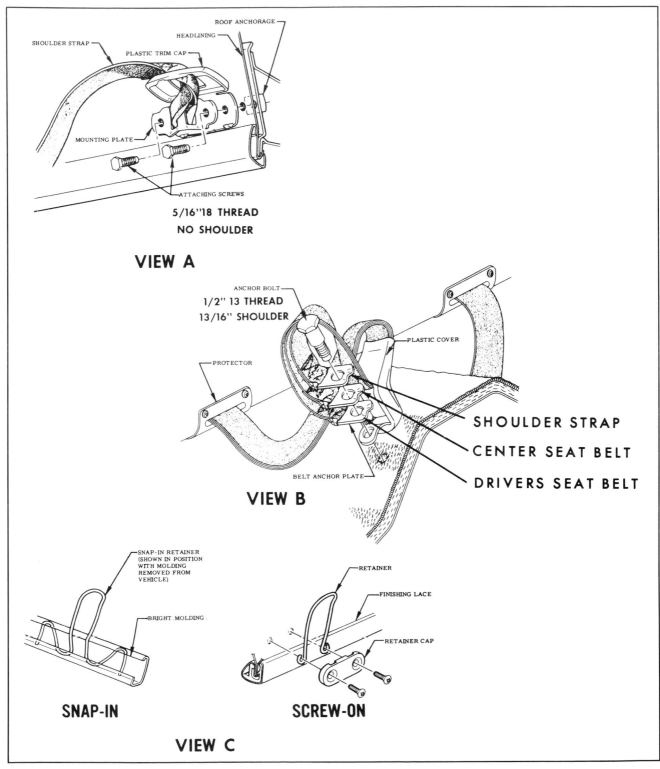

*Front shoulder belts.*

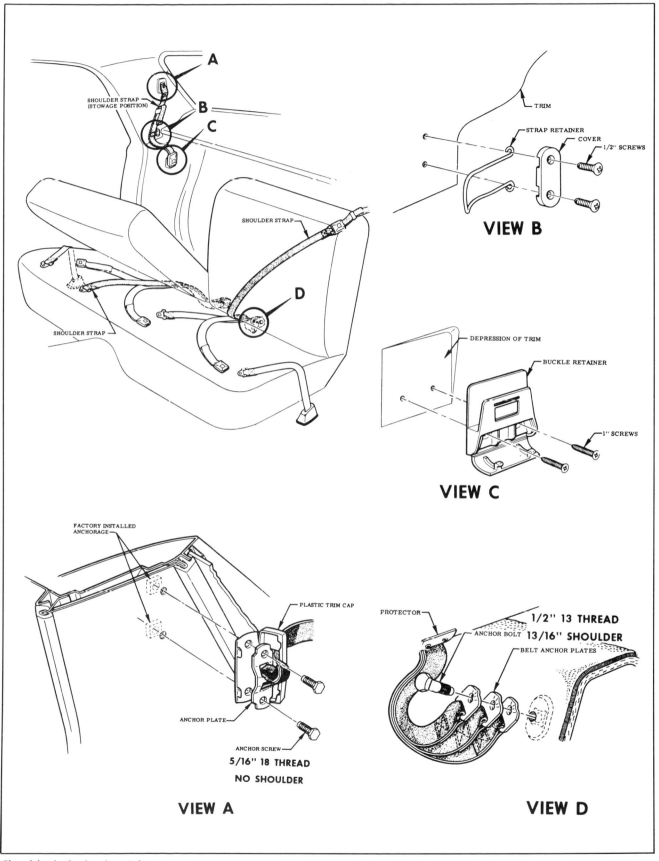

VIEW B

VIEW C

VIEW A

VIEW D

*Shoulder belts for the pickup.*

painted the same color as the interior trim, including white interior trim, in 1964, and the same color as the instrument panel in 1965. The console was mounted to the floor with chrome-plated Phillips-head screws.

### 1966-1967

The console was made optional, as RPO D55, in 1966 and was available with all transmissions except the standard three-speed manual. Its design and part numbers were identical in both 1966 and 1967.

The automatic console used base part number 3876408 and a front trim cover molded in the same color as the interior trim except with white inte-

riors, which had it molded in black. The base should be painted in a 60 degree gloss matching the front trim plate. A shallow compartment bin, part number 3878156, was also used with this base.

A green lens with green letters, part numbers 3880904 with the Powerglide and 3909548 with the Turbo Hydra-matic (1967 only), was used both years. A seal, part number 3878480, was placed behind it. These parts were then sandwiched between a natural appearing retainer cup, part number 3880939, and a bright two-part escutcheon plate, part numbers 3882789-LH and 3882790-RH, with two Phillips-head screws.

Four-speed transmissions used a different base, part number 3876407, and a sloping front

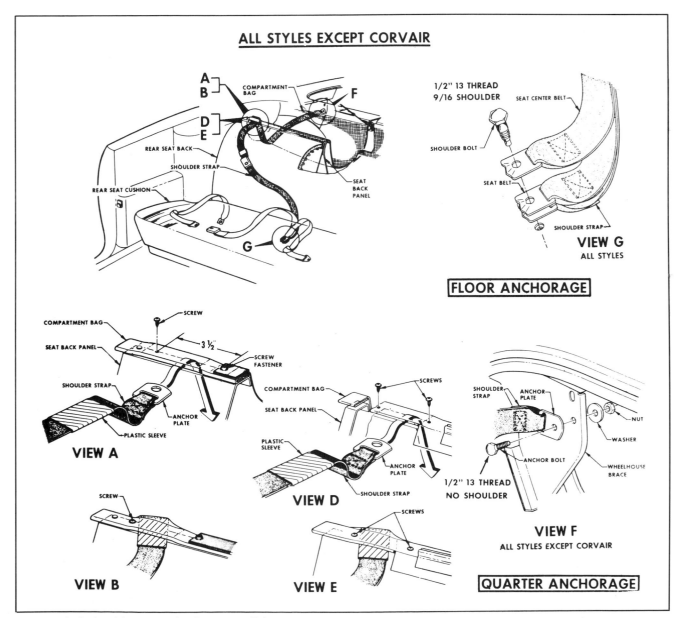

*Rear seatbelt shoulder straps for the convertible.*

176

trim plate. This plate was molded in the same color as the interior trim except with the white interior, which had it molded in black.

The four-speed console used an upper shift boot, part number 3907663, and a lower shift boot, part number 3903917. The upper seal was held with a retainer, part number 3878413, and Phillips-head screws. Another retainer, part number 3842927, was used on the lower seal. A shift pattern, part number 3880912, was installed to the right of the shifter opening.

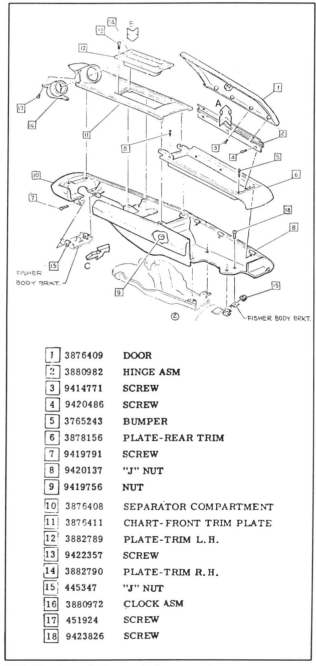

| | | |
|---|---|---|
| 1 | 3876409 | DOOR |
| 2 | 3880982 | HINGE ASM |
| 3 | 9414771 | SCREW |
| 4 | 9420486 | SCREW |
| 5 | 3765243 | BUMPER |
| 6 | 3878156 | PLATE-REAR TRIM |
| 7 | 9419791 | SCREW |
| 8 | 9420137 | "J" NUT |
| 9 | 9419756 | NUT |
| 10 | 3876408 | SEPARATOR COMPARTMENT |
| 11 | 3876411 | CHART-FRONT TRIM PLATE |
| 12 | 3882789 | PLATE-TRIM L. H. |
| 13 | 9422357 | SCREW |
| 14 | 3882790 | PLATE-TRIM R. H. |
| 15 | 445347 | "J" NUT |
| 16 | 3880972 | CLOCK ASM |
| 17 | 451924 | SCREW |
| 18 | 9423826 | SCREW |

*1966-67 automatic transmission console.*

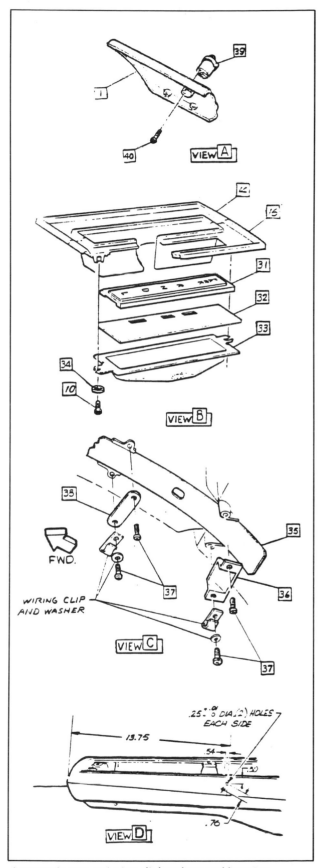

*Automatic transmission dial and control housing.*

*This console is incorrect for the Chevelle; it is an Impala unit.*

Both consoles used the same compartment door, part number 3876409, and it should be painted to match the rest of the console. A Rallye clock, part number 3880972, was also included with both consoles, as was a courtesy lamp at the rear. The housing and lens were listed as one part, part number 3880913. The console was mounted to the floor with hex-head screws.

### 1968-1969

The console was redesigned in 1968. The base, part number 3919941, was used with all transmissions. It should be painted to match the interior trim in a 30 degree gloss finish except with parchment interiors, which had it painted 30 degree gloss-black.

The console door, part number 3920080, featured a molding, part number 3920086, that ran down the center of it. This door also used a simple

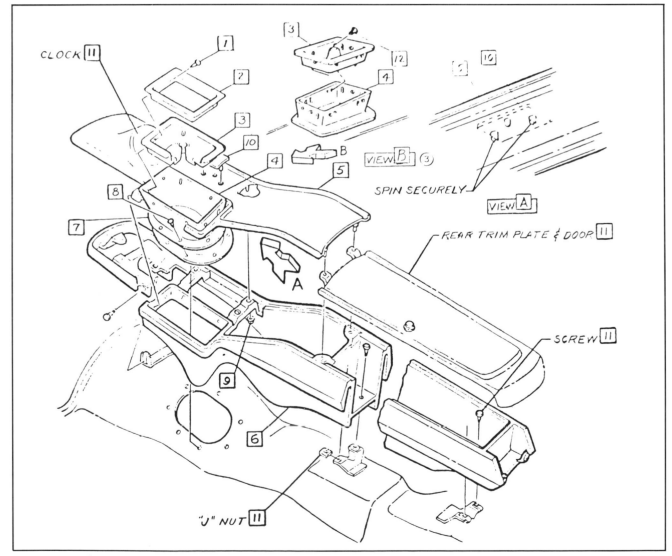

*1966-67 console used with the four-speed manual.*

spring locking device, part number 3920084, to keep it closed. The door should be finished to match the base, and the locking device was natural metal.

Automatic consoles used a brushed aluminum front trim plate, part number 3926727, with the outer edges trimmed with 0 degree gloss-satin-black. The shift escutcheon plate, part number 3926729, was also brushed aluminum with black accents. The plates were mounted with ½ in. number 8 Phillips-head screws; the heads of the screws should be painted to match the black accents.

Two green shift lenses were available in 1968. The Powerglide used part number 3921413 with white letters, and the Turbo Hydra-matic used part number 3921428 with green letters. A backing plate, part number 3921414, was used behind both lenses. This assembly was held together with a seal, part number 3922816, and a retainer, part number 3921415, with four nuts. A pair of seals, part number 3922817, were held with retainers, part number 3922818, along the insides of the base. The

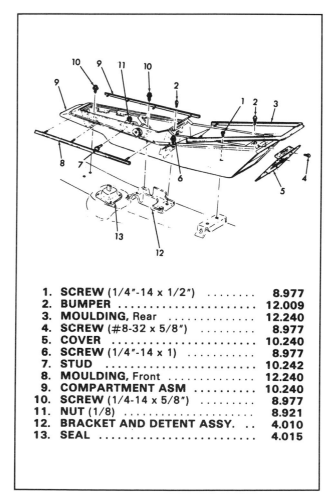

| | | |
|---|---|---|
| 1. | SCREW (1/4"-14 x 1/2") | 8.977 |
| 2. | BUMPER | 12.009 |
| 3. | MOULDING, Rear | 12.240 |
| 4. | SCREW (#8-32 x 5/8") | 8.977 |
| 5. | COVER | 10.240 |
| 6. | SCREW (1/4"-14 x 1) | 8.977 |
| 7. | STUD | 10.242 |
| 8. | MOULDING, Front | 12.240 |
| 9. | COMPARTMENT ASM | 10.240 |
| 10. | SCREW (1/4-14 x 5/8") | 8.977 |
| 11. | NUT (1/8) | 8.921 |
| 12. | BRACKET AND DETENT ASSY. | 4.010 |
| 13. | SEAL | 4.015 |

*1968-69 console base.*

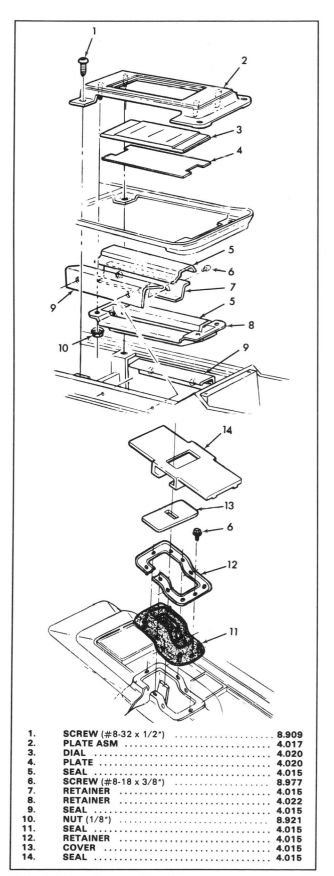

| | | |
|---|---|---|
| 1. | SCREW (#8-32 x 1/2") | 8.909 |
| 2. | PLATE ASM | 4.017 |
| 3. | DIAL | 4.020 |
| 4. | PLATE | 4.020 |
| 5. | SEAL | 4.015 |
| 6. | SCREW (#8-18 x 3/8") | 8.977 |
| 7. | RETAINER | 4.015 |
| 8. | RETAINER | 4.022 |
| 9. | SEAL | 4.015 |
| 10. | NUT (1/8") | 8.921 |
| 11. | SEAL | 4.015 |
| 12. | RETAINER | 4.015 |
| 13. | COVER | 4.015 |
| 14. | SEAL | 4.015 |

*1968-70 shifter plates and bezels.*

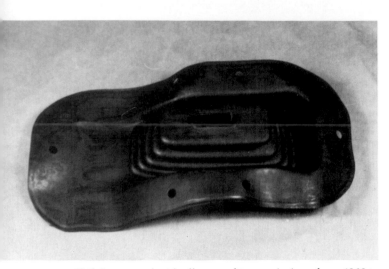

*Shift boot used with all manual transmissions from 1968 to 1972 with a console.*

retainers were held to the console with Phillips-head screws.

Manual transmissions used front trim plate part number 3934153; it too was brushed aluminum and accented with black paint. A black cover, part number 3903522, was placed over the top of

the shift boot. Another rubber seal, part number 3922820, was placed under the front trim plate, at the shifter opening.

A solid chrome knob was installed with all transmissions. The shift pattern was on a plate mounted behind the shift lever. Two plates were available: the standard transmission used part number 3919910, and all four-speeds used part number 3919914.

Chrome moldings were used along the sides, part number 3919941, and the rear, part number 3922814 (this piece wrapped around the sides), and were held in place with ⅛ in. nuts. The base was mounted to the floor of the cars using existing brackets and 32 thread ⅝ in. number 8 screws at the rear and 14 thread ¼×1 in. bolts at the front.

The console was virtually identical in 1969 except for a few minor changes. The door was restyled and consisted of two parts: an outer shell, part number 3953095, and an inner shell, part number 3953091. The simple spring lock was replaced with a more conventional type that was hid from view by the inner door panel. The hinge was listed as part number 3920082 and was mounted as in previous years with standard-head screws.

The door required a striker, part number 3954583, inside the compartment, and two small holes were drilled in the base, which was given part number 3953094. This base cannot be used in 1968 SS 396s. Finishing should be identical to that used in 1968.

Except for the deletion of the Powerglide dial, the automatic components were the same as in 1968. The shifter assembly was listed as part number 3952863. This was the same shifter used with all Powerglides and Turbo Hydra-matics with floor shift. Also available in 1969 was the Sports shifter, M08 (see Automatic Shift Levers in Chapter 3 for details).

The manual transmission components were similar, but part numbers were changed. The top shift boot was listed as part number 3931688 with retainer part number 3926744. The cover and top seal were identical. A chrome knob, part number 3922525, with ⅜ in. thread was now used exclusively.

**1970-1972**

Console base part number 3968566 was used from 1970-1972. The console door was restyled; the lock button was bigger and moved to the side. This caused the striker plate to be moved and thus required a change in the base.

**1970-1972 Console Base and Lock Part Numbers**

Door

| | |
|---|---|
| Outer | 3972990 |
| Inner | 3972991 |

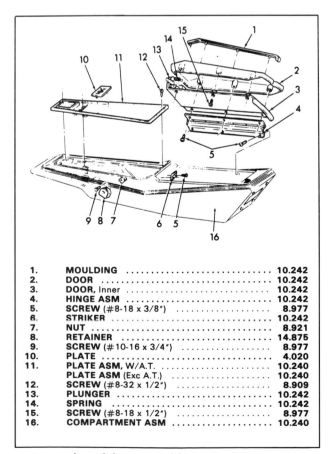

| | | |
|---|---|---|
| 1. | MOULDING | 10.242 |
| 2. | DOOR | 10.242 |
| 3. | DOOR, Inner | 10.242 |
| 4. | HINGE ASM | 10.242 |
| 5. | SCREW (#8-18 x 3/8") | 8.977 |
| 6. | STRIKER | 10.242 |
| 7. | NUT | 8.921 |
| 8. | RETAINER | 14.875 |
| 9. | SCREW (#10-16 x 3/4") | 8.977 |
| 10. | PLATE | 4.020 |
| 11. | PLATE ASM, W/A.T. | 10.240 |
| | PLATE ASM (Exc A.T.) | 10.240 |
| 12. | SCREW (#8-32 x 1/2") | 8.909 |
| 13. | PLUNGER | 10.242 |
| 14. | SPRING | 10.242 |
| 15. | SCREW (#8-18 x 1/2") | 8.977 |
| 16. | COMPARTMENT ASM | 10.240 |

*1969 console and door assembly.*

## 1970-1972 Console Base and Lock Part Numbers

| | |
|---|---|
| Hinge | 3972997 |
| Outer molding | 3920086 |
| Lock | |
| Cylinder | 3972993 |
| Retainer | 3972994 |
| Screw | 4598271 |

The trim plates were identical to the ones used in 1969. Shifter components were unchanged for the automatic transmission. The upper seal and cover on the automatic were replaced with an extension panel, part number 3975357, and the upper shift boot was now listed as part number 3975356 with retainer part number 3975358. A few late-model 1969 SS 396s may have been built with these seals and extensions.

The shift knobs were chrome for all transmissions with a console. Chrome trim and floor mounting of the base were the same as in 1968-69.

## Rear Compartment

### 1964-1965

The interior of the trunk on all models was painted with a gray and green spatter finish—part numbers Rinshed Mason 828, Ditzler SX-1676 and DuPont 389-195. A one-piece rubber mat with a gray and black grain pattern was used in both 1964 and 1965.

The spare tire was mounted on the right-hand side of the trunk floor. The bumper jack was positioned under it, along with the lug wrench, according to the jacking instruction decal affixed to the underside of the deck lid on the right-hand side. The jack base was painted gray and measured 6×6 in.

A spare wheel lock was optional, as RPO P19, in 1965 from the factory or as a dealer-installed accessory. The lock case should have a natural appearance. When it was ordered, an extra decal was affixed to the underside of the deck lid next to the jacking instructions.

A spare tire cover was available as a dealer-installed option in 1965 only. It matched the pattern of the floor mat.

### 1966-1967

A one-piece trunk mat with the same pattern and material as in 1964-65 was used again in 1966. The lining of the trunk was painted in a black, gray and aqua spatter finish—part numbers Ditzler DX1758, Rinshed Mason 844 Multiflex and DuPont 389-259—both years. The mat was changed to a

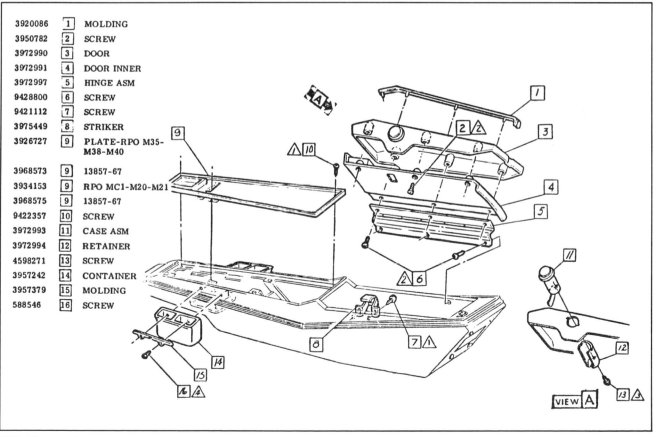

| | | |
|---|---|---|
| 3920086 | 1 | MOLDING |
| 3950782 | 2 | SCREW |
| 3972990 | 3 | DOOR |
| 3972991 | 4 | DOOR INNER |
| 3972997 | 5 | HINGE ASM |
| 9428800 | 6 | SCREW |
| 9421112 | 7 | SCREW |
| 3975449 | 8 | STRIKER |
| 3926727 | 9 | PLATE-RPO M35-M38-M40 |
| 3968573 | 9 | 13857-67 |
| 3934153 | 9 | RPO MC1-M20-M21 |
| 3968575 | 9 | 13857-67 |
| 9422357 | 10 | SCREW |
| 3972993 | 11 | CASE ASM |
| 3972994 | 12 | RETAINER |
| 4598271 | 13 | SCREW |
| 3957242 | 14 | CONTAINER |
| 3957379 | 15 | MOLDING |
| 588546 | 16 | SCREW |

*1970-72 console.*

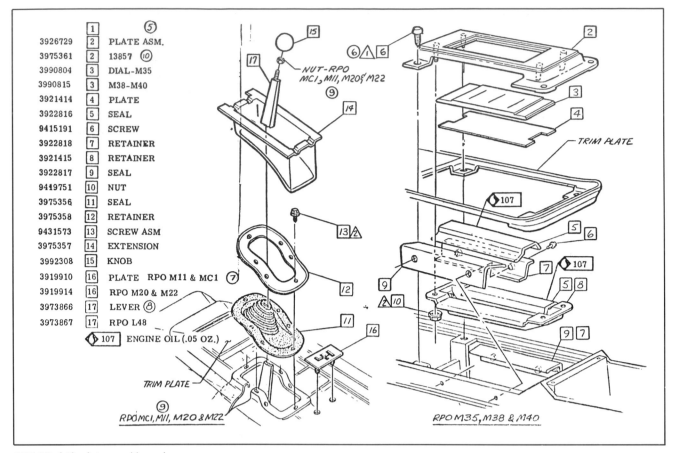

| | | | |
|---|---|---|---|
| | 1 | | |
| 3926729 | 2 | PLATE ASM. | |
| 3975361 | 2 | 13857 | |
| 3990804 | 3 | DIAL-M35 | |
| 3990815 | 3 | M38-M40 | |
| 3921414 | 4 | PLATE | |
| 3922816 | 5 | SEAL | |
| 9415191 | 6 | SCREW | |
| 3922818 | 7 | RETAINER | |
| 3921415 | 8 | RETAINER | |
| 3922817 | 9 | SEAL | |
| 9419751 | 10 | NUT | |
| 3975356 | 11 | SEAL | |
| 3975358 | 12 | RETAINER | |
| 9431573 | 13 | SCREW ASM | |
| 3975357 | 14 | EXTENSION | |
| 3992308 | 15 | KNOB | |
| 3919910 | 16 | PLATE   RPO M11 & MC1 | |
| 3919914 | 16 | RPO M20 & M22 | |
| 3973866 | 17 | LEVER | |
| 3973867 | 17 | RPO L48 | |
| 107 | ENGINE OIL (.05 OZ.) | | |

*1971-72 shift plates and bezels.*

turquoise and black hound's-tooth pattern for 1967.

The spare tire was placed on the right-hand side of the trunk floor both years. The jack—base part number 3841909—was the part used in previous years. The base was still painted gray, as was the combination jack handle and lug wrench. The base was secured in place with a natural metal wing nut, part number 9785616. Jacking instructions were affixed to the underside of the deck lid in the lower center depression both years.

A spare wheel cover was available for 1966 only as a dealer-installed option; it was identical to the one used in 1965. A spare wheel lock was available as a factory option for 1966 only; it was available as a dealer-installed option, package part number 9870848, both years.

### 1968-1972

The inside of the trunk was finished with the same pattern in 1968-72 as in 1966-67. A one-piece foam trunk mat with a gray grain pattern was used all five years. However, the 1971–72 mat was slightly different shaped. A trunk mat was not standard with the 1969 300 based SS 396s; a dealer-installed mat was available, and it was black rubber.

The jack and handle-wrench were placed in a black rubber sleeve, part number 9781956. El Caminos used a different jack and no sleeve. The jacking instructions were affixed to the underside

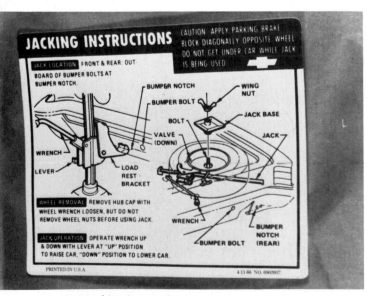

*1967 jacking instructions.*

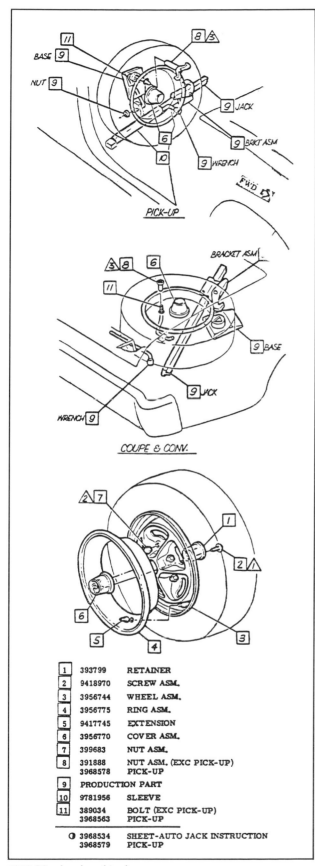

| | | |
|---|---|---|
| 1 | 393799 | RETAINER |
| 2 | 9418970 | SCREW ASM. |
| 3 | 3956744 | WHEEL ASM. |
| 4 | 3956775 | RING ASM. |
| 5 | 9417745 | EXTENSION |
| 6 | 3956770 | COVER ASM. |
| 7 | 399683 | NUT ASM. |
| 8 | 391888 | NUT ASM. (EXC PICK-UP) |
| | 3968578 | PICK-UP |
| 9 | | PRODUCTION PART |
| 10 | 9781956 | SLEEVE |
| 11 | 389034 | BOLT (EXC PICK-UP) |
| | 3968563 | PICK-UP |
| ☮ | 3968534 | SHEET-AUTO JACK INSTRUCTION |
| | 3968579 | PICK-UP |

*1969 SS wheel and jack.*

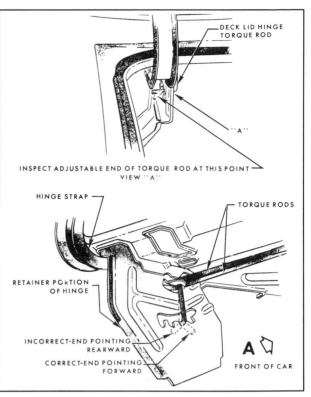

The torque rods of the trunk lid were color-coded. The right-hand rod was silver and the left-hand rod was light green on convertibles. On coupes the right-hand rod was red and the left-hand rod was white.

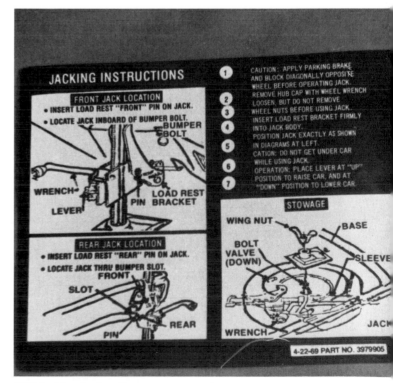

*1970 jacking instructions.*

183

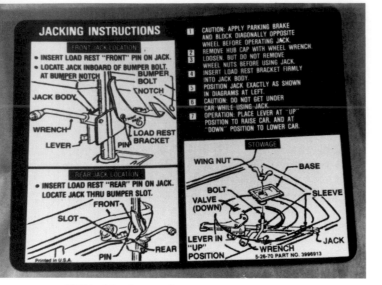

*1971 jacking instructions.*

*1964-71 ½ Positraction rear axle warning decal.*

of the deck lid on cars and to the rear wall on the pickup. Jack bases were now painted gloss-black; the jack differed each year.

### 1968–1972 Jack Part Numbers

| Year | Coupe and Convertible | Pickup |
|------|-----------------------|--------|
| 1968 | 3930139 | 3903877 |
| 1969 | 3903902 | 3903902 |
| 1970–72 | 3949206 | 3920034 |

A screwdriver, part number 3760276, came with the 1969 jack and was stored in the rubber sleeve along with the combination handle and lug wrench. It used the standard anchor bolt and wing nut. A center wheel cap was not included with the spare tire.

At the end of February 1969 these items were changed. The sleeve was eliminated except on the pickup, as was the screwdriver. A longer anchor bolt (part number 3916608, 3920026 for the El Camino) with a special retaining nut (part number 391888, 3968578 for the pickup) was positioned through one of the lug holes in the wheel. The base of the jack was placed under the tire, supported with the anchor bolt on the pickup. A center wheel cap was included with the spare tire. The lug wrench was positioned between the tire and the rear wall on the car and in the sleeve on the pickup. This arrangement was replaced with the more conventional one in 1970, and the spare center hub was again not included.

*1972 jacking instructions.*

*The 1971 ½ and 1972 Positraction warning decal change occurred after build date 03B 1971.*

Jacking instructions from 1970 to 1972 were moved to the upper left-hand corner of the underside of the deck lid in the second indentation from the left. The sleeve was now two bands of black rubber, part number 3975438, and secured the lug wrench.

A wheel cover was included with the El Camino with bucket seats that matched the interior trim. A cover was not available for the cars. A spare wheel lock was available as a dealer-installed option only all three years.

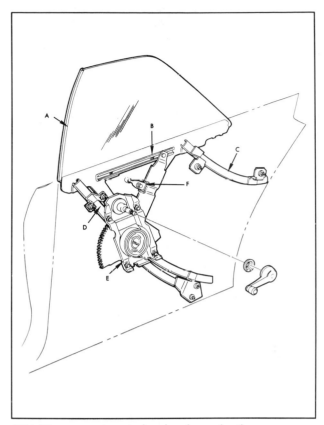

*1964-65 rear quarter window hardware for the coupe.*

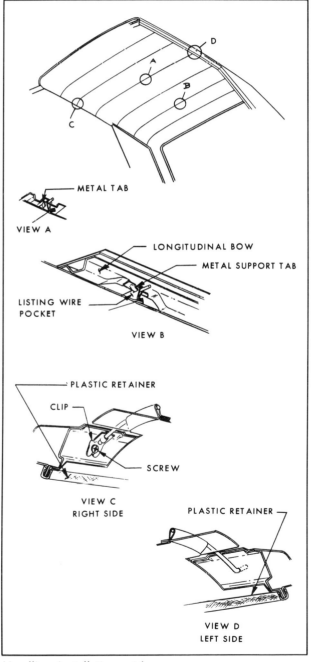

*Headliner installation guide.*

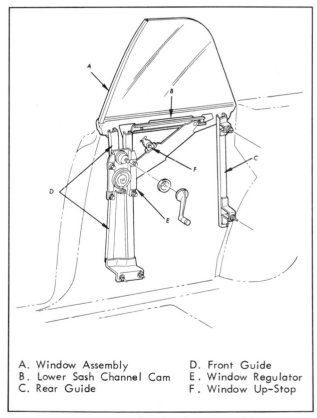

| A. | Window Assembly | D. | Front Guide |
| B. | Lower Sash Channel Cam | E. | Window Regulator |
| C. | Rear Guide | F. | Window Up-Stop |

*1964-65 rear quarter window for the convertible.*

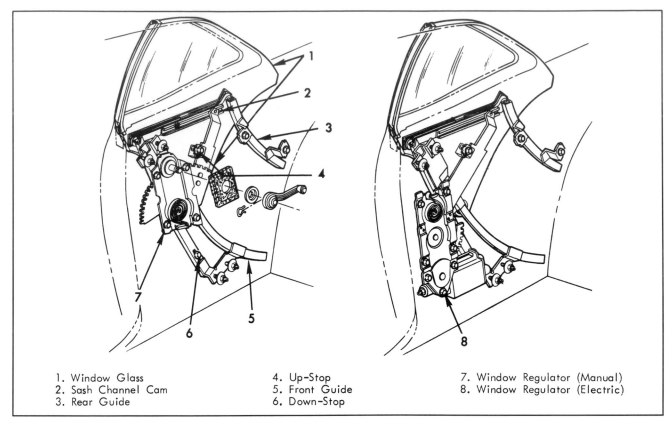

| | | |
|---|---|---|
| 1. Window Glass | 4. Up-Stop | 7. Window Regulator (Manual) |
| 2. Sash Channel Cam | 5. Front Guide | 8. Window Regulator (Electric) |
| 3. Rear Guide | 6. Down-Stop | |

*1966-67 rear quarter window for the hardtop.*

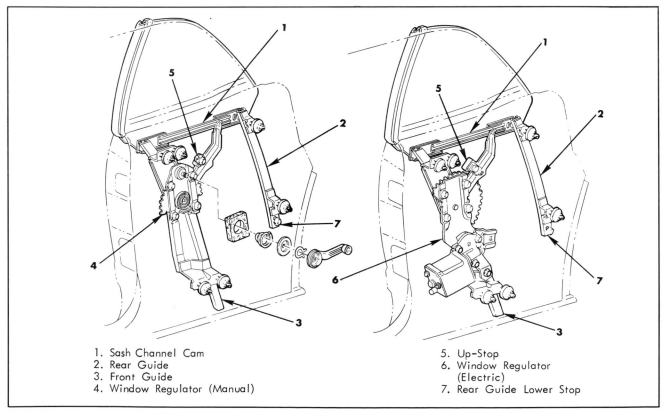

| | |
|---|---|
| 1. Sash Channel Cam | 5. Up-Stop |
| 2. Rear Guide | 6. Window Regulator (Electric) |
| 3. Front Guide | 7. Rear Guide Lower Stop |
| 4. Window Regulator (Manual) | |

*1966-67 rear quarter window for the convertible.*

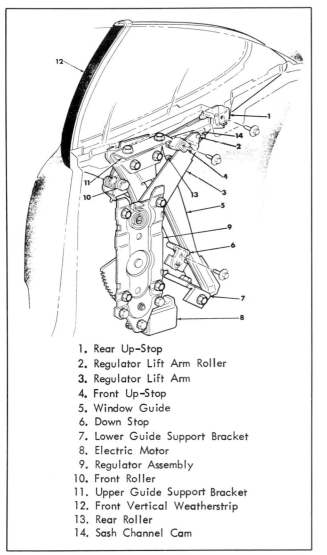

1. Rear Up-Stop
2. Regulator Lift Arm Roller
3. Regulator Lift Arm
4. Front Up-Stop
5. Window Guide
6. Down Stop
7. Lower Guide Support Bracket
8. Electric Motor
9. Regulator Assembly
10. Front Roller
11. Upper Guide Support Bracket
12. Front Vertical Weatherstrip
13. Rear Roller
14. Sash Channel Cam

*1968-72 rear quarter window for all coupes.*

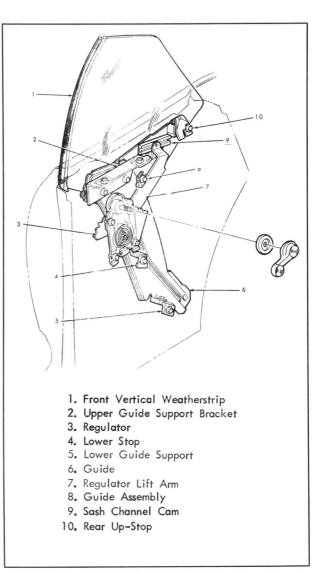

1. Front Vertical Weatherstrip
2. Upper Guide Support Bracket
3. Regulator
4. Lower Stop
5. Lower Guide Support
6. Guide
7. Regulator Lift Arm
8. Guide Assembly
9. Sash Channel Cam
10. Rear Up-Stop

*1968-72 rear quarter window hardware for the convertible.*

## 1964 Interior Codes and Combinations

| Code | Seating | | Door Trim | | Carpet | Headliner |
| | Style | Color | Panel | Upper Paint* | | Basket Weave |
|------|---------|-------|-------|--------------|--------|--------------|
| 710 | Buckets | Saddle | Saddle | Dark Saddle | Dark Saddle | Light Saddle |
| 714 | Buckets | Black | Black | Black | Black | Silver |
| 722 | Buckets | Aqua | Aqua | Aqua | Dark Aqua | Light Aqua |
| 729 | Buckets | White | White | White | Red | White |
| 770 | Buckets | Fawn | Fawn | Dark Saddle | Dark Fawn | Fawn |
| 786 | Buckets | Red | Red | Red | Red | Red |

*60-degrees gloss also applies to windlace trim

## 1965 Interior Codes and Combinations

| Code | Seating | | Door Trim | Carpet | Headliner |
| | Style | Color | Panel | | Basket Weave |
|------|---------|-------|-------|--------|--------------|
| 710 | Buckets | Saddle | Saddle | Dark Saddle | Light Saddle |
| 714 | Buckets | Black | Black | Black | Silver |
| 741 | Buckets | Blue | Blue | Blue | Light Blue |

## 1965 Interior Codes and Combinations

| Code | Seating | | Door Trim | Carpet | Headliner |
|------|---------|-------|-----------|--------|-----------|
| | Style | Color | Panel | | Basket Weave |
| 770 | Buckets | Fawn | Fawn | Dark Fawn | Fawn |
| 786 | Buckets | Red | Red | Red | Red |
| 729 | Buckets | White | White/Aqua | Aqua | Light Aqua |
| 796 | Buckets | White | White/Black | Black | Parchment |
| 799 | Buckets | Slate | Light Slate | Dark Slate | Light Slate |

## 1966 Interior Codes and Combinations

| Code | Seating | | Door Trim | Carpet | Headliner |
|------|---------|-------|-----------|--------|-----------|
| | Style | Color | Panel | (1) | Diamond Weave |
| 709 | Bench | Light Fawn | Light Fawn | Fawn | Medium Fawn |
| 712 | Bucket | Light Fawn | Light Fawn | Medium Dark Fawn | Medium Fawn |
| 731 | Bucket | Bright Blue | Bright Blue | Dark Blue | Dark Blue |
| 732 | Bench | Bright Blue | Bright Blue | Dark Blue | Dark Blue |
| 747 | Bench | Red | Red | Dark Red | Red |
| 750 | Bucket | Red | Red | Dark Red | Red |
| 761 | Bench | Black | Black | Black | Black |
| 763 | Bucket | Black | Black | Black | Black |
| 776 | Bench | Turquoise | Turquoise | Dark Turquoise | Turquoise |
| 787 | Bench | Bronze | Bronze | Bronze | Bronze |
| 790 | Bucket | Bronze | Bronze | Bronze | Bronze |
| 798 | Bench | White | White | Black | White |
| 797 | Bucket | White | White | Black | White |

(1)-Carpet strip on lower portion of door panel and floor.

## 1967 Interior Codes and Combinations

| Code | Seating | | Door Trim | Carpet | Headliner |
|------|---------|-------|-----------|--------|-----------|
| | Style | Color | Panel | (1) | Ribbed Pattern |
| 723 | Bench | Bright Blue | Bright Blue | Dark Bright Blue | Bright Blue |
| 729 | Bench | Blue | Blue | Dark Blue | Blue |
| 731 | Bucket | Bright Blue | Bright Blue | Dark Bright Blue | Bright Blue |
| 738 | Bucket | Blue | Blue | Dark Blue | Blue |
| 747 | Bench | Red | Red | Dark Red | Red |
| 750 | Bucket | Red | Red | Dark Red | Red |
| 761 | Bench | Black | Black | Black | Black |
| 763 | Bucket | Black | Black | Black | Black |
| 776 | Bench | Turquoise | Turquoise | Dark Turquoise | Turquoise |
| 778 | Bucket | Turquoise | Turquoise | Dark Turquoise | Turquoise |

(1)-Carpet strip on lower portion of door panel and floor.

## 1968 Interior Codes and Combinations

| Code | Seating | | Door Trim | Pillar | Carpet | Headliner |
|------|---------|-------|-----------|--------|--------|-----------|
| | Style | Color | Panel | Color | Color | Leatherette |
| 754 | Bench | Gold | Gold | Dark Gold | Dark Gold | Gold |
| 755 | Bench | Teal | Teal | Blue | Blue | Light Blue |
| 756 | Bucket | Gold | Gold | Dark Gold | Dark Gold | Gold |
| 757 | Bucket | Teal | Teal | Blue | Blue | Light Blue |
| 765 | Bench | Black | Black | Black | Black | Black |
| 766 | Bucket | Black | Black | Black | Black | Black |
| 793 [b] | Bench | Parchment | Parchment | Parchment | Black | Parchment |
| 794 | Bucket | Parchment | Parchment | Parchment | Black | Parchment |
| 795 [a] | Bench | Red | Red | Red | Red | Red |

[a]-Convertible only; not available for pickup or coupe
[b]-Coupe only

# 1969 Interior Codes and Combinations

| Code | Style | Seating Color | Door Trim Panel | Pillar Color | Carpet | Headliner Perforated # |
|---|---|---|---|---|---|---|
| | | | **Cloth and Vinyl; 300 Based** | | | |
| 751 | Bench | Black | Black | Black | Black | Black |
| 760 | Bench | Medium Blue | Medium Blue | Blue | Blue | Medium Blue |
| 786 | Bench | Medium Green | Medium Green | Green | Green | Medium Green |
| | | | **Malibu Based** | | | |
| 753 | Bench | Black | Black | Black | Black | Black |
| 762 | Bench | Dark Blue | Dark Blue | Dark Blue | Dark Blue | Blue |
| 779 | Bench | Medium Turquoise | Medium Turquoise | Dark Turquoise | Dark Turquoise | Medium Turquoise |
| 782 | Bench | Dark Green | Dark Green | Dark Green | Dark Green | Dark Green |
| 783 | Bench | Medium Green | Medium Green | Dark Green | Medium Green | Medium Green |
| | | | **All Vinyl; 300 Based** | | | |
| 752 | Bench | Black | Black | Black | Black | Black |
| | | | **Malibu Based (Standard Convertible and El Camino)** | | | |
| 755 | Bench | Black | Black | Black | Black | Black |
| 756 | Bucket | Black | Black | Black | Black | Black |
| 764 | Bench [a] | Dark Blue | Dark Blue | Dark Blue | Dark Blue | Dark Blue |
| 765 | Bucket [b] | Dark Blue | Dark Blue | Dark Blue | Dark Blue | Dark Blue |
| 784 | Bench [c] | Medium Green | Medium Green | Dark Green | Medium Green | Medium Green |
| 785 | Bucket [c] | Medium Green | Medium Green | Dark Green | Medium Green | Medium Green |
| 795 | Bench [c] | Dark Green | Dark Green | Dark Green | Dark Green | Dark Green |
| 796 | Bucket [c] | Dark Green | Dark Green | Dark Green | Dark Green | Dark Green |
| 787 | Bench [d] | Medium Red | Medium Red | Dark Red | Medium Red | Medium Red |
| 788 | Bucket [d] | Medium Red | Medium Red | Dark Red | Medium Red | Medium Red |
| 790 | Bench [d] | Parchment | Parchment | Parchment | Black | Parchment |
| 773 | Bench [e] | Saddle | Saddle | Dark Saddle | Saddle | Saddle |
| 771 | Bucket [e] | Saddle | Saddle | Dark Saddle | Saddle | Saddle |

#-Early 1969 used the leatherette pattern headliner
[a]-convertible only
[b]-coupe and pickup only
[c]-coupe only
[d]-coupe and convertible only
[e]-pickup only

# 1970 Interior Codes and Combinations

| Code | Style | Seating Color | Door Trim Panel | Pillar Color | Carpet Color | Headliner Perforated # |
|---|---|---|---|---|---|---|
| | | | **Cloth and Vinyl; Coupe only** | | | |
| 753 | Bench | Black | Black | Black | Black | Black |
| 762 | Bench | Medium Blue | Medium Blue | Dark Blue | Dark Blue | Medium Blue |
| 782 | Bench | Dark Green | Dark Green | Dark Green | Dark Green | Dark Green |
| 776 | Bench | Medium Gold | Medium Gold | Dark Gold | Medium Gold | Medium Gold |
| | | | **All Vinyl Standard Convertible and Pickup** | | | |
| 755 | Bench | Black | Black | Black | Black | Black |
| 756 | Bucket | Black | Black | Black | Black | Black |
| 764 | Bench [b] | Medium Blue | Medium Blue | Dark Blue | Dark Blue | Medium Blue |
| 765 | Bucket [b] | Medium Blue | Medium Blue | Dark Blue | Dark Blue | Medium Blue |
| 770 | Bench | Saddle | Saddle | Dark Saddle | Saddle | Saddle |
| 771 | Bucket | Saddle | Saddle | Dark Saddle | Saddle | Saddle |
| 787 | Bench [d] | Red | Red | Dark Red | Dark Red | Red |
| 788 | Bucket [d] | Red | Red | Dark Red | Dark Red | Red |
| 795 | Bench [c] | Dark Green | Dark Green | Dark Green | Dark Green | Dark Green |
| 790 | Bench [d] | Ivory | Ivory | Black | Black | Ivory |
| 791 | Bucket [d] | Ivory | Ivory | Black | Black | Ivory |

[b]- convertible and pickup    [d]-not available on pickup
[c]- coupe only

# 1971 Interior Codes and Combinations

| Code | Seating Style | Seating Color | Door Trim Panel | Pillar Color | Carpet Color | Headliner Perforated # |
|---|---|---|---|---|---|---|
| **Cloth and Vinyl; Coupe only** | | | | | | |
| 704 | Bench | Black | Black | Black | Black | Black |
| 725 | Bench | Dark Blue | Dark Blue | Dark Blue | Dark Blue | Dark Blue |
| 730 | Bench | Dark Jade | Dark Green | Dark Green | Dark Green | Dark Green |
| 718 | Bench | Sandalwood | Sandalwood | Medium Beige | Beige | Sandalwood |
| **All Vinyl Standard Convertible and Pickup** | | | | | | |
| 705 | Bench | Black | Black | Black | Black | Black |
| 706 | Bucket | Black | Black | Black | Black | Black |
| 731 | Bench | Dark Jade | Dark Green | Dark Green | Dark Green | Dark Green |
| 732 | Bucket | Dark Jade | Dark Green | Dark Green | Dark Green | Dark Green |
| 714 | Bench [f] | Sandalwood | Sandalwood | Medium Beige | Beige | Sandalwood |
| 715 | Bucket [f] | Sandalwood | Sandalwood | Medium Beige | Beige | Sandalwood |
| 721 | Bench | Dark Saddle | Dark Saddle | Dark Saddle | Dark Saddle | Dark Saddle |
| 722 | Bucket | Dark Saddle | Dark Saddle | Dark Saddle | Dark Saddle | Dark Saddle |

[f]–Not available on convertible

# 1972 Interior Codes and Combinations

| Code | Seating Style | Seating Color | Door Trim Panel | Pillar Color | Carpet Color | Headliner Perforated # |
|---|---|---|---|---|---|---|
| **Cloth and Vinyl; Coupe only** | | | | | | |
| 703 | Bench | Black | Black | Black | Black | Black |
| 720 | Bench | Medium Tan | Medium Tan | Dark Tan | Dark Tan | Medium Tan |
| 724 | Bench | Dark Blue | Dark Blue | Dark Blue | Dark Blue | Dark Blue |
| 730 | Bench | Light Covert | Light Covert | Beige | Beige | Light Covert |
| **All Vinyl Stand Convertible and Pickup** | | | | | | |
| 704 | Both | Black | Black | Black | Black | Black |
| 713 | Both | Dark Green | Dark Green | Dark Green | Dark Green | Dark Green |
| 720 | Both [f] | Medium Tan | Medium Tan | Dark Tan | Dark Tan | Medium Tan |
| 732 | Both [f] | Light Covert | Light Covert | Beige | Beige | Light Covert |
| 743 | Both [d] | White | White | Black | Black | Black |

[d]–Coupe and convertible only
[f]–Coupe and pickup only

## 1964 Seat Belt Colors

| Interior | Standard Belts | Deluxe RPO A49 |
|---|---|---|
| Black | Black | Black |
| Red | Red | Red |
| Aqua | Blue | Blue |
| White | Red | White |
| Fawn | Fawn | Dark Fawn |
| Saddle | Black | Dark Fawn |

All used the Fisher Coach emblem.

Standard belts were optional till December 1964, then made standard.

## 1965 Seat Belt Colors

| Interior | Standard Belts | Deluxe RPO A49 |
|---|---|---|
| Red | Red | Red |
| Blue | Blue | Blue |
| Black | Black | Black |
| Slate | Black | Dark Blue |

## 1964 Seat Belt Colors

| Interior | Standard Belts | Deluxe RPO A49 |
|---|---|---|
| White/blue | Black | Blue |
| White/black | Black | Black |
| Saddle | Fawn | Fawn |
| Fawn | Fawn | Fawn |

## 1966 Seat Belt Colors

| Interior | Standard Belts | Deluxe RPO A49 |
|---|---|---|
| Light Fawn | Black | Dark Fawn |
| Turquoise | Black | Turquoise |
| Red | Red | Red |
| Bright Blue | Blue | Blue |
| Black | Black | Black |
| White | Black | Black |
| Bronze | Black | Bronze |

## 1967 Seat Belt Colors

| Interior | Standard Belts | Deluxe RPO A49 |
|---|---|---|
| Black | Black* | Black |
| Fawn | Black | Dark Fawn |
| Red | Black | Red |
| Blue | Blue | Blue |
| Bright Blue | Blue | Bright Blue |
| Gold | Gold | Gold |
| Turquoise | Turquoise | Turquoise |

Fisher Coach emblem buckle used on all.

*-Also available with GM logo buckle. Later version had the words "Mark of Excellence" added.

## 1968 Seat Belt Colors

| Interior | Standard Belts | Deluxe RPO A49 |
|---|---|---|
| Black | Black | Black |
| Gold | Gold | Dark Gold |
| Parchment | Black | Black |
| Blue | Blue | Dark Blue |
| Red | Black | Red |
| Teal | Blue | Teal |

All used GM "Mark of Excellence" emblem; custom belts are brushed aluminum.

## 1969 Seat Belt Colors

| Interior | Standard Belts | Deluxe RPO A49 |
|---|---|---|
| Black (4) | Black | Black |
| Dark Blue (3) | Dark Blue | Dark Blue |
| Medium Green (1) | Dark Green | Dark Green |
| Dark Green | Dark Green | Medium Green |
| Medium Turquoise | Black | Dark Turquoise |
| Medium Red | Black | Dark Red |
| Parchment | Black | Black |
| Saddle (2) | Black | Dark Saddle |
| Medium Blue (1) | Dark Blue | Dark Blue |

All used GM "Mark of Excellence" emblem; custom belts are brushed aluminum.

Belts are limited to Malibu base except as noted:

(1)–300 base only
(2)–El Camino base only
(3)–Malibu and El Camino base only
(4)–Available in all bases

## 1970 Seat Belt Colors

| Interior | Standard Belts | Deluxe RPO A49 |
|---|---|---|
| Black | Black | Black |
| Medium Saddle | Black | Medium Saddle |
| Medium Blue | Dark Blue | Dark Blue |
| Dark Green | Dark Green | Dark Green |
| Ivory | Black | Black |
| Medium Red | Black | Medium Red |
| Medium Gold | Medium Gold | Medium Gold |
| Medium Turquoise | Black | Dark Turquoise |

Standard belt buckles are plastic, same color as the belts. Custom belt buckles have brushed finish.

## 1971 Seat Belt Colors

| Interior | Standard Belts | Deluxe RPO A49 |
|---|---|---|
| Dark Jade | Black | Jade |
| Saddle | Black | Saddle |
| Dark Blue | Black | Blue |
| Sandalwood | Black | Black |

All standard belt and shoulder belts have black plastic and black webbing. Custom belts are color-keyed with buckles with a brushed finish.

## 1972 Seat Belt Colors

| Interior | Standard Belts | Deluxe RPO A49 |
|---|---|---|
| Black | Black | Black |
| Dark Green | Black | Dark Green |
| Medium Tan | Black | Tan |
| Dark Blue(1) | Black | Dark Blue |
| Light Covert | Black | Covert |
| White (1) | Black | Black |

Early models used the four point system and no sensor warning. Later models used the three-point design with sensor warning. They were available in the same colors as above. However with standard belts, two types of buckles were used. Bench seats used a plastic buckle, bucket seats used a vinyl, sprayed buckle. Deluxe belts retained their brushed finish.

(1)–Not available on the El Camino

# Chapter 9

# Electrical Systems

## Battery and Battery Cables

### 1964-1965

The standard battery in both 1964 and 1965 was the Delco DC-12 tar top with yellow caps. A 61 amp heavy-duty battery, RPO T60, was optional both years; it was standard on the 1965 327 and 396 ci engines. Both batteries used the same gloss-black tray, part number 3838454, and top retainer, part number 3848480. However, the side retainer bolts for the heavy-duty battery were longer than the standard part, because the optional battery was taller. The side retainer bolts should also be painted gloss-black.

### 1964-1965 Side Retainer Bolt Part Numbers

| Part | Standard Production | Heavy-duty T60 |
|---|---|---|
| Rear bolt | 3848488 | 3848495 |
| Front bolt | 3826708 | 3714197 |
| Front bolt nut | 120376 | 120376 |
| Front bolt washer | 446363 | 446363 |

The 6 gauge positive battery cable, part number 2987260, was routed from the battery to the B-terminal of the solenoid. It was supported by two clips on the oil pan and a black plastic clip, part number 3857706, on the frame rail. The standard cable was listed as part number 2987288 in 1965 and included a 10 gauge red pigtail wire that was routed to a junction block, part number 3882795, on the radiator support.

Different cables were used on the heavy-duty battery both years. In 1964 positive cable part number 29865623 was used. This cable employed a pigtail wire that was routed like the 1965 production cable. It was routed down and under the tray assembly. In 1965 part number 2987293 was used. The pigtail wire was routed along the side of the battery behind the retainer bolt, then to the junction block.

A 6 gauge black wire was also used for the negative cable. A single cable, part number 2985611, was grounded to the water pump. The 1965 cable, part number 2897288, included a 12 gauge black pigtail wire routed to the radiator support wall.

A short pigtail was used on the 1964 heavy-duty cable, part number 2985623, in 1964 and was attached to the right front fender with a screw and lock washer. Two different cables were available with the T60 battery in 1965; both used the same route and included a pigtail that was rerouted to the radiator support wall.

### 1965 T60 Battery Cable Part Numbers

| | |
|---|---|
| 283 V-8 | 2987295 |
| 327 V-8 | 2987294 |

The heavy-duty battery was included with the air conditioning and Z16 packages.

### 1966-1967

Early 1966 models used the 1965 tray and retaining system. Later models used tray part number 3885938, hold-down clamp part number 3887588 and a $5/16 \times 7/8$ in. tap screw with 18 threads to secure the battery. The tray, clamp and screw should be painted gloss-black.

A heavy-duty Delco battery was standard with the 396 engine. The case and caps were black with Delco written on them in yellow letters. Late 1966 models and all 1967 SS 396s were standard with the heavy-duty Delco Energizer R59S and rated at 61 amps. Molded into the top of the case was the name Delco Energizer. The caps were black with the name Delco on top.

A 6 gauge black positive cable, part number 6289132, with a 12 gauge red pigtail wire was used in 1966 and was routed the same as in 1965. This cable was supported with a special clip, part number 3866188, that was held to the frame by a hex-head screw and lock washer. Early models did not have this clip, but during hard turns the cable would sometimes get caught in the fan belt, so dealers installed the clip on earlier models for their customers.

The above black plastic clip was also used with the 1967 positive cable, part number 6290595, but was positioned farther forward on the frame rail. The cable was the same as in 1966.

Negative cable part number 2987294 was used in 1966 and included a long 12 gauge black pigtail wire that was grounded to the radiator support wall. A cable, part number 2987294, with a shorter pigtail that grounded to the right front fender was used in 1967. Both cables were black.

### 1968-1969

The 1968 battery was identical to that used in 1967. The support tray was redesigned in 1968 and was listed as part number 3915473 in both 1968 and 1969. However, the retaining clamp and ½ in. hex-head bolt were the same as before. The tray clamp and bolt should be gloss-black.

Both years the battery used a felt washer, part number 378082, on each post. The positive cable was listed as part number 6296701 in 1968, 6296787 in 1969; its route was the same as in 1967. The support clip, part number 3732015, was re-styled and attached to the side of the right front frame rail with a single bolt. Both years a brown pigtail wire was used on the cables.

The negative cables were different each year. The 1968 cable, part number 6296700, featured a longer pigtail that was grounded on the radiator support wall. The 1969 cable, part number 6296751, had a shorter pigtail wire that was grounded on the right-hand front fender, as in 1967.

The main ground of the negative cable was in the block under and to the right of the alternator instead of on the water pump as in years before.

### 1970-1972

A top post Delco Energizer was standard in 1970 for both SS packages except with the LS6 engine. An 80 amp heavy-duty side post battery was optional and standard with air conditioning and the LS6 engine package.

Several different cables and routes were used in 1970 on the L34 and LS5 engines. Early cars, built in the first month, used the same route and cables as in 1969. Cars built in the next two months used a different positive cable, part number 6296791, with the addition of a clip on the engine mount.

Most SSs used positive cable part number 8901074 and negative cable part number 8901083. The positive cable was supported by a special clip, part number 3973690; the side rail clip was eliminated. The negative cable was now grounded at the generator bracket. The pigtail on the negative cable was grounded as in 1969. The pigtail on the positive cable was connected to a junction block on the radiator support wall to the left of the battery. Both pigtails should have a fused link.

Side mount cables were used with the heavy-duty battery and the LS6 Chevelle. They should have red connectors and black cables. Different cables were used on early 1970 396 engines, but

positive cable part number 8901624 and negative cable part number 8901637 were used with all engines beginning in December 1969 and are correct replacements.

The side mount Delco battery was phased into production at the end of the 1970 model year, so some 1970 SSs without the T60 option could use it. All 1971 and 1972 Chevelles used the side mount battery.

Both small-blocks and the LS3 engine were standard with a 61 amp battery; the LS5 engine used a 63 amp unit, and this was also standard with air conditioning. The 80 amp heavy-duty battery was still optional and standard with the LS6 engine. This same battery became a required option in 1972 with the LS5 454 ci engine.

Several different cables were used depending on the engine and battery. The route was the same as in 1970.

### 1971-1972 Battery Cable Part Numbers

L48, L65
| | |
|---|---|
| Positive | 8901623 |
| Negative | 8901636 |

LS3, LS5
| | |
|---|---|
| Positive | 8908072 |
| Negative | 8901866 |

Heavy-duty battery & 1971 LS6
| | |
|---|---|
| 1971 positive | 8901932 |
| 1972 positive | 8908072 |
| Negative | 8901866 |

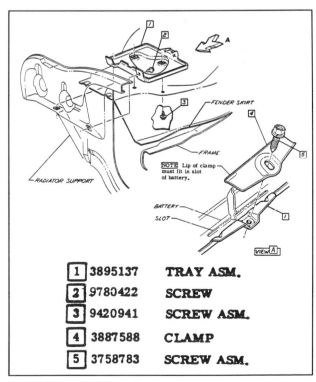

| | | |
|---|---|---|
| 1 | 3895137 | TRAY ASM. |
| 2 | 9780422 | SCREW |
| 3 | 9420941 | SCREW ASM. |
| 4 | 3887588 | CLAMP |
| 5 | 3758783 | SCREW ASM. |

*1966-67 second-design battery support tray.*

The support tray and clamp were identical all three years and were the same parts as in 1968-69. They should be painted gloss-black.

## Standard Ignition Systems

### 1964-1965

Two types of ignition systems were available in 1964: the standard and the transistor (which will be covered later). Only one coil, part number 1115115, was used with all V-8s in 1964 with standard ignition; it was manufactured by Delco Remy. The high-tension lead was listed as part number 2983719.

Four distributors were used. Each was unique in design and cannot be interchanged. A red part number band was used around each distributor for identification.

### 1964 Distributor Part Numbers

| | |
|---|---|
| 2 bbl 283 ci | 1111015 |
| 4 bbl 283 ci | 1111051 |
| 250 hp 327 ci | 1111016 |
| 300 hp 327 ci | 1111060 |

Natural metal shields were installed on the exhaust manifolds to protect the spark plug wires. Three parts were needed: left side section, part

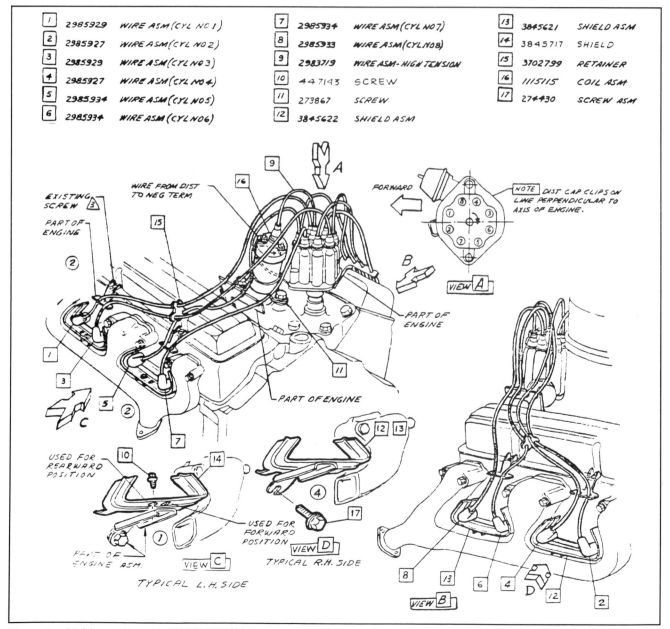

Plug wire shields used on the 1964-65 small-block engine.

194

number 345717; right side forward section, part number 3845622; and right side rear section, part number 3845621.

Three different coils were available. The 283 ci V–8s and the 250 and 300 hp 327 ci engines used the same coil, part number 1115204. The L79 350 hp 327 ci engine used part number 1115202. The 396 ci V–8 powerplant used part number 1115210.

The typical mount was to the left of the distributor except with the L79 engine, where it was to the right of the distributor housing. A special brace support, part number 3858859, was used on early models. Cars built after the fifth week in October 1964 used a different bracket, part number 3870320, that mounted the coil on its side with the nose facing the firewall. Both of these supports should have a natural finish.

Four conventional distributors were used in 1965. As in 1964, a red part number band was used around each one. All distributors were manufactured by Delco Remy.

## 1965 Distributor Part Numbers

| | |
|---|---|
| All 283 ci | 1111015 |
| 250 & 300 hp 327 ci | 1111075 |
| 350 hp 327 ci | 1111072 |
| 375 hp 396 ci | 1111100 |

### 1966–1967

For most of 1966 coil part number 1115204 was used; however, from mid February to mid March part number 1115242 was used. The first part number is the correct replacement. When installed correctly the positive post of the coil should face the firewall.

The high-tension lead was listed as part number 2989408 and was routed to the center of the distributor cap. Three distributors were available with conventional ignition. All used a red part number band and a thin black wire that was connected to the negative terminal of the coil.

## 1966 Distributor Part Numbers

| | |
|---|---|
| 325 hp 396 ci | 1111109 |
| 360 hp 396 ci | 1111138 |
| 375 hp 396 ci | 1111100 |

Nontapered AC/Delco 43N spark plugs were standard; 42N is recommended by Chevrolet for normal service. Plug wires were also manufactured by AC.

## 1966 Plug Wire Part Numbers

| Cylinder | Part Number |
|---|---|
| 1 & 2 | 2989400 |
| 3 | 2989401 |
| 4 | 2989402 |
| 5 | 2989403 |
| 6 | 2989404 |
| 7 | 2989407 |
| 8 | 2989408 |

Small retainers, part number 2977995, were mounted on each valve cover and supported two wires each. The left-hand side supported cylinders 1 and 3, and the right-hand side supported cylinders 2 and 4. A two-piece tower retainer, part numbers 2965950–LH and 2977555–RH, was used at the rear of the engine and supported all four wires. An additional support, part number 2965736, was employed on the right-hand side between the tower and the valve cover supports.

The ignition switch was mounted in the upper instrument panel. No engraved bezel was used; it was installed in the 300 series but is incorrect for the SS.

The ignition coil was listed as part number 1115242 in 1967; a few early models used the 1966 coil. The high-tension lead and spark plug cables used the same part numbers as in 1966.

Three distributors were installed with the 396 engine. The base 325 hp used part number 1111195, the L34 350 hp used part number 1111169 and the L78 375 hp used part number 1111170.

The spark plug supports and ignition switch were the same as in 1966.

### 1968–1969

The battery cables used the same part numbers in 1968 as in 1966–67. However, the 1968 coil was listed as part number 1115267. It should be mounted the same as in previous years.

The part number of each of the four distributors was found on a red band around the housing. The base 325 hp engine used part number 1111444 with manual transmission and part number 1111169 with automatic. The L34 350 hp engine used part number 1111277 with all transmissions. The L78 375 hp engine used part number 1111170 only.

The ignition switch was deeply recessed into the instrument carrier in 1968. In 1969 it was moved to the steering column. For 1969 all Chevelle cylinders are interchangeable except with the tilt wheel, which requires a special part.

The coil, tension lead and spark plug wires were the same parts as in 1968. More distributors were added in 1969 and were used according to the type of transmission and power rating of the engine.

## 1969 Distributor Part Numbers

| | |
|---|---|
| L34 350 hp | |
| Manual | 1111498 |
| Automatic | 1111499 |
| Base L35 325 hp | |
| Manual | 1111497 |
| Automatic | 1111497 |
| L78 375 & 425 hp 427 ci | |
| Manual & automatic | 1111499 |

## 1970-1972

In 1970 the coil was standard production part number 1115293. The high-tension lead was the same as before, but the spark plug cables were changed.

### 1970 Plug Wire Part Numbers

| Cylinder | Part Number |
|----------|-------------|
| 1 & 2 | 8901007 |
| 3 | 8901008 |
| 4 | 8901009 |
| 5 | 8901010 |
| 6 | 8901011 |
| 7 | 8901004 |
| 8 | 8901012 |

A unique retainer, part number 3702799, on the valve covers grouped three wires together: the wires for cylinders 1, 3 and 5 on the left-hand side and the wires for cylinders 2, 4 and 6 on the right-hand side. Heat shields were also used on the exhaust manifolds. They fit either side and were listed as part numbers 3845622 front and 3845621 rear. They were held with two small bolts.

The distributors were identified the same way as in previous years with the red part number band.

### 1970 Distributor Part Numbers

L34 350 hp
| | |
|---|---|
| Manual | 1111999 |
| Automatic | 1112000 |

L78 375 hp
| | |
|---|---|
| Manual & automatic | 1112000 |

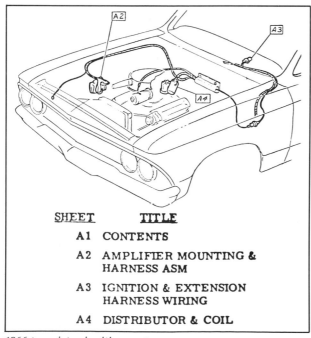

| SHEET | TITLE |
|-------|-------|
| A1 | CONTENTS |
| A2 | AMPLIFIER MOUNTING & HARNESS ASM |
| A3 | IGNITION & EXTENSION HARNESS WIRING |
| A4 | DISTRIBUTOR & COIL |

*1966 transistor ignition system.*

LS5 360 hp 454
| | |
|---|---|
| All transmissions | 1112000 |

LS6 450 hp 454
| | |
|---|---|
| Manual & automatic | 1111437 |

The coil assembly was changed to part number 1115293 for 1971 and 1972. A total of eight distributors were used in 1971. In 1972 that choice was narrowed to four.

### 1971 Chevelle SS Distributors

| Engine Size | Transmission | Part Number |
|-------------|--------------|-------------|
| 350/245 hp | Manual | 1112042 |
| 350/245 hp | Automatic | 1112005 |
| 350/270 hp | Manual | 1112044 |
| 350/270 hp | Automatic | 1112045 |
| 402/300 hp* | All | 1112057 |
| 454/365 hp | All | 1112052 |
| 454/425 hp | Manual | 1112075 |
| 454/425 hp | Automatic | 1112054 |

*-Listed as Turbo-Jet 400

### 1972 Chevelle SS Distributors

| Engine Size | Transmission | Part Number |
|-------------|--------------|-------------|
| 350/165 hp | All | 1112005 |
| 350/175 hp | Manual | 1112044 |
| 350/175 hp | Automatic | 1112045 |
| 402/240 hp | All | 1112057 |
| 454/270 hp | All | 1112052 |

### Transistor Ignition

#### 1964-1966

Transistorized ignition was not available in 1964. For 1965 this option, RPO K66, was available only with the L79 350 hp 327 ci V-8 powerplant and not with any other engine choice including the L37 396 ci big-block. The distributor was listed as part number 111072. The amplifier was part number 1115005 and was manufactured by Delco Remy. It was mounted on the hood release support. This required a special harness, part number 2988987. A black wire was grounded to the support wall on the left-hand side just above the headlamps.

The coil was listed as part number 1115207, and special tachometer part number 6412735 was incuded with the package. A 42 amp alternator, part number 1100696, was also included; if air conditioning was ordered, the RPO K81 alternator was used.

The K66 option made its last appearance in 1966. It was available only on the SS 396. The amplifier was again the same part as in 1965 but was mounted to the lower right-hand front fender skirt. The harness was listed as part number 6289488. It was routed along the firewall, where it connected to the main harness, then upward into the right front fender. A 0.26 in. diameter exit hole was drilled for the harness so that the leads could connect to the amplifier. A ground wire was connected to the radiator support wall with a production screw.

Three distributors were offered: the base L35 used part number 1111109, the L34 engine used part number 1111139 and the L78 engine used part number 1111074. The coil was listed as part number 1115210. The tachometer was again included with the option package, and three were available: The base engine used part number 6412765, the L34 engine used part number

6412817 and the L78 engine used part number 6412766.

## Charging Systems

### 1964-1965

The standard alternator in 1964 was rated at 37 amps and was listed as part number 1100668 with a natural fan. A 55 amp alternator, RPO K77, part number 1100665, was included with the air conditioning package; the fan was painted gloss-black. A 42 amp alternator, RPO K79, part number

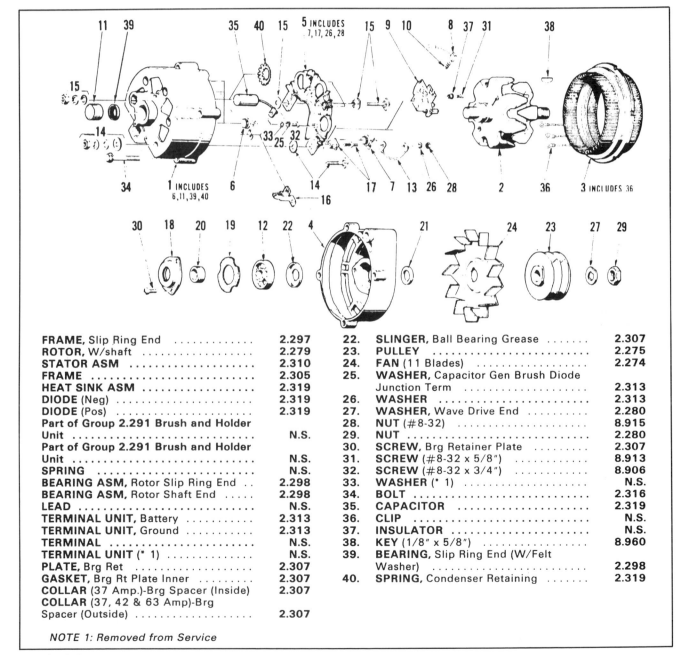

| | | | |
|---|---|---|---|
| **FRAME,** Slip Ring End | 2.297 | 22. **SLINGER,** Ball Bearing Grease | 2.307 |
| **ROTOR,** W/shaft | 2.279 | 23. **PULLEY** | 2.275 |
| **STATOR ASM** | 2.310 | 24. **FAN** (11 Blades) | 2.274 |
| **FRAME** | 2.305 | 25. **WASHER,** Capacitor Gen Brush Diode | |
| **HEAT SINK ASM** | 2.319 | Junction Term | 2.313 |
| **DIODE** (Neg) | 2.319 | 26. **WASHER** | 2.313 |
| **DIODE** (Pos) | 2.319 | 27. **WASHER,** Wave Drive End | 2.280 |
| **Part of Group 2.291 Brush and Holder** | | 28. **NUT** (#8-32) | 8.915 |
| Unit | N.S. | 29. **NUT** | 2.280 |
| **Part of Group 2.291 Brush and Holder** | | 30. **SCREW,** Brg Retainer Plate | 2.307 |
| Unit | N.S. | 31. **SCREW** (#8-32 x 5/8") | 8.913 |
| **SPRING** | N.S. | 32. **SCREW** (#8-32 x 3/4") | 8.906 |
| **BEARING ASM,** Rotor Slip Ring End | 2.298 | 33. **WASHER** (* 1) | N.S. |
| **BEARING ASM,** Rotor Shaft End | 2.298 | 34. **BOLT** | 2.316 |
| **LEAD** | N.S. | 35. **CAPACITOR** | 2.319 |
| **TERMINAL UNIT,** Battery | 2.313 | 36. **CLIP** | N.S. |
| **TERMINAL UNIT,** Ground | 2.313 | 37. **INSULATOR** | N.S. |
| **TERMINAL** | N.S. | 38. **KEY** (1/8" x 5/8") | 8.960 |
| **TERMINAL UNIT** (* 1) | N.S. | 39. **BEARING,** Slip Ring End (W/Felt | |
| **PLATE,** Brg Ret | 2.307 | Washer) | 2.298 |
| **GASKET,** Brg Rt Plate Inner | 2.307 | 40. **SPRING,** Condenser Retaining | 2.319 |
| **COLLAR** (37 Amp.)-Brg Spacer (Inside) | 2.307 | | |
| **COLLAR** (37, 42 & 63 Amp)-Brg | | | |
| Spacer (Outside) | 2.307 | | |

*NOTE 1: Removed from Service*

*Standard alternator.*

1100669, was included with transistor ignition; the fan was painted red. Also optional was a 60 amp heavy-duty alternator, RPO K81, part number 1117765. A double-groove pulley, part number 3825453, was used with this alternator.

All except the K81 alternator used regulator part number 1119515. K81 used part number 1116366. Both were mounted on the left-hand corner of the radiator support wall. K81 required three extra holes to be drilled. A dark blue wire and a black and white wire were routed from the alternator to the regulator. A red wire was routed from the alternator to the horn relay mounted above the regulator. Except with the 60 amp alternator the red lead was clipped and taped back, and a heavier-gauge black wire was routed to the horn relay.

The alternator belt was listed as part numbers 3759202 without air conditioning and 3738437 with air conditioning. The 60 amp alternator used part number 3847703 with or without air conditioning.

Color-coded fans were eliminated for 1965. The line-up was the same as in 1964 except that the part numbers were changed and a 62 amp alternator, RPO K76, was added near the end of the year.

### 1965 Alternator Part Numbers

| | |
|---|---|
| 37 amp standard | 1100693 |
| 42 amp w/K66 | 1100696 |
| 55 amp w/C60 | 1100694 |
| 60 amp K81 | 1100697 |
| 62 amp K76 | 1117765 |

All but the K81 and K76 alternators used regulator part number 1111515. K81 and K76 used regulator part number 1116368 only, and this regulator was optional with the other alternators. The housing of the standard regulator should be the same as before: flat-black. The optional regulator was natural.

Braces were the same as in 1964. All but the heavy-duty alternators used part number 3873814. The heavy-duty units used a bar-shaped brace, part number 3846866, that was curved upward at the slotted end. Both braces should be painted gloss-black. Belts used the same part numbers as in 1964.

### 1966-1967

The 37 amp alternator, part number 1100693, was standard in both 1966 and 1967. The 42 amp alternator was standard with the L78 engine and the transistor ignition package. A 60 amp alternator, K76, part number 1100750, was included with all air conditioning packages. The 55 amp alternator was eliminated in 1966, and a 62 amp alternator, K81, part number 1117754, was optional for 1966 only.

The regulator for all but the K81 alternator was listed as part number 1119515 both years. The heavy-duty alternator used a special regulator, part number 1116378, with a ribbed natural finish outer case. The location was the same as in 1964-65. The black and white wire was now solid white.

The production belt was listed as part number 3893254, 3862776 with air conditioning. The L78 engine used a shorter belt, part number 3869978; when equipped with the K81 alternator it used part number 3863159. The base and L34 engines with this alternator used part numbers 3879951

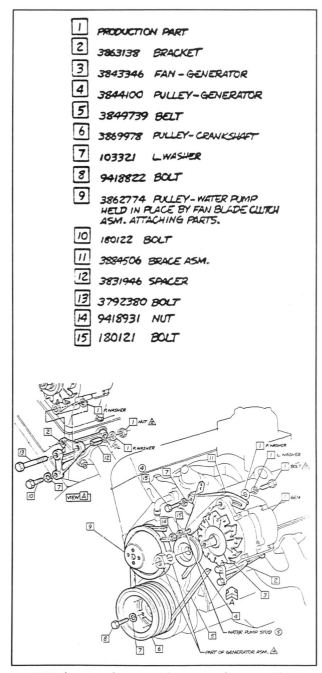

| | | |
|---|---|---|
| 1 | | PRODUCTION PART |
| 2 | 3863138 | BRACKET |
| 3 | 3843346 | FAN - GENERATOR |
| 4 | 3844100 | PULLEY - GENERATOR |
| 5 | 3849739 | BELT |
| 6 | 3869978 | PULLEY - CRANKSHAFT |
| 7 | 103321 | L.WASHER |
| 8 | 9418822 | BOLT |
| 9 | 3862774 | PULLEY - WATER PUMP HELD IN PLACE BY FAN BLADE CLUTCH ASM. ATTACHING PARTS. |
| 10 | 180122 | BOLT |
| 11 | 3884506 | BRACE ASM. |
| 12 | 3831946 | SPACER |
| 13 | 3792380 | BOLT |
| 14 | 9418931 | NUT |
| 15 | 180121 | BOLT |

*1965 L37 alternator braces and supports for use with Z16.*

198

without air conditioning and 3861956 with air conditioning.

### 1968-1969

Except for part numbers the alternators in 1968 were the same as in 1967. A 37 amp alternator was part number 1100813. A 42 amp alternator, part numbers 1100696 with manual transmissions and 1100795 with automatic transmissions, was included with air conditioning and the L78 engine. A 63 amp alternator, part numbers 1100810 with air conditioning and 1100818 without, was optional.

The regulator was mounted higher up on the radiator support wall in the left-hand corner. It was listed as part number 1119515. The standard belt was listed as part number 3845644, 3861952 with air conditioning. With the 63 amp alternator, belt part number 3917208 was used, and with air conditioning, part number 3928904 was used.

All alternators were mounted with the production braces, which consisted of a gloss-black top brace, part number 3884508, and a natural bottom brace, part number 3925526. The bottom brace was unique in design and fit the 396 ci engine only.

The alternator was mounted on the right-hand side of the engine in 1969 instead of the left as in previous years. The standard alternator was listed as part number 1100834. A 42 amp alternator, part number 1100837, was standard with the L78 and COPO 427 engines. A 61 amp alternator, part number 1100843, was included with air conditioning or as an option. A 63 amp heavy-duty alternator, RPO K85, part number 1100846, was also available with or without air conditioning.

The regulator was still mounted in the left-hand corner of the radiator support wall. The braces were restyled to accommodate the right-hand side mounting. The gloss-black top brace, part number 3940941, shielded over the alternator and featured an adjustable slot. The bottom brace consisted of a gloss-black outer plate, part number 3940939, and a threaded stud, part number 3940944, that was mounted in the head. A rear brace bar, part number 3940942, and a spacer, part number 3940943, both of which should have a natural appearance, were also used.

### 1970-1972

The standard alternator with all engines was listed as part number 1100834 in 1970. It was rated at 37 amps and built by Delco Remy, as in years before. With air conditioning, a 61 amp alternator, part number 1100843, was standard. The only optional alternator was the K85 63 amp, part number 11000847, 1000846 with air conditioning.

The regulator was identical to the 1969 unit and in the same location. The forward wiring harness, part number 8901301, was routed along the

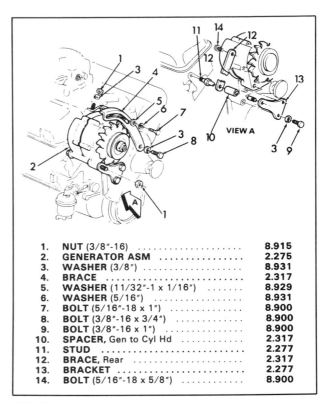

| | | |
|---|---|---|
| 1. | NUT (3/8"-16) | 8.915 |
| 2. | GENERATOR ASM | 2.275 |
| 3. | WASHER (3/8") | 8.931 |
| 4. | BRACE | 2.317 |
| 5. | WASHER (11/32"-1 x 1/16") | 8.929 |
| 6. | WASHER (5/16") | 8.931 |
| 7. | BOLT (5/16"-18 x 1") | 8.900 |
| 8. | BOLT (3/8"-16 x 3/4") | 8.900 |
| 9. | BOLT (3/8"-16 x 1") | 8.900 |
| 10. | SPACER, Gen to Cyl Hd | 2.317 |
| 11. | STUD | 2.277 |
| 12. | BRACE, Rear | 2.317 |
| 13. | BRACKET | 2.277 |
| 14. | BOLT (5/16"-18 x 5/8") | 8.900 |

*1971-72 alternator mount.*

left front fender well and secured with two black plastic clips, part number 3977640, then curled upward into the fender cavity and finally routed across the radiator support wall to the alternator. The braces were also the same as those used in 1969 and followed the same painting techniques.

The standard alternator in 1971 was identical to that in 1970 except with the SS 350s, which used part number 1100566, although both alternators were rated at 37 amps. The standard alternator with air conditioning was now rated at 63 amps and listed as part number 1100917. This unit was also optional without air conditioning.

The 400 Turbo-jet and 454 engines used the same braces as in 1969 and 1970. However, the 350 used different braces. The front brace, part number 3973396, had more curl on the lip; a long bolt instead of a threaded shaft secured the alternator at the bottom; and the outer plate, part number 3951500, was shaped different. The braces should be painted the same as those used with the big-blocks. These are the same braces used with all small-blocks since 1969.

At the beginning of production the Turbo-Jets used a different alternator, part number 1102454, than the 350s. After March 1972 all V-8 engines used part number 1102440. This alternator was used all year on the small-block engines and is the correct replacement part number for all 1972 Chevrolet engines.

*This wiper motor is identified as a standard two-speed motor for 1966, part number 5045430. It is installed in a 1965 El Camino, which makes it incorrect. The hood springs are also incorrectly painted black; they should be natural.*

Air-conditioned models, regardless of engine size, used a 63 amp alternator, part number 1102463; early models used part number 1102464. Both of these alternators were available as optional equipment without air conditioning.

The rear alternator braces were redesigned and will not interchange with earlier models. The

*A white washer jar was standard in a bracket that mounted to the inside of the left-hand front fender as shown. A black washer jar was also available.*

SS 350s used part number 6262934; it was shorter than before. The big-block engines used part number 6262938; it was bent and short in length. Both braces should have a natural metal appearance. The top braces were the same as in previous years and should be painted gloss-black.

## Windshield Wipers

### 1964-1965

Single-speed dual-arm wipers were standard in both 1964 and 1965. Two-speed washer-wipers were available both years as part of the comfort and convenience option. The motor and pump assembly was listed as part number 5044582; the housing should be painted gloss-black.

An opaque white washer bottle, part number 3640083, and a black cap, part number 3798372, were mounted in a gloss-black bracket, part number 548935, on the radiator support wall on the left-hand side. The hose was routed along the left-hand fender and supported with three clips, part number 3830786. A natural appearing nozzle, part number 3840766, was placed on each side. A windshield washer was also available with the single-speed motor as a dealer-installed option both years.

The wiper arms were stainless steel, part number 3832847, for both the standard and two-speed wipers. A two-speed switch was listed as part number 1993665, 1993678 in 1965. The standard knob, part number 3837947, 3859221 in 1965, was round and chrome-plated; the two-speed knob was flat on the end and was listed as part number 3837946, 3859322 in 1965. All knobs were mounted with a setscrew.

### 1966-1967

Two-speed washer-wipers were made standard in 1966 and continued in 1967. Part numbers were listed as 4914507 in 1966 and 5045430 in 1967 for the wiper motor assembly. The case was painted gloss-black and mounted to the left-hand side of the firewall.

Stainless steel wiper arms were identical both years; however, the 1966 arms used part number 3887573, and the 1967 arms used part number 393832. Both arms came with the same blade, part number 3888296.

A white washer jar was standard and listed as part number 3840083 both years. A black plastic jar was also a special order option. Both jars used the same cap, part number 3798372, and gloss-black bracket, part number 548935. The location was the same as in 1964-65: on the left-hand corner of the radiator support wall.

The hose route was up inside the left front fender with the wiring harness. Two natural nozzles, part number 3880753, were used on the cowl. The nozzle should be inserted through a slit in the hood-cowl seal.

## 1968-1969

The wiper motor was restyled in 1968 and listed as part number 5044681. This same motor was also used on all Malibu-based SS 396s and El Caminos in 1969, but the 300 based SS 396 used nonconcealed wipers and motor part number 5045573. Concealed wipers were optional, as RPO C24, on the 300 series.

The washer jar, part number 3840083, was restyled in 1968 and remained unchanged in 1969. The black cap was listed as part number 3798372 both years. The mounting bracket was also restyled and was listed as part number 548935. It was mounted to the left-hand fender skirt. The bracket should be painted gloss-black. A black plastic washer fluid jar remained as a special order option both years.

The washer hoses were routed along the left front fender well to the washer pump both years. Each hose was supported by two clips that also supported the engine harness. The wiper arms for all 1968 vehicles and for 1969 Malibu- and El Camino-based SS 396s were listed as part number 3918247. The 300 based SS 396s in 1969 used part number 3913611 if concealed wipers were ordered, and it also came with the same arms as the Malibu.

The nozzles, part number 3928766, were restyled in 1968 and were mounted to the underside of the hood and held with two 16×⅜ in. number 10 hex-head screws. The location was determined by two existing holes. Two 5/32 in. ID hoses were rerouted through two holes in the firewall, then up through the hood. The left hose was supported by a clip, part number 9793032, on the hood. Both hoses must be looped before reaching the nozzles to avoid stress on the hoses when the hood is fully open. Also, the hoses must not rest on the cowl seal when the hood is closed.

The switch was located in the far upper left-hand corner of the instrument carrier both years; however, it was different each year. The 1968 version used a rotary switch, part number 1993442, with a bright bezel, part number 3927331, and a long, thin bright knob, part number 3943622. The word *wipers* was imprinted on the carrier under the switch in white.

Two switches were used in 1969. Both were slide type. The Malibu- and El Camino based SS 396s and all COPO cars used part number 1993465 with a chrome knob. The 300 based SS 396 used part number 1993464 with a black knob. Both switches were attached to a ground strap, part number 3937641, that was grounded in the instrument panel cluster.

## 1970-1972

Hideaway wipers were standard and motor assembly part number 5044756 was used from 1970 to 1972. This assembly should be painted

*Standard washer-wiper switch for 1970-72 Chevelle SSs. The lettering on the carrier was done in silver.*

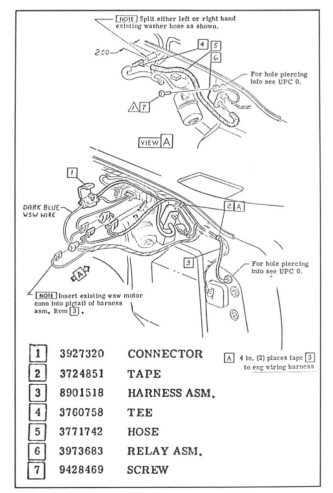

| | | |
|---|---|---|
| 1 | 3927320 | CONNECTOR |
| 2 | 3724851 | TAPE |
| 3 | 8901518 | HARNESS ASM. |
| 4 | 3760758 | TEE |
| 5 | 3771742 | HOSE |
| 6 | 3973683 | RELAY ASM. |
| 7 | 9428469 | SCREW |

*Hose routes and firewall with the CD3 option.*

201

according to previous instructions. The wipers were restyled and uniquely fitted to each side. The driver's side used part number 3913613, and the passenger's side part number 3913612.

The reservoir jar was completely redesigned for 1970 and was listed as part number 3961557. Only the opaque white jar remained. The design enabled the jar to be bolted to the left front fender skirt without a bracket. Shortly after the start of production in 1971 the jar was changed to part number 3990892, which was used till 1972. The jars were identical. A black cap, part number 3798372, was used with both jugs.

The hose route was the same all three years. A $^7\!/_{32}$ in. ID hose was routed from the pump; around behind the wiper motor; across the firewall, being supported with a black plastic engine harness clip; then forward between the engine harness and the left front fender to the lid on the jar.

The smaller $^5\!/_{32}$ in. diameter spray hoses were routed through the firewall; up through the cowl; through holes in the underside of the hood (an extra amount of hose should be looped here to avoid stretching when the hood is fully open); then on to the nozzles, part number 3976328. The nozzles should have a natural appearance. Each nozzle was attached with a single $16 \times \frac{3}{8}$ in. number 10 hex-head screw.

The standard wiper switch was listed as part number 1994131 and was located on the lower left-hand side of the instrument carrier under the tachometer, or under the fuel gauge on vehicles without the instrument package. It was a slide-type switch similar to that used in 1969.

A rare and unique option for 1970 only was RPO CD3 Electrotip wipers. These were activated by a small button on the signal lever, part number 3873684. The wires were routed down the steering column. A black cover, part number 7806271, protected wires on the column. Three extra holes were drilled in the firewall. A single 0.75 in. diameter hole was drilled to the left top corner of the fuse panel where the harness assembly, part number 8901518, was routed through a rubber grommet that was used for protection. Two smaller, 0.147 in. diameter holes were drilled into the firewall next to the windshield wiper motor assembly to support the relay switch, part number 3973683.

Also used in 1970 only was RPO CD2, which monitored the washer fluid level. A small black housing unit, part number 8900644, was mounted on the underside of the instrument panel on the left-hand side. A 0.75 in. hole was drilled into the jug to accommodate the sending unit, part number 8900646. A light blue lead wire was connected to the sender. It traced the route of the washer hoses

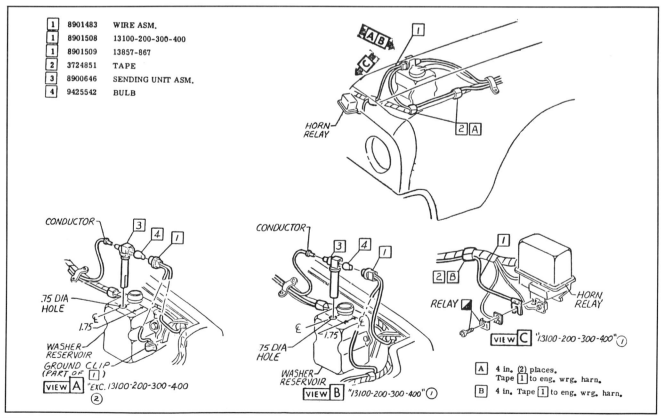

*Wiring route on the steering column with CD3.*

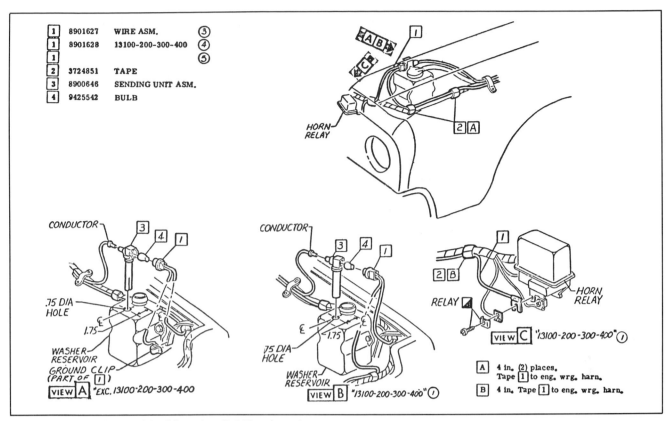

| | | |
|---|---|---|
| 1 | 8901627 | WIRE ASM. |
| 1 | 8901628 | 13100-200-300-400 |
| 1 | | |
| 2 | 3724851 | TAPE |
| 3 | 8900646 | SENDING UNIT ASM. |
| 4 | 9425542 | BULB |

HORN RELAY

CONDUCTOR

.75 DIA HOLE

1.75

WASHER RESERVOIR

GROUND CLIP (PART OF [1])

VIEW [A] *EXC. 13100-200-300-400

CONDUCTOR

.75 DIA HOLE

1.75

WASHER RESERVOIR

VIEW [B] "13100-200-300-400" (1)

HORN RELAY

RELAY

VIEW [C] "13100-200-300-400" (1)

[A] 4 in. (2) places. Tape [1] to eng. wrg. harn.

[B] 4 in. Tape [1] to eng. wrg. harn.

Connector route for windshield washer fluid level monitor option, CD2.

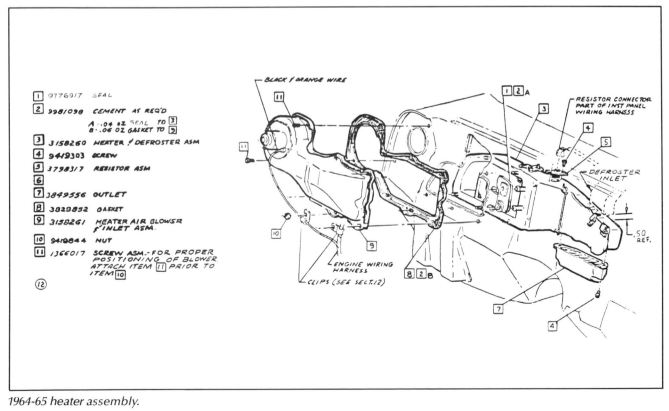

| | | |
|---|---|---|
| 1 | 9776917 | SEAL |
| 2 | 9981098 | CEMENT AS REQ'D |
| | | A - .04 OZ SEAL TO [3] |
| | | B - .06 OZ GASKET TO [9] |
| 3 | 3158260 | HEATER / DEFROSTER ASM. |
| 4 | 9419303 | SCREW |
| 5 | 3798317 | RESISTOR ASM. |
| 6 | | |
| 7 | 3849556 | OUTLET |
| 8 | 3828852 | GASKET |
| 9 | 3158261 | HEATER AIR BLOWER / INLET ASM. |
| 10 | 9419844 | NUT |
| 11 | 1366017 | SCREW ASM.-FOR PROPER POSITIONING OF BLOWER ATTACH ITEM [11] PRIOR TO ITEM [10] |
| 12 | | |

BLACK / ORANGE WIRE

RESISTOR CONNECTOR PART OF INST PANEL WIRING HARNESS

DEFROSTER INLET

.50 REF.

ENGINE WIRING HARNESS

CLIPS (SEE SECT. 12)

1964-65 heater assembly.

on the fender, then passed through the firewall. A 0.5 in. diameter hole was drilled just above the fuse panel opening. When the fluid level was low a small green light would warn the driver. This option was also included in the auxiliary lighting package.

## Heaters and Defrosters

### 1964–1965

The heater-blower assembly was listed as part number 3158261, 3002180 in 1965. In both 1964 and 1965 it was mounted on the right-hand side of the firewall. The entire housing should be painted gloss-black for detail. A black and orange wire from the engine harness was attached to the motor. The wire was supported with a single clip, part number 3799990, attached to the housing with a production nut. The engine harness was also supported with this clip on the outer left-hand side of the blower housing.

The defroster—part number 3158260, 30023343 in 1965—was placed up under the instrument panel and attached to the motor-blower assembly. An end outlet, part number 3849556, was used both years.

A control assembly, part number 3843244, with three chrome-plated slide switches was used both years. The far left knob controlled the airflow, the center knob the defroster, and the right knob the temperature. This panel was installed in a portion of the instrument panel and except for the knobs and control levers was painted the same color as the instrument panel. A bezel, part number 3843461 both years, was placed around the opening. The heater could be deleted both years.

If air conditioning was ordered, a different heater control assembly, part number 3843997, was used. It featured four knobs and was recessed. No bezel was installed, and the assembly was bright-plated. The motor-blower assembly was changed to part number 3001100, 3002455 in 1965, and the defroster assembly to part number 3001103, 3002375 in 1965. The end outlet was the same as the production unit.

Custom Deluxe air conditioning, RPO C65, was available from the factory in 1964 only. It used a different motor assembly, part number 3844141, and defroster, part number 3840942, with an air duct, part number 3840954, attached to the front.

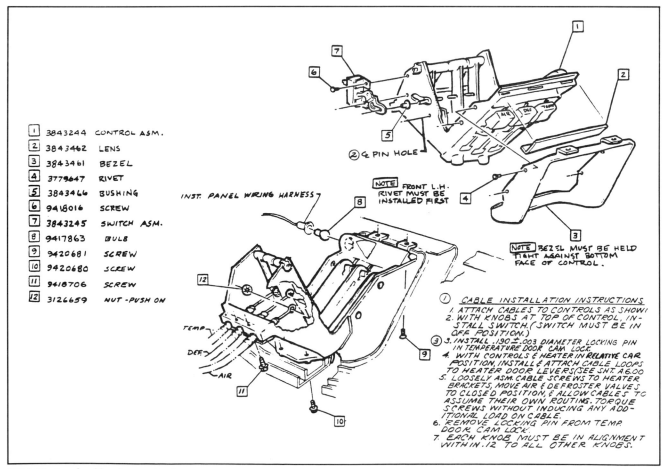

*1964-65 standard heater controls.*

204

This system also used standard kick panels and vents. The grille was changed to part number 3852448. An evaporator assembly, part number 3840947, was placed underneath the instrument panel in the center.

A special grommet, part number 3834892, protected the coolant lines as they passed through the firewall.

### 1966-1967

The DeLuxe heater remained standard on the 1966 Chevelle. The motor-blower assembly was listed as part number 3002180. It was mounted to the firewall on the passenger's side with bolts, space washers and nuts on the studs that protruded from the core-defroster, assembly part number 3006209, into the interior.

The heater wire was now solid orange and was supported with the same clips as in 1964-65. If air conditioning, RPO C60, was ordered, the blower assembly was changed to part number 3005785, and the core to 3008860, both of which are larger than the production units. Both the C60 and production blower housings should be painted gloss black. The core assemblies should be painted 30 degree gloss black.

Heater hoses were stacked vertically. The top hose (outlet) part number 3798599 was routed to the water pump. The bottom hose (inlet) part number 3883895 was routed to the front of the intake. Both hoses were retained with a gloss black clip, part number 3770259, mounted on the right-hand front fender skirt. The hoses used wire ring clamps on each end.

Heater delete option RPO C48 continued to be available. When it was selected, the openings in the firewall were covered over with plates. The opening in the dash was also covered over, and plugs were placed in the hose provisions on the engine. The firewall plates should be painted gloss-black, and the interior plate should be painted to match the instrument panel.

Except for the heater core being listed as part number 3012538 everything else was the same in 1967, including the part numbers and the C48 option. The defroster outlet assembly both years was listed as part number 3870273 and bolted to the top of the heater core.

### 1968-1969

Both the heater motor and the core assembly were made larger for 1968 and will not fit earlier models. The motor-blower assembly was listed as part number 3014734 for both 1968 and 1969. It should be painted gloss-black. An orange wire was routed to the motor as in previous years.

The heater core was listed as part number 3013622 for both years, and the end outlet was

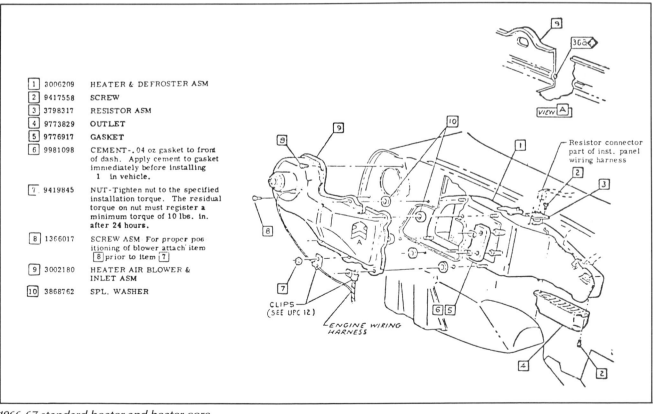

| | | |
|---|---|---|
| 1 | 3006209 | HEATER & DEFROSTER ASM |
| 2 | 9417558 | SCREW |
| 3 | 3798317 | RESISTOR ASM |
| 4 | 9773829 | OUTLET |
| 5 | 9776917 | GASKET |
| 6 | 9981098 | CEMENT-.04 oz gasket to front of dash. Apply cement to gasket immediately before installing 1 in vehicle. |
| 7 | 9419845 | NUT-Tighten nut to the specified installation torque. The residual torque on nut must register a minimum torque of 10 lbs. in. after 24 hours. |
| 8 | 1366017 | SCREW ASM. For proper positioning of blower attach item 8 prior to item 7 |
| 9 | 3002180 | HEATER AIR BLOWER & INLET ASM |
| 10 | 3868762 | SPL. WASHER |

*1966-67 standard heater and heater core.*

1. Left Blower Location
2. Right Blower Location
3. Blowers Before Installation
4. Upper Support Attaching Studs
5. Lower Support
6. Grommet
7. Motor Ground
8. Electrical Connector
9. Front Plenum Chamber

*1970-72 high-level ventilation motors.*

part number 9790487. The dual defroster duct was part number 3906067 in 1968, with no change in 1969.

The heater motor was the same with air conditioning, but the evaporator was combined with the blower unit and listed as part number 3955901. The inside core was listed as part number 3946934 with air conditioning. The intermediate duct was listed as part number 3917357. The lower duct, part number 3949816, featured two chrome air vents.

The center vent consisted of two main parts: the duct, part number 3942683, and the outlet,

part number 3942682. A foam seal, part number 3946903, was placed between the two.

The heater hoses were arranged the same as in 1966–67. In 1968 the top hose was listed as part number 3798599, and the bottom hose as part number 3883895. In 1969 the hoses were listed as

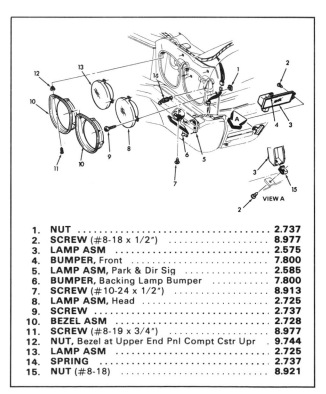

| | | |
|---|---|---|
| 1. | NUT | 2.737 |
| 2. | SCREW (#8-18 x 1/2") | 8.977 |
| 3. | LAMP ASM | 2.575 |
| 4. | BUMPER, Front | 7.800 |
| 5. | LAMP ASM, Park & Dir Sig | 2.585 |
| 6. | BUMPER, Backing Lamp Bumper | 7.800 |
| 7. | SCREW (#10-24 x 1/2") | 8.913 |
| 8. | LAMP ASM, Head | 2.725 |
| 9. | SCREW | 2.737 |
| 10. | BEZEL ASM | 2.728 |
| 11. | SCREW (#8-19 x 3/4") | 8.977 |
| 12. | NUT, Bezel at Upper End Pnl Compt Cstr Upr | 9.744 |
| 13. | LAMP ASM | 2.725 |
| 14. | SPRING | 2.737 |
| 15. | NUT (#8-18) | 8.921 |

*1970 Chevelle headlamps and front turn lamps. The front bumper turn lens should be clear for SS models.*

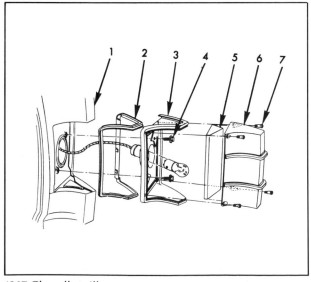

*1967 Chevelle taillamps.*

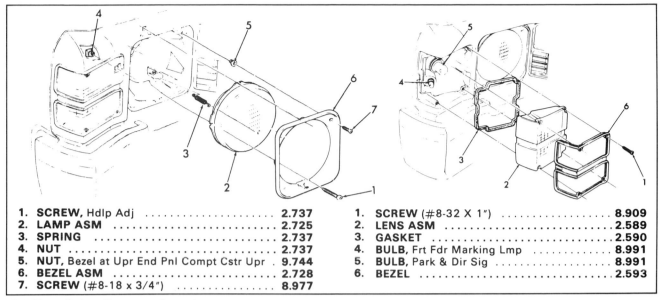

| 1. SCREW, Hdlp Adj | 2.737 | 1. SCREW (#8-32 X 1") | 8.909 |
|---|---|---|---|
| 2. LAMP ASM | 2.725 | 2. LENS ASM | 2.589 |
| 3. SPRING | 2.737 | 3. GASKET | 2.590 |
| 4. NUT | 2.737 | 4. BULB, Frt Fdr Marking Lmp | 8.991 |
| 5. NUT, Bezel at Upr End Pnl Compt Cstr Upr | 9.744 | 5. BULB, Park & Dir Sig | 8.991 |
| 6. BEZEL ASM | 2.728 | 6. BEZEL | 2.593 |
| 7. SCREW (#8-18 x 3/4") | 8.977 | | |

*1971 Chevelle headlamps and turn lamps.*

part numbers 3955929 top and 3955926 bottom. Tower clamps were used on the 1969 models. These clamps were phased in at the end of the 1968

*Amber turn lens. Before build date 11D 71, SSs used a clear lens, part numbers 5965269-LH and 5965270-RH, with an amber bulb. Pickups used part numbers 5965275-LH and 5965276-RH.*

model year, so a few late 1968 models could have them; most 1968 models used ring clamps.

A clip, part number 3940246, held the hoses together on the right front fender as in 1966–67. This clip should be painted gloss-black. Early 1969 production models featured an extra clip at the alternator bracket, but because of restriction problems it was removed. A service bulletin alerted service departments to take the clip off.

### 1970-1972

The same heater motor, part number 3014734, and heater core, part number 3013622, were used

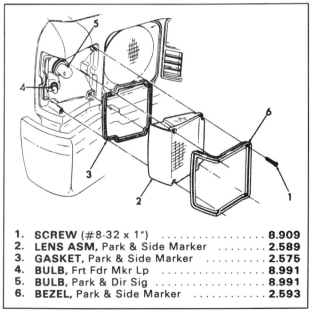

| 1. SCREW (#8-32 x 1") | 8.909 |
|---|---|
| 2. LENS ASM, Park & Side Marker | 2.589 |
| 3. GASKET, Park & Side Marker | 2.575 |
| 4. BULB, Frt Fdr Mkr Lp | 8.991 |
| 5. BULB, Park & Dir Sig | 8.991 |
| 6. BEZEL, Park & Side Marker | 2.593 |

*1972 Chevelle turn lamps.*

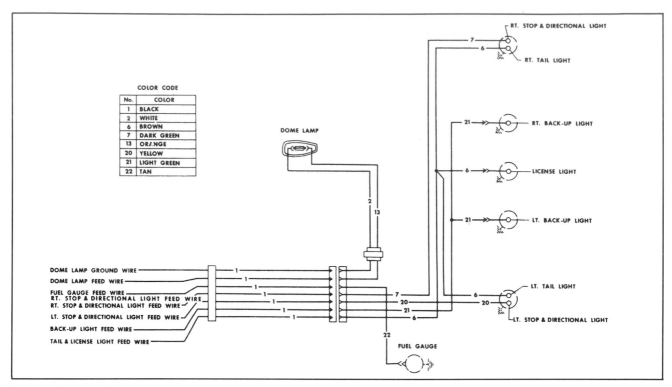

*Front end wiring diagram.*

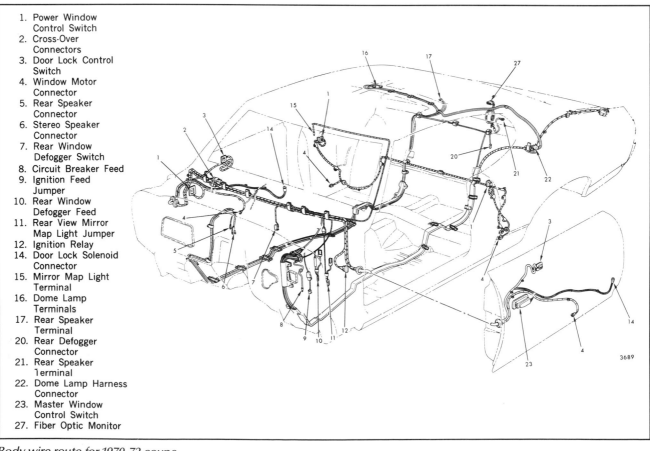

1. Power Window Control Switch
2. Cross-Over Connectors
3. Door Lock Control Switch
4. Window Motor Connector
5. Rear Speaker Connector
6. Stereo Speaker Connector
7. Rear Window Defogger Switch
8. Circuit Breaker Feed
9. Ignition Feed Jumper
10. Rear Window Defogger Feed
11. Rear View Mirror Map Light Jumper
12. Ignition Relay
14. Door Lock Solenoid Connector
15. Mirror Map Light Terminal
16. Dome Lamp Terminals
17. Rear Speaker Terminal
20. Rear Defogger Connector
21. Rear Speaker Terminal
22. Dome Lamp Harness Connector
23. Master Window Control Switch
27. Fiber Optic Monitor

*Body wire route for 1970-72 coupe.*

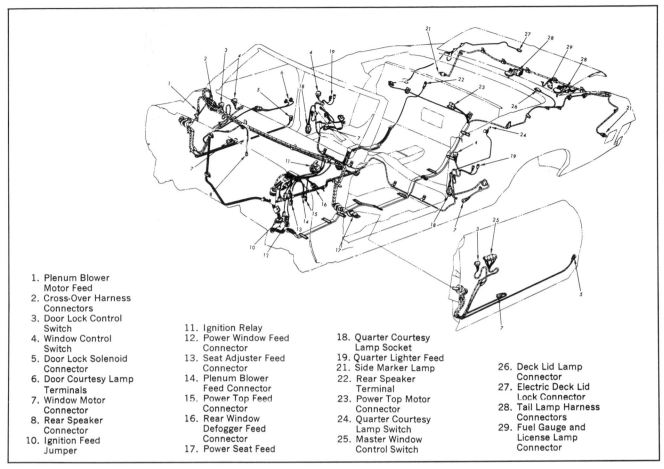

1. Plenum Blower Motor Feed
2. Cross-Over Harness Connectors
3. Door Lock Control Switch
4. Window Control Switch
5. Door Lock Solenoid Connector
6. Door Courtesy Lamp Terminals
7. Window Motor Connector
8. Rear Speaker Connector
10. Ignition Feed Jumper

11. Ignition Relay
12. Power Window Feed Connector
13. Seat Adjuster Feed Connector
14. Plenum Blower Feed Connector
15. Power Top Feed Connector
16. Rear Window Defogger Feed Connector
17. Power Seat Feed

18. Quarter Courtesy Lamp Socket
19. Quarter Lighter Feed
21. Side Marker Lamp
22. Rear Speaker Terminal
23. Power Top Motor Connector
24. Quarter Courtesy Lamp Switch
25. Master Window Control Switch

26. Deck Lid Lamp Connector
27. Electric Deck Lid Lock Connector
28. Tail Lamp Harness Connectors
29. Fuel Gauge and License Lamp Connector

*Body wire route for 1970-72 convertible.*

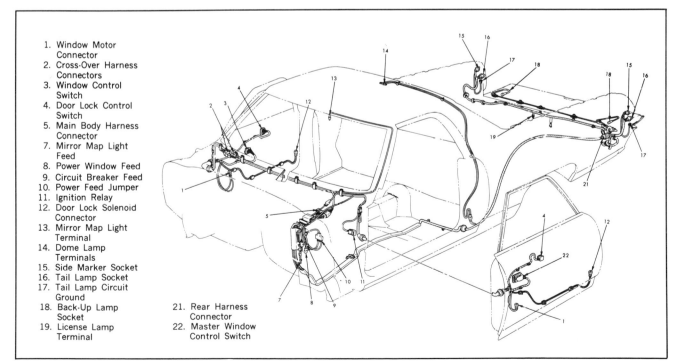

1. Window Motor Connector
2. Cross-Over Harness Connectors
3. Window Control Switch
4. Door Lock Control Switch
5. Main Body Harness Connector
7. Mirror Map Light Feed
8. Power Window Feed
9. Circuit Breaker Feed
10. Power Feed Jumper
11. Ignition Relay
12. Door Lock Solenoid Connector
13. Mirror Map Light Terminal
14. Dome Lamp Terminals
15. Side Marker Socket
16. Tail Lamp Socket
17. Tail Lamp Circuit Ground
18. Back-Up Lamp Socket
19. License Lamp Terminal

21. Rear Harness Connector
22. Master Window Control Switch

*Body wire route for 1970-72 pickup.*

209

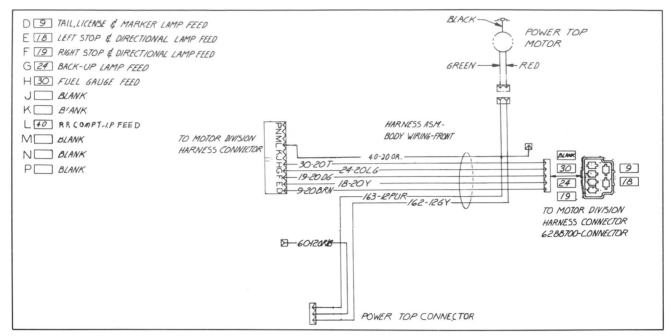

D [9] TAIL, LICENSE & MARKER LAMP FEED
E [18] LEFT STOP & DIRECTIONAL LAMP FEED
F [19] RIGHT STOP & DIRECTIONAL LAMP FEED
G [24] BACK-UP LAMP FEED
H [30] FUEL GAUGE FEED
J [ ] BLANK
K [ ] BLANK
L [40] R.R. COMPT.-L.P. FEED
M [ ] BLANK
N [ ] BLANK
P [ ] BLANK

*1971-72 power folding top circuit diagram.*

from 1970 to 1972. Few people know that the heater wire was rerouted midway through the 1970 model year. Early 1970 models used the same route as 1969 models, but later 1970 models and all 1971 and 1972 cars used a different route. The orange wire was wrapped around the wiring harness, which was supported with a clip to the blower, eliminating the need for the second clip.

The defroster ducts were redesigned and listed as part number 3984680. Early 1970 models used part number 3963756, which had less curve at the base of the assembly.

Air-conditioned cars used core part number 3984650 and a front distribution duct, part number 3992154, all three years. Painting should be done according to earlier instructions. Lap coolers, part numbers 3992196 for the passenger's side and 3992195 for the driver's side, were used with air conditioning. They were mounted on the underside of the instrument panel. They should be painted to match the lower portion of the instrument panel in a 30 degree gloss finish except the vents themselves. The bezel was chrome, and the inner fins were dull black plastic.

Early 1970 SSs used the same hoses as 1969 models, but later production used different part numbers. Different hoses were installed for the 350 engines.

### 1970-1972 Heater Hose Part Numbers

| L34, LS3, LS5 & LS6* | |
| --- | --- |
| Outlet | 483026 |
| Inlet | 482999 |
| L48 & L65 | |
| Outlet | 483024 |
| Inlet | 482997 |

An extra clip, part number 3940246, should retain the heater hoses on both 350 ci engines at the alternator bracket. It should be positioned 3 in. from the end of the inlet hose. This was the same bracket that was used on the front fender and should be painted gloss-black.

In 1972 this bracket was also used on the big-block engines and was secured with a hex-head screw in the second hole from the rear in the alternator bracket. On 350 ci engines it was installed in the rearmost hole.

*—1970–71 only.

*This photo shows the support clip used in 1972 on the alternator to support the heater hoses.*

# Chapter 10

# Regular Production Options

Some options are covered throughout this book where they replaced the standard production part, such as with remote control side mirrors or transmissions. However, some options were unique on their own and are covered in this chapter. The options discussed here were available only with the SS; others that were available on the Chevelle but not the SS are not listed.

## RPOs A90 and A91 Remote Deck Lid Release

### 1967-1972

A vacuum release system, RPO A90, was available for 1967 for a short time. The option was canceled in March 1967, and it was not available in 1968 or 1969. From 1970 to 1972 electrical deck lid release RPO A91 was available.

In 1967 a chrome release lever, part number 3868724, was mounted in the glove compartment. A 3/32 in. ID hose was connected to this and was then routed to a reducer; from there a 3/16 in. ID hose ran to a vacuum release cylinder, part number 3825538, in the trunk compartment, which was mounted to a reinforcement and a two-part bracket. A special coupler, part number 3885954, was placed over the standard lock cylinder.

Electrical locks were used in 1970-72, and a small button was placed in the glove compartment. A wire, part number 9792899, was routed from this switch to the trunk lock. A 32 in. wire, part number 9788060, was routed from the main harness to the glove compartment switch. The electric lock, part number 7660686, replaced the standard lock assembly.

## RPOs A93 and AU3 Power Door Locks

### 1969-1972

Vacuum power door locks, RPO A93, were available in 1969 only. For 1970-72 door locks were electric, RPO AU3. A vacuum tank, part number 3917463, was bolted to the left front fender wheel skirt. The canister should be painted gloss-black. A white hose was routed from the end of the tank

through the firewall to a remote valve. Here vacuum lines were routed to the actuator in the doors, then to the selector switches in the door panels.

A black rubber hose, part number 3926845, was routed from the tank to a fitting in the intake manifold. It was supported with three straps that held both hoses together. Six different fittings were used.

## 1969-1972 Power Door Lock Hose Fitting Part Numbers

| | |
|---|---|
| Door locks only | 3891523 |
| W/C60 or automatic | 3891524 |
| W/C60 & automatic | 3891527 |
| W/power brakes, & C60 or automatic | 3905374 |
| W/power brakes & C60 & automatic | 3905376 |
| W/power brakes only | 3905372 |

When electrical locks were ordered in 1970-72 another option, electrical seatback release RPO

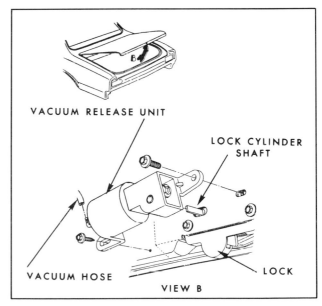

*Vacuum release unit.*

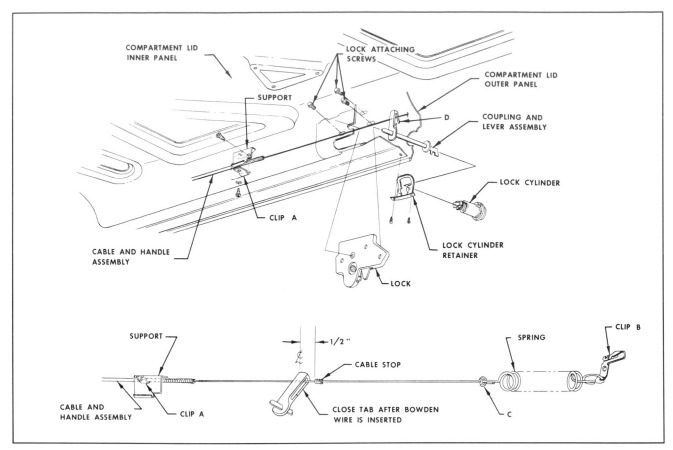

Trunk lid release unit (manual release).

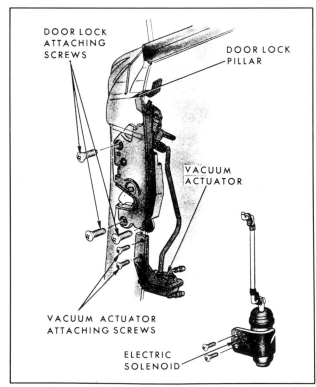

Front door lock actuator with vacuum door locks.

AQ2, could also be ordered. It was available for the coupe and convertible only, with or without bucket seats. When the door was opened, the seatback locks were automatically released.

The electrical locks were activated by an electrical-powered actuator, part numbers 9633794-LH and 9633793-RH, in the doors. Con-

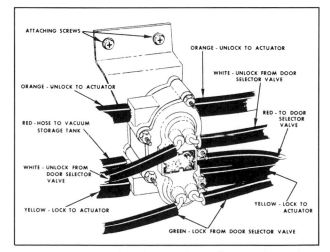

Remote lock control in driver's door. The rear door's lines are eliminated for use in the SS 396.

212

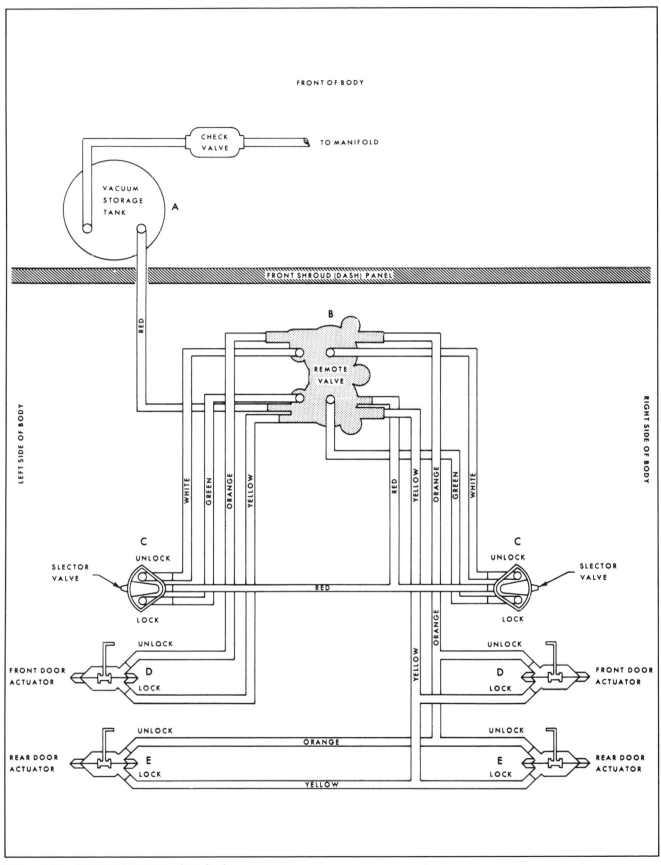

*Vacuum line diagram for power door locks.*

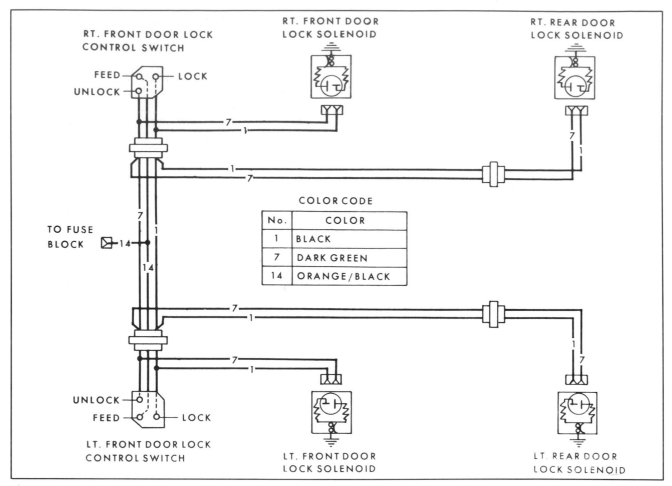

*Electrical door locks wiring diagram. Only the front doors apply to the SS.*

trol switches were listed as part numbers 8789693 for the driver's side and 8789693 for the passenger's side.

## RPO CE1 Headlamp Washers

### 1969

A rare and unusual option was available for all of 1969 and the first month of production in 1970: RPO CE1 headlamp washers. A special windshield wiper motor—part number 5044739, 5045606 with 300s without hidden wipers—was used. This pump was recognizable by the extra provision on it for the headlamps. A black rubber hose, part number 3837619, was routed down the left front fender wheelwell along the windshield. This hose was supported by four straps, part number 9422033, to a tee, part number 4919503, where it branched off to the other side.

The hose on the other side of the tee was listed as part number 3957037 and was routed along the top of the radiator support wall. This hose was supported by three of the same straps. At each

headlight a tee, part number 3760758, and two small short hoses, part number 3776838, were connected to a spray nozzle, part number 3957029. These nozzles were mounted in two special outboard headlamp bezels, part numbers 3957035-LH and 3957036-RH. The washers were activated by the wiper switch.

## RPO C50 Rear Window Defroster

### 1964-1965

The two-speed blower, RPO C50, part number 3157073, was used in 1964 and was mounted in the left-hand side of the rear shelf. The grille, part number 3863251, was painted to match the rear shelf in a 60 degree gloss finish.

Blower switch part number 3001071 was mounted on the underside of the instrument panel on the left-hand side. The switch used a round black plastic knob, part number 3848080, that was secured with a setscrew. The wire harness was routed under the carpet and pad and secured with the existing wire harness clips.

214

The same grille was used in 1965, but the blower unit was listed as part number 3003268. The blower location was the same. The blower switch, part number 3861697, was restyled. The black plastic knob, part number 3825815, was longer and thinner in shape. The blower option was available only on the coupe both years.

### 1966-1967

The two-speed blower was available on only the coupe in both 1966 and 1967. It was also available as a dealer-installed option and used accessory package part number 986942 both years.

The blower housing, part number 3003268, was located on the left side of the rear shelf tray. The grille, part number 3863251, was painted the same color as the tray in a 60 degree gloss. Both the blower assembly and the grille were supplied by Fisher Body and used in all GM A-bodies.

The blower switch was located underneath the instrument panel to the left of the steering column. A black knob was used in 1966, and a chrome knob in 1967. The wiring route was under the carpet. A pigtail wiring harness was used at the switch to connect the wire to the fuse panel.

### 1968-1969

The convertible was available with a rear window defroster in 1968. The blower was located in the center of the rear shelf tray, and the grille was painted to match the rear shelf in a 30 degree gloss finish.

The switch, part number 3861197, was in the same location as before, but when it was installed in the convertible an extension bracket, part number 3919567, held the control past the power top switch. The bracket should be painted 30 degree gloss-black. The knob was also redesigned; it was a large round black plastic knob and was listed as part number 3899716.

The blower switch was relocated in 1969, now installed in the dash panel on the right side next to the fuel gauge. The switch used a chrome bezel. The cutout in the dash required to mount the switch looked similar to the bow-tie emblem.

Switch part number 3959229 was placed in a housing, part number 3937659, and was secured with a special clip, part number 4154886. When used on the convertible with a power top, the blower switch was placed under the power top switch. Convertibles with a manual top used the

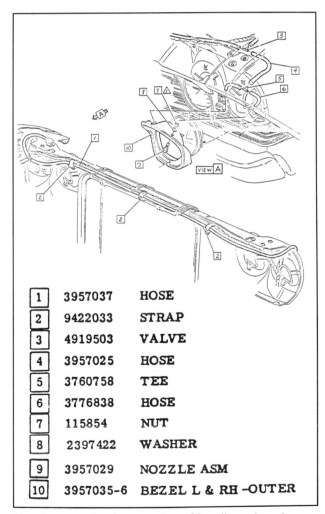

| 1 | 3957037 | HOSE |
| 2 | 9422033 | STRAP |
| 3 | 4919503 | VALVE |
| 4 | 3957025 | HOSE |
| 5 | 3760758 | TEE |
| 6 | 3776838 | HOSE |
| 7 | 115854 | NUT |
| 8 | 2397422 | WASHER |
| 9 | 3957029 | NOZZLE ASM |
| 10 | 3957035-6 | BEZEL L & RH –OUTER |

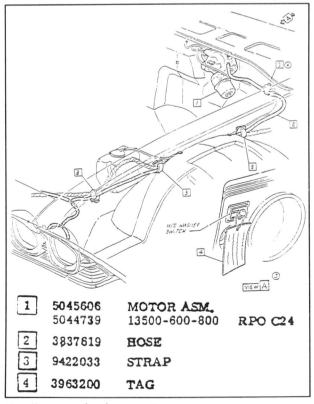

| 1 | 5045606 | MOTOR ASM. |
| | 5044739 | 13500-600-800 RPO C24 |
| 2 | 3837619 | HOSE |
| 3 | 9422033 | STRAP |
| 4 | 3963200 | TAG |

*Headlamp washer hose route.*

*Headlamp washer hose route and headlamp bezels.*

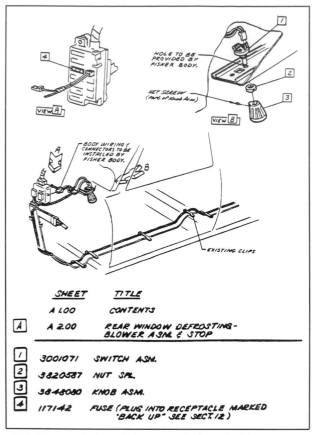

| SHEET | TITLE |
|---|---|
| A 1.00 | CONTENTS |
| A 2.00 | REAR WINDOW DEFROSTING-BLOWER ASM. & STOP |

| | | |
|---|---|---|
| 1 | 3001071 | SWITCH ASM. |
| 2 | 3820587 | NUT SPL. |
| 3 | 3848080 | KNOB ASM. |
| 4 | 117142 | FUSE (PLUG INTO RECEPTACLE MARKED 'BACK UP" SEE SECT. 12) |

*1964-65 rear window defroster switch and wiring route.*

same blower switch location as the coupe. The knob was part of the switch.

### 1970-1972

The switch was again relocated in 1970 and was used in the same place from 1970 to 1972. It was installed in the instrument carrier on the lower right-hand side to the left of the radio opening. Approximately 5.6 in. separated the switch and the radio from centerline to centerline.

A chrome bezel, part number 3973643, used a 1.52 in. diameter hole and a 1.06 in. square top. The switch, part number 3973646, was mounted with a natural bracket, part number 3973645. A chrome-plated togglelike knob was part of the switch.

The pigtail wire should be plugged into the fuse panel in the receptacle marked AC or Ign; either is correct.

## RPO C60 Air Conditioning

### 1964-1972

C60 air conditioning was a complex option. The following discussion is a general overview, with only the major component part numbers given. For further reference check an assembly or repair manual for your particular year.

In 1964 a total of three different air conditioning systems were available on the Chevelle. From the factory were RPO C60 All Weather air condi-

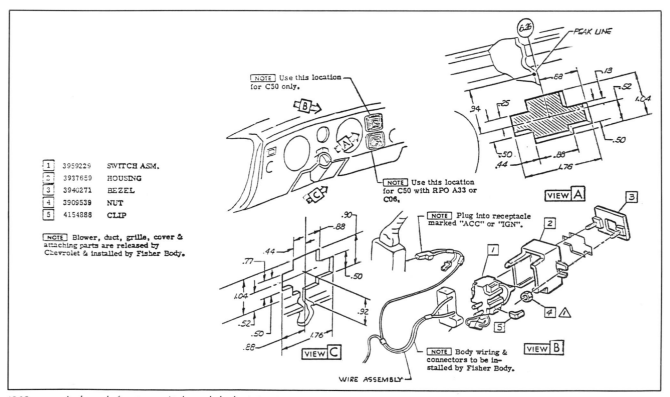

| | | |
|---|---|---|
| 1 | 3959229 | SWITCH ASM. |
| 2 | 3937659 | HOUSING |
| 3 | 3940271 | BEZEL |
| 4 | 3909539 | NUT |
| 5 | 4154886 | CLIP |

NOTE Blower, duct, grille, cover & attaching parts are released by Chevrolet & installed by Fisher Body.

*1969 rear window defroster switch and dash cutout.*

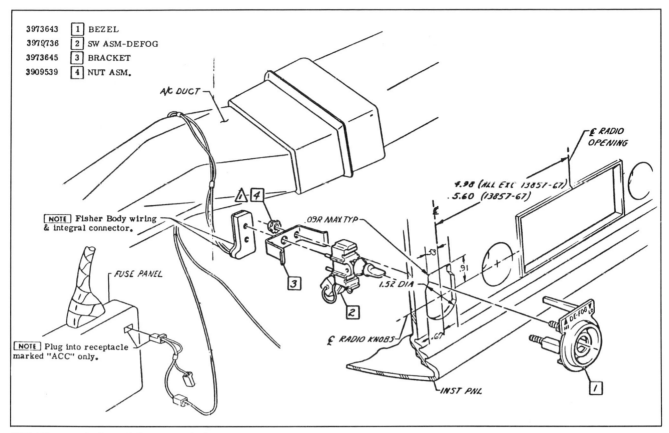

| 3973643 | 1 | BEZEL |
| 3979736 | 2 | SW ASM-DEFOG |
| 3973645 | 3 | BRACKET |
| 3909539 | 4 | NUT ASM. |

*1970-72 rear window defroster switch.*

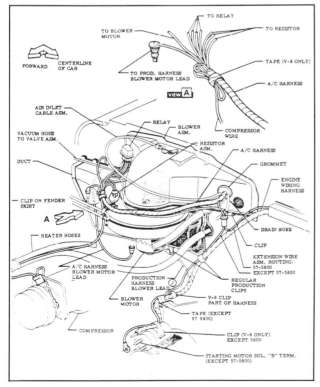

*1964-67 air conditioning blower assembly and wiring route.*

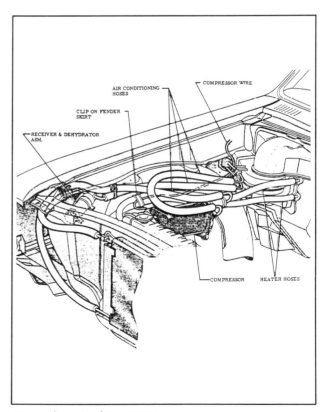

*Air conditioning hose route.*

tioning and RPO C65 Deluxe air conditioning. A dealer-installed Custom unit was also offered.

For 1965 RPO C65 was eliminated but the dealer-installed option remained. Air conditioning was not available with the L78 375 hp engine option till December 1965, as the engine was not available.

Four Season was the only factory air conditioning option available in 1966. It differed greatly from earlier designs, as it was completely integrated into the heater. The dealer-installed option continued and used a general-purpose GM unit with the Chevrolet name.

In 1967 the dealer-installed system was renamed Comfort-Car.

The compressor, part number 6550133 in both 1966 and 1967, was manufactured by Frigidaire. It was mounted on the right-hand side of the engine with special brackets. The brackets should be painted 60 degree gloss-black, as should the compressor housing.

A bow-tie-shaped Air Conditioned decal was placed on the inside of the rear window in the lower right-hand corner on all models except the convertibles, in which it was placed on the right side rear quarter window.

The Four Season air conditioning unit was slightly restyled for 1968. The air duct hoses were mounted up in the dash and were connected to the side vents in the instrument panel and to each side of the upper duct, part number 3937110.

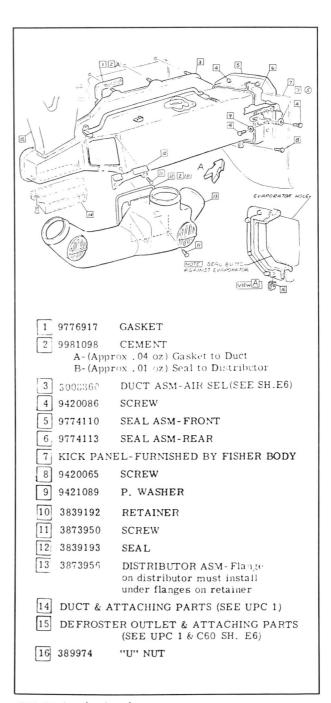

| 1 | 9776917 | GASKET |
| 2 | 9981098 | CEMENT |
| | | A-(Approx .04 oz) Gasket to Duct |
| | | B-(Approx .01 oz) Seal to Distributor |
| 3 | 5008860 | DUCT ASM-AIR SEL(SEE SH.E6) |
| 4 | 9420086 | SCREW |
| 5 | 9774110 | SEAL ASM-FRONT |
| 6 | 9774113 | SEAL ASM-REAR |
| 7 | | KICK PANEL-FURNISHED BY FISHER BODY |
| 8 | 9420065 | SCREW |
| 9 | 9421089 | P. WASHER |
| 10 | 3839192 | RETAINER |
| 11 | 3873950 | SCREW |
| 12 | 3839193 | SEAL |
| 13 | 3873956 | DISTRIBUTOR ASM-Flange on distributor must install under flanges on retainer |
| 14 | | DUCT & ATTACHING PARTS (SEE UPC 1) |
| 15 | | DEFROSTER OUTLET & ATTACHING PARTS (SEE UPC 1 & C60 SH. E6) |
| 16 | 389974 | "U" NUT |

*1966-67 air selection ducts.*

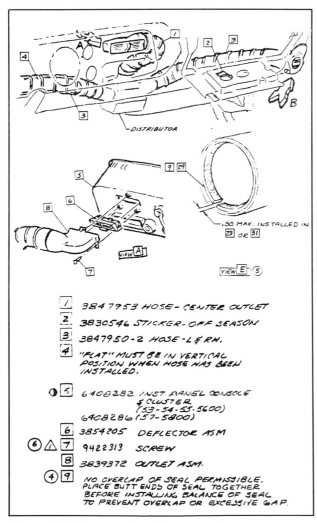

1. 3847953 HOSE - CENTER OUTLET
2. 3830546 STICKER - OFF SEASON
3. 3847950-2 HOSE - L & RH.
4. "FLAT" MUST BE IN VERTICAL POSITION WHEN HOSE HAS BEEN INSTALLED.
5. 6408282 INST. PANEL CONSOLE & CLUSTER (53-54-55-5600) 6408286 (57-5800)
6. 3854205 DEFLECTOR ASM
7. 9422313 SCREW
8. 3839372 OUTLET ASM.
9. NO OVERLAP OF SEAL PERMISSIBLE. PLACE BUTT ENDS OF SEAL TOGETHER BEFORE INSTALLING BALANCE OF SEAL TO PREVENT OVERLAP OR EXCESSIVE GAP.

*Air conditioning console and center outlet.*

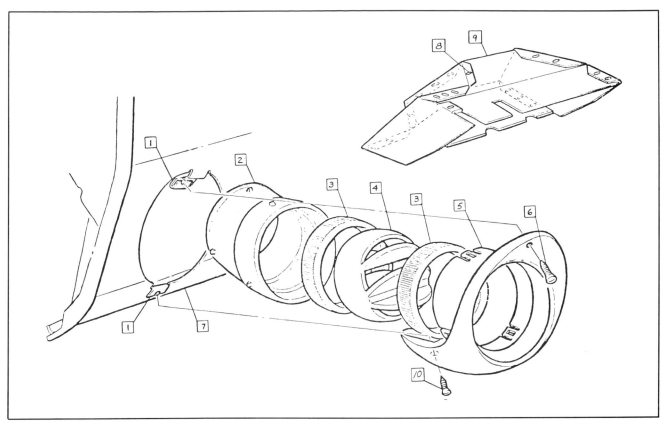

*1966-67 dash bezels with air conditioning.*

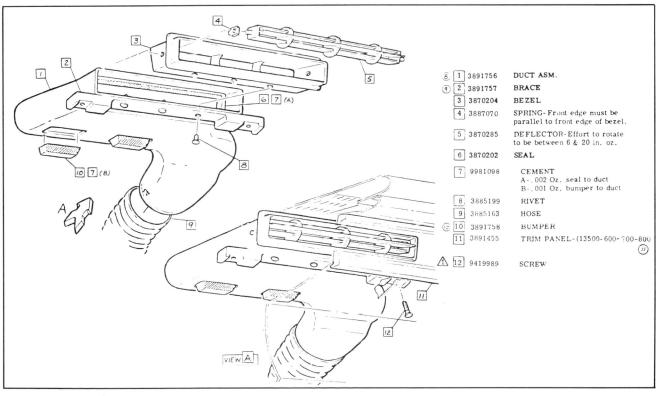

| | | | |
|---|---|---|---|
| (8) | 1 | 3891756 | DUCT ASM. |
| (9) | 2 | 3891757 | BRACE |
| | 3 | 3870204 | BEZEL |
| | 4 | 3887070 | SPRING-Front edge must be parallel to front edge of bezel. |
| | 5 | 3870285 | DEFLECTOR-Effort to rotate to be between 6 & 20 in. oz. |
| | 6 | 3870202 | SEAL |
| | 7 | 9981098 | CEMENT A-.002 Oz. seal to duct B-.001 Oz. bumper to duct |
| | 8 | 3885199 | RIVET |
| | 9 | 3885163 | HOSE |
| (12) | 10 | 3891758 | BUMPER |
| | 11 | 3891455 | TRIM PANEL-(13500-600-700-800 |
| ⚠ | 12 | 9419989 | SCREW |

*1966-67 center air duct.*

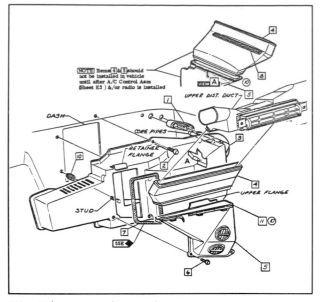

*1968-69 lower air selection ducts.*

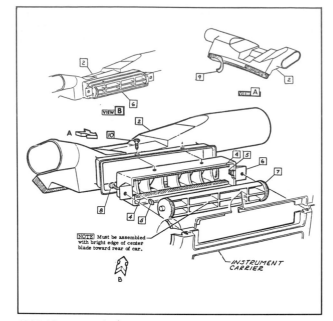

*1968-69 center air ducts.*

Chrome plastic regulator vents were in the center of the dash on each side. The side vent bezels were painted the same color as the instrument panel in a flat finish for 1968 and 1969.

The compressor was manufactured by Frigidaire and listed as part 6550133 in 1968. Two different compressors were available in 1969:

manual-transmission-equipped cars used part number 5910688, and cars with the Turbo 400 transmission used part number 5910687. The mounting location was also changed in 1969 to the left-hand side of the engine. Braces were the same in 1968 as in 1967 but were redesigned in 1969.

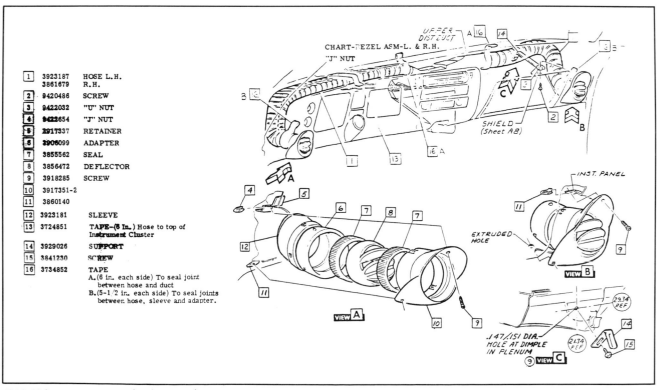

| | | |
|---|---|---|
| 1 | 3923187 | HOSE L.H. |
| | 3861679 | R.H. |
| 2 | 9420486 | SCREW |
| 3 | 9422032 | "U" NUT |
| 4 | 9422654 | "J" NUT |
| 5 | 2917337 | RETAINER |
| 6 | 3906099 | ADAPTER |
| 7 | 3855562 | SEAL |
| 8 | 3856472 | DEFLECTOR |
| 9 | 3918285 | SCREW |
| 10 | 3917351-2 | |
| 11 | 3860140 | |
| 12 | 3923181 | SLEEVE |
| 13 | 3724851 | TAPE-(8 In.) Hose to top of Instrument Cluster |
| 14 | 3929026 | SUPPORT |
| 15 | 3841230 | SCREW |
| 16 | 3734852 | TAPE |

A.(6 in. each side) To seal joint between hose and duct
B.(5-1/2 in. each side) To seal joints between hose, sleeve and adapter.

*1968-69 instrument panel selection ducts.*

*Air compressor decal.*

## 1969 Air Conditioning Brace Part Numbers

| | |
|---|---|
| Front bracket | 3940949 |
| Front bracket support | 3940946 |
| Rear bracket | 3932493 |
| Rear bracket support | 3940946 |
| Rear brace | 3940947 |

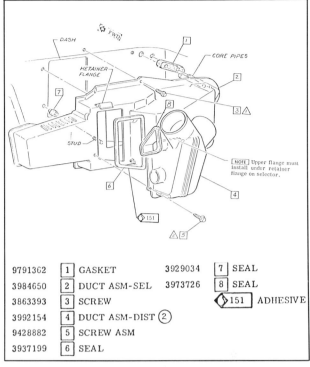

| | | | | | |
|---|---|---|---|---|---|
| 9791302 | 1 | GASKET | 3929034 | 7 | SEAL |
| 3984650 | 2 | DUCT ASM-SEL | 3973726 | 8 | SEAL |
| 3863393 | 3 | SCREW | | ⬦151 | ADHESIVE |
| 3992154 | 4 | DUCT ASM-DIST ② | | | |
| 9428882 | 5 | SCREW ASM | | | |
| 3937199 | 6 | SEAL | | | |

*1970-72 air conditioning lower air ducts.*

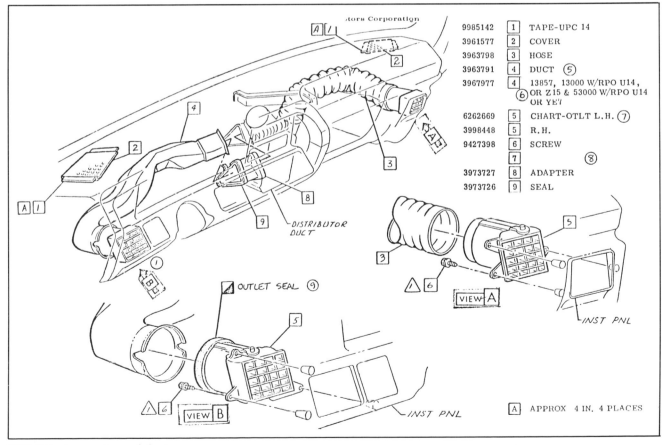

| | | | |
|---|---|---|---|
| 9985142 | 1 | TAPE-UPC 14 | |
| 3961577 | 2 | COVER | |
| 3963798 | 3 | HOSE | |
| 3963791 | 4 | DUCT ⑤ | |
| 3967977 | 4 | 13857, 13000 W/RPO U14, ⑥ OR Z15 & 53000 W/RPO U14 OR YE7 | |
| 6262669 | 5 | CHART-OTLT L.H. ⑦ | |
| 3998448 | 5 | R.H. | |
| 9427398 | 6 | SCREW | |
| | 7 | | ⑧ |
| 3973727 | 8 | ADAPTER | |
| 3973726 | 9 | SEAL | |

*1970-72 instrument panel ducts.*

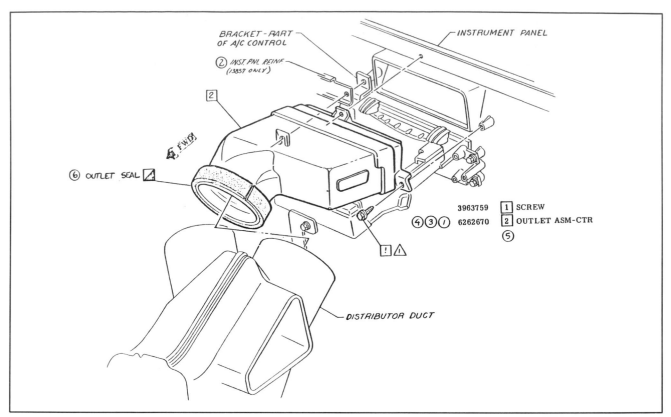

BRACKET - PART OF A/C CONTROL

② INST. PNL. REINF.
(13857 ONLY)

INSTRUMENT PANEL

②

FWD

⑥ OUTLET SEAL

| | | | |
|---|---|---|---|
| | 3963759 | 1 | SCREW |
| ④③① | 6262670 | 2 | OUTLET ASM-CTR |
| | | 5 | |

! ⚠

DISTRIBUTOR DUCT

*1970-72 air conditioning center outlet ducts.*

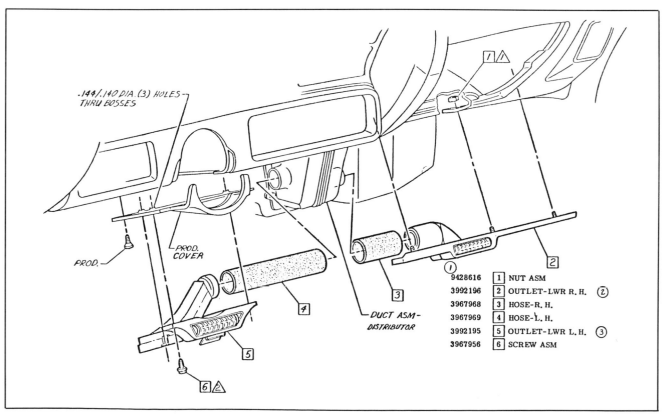

.144/.140 DIA. (3) HOLES
THRU BOSSES

! ⚠

PROD.
COVER

PROD.

DUCT ASM-
DISTRIBUTOR

4

3

①

2

5

6 ⚠

| | | | |
|---|---|---|---|
| 9428616 | 1 | NUT ASM | |
| 3992196 | 2 | OUTLET-LWR R. H. | ② |
| 3967968 | 3 | HOSE-R. H. | |
| 3967969 | 4 | HOSE-L. H. | |
| 3992195 | 5 | OUTLET-LWR L. H. | ③ |
| 3967956 | 6 | SCREW ASM | |

*1970-72 lap coolers.*

The brackets were attached to the previous alternator mounting positions. The rear brace was specially designed for the 396 and was attached to the third and fourth bolts on the intake manifold. The compressor, brace and bracket should be painted 60 degree gloss-black.

The instrument panel side ducts were redesigned in 1970 to be rectangular in shape with four black horizontal flaps that directed the airflow. When not needed, the flaps could be closed. Lap coolers were also used from 1970 to 1972.

## RPO U46 Lamp Monitoring System

### 1967-1970

Many believe that the lamp monitoring system, RPO U46, was not available until 1968, as it was not displayed in the 1967 sales catalog. However, it was offered on late-model 1967 Chevelles, although few were built with it.

The system used fiber optics to monitor for condition of the exterior lamps from the driver's seat. Conductors with chrome-plated housings were placed on the front fenders. The rear lamps were monitored by a conductor mounted in the middle on the forward edge of the rear package shelf.

A special wiring harness connected the conductors into the lamps. When U46 was used, special front signal lamp assemblies were also installed. Wires from the rear conductor were

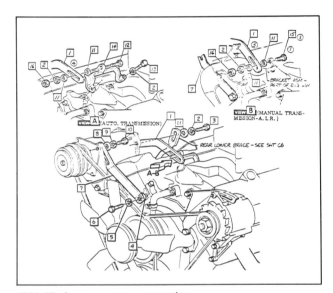

*1966-67 air compressor mounting.*

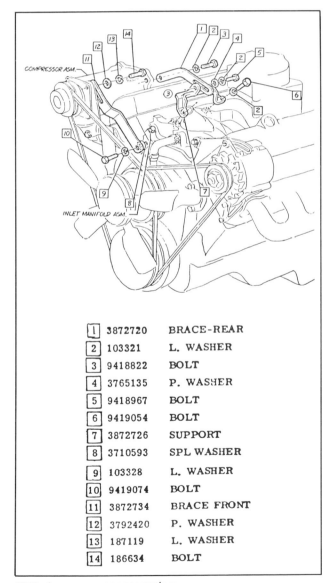

| | | |
|---|---|---|
| 1 | 3872720 | BRACE-REAR |
| 2 | 103321 | L. WASHER |
| 3 | 9418822 | BOLT |
| 4 | 3765135 | P. WASHER |
| 5 | 9418967 | BOLT |
| 6 | 9419054 | BOLT |
| 7 | 3872726 | SUPPORT |
| 8 | 3710593 | SPL WASHER |
| 9 | 103328 | L. WASHER |
| 10 | 9419074 | BOLT |
| 11 | 3872734 | BRACE FRONT |
| 12 | 3792420 | P. WASHER |
| 13 | 187119 | L. WASHER |
| 14 | 186634 | BOLT |

*1968 air compressor mounting.*

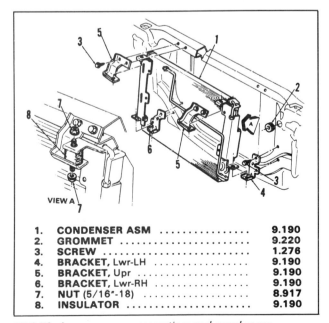

| | | |
|---|---|---|
| 1. | CONDENSER ASM | 9.190 |
| 2. | GROMMET | 9.220 |
| 3. | SCREW | 1.276 |
| 4. | BRACKET, Lwr-LH | 9.190 |
| 5. | BRACKET, Upr | 9.190 |
| 6. | BRACKET, Lwr-RH | 9.190 |
| 7. | NUT (5/16″-18) | 8.917 |
| 8. | INSULATOR | 9.190 |

*1970-72 air compressor mounting and condenser.*

| | | |
|---|---|---|
| 1. | BOLT (5/16"-18 x 5/8") | 8.900 |
| | WASHER (5/16") | 8.931 |
| 2. | RETAINER | 9.170 |
| 3. | DAMPER ASM | 9.170 |
| 4. | NUT | 9.181 |
| 5. | RING, A/C Comp Drive Shaft Dr Hub Ret | 9.175 |
| 6. | SPACER | 9.181 |
| 7. | PLATE | 9.188 |
| 8. | RING, A/C Comp Brg to Pulley Hub Ret | 9.181 |
| 9. | RING, A/C Comp Pulley Brg to Hd Ret | 9.181 |
| 10. | BEARING ASM | 9.181 |
| 11. | PULLEY | 9.180 |
| 12. | RING, A/C Comp Coil Hsg Retaining | 9.175 |
| 13. | COIL | 9.186 |
| 14. | SHELL ASM | 9.170 |
| 15. | GASKET | 9.177 |
| | SCREW | 9.177 |
| 16. | RETAINER | 9.175 |
| 17. | SEAL | 9.175 |
| 18. | RING (A/C Comp Drive Shaft Seal)(Pt of SEAL UNIT #22) | 9.175 |
| 19. | SEAL | N.S. |
| 20. | SEAL | N.S. |
| 21. | SEAL | N.S. |
| 22. | SEAL UNIT | 9.175 |
| 23. | HEAD | 9.174 |
| 24. | SEAL | N.S. |
| 25. | VALVE PLATE, Frt | 9.172 |
| 26. | VALVE | 9.172 |
| 27. | SLEEVE | 9.172 |
| 28. | SEAL | N.S. |
| 29. | BEARING | 9.172 |
| 30. | PIN | 9.178 |
| 31. | RACE (Stamped 5) | 9.172 |
| | RACE (Stamped 0) | 9.172 |
| | RACE (Stamped 5.5) | 9.172 |
| | RACE (Stamped 6) | 9.172 |
| | RACE (Stamped 6.5) | 9.172 |
| | RACE (Stamped 7) | 9.172 |
| | RACE (Stamped 7.5) | 9.172 |
| | RACE (Stamped 8) | 9.172 |
| | RACE (Stamped 8.5) | 9.172 |
| | RACE (Stamped 9) | 9.172 |
| | RACE (Stamped 9.5) | 9.172 |
| | RACE (Stamped 10) | 9.172 |
| | RACE (Stamped 10.5) | 9.172 |
| | RACE (Stamped 11) | 9.172 |

| | | | |
|---|---|---|---|
| | RACE (Stamped 15.5) | | 9.172 |
| | RACE (Stamped 12) | | 9.172 |
| 32. | BEARING | | 9.172 |
| 33. | COVER | | 9.172 |
| 34. | KEY | | 9.188 |
| 35. | TUBE UNIT | | 9.172 |
| 36. | RING, A/C Comp. Piston | | 9.172 |
| 37. | PISTON | | 9.172 |
| 38. | SHAFT ASM | | 9.170 |
| 39. | BALL | | 9.172 |
| 40. | SEAT (Stamped 0) | | 9.172 |
| | SEAT (Stamped 17.5) | | 9.172 |
| | SEAT (Stamped 18) | | 9.172 |
| | SEAT (Stamped 18.5) | | 9.172 |
| | SEAT (Stamped 19) | | 9.172 |
| | SEAT (Stamped 19.5) | | 9.172 |
| | SEAT (Stamped 20) | | 9.172 |
| | SEAT (Stamped 20.5) | | 9.172 |
| | SEAT (Stamped 21) | | 9.172 |

| | | |
|---|---|---|
| | SEAT (Stamped 21.5) | 9.172 |
| | SEAT (Stamped 22) | 9.172 |
| 41. | SEAL | 9.172 |
| 42. | TUBE | 9.172 |
| 43. | VALVE PLATE, Rr | 9.172 |
| 44. | PUMP UNIT | 9.172 |
| 45. | SCREEN | 9.172 |
| 46. | HEAD | 9.174 |
| 47. | VALVE ASM | 9.178 |
| 48. | SEAL | 9.226 |
| 49. | NUT UNIT | 9.170 |
| 50. | CYLINDER ASM, A/C Comp W/Drive Shaft Brg | 9.170 |
| | CYLINDER ASM, A/C Comp W/Piston | 9.170 |
| 51. | SEAL KIT | 9.170 |
| 53. | RETAINER | 9.172 |
| 54. | RING, A/C Comp Super Heat Switch | 9.172 |
| 55. | SWITCH | 9.172 |

*1971-72 compressor.*

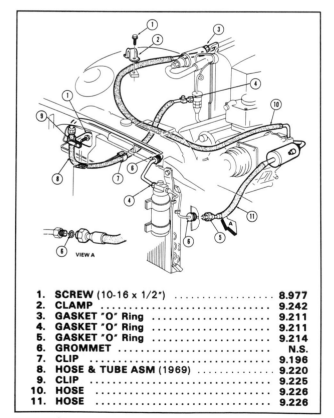

| | | |
|---|---|---|
| 1. | SCREW (10-16 x 1/2") | 8.977 |
| 2. | CLAMP | 9.242 |
| 3. | GASKET "O" Ring | 9.211 |
| 4. | GASKET "O" Ring | 9.211 |
| 5. | GASKET "O" Ring | 9.214 |
| 6. | GROMMET | N.S. |
| 7. | CLIP | 9.196 |
| 8. | HOSE & TUBE ASM (1969) | 9.220 |
| 9. | CLIP | 9.225 |
| 10. | HOSE | 9.226 |
| 11. | HOSE | 9.226 |

*1969-72 hose route.*

supported by black clips on the rear seatback supports and around the outline of the trunk. A special license plate lamp was also used.

The system was offered until 1969 unchanged except for part numbers. In 1970 it returned but used only the front monitors. Problems with visibility of the rear unit caused it to be canceled. U46 was not available on the pickup except in 1970. The entire system was canceled in 1971.

## RPOs U57, U60, U63 and U69 Radios

### 1964-1965

Only a manual-tune radio, RPO U60, and a push-button AM radio, RPO U63, were available in 1964. Both used chrome tuning knobs, part numbers 3839324 for the selector and 3839323 for the volume. The selector knob featured a speaker control knob.

With the regular production alternator a capacitor, part number 194752, was attached to the coil bracket and the positive pole of the coil. With the RPO K79 and RPO K82 alternators capacitor part number 1964086 was attached to the production regulator and ground wire. This same capacitor was used with the K81 alternator, but it was plugged into the fifth tab on the optional regulator.

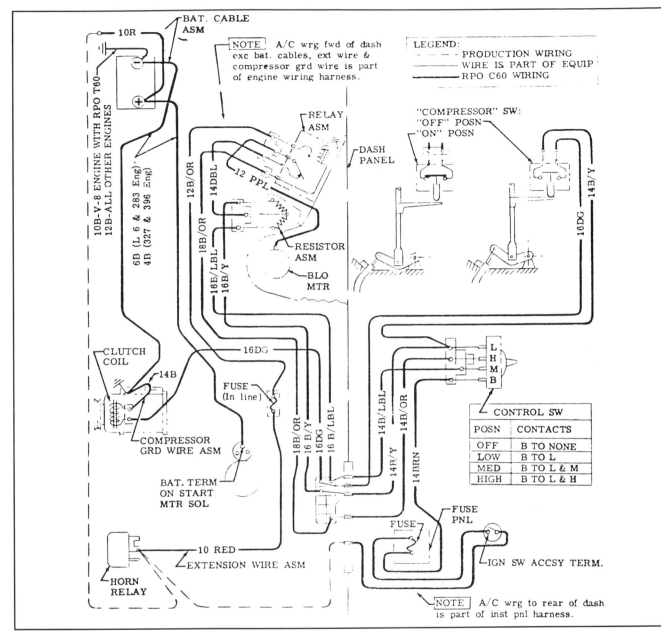

*1964-67 air conditioning wiring diagram.*

## Part Numbers of U46 Accessories

| Item | 1967 | 1968 | 1969 | 1970 |
|---|---|---|---|---|
| **Front Conductor** | | | | |
| Left | 6290682 | 6295131 | 6297563 | 8901375 |
| Right | 6290683 | 6295132 | 6297564 | 8901376 |
| **Rear Conductor** | | | | |
| Coupe | 6293386 | 6295139 | 6295139 | n/a |
| Convertible | same | 6295137 | 6295137 | n/a |
| **Front Park Lamp** | | | | |
| Left | 916141 | 916355 | 910407 | 911407 |
| Right | 916142 | 916356 | 910408 | same |
| **License Lamp** | | | | |
| | 916143 | 91664 | 916999 | n/a |

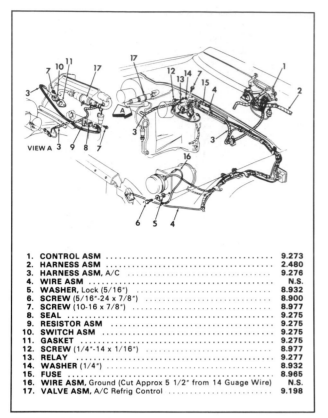

| | | |
|---|---|---|
| 1. | CONTROL ASM | 9.273 |
| 2. | HARNESS ASM | 2.480 |
| 3. | HARNESS ASM, A/C | 9.276 |
| 4. | WIRE ASM | N.S. |
| 5. | WASHER, Lock (5/16") | 8.932 |
| 6. | SCREW (5/16"-24 x 7/8") | 8.900 |
| 7. | SCREW (10-16 x 7/8") | 8.977 |
| 8. | SEAL | 9.275 |
| 9. | RESISTOR ASM | 9.275 |
| 10. | SWITCH ASM | 9.275 |
| 11. | GASKET | 9.275 |
| 12. | SCREW (1/4"-14 x 1/16") | 8.977 |
| 13. | RELAY | 9.277 |
| 14. | WASHER (1/4") | 8.932 |
| 15. | FUSE | 8.965 |
| 16. | WIRE ASM, Ground (Cut Approx 5 1/2" from 14 Guage Wire) | N.S. |
| 17. | VALVE ASM, A/C Refrig Control | 9.198 |

*1970-72 wiring route.*

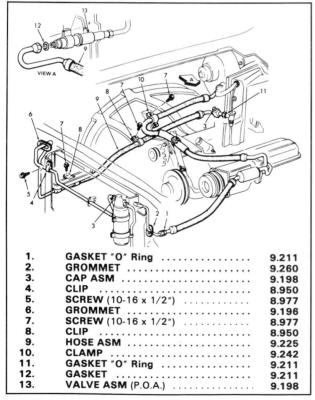

| | | |
|---|---|---|
| 1. | GASKET "O" Ring | 9.211 |
| 2. | GROMMET | 9.260 |
| 3. | CAP ASM | 9.198 |
| 4. | CLIP | 8.950 |
| 5. | SCREW (10-16 x 1/2") | 8.977 |
| 6. | GROMMET | 9.196 |
| 7. | SCREW (10-16 x 1/2") | 8.977 |
| 8. | CLIP | 8.950 |
| 9. | HOSE ASM | 9.225 |
| 10. | CLAMP | 9.242 |
| 11. | GASKET "O" Ring | 9.211 |
| 12. | GASKET | 9.211 |
| 13. | VALVE ASM (P.O.A.) | 9.198 |

*1971-72 hose route.*

A pair of ground straps, part number 2985648, were attached to the spark plug wire supports and the firewall. Be sure that the open end of each strap is under the wire supports.

A front antenna was standard, and rear antenna RPO U70 was optional and mounted on the right-hand side. The bezel was listed as part number 3849190; this part was used solely with the coupe and convertible body styles. It is recognizable by a notch on the outer rim. A dummy antenna was available as a dealer-installed option and mounted on the left-hand side.

A single auxiliary rear speaker, RPO Z02, part number 7282605, was available with the push-button radio. A special baffle, part number 38597194, was placed under the speaker and attached to the rear seatback diagonal brace. The rear package tray was cut to fit, and a grille, part number 7273051, was placed over the opening. This option was available for the coupe only.

The balance between the rear and front speakers was controlled by a knob, part number 7288421, on the radio shaft. This required a different selector knob, part number 3839323, to be used. The balance knob matched the volume knob in design.

An AM/FM radio, RPO U69, and a stereo converter, RPO U79, were added in 1965. The U79 stereo was available with all radios. The adapter assembly was listed as part number 7293671 and was placed under the instrument panel in the center. It was supported with a bracket, part number

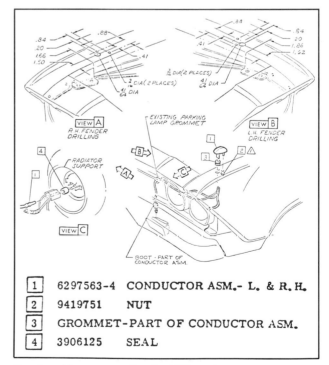

| | | |
|---|---|---|
| 1 | 6297563-4 | CONDUCTOR ASM.- L. & R.H. |
| 2 | 9419751 | NUT |
| 3 | | GROMMET-PART OF CONDUCTOR ASM. |
| 4 | 3906125 | SEAL |

*Front end lamp mounting for U46 option.*

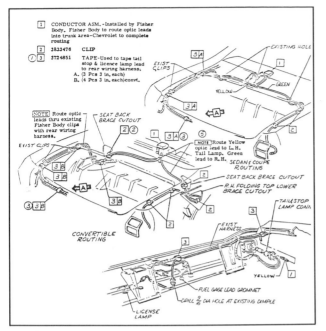

*Rear lamp monitors.*

*This radio is incorrect. The radio bezel is also incorrect; it should be dull aluminum, not black-accented as shown.*

7292694, and hex-head screws. Front speakers, part number 7292488, were placed in the kick panels. The speaker grilles, part number 3879567, were painted the same color as the kick panels.

Two rear speakers were installed in the rear shelf on each side. The rear defroster could not be ordered with the stereo option. The speaker grilles were part number 7264992 and were painted the same color as the shelf in a 60 degree gloss.

In 1965 the single rear seat speaker was listed as RPO U80. It was available with all three radios. The tri-pointed knob, part number 7290901, that

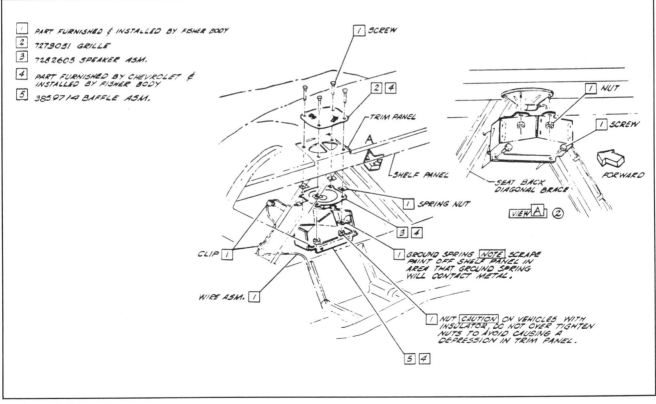

*1964 rear shelf speaker.*

*1967 radio bezel. Note the two thin black stripes, which are correct.*

controlled the balance was placed over the right-hand control knob.

Since the AM/FM radio option was added late in the 1964 model year, a few 1964 models could have been built with either of these options. However, anything earlier than build date 05 64 would be incorrect.

The standard antenna was still mounted on the right front fender. A rear manual antenna was optional. No power antenna was available.

### 1966-1967

No radio was standard with the 1966 Chevelle, and only two radios were available. The manual-tune AM radio, U60, was eliminated May 20, 1965.

The basic radio was the U63 push-button AM unit. It used four black plastic buttons to locate the dial indicator. Of all the radios this is the most common unit.

Also optional was the U69 AM/FM radio. With this unit the wiring harness was installed sideways instead of directly into the back of the unit as with the AM radio.

Both radios were mounted with a dull silver bezel, part number 3876588. The front dash speaker measured 4×10 in. and was rated at 10 ohms.

When the radio was not ordered, a blocking plate, part number 3874743, was used. This plate was painted to match the adjoining trim. A few early models came with a different plate, part number 3874741, that was painted to match the interior color.

Chrome knobs and bezels that matched the other knobs were used on both radios. Rear speaker U80, part number 7294892, was again available. It measured 6×9 in. and was rated at 10 ohms. It was covered with a grille, part number 7296871, and was painted 60 degree gloss in a color that matched the interior except with white interiors, which had it painted in 60 degree gloss-black. This speaker was available on the coupe all year and on convertibles built after the second week of

May 1966. On the convertible it was placed in an enclosure, part number 3880726, behind the rear seat. A baffle, part number 9776185, like the one used in 1965, was placed over the speaker; it attached to the speaker magnet with a clip.

The radios were usually grounded on the left-hand side of the engine to the spark plug wire support. When transistor ignition was used, they were grounded on the right-hand side. The AM/FM radio should be grounded to the frame on the right-hand side of the car.

Noise suppressors were unique to the type of accessories that were installed. With standard production items and the push-button AM radio, the suppressor and bracket, part number 1947452, were attached to the coil bracket and the lead to the positive post of the coil.

With transistor ignition or the L78 engine, the capacitor was mounted to the side of the voltage regulator were the ground wire attached. The ground wire should be installed last, and the lead should be connected to a pin on the regulator. The suppressor was listed as part number 1964086; it was also used with the 61 amp alternator, K81.

The AM/FM radio used a unique capacitor, part number 3886965. It featured two long leads and was attached to the outermost lower stud on the heater-blower assembly. One lead was looped around and connected to the blower; the other was connected to the existing orange wire. Slack in the production wire should be taken up in the clip on the firewall.

When air conditioning was used with the AM/FM radio, the suppressor was attached to the bottom of the blower housing with a Phillips-head screw. One lead was connected to the terminal on the blower, and the other to the production wire. Four inches of tape should hold the lead and the orange production wire together.

A power-operated antenna was available in 1966 and was listed as RPO U75. It was mounted on the right-hand rear fender. The motor and body assembly was listed as part number 3879544. The toggle switch, part number 3866170, was mounted on the underside of the instrument panel to the left of the steering column and used a bright knob. The wires were routed along with the main wiring harness and supported with tape.

The toggle switch's hot lead was connected into the receptacle marked Ign Fused; if the car was equipped with a tachometer a jumper connector had to be used. The antenna lead, part number 3880975, was 188 in. long.

The stereo converter was available only from the dealer in 1966. It remained pretty much a copy of the 1965 factory unit.

Few visible changes were made in 1967, although the knobs were restyled to match the 1967 interior. The push-button AM and AM/FM radios were still available and used a different bezel, part number 3897321. This bezel featured a ribbed design with two thin black stripes.

When no radio was used, a blocking plate, part number 3897549, was installed. It matched the adjoining trim above the glove compartment in design and color. The speakers were identical to those used in 1966, as were the capacitors.

A new option appeared for 1967: the RPO U57 stereo tape player. It was available with or without the radio. The system consisted of the tape player and four speakers.

The tape player, part number 7300481, was mounted to the underside of the instrument panel in the center with a natural bracket, part number 3909582, and Phillips-head screws. A rear brace, part number 7301820, was also used for added support. When the heater delete option, C48, was ordered, the bracket was mounted with hex-head screws, washers and nuts. The player assembly was held to the bracket in either case with Phillips head screws.

A cover, part number 7301634, was placed over the player assembly and held with two Phillips-head screws and lock washers. The cover was flat-black, featuring a brushed aluminum faceplate trimmed in black and printed with the controls. Four knurled chrome knobs, part number 7301181, were used.

Front speakers, part number 7300731, were installed into the kick panel and covered with grilles, part number 3901622, which were painted the same color as the kick panel in a 60 degree gloss finish. A speaker extension harness, part number 7290858, was routed along the bottom rail of the instrument panel and secured with tape—two pieces on the right and one on the left.

Two rear speakers, part number 7300614, were installed in the rear shelf tray, one on each side, and covered with a grille, part number 7296871, which should be painted to match the rear shelf in a 60 degree gloss finish. On the convertible the rear speakers were enclosed in housing units, part number 3919044, and placed behind the rear seat.

Option U57 was not available with the rear speaker option, U80, or the rear defroster. However, it was available as dealer-installed equipment in separate packages, so a tape player with only rear speakers could have been installed. Either way it is a rare option today. Also included with the player was a free eight-track tape.

The stereo Multi-plex system continued, but only as a dealer-installed option, as accessory package part number 986975, and was nearly a carbon copy of the 1965 unit available from the factory. This system used the same speakers as the tape player. A power-operated antenna was not available in 1967; the manual rear-mounted antenna was still optional.

## 1968-1969

The push-button AM and AM/FM radios continued in 1968. The AM radio used capacitor part number 1964086 and was mounted to the regulator on the radiator support wall. The AM/FM radio used two different capacitors. Without air conditioning, part number 3847975 was installed. This suppressor featured two long leads and was mounted to the outermost lower stud on the heater-blower assembly. One lead was connected to the blower terminal, and the other to the production heater wire.

Because the evaporator was redesigned in 1968 a special capacitor, part number 3847975, was used with the AM/FM radio and air conditioning. Like the unit used without air conditioning, it featured two long leads. One end connected to the blower terminal. The other end had a loop connector and was placed on a terminal on the evaporator; the production lead was connected to it.

The stereo radio converter was again listed as factory option U79 in 1968. It consisted of four speakers—two front, two rear—and an adapter unit, part number 7304621, that was mounted to the bottom of the instrument panel, just below the ashtray. Two brackets, part numbers 3927325-LH and 3927326-RH, were used for mounting. These brackets should be painted black to match the converter assembly.

The eight-track tape deck was redesigned in 1968 and made more compact. Two different players were available: without the stereo radio adapter, part number 7305301 was used; with the adapter, part number 7305311 was used. The players are distinguishable by part number 7305311's extra provision for the adapter's lead.

Both players were mounted by a pair of unique brackets, part numbers 3934237-LH and 3934238-RH. The left-hand bracket wrapped around to support the right-hand bracket. Early cars used a different set of brackets that were two separate pieces—the left-hand bracket did not wrap around. The second-design left-hand bracket was mounted to the instrument panel with a single hex-head screw. The right-hand bracket was mounted to the left-hand bracket with a Phillips-head screw. Phillips-head screws, two on each side, were also used to mount the player to the brackets.

When the eight-track player was ordered with the stereo radio converter, U79, a special adapter assembly, part number 7306361, was placed on the right-hand side of the car above the glove compartment. It was mounted with a pair of natural brackets, part numbers 3927335 and 3927336. Two leads were affixed to this adapter, the top lead to the tape player and the bottom lead to the radio.

A manual antenna mounted on the right front fender was part of the radio package from the factory. The rear manual antenna, RPO U73, was relocated farther back and used the same parts as the front-fender-mounted unit except for the bezel, part number 3923952, and ground ring, part number 3923953.

A fixed-height front antenna was a dealer-installed option, as were manually adjustable front- and rear-mounted antennas. A single rear speaker continued as both a factory option and a dealer option. The AM radio with manual front-fender-mounted antenna and an AM/FM radio with fixed-height antenna were also available as dealer-installed options. The power antenna was not available on the Chevelle.

Not much changed in 1969. The same radios were again offered. The stereo eight-track tape player was listed as part number 7307341, 7310021 when equipped with the stereo radio option. It was now located under the ashtray, so the brackets, part numbers 3951221-LH and 3951222-RH, were restyled and made smaller. They were mounted to the instrument panel with Phillips-head screws on the left-hand side and a hex-head screw and J-nut, part number 3885999, on the right side. A rear support brace, part number 3954289, was also used. It too employed the same J-nut and a hex-head screw.

To open the ashtray a special handle, part number 3951224, had to be riveted to it. Two 0.125 in. diameter holes were drilled at the points marked M in the tray assembly. A special spacer-cover, part number 3961220, was used between the tape player and the ashtray. A seal, part number 3984245, was installed between the cover unit and the tape player. Both the ashtray handle and the spacer-cover assembly should be painted to match the instrument panel.

The stereo radio amplifier, part number 7308161, was mounted up under the instrument panel just below the radio and to the left with hex-head screws and J-nuts.

The rear seat speaker option, U80, was still available but not for the pickup either year. A switch, part number 7309211, and a knob, part number 3954239, were used to control the speaker on the right-hand radio control shaft. As in previous years, a baffle made from cardboard and lined with insulation was used with this speaker.

Capacitors were the same as in 1968, but the AM/FM suppressor with air conditioning was eliminated. The front antenna was standard with any radio. The manual rear antenna was available with the AM radio only. This antenna was offered with all body styles except the pickup.

## 1970-1972

The most noticeable change in 1970 was that the eight-track tape player was integrated into the radio. It was available in two forms: RPO UM1 with an AM radio and RPO UM2 with an AM/FM radio; both were stereophonic. With either system Chevrolet tossed in a tape entitled *Great Sound Stereo* from RCA, part number 349.

The push-button AM radio used part number 7313491, and the push-button AM/FM radio was listed as part number 7312321. Also available was a stereo AM/FM radio, U79; it consisted of two speakers mounted on the instrument panel and two speakers mounted on the rear shelf.

All factory-installed radios used the Hidden Radio Antenna, which consisted of two thin wires laminated in between the layers of glass in the windshield. Dealer-installed radios used the antenna mounted outside on the right front fender.

Speakers on all nonstereo radios without air conditioning were located in the center of the instrument panel. However, if air conditioning was selected, two speakers were used, one on each end of the instrument panel. The driver's-side speaker—part number 7313131, 7933761 after March 19, 1970—and speaker bracket were unique to the SS package and differed from production Chevelle units. The right side speaker, part number 7313151, and bracket, part number 3961580, were the same as production Chevelle parts with air conditioning. The special driver's-side bracket and speaker were also used in all Monte Carlos.

In 1971-72 all SSs used soft black knobs with special white symbols to identify the controls. A white sixteenth note was used on knob part number 3986872 to signify the volume control. A chrome speed knob, part number 3986874, was also used to control bass and treble. The tuning control knob was part number 3986829, and it featured a white horn-shaped figure with sound waves. With a stereo radio another chrome speed knob, part number 3986874, was used to control the balance to the speakers.

The rear seat speaker option was still available in 1970 but not with a stereo radio system. It was also offered as a dealer-installed option. The windshield antenna, RPO U76, could be ordered without a radio all three years, from 1970 to 1972.

The following radios were available in 1971 and 1972 from the factory and as dealer-installed options.

### 1971-1972 Radio Part Numbers

| | |
|---|---|
| AM radio | 7933241 |
| AM/FM radio | 7933251 |
| AM/FM stereo | 7933261 |
| AM radio w/8 track player | NA |
| AM/FM radio w/8 track player | NA |

Two different rear seat speakers were available: part number 7933501 with AM radios and part number 7933511 with AM/FM radios. These options were not offered with the tape players or the stereo radio. No rear-mounted antenna was available for all three years.

## RPO V75 Traction Dispenser

### 1969

A rare and little-known option was the traction dispenser. It was available for 1969 only and was available for all SS 396s except the pickup.

This option consisted of a traction dispenser, part number 6440708, that was mounted into each rear wheelwell and dispensed a traction compound, part number 1550521, on the rear tires. The system was activated by a switch, part number 1378545, mounted on the lower portion of the instrument panel to the right of the steering column.

Vacuum was drawn from the engine by a fitting in the intake manifold. A total of four fittings were used.

### 1969 Traction Dispenser Vacuum Fitting Part Numbers

| | |
|---|---|
| W/C60 | 3891523 |
| W/automatic | 3891524 |

W/power brakes 3905372
W/automatic & power brakes 3905374

If any other accessories—such as air conditioning with an automatic transmission—were ordered, a special tee, part number 3929022, had to be used to split the rubber hoses to the accessories and the traction compound dispenser. If no optional accessory was used, an adapter, part number 3955040, was required with all fittings. The vacuum hose from the engine to the switch was listed as part number 3739667.

This option was sold mostly in the northern states, and most cars equipped with it were four-door sedans. It is unclear if any SS 396s were built with it.

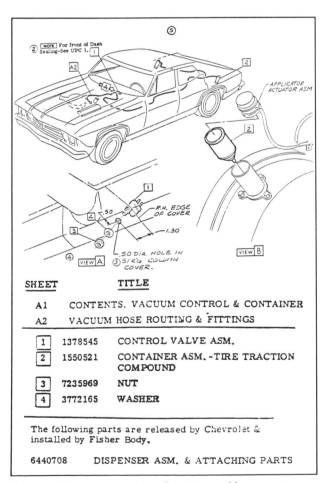

| SHEET | TITLE |
|---|---|
| A1 | CONTENTS. VACUUM CONTROL & CONTAINER |
| A2 | VACUUM HOSE ROUTING & FITTINGS |

| | | |
|---|---|---|
| 1 | 1378545 | CONTROL VALVE ASM. |
| 2 | 1550521 | CONTAINER ASM. -TIRE TRACTION COMPOUND |
| 3 | 7235969 | NUT |
| 4 | 3772165 | WASHER |

The following parts are released by Chevrolet & installed by Fisher Body.

6440708 DISPENSER ASM. & ATTACHING PARTS

*Traction dispenser container location and hose route.*

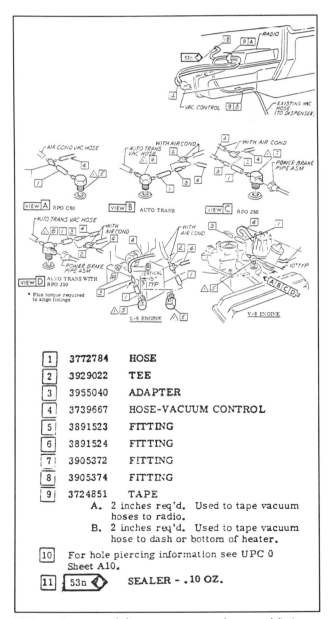

| | | |
|---|---|---|
| 1 | 3772784 | HOSE |
| 2 | 3929022 | TEE |
| 3 | 3955040 | ADAPTER |
| 4 | 3739667 | HOSE-VACUUM CONTROL |
| 5 | 3891523 | FITTING |
| 6 | 3891524 | FITTING |
| 7 | 3905372 | FITTING |
| 8 | 3905374 | FITTING |
| 9 | 3724851 | TAPE |
| | A. | 2 inches req'd. Used to tape vacuum hoses to radio. |
| | B. | 2 inches req'd. Used to tape vacuum hose to dash or bottom of heater. |
| 10 | | For hole piercing information see UPC 0 Sheet A10. |
| 11 | 53n | SEALER - .10 OZ. |

*V75 traction control dispenser vacuum hose and fittings.*

*Standard Rally wheel with Heavy Chevy option package. A touch of green paint should be added to the silver wheel color for correctness.*

## RPO YF3 Heavy Chevy

### 1971

Often called a poor person's SS, the Heavy Chevy package, RPO YF3, offered the SS grille and hood on two Chevelle coupe models. No Heavy Chevy Malibus were built.

This option started with build date 04 A 71 as a 1971 model. Special black side stripes and decals were part of the package. The side stripes were located 0.22 in. above the center crease line in the body and remained constant. A Heavy Chevy decal, part number 6261947, was placed on the front fender; the correct position was 1 in. from the door edge and 16.25 in. from the bottom of the rocker sill to the bottom of the decal. This same decal was placed on the rear deck lid on the right-hand side;

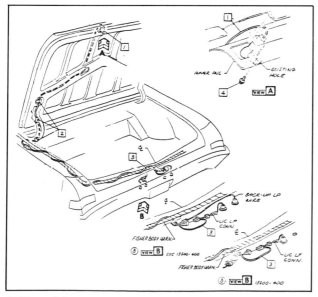

*1969 trunk lamp.*

it should be located 0.55 in. from the right edge of the deck and 0.85 in. from the deck opening. A smaller Heavy Chevy decal, part number 6261932, was located 0.55 in. left of the first hood crease and 1 in. from the front edge of the hood.

These stripes and decals were also optional in white, as RPO ZR8. The deck fender decal was listed as part number 6261946, and the hood decal as part number 6261931. Black stripes were standard with all exterior colors except Tuxedo Black, which came with white stripes. White stripes could not be ordered with a white exterior.

## RPOs Z19 and ZJ9 Auxiliary Lighting

### 1964-1965

An underhood lamp, a trunk lamp and an ashtray lamp were available only as separate dealer-installed options in 1964 and 1965. Spot lamps were also available from the dealer.

### 1966-1967

Auxiliary lighting was part of the RPO Z19 comfort and convenience package in 1966. It consisted of an underhood lamp—part number 3901639, superseded by part number 3981639. The first lamp used a rubber bumper, part number 3762180; the second lamp used a lock washer between it and the hood. Both lamps were located 7.5 in. to the right of the centerline of the hood, measured from the centerline of the lamp. The lamp should be painted flat-black.

The underhood lamp wire was routed from the lamp to the horn relay following the route of the forward lamp harness and was secured to the lamp with three black plastic clips.

A luggage compartment lamp, part number 3878110, was also included in the Z19 package and was located in a recess at the rear end of the deck lid. The wiring route followed the rear body harness and connected into the license plate.

In 1967 the lighting package was listed as separate items or as part of the RPO ZJ9 auxiliary lighting group. Underhood lamp RPO U26, part number 3901639, was located 17.75 in. to the right of the centerline of the hood. The trunk lamp was listed as RPO U25, part number 3886947, but was identical to that used in 1966.

An ashtray lamp, RPO U28, part number 3900506, was also included in the ZJ9 package. It was mounted to the top of the ashtray retainer, then connected to the fuse panel in the receptacle marked Lamps.

All these items were also available as dealer-installed options both years.

### 1968-1969

Auxiliary light group ZJ9 continued for 1968 and 1969. The underhood lamp was redesigned, given part number 3916763 and relocated on the

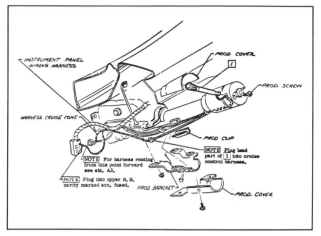

*1967 cruise control switch.*

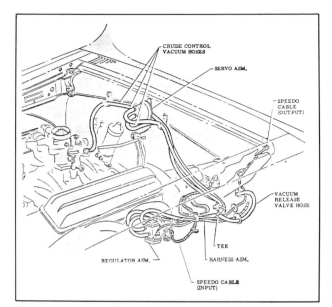

*1967 cruise control hose and wire route.*

lower edge of the hood in the center. It was mounted with two ¼ in. cadmium bolts. The lamp house should be painted flat-black.

The luggage compartment lamp was located in the same place as in previous years but was given part number 3916767 because the wiring route was changed. Convertibles were routed as before, but the wire should wrap around the rear body harness to be correct. Coupes followed a different route, as the lead was connected to a wire that ran to the dome lamp.

For most of the 1968 model year the ashtray lamp was the same as in 1967, but in late March 1968 fiber-optic filaments were used and the lamp option consisted of a conductor, part number 6295160, and a retainer, part number 6288831. The other end of the conductor was connected to the instrument panel. These same parts were used unchanged in 1969.

On 300 Deluxe based models in 1969 this package also included a glove compartment lamp

and instrumentation lighting, all of which were standard on the Malibu- and El Camino based packages.

**1970-1972**

A map light and rearview mirror assembly, part number 911224, was added to the ZJ9 package in 1970. The underhood lamp—part number 3980125, 62622656 in 1971 and 1972—was located on the left side of the hood from 1970 to 1971. It should be painted according to the 1969 specifications.

The luggage compartment lamp was identical to that used in 1969; its wire route was the same too. The ashtray lamp conductor was now listed as

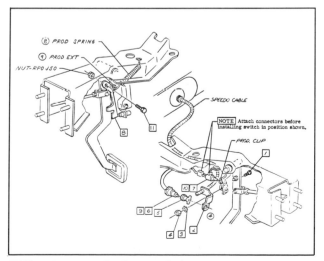

*1967 cruise control release switch.*

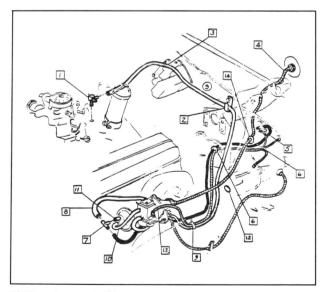

*1968 cruise control hose route.*

233

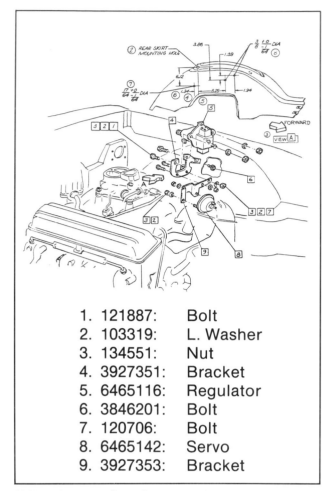

1. 121887: Bolt
2. 103319: L. Washer
3. 134551: Nut
4. 3927351: Bracket
5. 6465116: Regulator
6. 3846201: Bolt
7. 120706: Bolt
8. 6465142: Servo
9. 3927353: Bracket

*1968 cruise control regulator mounting.*

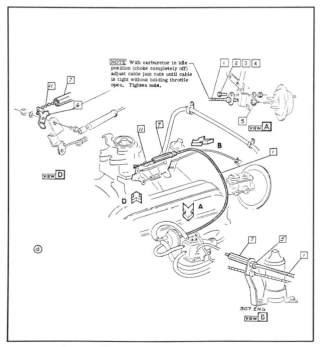

*1968 speed control with automatic transmission.*

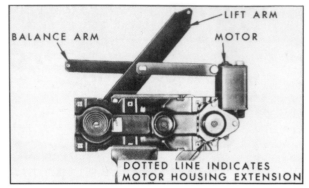

*Power window regulator.*

part number 6297516, 8901757 in 1971–72, and was housed in a socket, part number 6288601, all three years.

These items were available as a group or as separate options in 1970. However, in 1971 and 1972 the only way to get them from the factory was in the auxiliary lighting group. They were still available as dealer-installed options all three years.

## RPO Z16 Special Sport Equipment

### 1965

The most-sought-after SS option was RPO Z16. Only 201 were made: 200 hardtop coupes and one convertible. The whereabouts of this ragtop are unknown.

Not all Z16 Chevelles were assembled at the Kansas City, Missouri, plant. Two Chevelle coupes were pulled from the Baltimore plant and then assembled in Warren. These two cars still retained their assembly plant code for the Baltimore plant. They were used as test cars for magazines.

The Z16 package retailed for $1,501.05 and contained the following parts: a special reinforced frame, larger drum brakes, a special suspension

*1966-67 power window control assembly.*

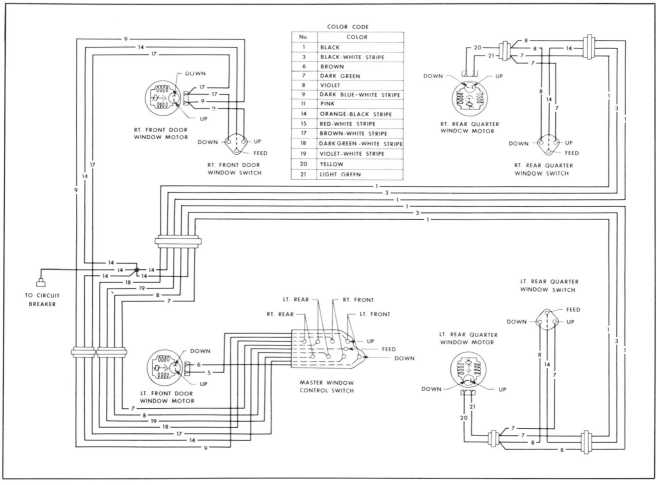

Power window circuit diagram.

The following color code table appears in the diagram:

| No. | COLOR |
|-----|-------|
| 1 | BLACK |
| 3 | BLACK-WHITE STRIPE |
| 6 | BROWN |
| 7 | DARK GREEN |
| 8 | VIOLET |
| 9 | DARK BLUE-WHITE STRIPE |
| 11 | PINK |
| 14 | ORANGE-BLACK STRIPE |
| 15 | RED-WHITE STRIPE |
| 17 | BROWN-WHITE STRIPE |
| 18 | DARK GREEN -WHITE STRIPE |
| 19 | VIOLET-WHITE STRIPE |
| 20 | YELLOW |
| 21 | LIGHT GREEN |

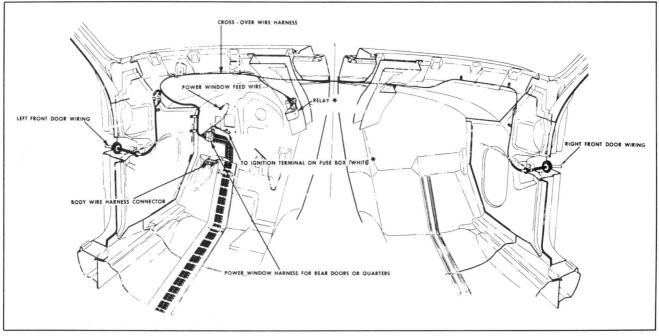

Front end power window wiring route.

with front and rear sway bars, simulated magnesium wheel covers, 14×6 in. steel wheels, 7.75×14 Firestone Gold Stripe tires, special molding and nameplates, and special instrumentation with a 160 mph speedometer and a tachometer that redlined at 6500 rpm. Mandatory options included the following:

### 1965 Z16 Mandatory RPO Codes

| | |
|---|---|
| Rear seatbelts | A47 |
| Custom Deluxe front seatbelts w/retractors | A49 |
| Instrument panel pad | B70 |
| Power brakes | J50 |
| 375 hp 396 ci engine | L37 |
| Wide-ratio 4 speed manual | M20 |
| Special-ratio power steering | N40 |
| Tachometer | U16 |
| AM/FM radio | U69 |
| Stereo converter | U79 |
| Comfort & convenience package w/remote control side mirror | Z13 |

Although usually seen, the black vinyl top was not part of the option. Also, black was not the only interior color offered; buyers had the choice of a red, black or white interior with a red, black or yellow exterior. A red interior was not available in a yellow car.

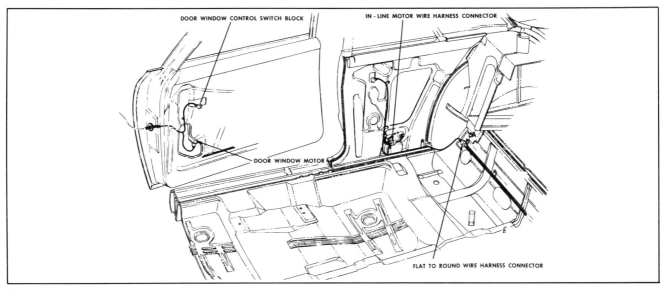

*Right side power window wiring route.*

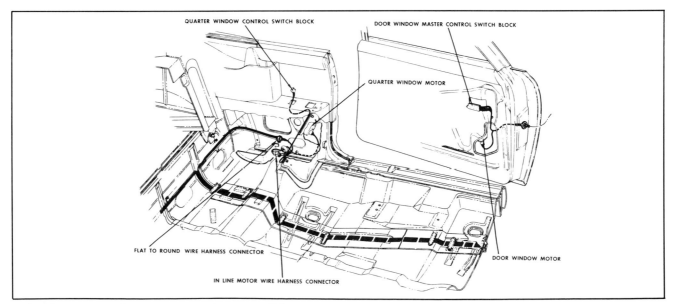

*Left side power window wiring route for convertibles.*

# Appendix A

# Appendix B

**1964–1972 Chevelle SS Production Totals**

| Year | Body Style | Production | Remarks |
|------|-----------|-----------|---------|
| 1964 | Coupe, convertible | 76,860 | Most were V-8 powered |
| 1965 | Coupe, convertible | 81,812 | 201 came w/the Z16 option |
| 1966 | Coupe, convertible | 72,272 | 5,429 were convertibles |
| 1967 | Coupe, convertible | 63,006 | 3,321 were convertibles |
| 1968 | Coupe, convertible, pickup | 62,785 | 5,190 were El Caminos |
| 1969 | Coupe, convertible, pickup | 86,307 | 948 were 300 Deluxe pillar coupes |
| 1970 | Coupe, convertible, pickup | 53,599 | 8,773 were SS 454s |
| 1971 | Coupe, convertible, pickup | 19,293 | Number of SS 350s is not known |
| 1972 | Coupe, convertible, pickup | 24,946 | Total includes SS 350s |

**Production According to Powerplant**

| Year | Cid | Hp | RPO Numbers | Production |
|------|-----|-----|-------------|-----------|
| 1966 | 396 | 325 | L35 (base) | 44,362 |
|      |     | 360 | L34 | 24,811 |
|      |     | 375 | L78 | 3,099 |
| 1967 | 396 | 325 | L35 (base) | 45,218 |
|      |     | 350 | L34 | 17,176 |
|      |     | 375 | L78 | 612 |
|      | 427 | 425 | * | 500† |
| 1968 | 396 | 325 | L35 (base) | 45,553 |
|      |     | 350 | L34 | 12,481 |
|      |     | 375 | L78 | 4,475 |
| 1969 | 396 | 325 | L35 (base) | 59,463 |
|      |     | 350 | L34 | 17,358 |
|      |     | 375 | L78 | 9,486 |
|      | 427 | 425 | COPO | 358 |
| 1970 | 396 | 350 | L34 (base) | 53,599 |
|      |     | 375 | L78, L89 | 2,144 |
|      | 454 | 360 | LS5 | 4,298 |
|      |     | 450 | LS6 | 4,475 |
| 1971 | 350 | 245 | L65 | ‡ |
|      |     | 270 | L48 | ‡ |
|      | 400 | 300 | LS3 | 9,791 |
|      | 454 | 365 | LS5 | 6,044 |
|      |     | 425 | LS6 | 3,458 |
| 1972 | 350 | 165 | L65 | § |
|      |     | 175 | L48 | § |
|      | 400 | 240 | LS3 | 12,489 |
|      | 454 | 270 | LS5 | 5,333 |

*Built by Motion Performance.

†Estimate; 500 were needed to qualify for racing.

‡Small-block SSs were not counted.

§Total number of L65s and L48s is estimated at 7,124, with most being L48s.

# Appendix C

## Chevelle Part Suppliers

Antique Auto Battery Co.
2320 Old Mill Rd.
Hudson, OH 44236
  Reproduction battery and
  spring ring battery cables

Ausley's
300 S. Main
Graham, NC 27253
  Various reproduction and
  genuine GM parts

Auto Body Specialties
P.O. Box 455
Rte. 66
Middlefield, CT 06455
  Extensive selection of reproduction
and original sheet metal

C.A.R.S.
1964 W. 11 Mile Rd.
Berkley, MI 48072
  Trim parts and floor sheet metal

Chevelle Classics
17892 Gothard St.
Huntington Beach, CA 92647
  Various reproduction and
  genuine parts

Chevelle Magnum Automotive
Products
13578 Pumice St.
Northwalk, CA 90650
  Various restoration parts

Ciadella Chevrolet
3757 E. Broadway
Ste. 4
Phoenix, AZ 85040
  Interior parts

Classic Muscle Cars, Part &
Accessories
P.O. Box 294
Aurora, MO 65605
  Original, reproduction and
  NOS Chevelle parts

Convertible Service
5126 Walnut Grove Ave.
San Gabriel, CA 91776
  Convertible top parts

Custom Mold Dynamics
5161 Wolfpen Pleasant Hill Rd.
Milford, OH 45150
  Trim parts

Danchuk Manufacturing
3221 S. Halladay St.
Santa Ana, CA 92705
  Various reproduction parts

Harmon's
Hwy. 27 N.
Geneva, IN 46740
  Sheet metal, rubber and
  electrical parts

Holley Replacement Parts
11955 E. Nine Mile Rd.
Warren, MI 48089
  Carburetors

J.C. Whitney & Co.
1917-19 Archer Ave.
P.O. Box 8410
Chicago, IL 60680
  Door panels and convertible tops

Martz Classic Chevy Parts
R.D. 1, Box 199B
Thomasville, PA 17364
  Various parts for 1964-67 only

Metro Molded Parts
11610 Jay St.
P.O. Box 33130
Minneapolis, MN 55433
  Weather stripping

Mike's Chevy Parts
7716 Deering Ave.
Canoga Park, CA 91304
  Various restoration parts

National Parts Depot
3101 SW 40th Blvd.
Gainesville, FL 32608
  Various parts; ask for the company's
  Chevelle catalog

O.B. Smith Classic Cars & Parts
900 New Circle Rd. NW
P.O. Box 11703

Lexington, KY 40577
  Various parts

Jim Osborn Reproductions
101 Ridgecrest Dr.
Lawrenceville, GA 30245
  Reproduction decals

Sherman & Associates
27940 Groesbeck Hwy.
Roseville, MI 48066
  Replacement sheet metal

SoftSeal
104 May Dr.
Harrison, OH 45030
  Reproduction rubber parts

Southwestern Classic Chevrolet
1230 Dan Gould Dr.
Arlington, TX 76017
  Various parts

Steele
1601 Hwy. 150 E.
Denver, NC 28037
  Reproduction rubber parts

Stencils & Stripes Unlimited
1108 S. Crescent
Park Ridge, IL 66068
  Stencils and stripes

USA-1 Interiors
P.O. Box 691
Williamstown, NJ 08094
  Extensive interior selection

Volunteer State Chevy Parts
P.O. Drawer D
Greenbrier, TN 37073
  Various parts

Ted William's Chevelle Parts
5615 St.
Rte. 45 N.
Lisbon, OH 44432
  Various parts

Year One
P.O. Box 2023
Tucker, GA 30085
  Various parts

# Index